BARRON'S

AP*

ENGLISH LITERATURE AND COMPOSITION

4TH EDITION

George Ehrenhaft, Ed.D.
Former Chairman, English Department
Mamaroneck High School
Mamaroneck, New York

BARRON'S

*AP is a registered trademark of the College Board, which was not involved in the production of, and does not endorse, this product.

All inquiries should be addressed to:
Barron's Educational Series, Inc.
250 Wireless Boulevard
Hauppauge, New York 11788
www.barronseduc.com

ISBN: 978-0-7641-4696-1 (book only)
ISBN: 978-1-4380-7130-5 (book with CD-ROM)

ISSN 2163-9302 (book only)
ISSN 2163-9310 (book with CD-ROM)

PRINTED IN THE UNITED STATES OF AMERICA
9 8 7 6

10%
POST-CONSUMER
WASTE
Paper contains a minimum
of 10% post-consumer
waste (PCW). Paper used
in this book was derived
from certified, sustainable
forestlands.

Contents

To reach your goal of **5** on the AP English Literature and Composition exam, here are five essentials you **MUST** do:

Barron's Essential

1 **Familiarize yourself with literary terms.** For multiple-choice and essay questions you won't be asked about definitions. But you must recognize and be conversant with matters such as the structure, style, themes, imagery, symbolism, irony, and use of figurative language in works of imaginative literature.

2 **Develop the habit of close reading.** Choose fiction of recognized literary merit, and pick a page or a short passage to dissect. Read it once for an overall impression. Then go back resolved to draw out meanings that lie beneath the surface. Observe textual details, sentence structures, style, diction, syntax, and figures of speech. Describe the author's tone. This type of close reading, consistently done, boosts performance in both the multiple-choice and essay sections of the exam.

3 **Devour poetry.** A steady diet of poems builds appreciation and understanding of poetry, *a major subject on the AP exam.* Read poems daily. For each one, answer the ten essential questions on pages 119–122 designed to make clear the poet's purpose and meaning. With practice, you'll soon see how structure, sound, meter, and other elements give poems the power to move, entertain, and enlighten.

4 **Read widely and well.** Exam questions about literature range from the meaning of an entire novel or play to the use of a single word or phrase. Every dimension of literature is fair game. Be prepared by immersing yourself in high-quality works from various periods. Read thoroughly. Take nothing for granted. Assume that every component in the work contributes to the meaning of the work as a whole. Make an effort to contemplate and analyze:

- plot
- setting
- character
- narrative voice
- structure
- language
- . . . and much more

5 **Plan and practice an essay-writing process.** Develop a process for writing an essay in no more than 40 minutes. Build in time to read the question, pick a main idea, and decide how to support it. Before you start writing, list your ideas and arrange them in sensible order. While composing your essay, be sure to:

- introduce your topic
- develop coherent paragraphs
- vary sentence structures
- choose the best words to express ideas
- provide a brief conclusion

Set aside time for editing and proofreading.

Introducing the
AP English Literature
and Composition Exam

The AP English Literature and Composition exam tests your ability to compre-hend and interpret the form and substance of poems and prose passages. In addition, it asks you to write clear, concise, and persuasive analytical essays that demonstrate your understanding of literary techniques used by poets and authors of fiction.

The exam takes three hours and is divided into two sections. Section 1, which lasts an hour, consists of multiple-choice questions and counts for 45 percent of your total score. The second section is two hours long and requires you to write three essays. It comprises 55 percent of your grade.

Section I	Section II
Fifty-five multiple-choice questions based on your reading of two or three prose fiction passages and two or three poems. (One hour)	Three essays: one on a given poem, one on a passage of prose fiction—each analyzing how form and content relate to the meaning—and a third essay on your choice of novel or play. (Two hours)

Your score on the exam is reported on a scale of 1–5. In general, the numbers are interpreted to mean

5 extremely well qualified
4 well qualifed
3 qualified
2 possibly qualified
1 not recommended for AP credit

A high score on this exam demonstrates a proficiency in English at least on a par with college students who have done well in an introductory course in composition or literature. Recognizing this, many colleges and universities waive freshman English requirements for high-scoring students. Some give academic credit or permit you to take a more advanced course during freshman year. Because each college and university uses AP scores in its own way, be sure to check with the admissions office of the institution you hope to attend.

Part of this book will acquaint you with the multiple-choice questions on the exam and give you practical help in essay writing. Other parts will help you develop a flair for critically evaluating poems, novels, and plays.

If you teach an AP English class, use this book as a resource. It will lighten your load because it contains a great deal of what an AP Lit course typically contains, including selected reading passages, important literary terminology, analyses of prose and poetry, sample essays with evaluations, exam questions, and several practice AP tests with answers fully explained. The literature discussed in these pages may or may not already be part of your AP course. If it isn't, you might consider including it in the future. All titles come from existing AP curricula and have been used in AP classes across the country. Questions and exercises throughout the book are intended to stimulate thinking and inspire students to write the kinds of in-depth analyses required on AP exams.

If you are a student, use this book to prepare for the exam. Study each chapter. Take the practice tests and check your answers. Revel in the correct ones but let the wrong answers steer you to chapters in the book that you should probably review a bit more.

To all students preparing to take the AP English exam, best of luck.

George Ehrenhaft

PART 1

GETTING ACQUAINTED
WITH THE EXAM

Overview

CHAPTER 1

- Length of the exam
- Types of questions
- Format of questions

The analysis of poetry and prose fiction lies at the heart of the exam. The best preparation consists of being familiar with the format of the exam and having practiced critical reading and analysis of prose and poetry from roughly the sixteenth century to the present. Ideally, most of the works should have been written originally in English, but high-quality literature in translation, such as Greek drama and Russian novels, serve the purpose equally well.

On the exam you'll be asked to analyze a number of poems and prose passages by taking into account, among other things, their structure, style, and dominant themes. You may also be asked to recognize and discuss such elements as figurative language, imagery, point of view, and tone.

You should also be conversant with several works by established novelists such as Jane Austen, F. Scott Fitzgerald, John Updike, Toni Morrison, and Cormac McCarthy and plays by such dramatists as Shakespeare, Henrik Ibsen, Eugene O'Neill, David Mamet, and August Wilson. On the exam you'll be asked to choose a work of high quality—the kind you've probably studied in AP English—and write an analysis, taking into account such matters as meaning, form, structure, or the extent to which the work reflects the values of the time in which it was written.

TIP

To earn a top score on the exam, get into the habit of searching for the ways authors use language and literary form to convey meaning.

SECTION I

Section I of the exam lasts one hour and usually consists of 55 multiple-choice questions. It contains two, or sometimes three, passages of prose fiction excerpted from novels and short stories, but on occasion from a play or other genre. Along with the prose passages, you'll be given two or more short poems to read and analyze. More than half the questions relate to the prose passages, the rest to the poems.

Prose Passages

Unlike the SAT or ACT, this exam almost never asks basic comprehension questions about the passages. Because AP students are assumed to have little trouble comprehending what they read, questions focus not on what the passage says but on the author's linguistic and rhetorical choices. Emphasis is on literary technique, including, among other things, structure of the passage, effects of diction and syntax, point of view, and the relationship between parts of the passage. Instead of asking about the meaning of a particular sentence, questions may ask you to determine how the structure of that sentence relates to the theme or overall effect of the passage. Rather than identify the meaning of an allusion, you may be asked to determine its intent. Or you might be asked to discern why the author used a particular phrase, image, figure of speech, or word.

In short, you should be prepared to handle almost any type of analytical question. According to surveys of past AP exams, the most common questions, and therefore those you are most likely to encounter, pertain to:

- tone
- shifts in the writing style within the passage
- the effects of certain words and phrases, especially figures of speech
- the relationship of one sentence or idea to another
- the relationship of one sentence to the meaning of the passage as a whole
- the rhetorical stance of the narrator

The exam includes many other types of questions, too, all meant to test your analytical skills and perception as a reader. In addition, almost every exam contains at least one question on standard English grammar.

For a comprehensive review of what you are expected to know about prose fiction, please see Part 4.

Poetry

TIP

Rest assured that you won't be asked about archaic words or obscure allusions; should the poem contain any, they'll probably be explained in a footnote.

In addition to prose passages, you will be given two or sometimes three poems, each accompanied by roughly ten questions that focus on anything from the aesthetic intent of the poet to the implications of a single word. Whatever the poet has done to create the poem is grist for the test maker's mill. You could be asked to recognize structural components, types of language, tone, diction, themes, rhetorical devices, rhythms, meter, rhymes, and more.

A survey of several recent tests shows that the most common poetry questions asked students to identify the meaning of a word or phrase in context. Other frequently asked questions relate to the implication or meaning of figures of speech, to the tone, and to the effect of poetic techniques on the unity or meaning of the entire poem. If the poem contains a shift in the speaker's point of view or rhetorical stance, you can depend on a question about that. Technical questions on meter and rhythm show up occasionally but rarely more than once per exam.

See Part 3 for what you need to know about poetry for the AP exam.

Once Section I is finished, you may not return to it. Test booklets are sealed and collected, and after a five- to ten-minute break, Section II begins.

SECTION II

Section II consists of three essay questions to be completed in two hours. How you apportion your time is left up to you, but forty minutes is recommended for each essay.

Poetry

One essay is on poetry. After reading a given poem (or sometimes a pair of poems to compare and contrast), you must write an essay that explains the techniques the poet used to convey meaning. Sometimes the question will suggest that you consider specific poetic devices, such as the use of figurative language, irony, or structure. On some AP tests, the question may be more open-ended, allowing you to identify and explain any literary devices that you find important to the purpose and meaning of the poem.

Prose Passages

A second essay question asks you to analyze an excerpt from a novel or story—or possibly a series of letters, a speech in a play, or some other literary passage. The question, or "prompt," will specify the purpose of your analysis, but you are free to choose literary elements such as tone, language, structure, diction, and others to discuss.

Essay

The last question asks you to write an essay on a novel or play of your choice—never on a short story, a work of nonfiction, or other genre. The prompt usually makes a general observation about life or literature. Your job is to discuss the observation as it applies to a work of literature. The names of several appropriate titles are given, but you can choose any other book or play of "comparable literary merit," a phrase whose meaning is far from clear-cut but suggests titles that have endured and deserve to be read again and again. In all likelihood, a novel or play you studied in AP English class would serve well as a subject for this essay.

TIP

Avoid writing an essay on a best seller or popular fiction not read in school. And don't write about a film. You may, of course, choose a novel or play that's been made into a movie, but be sure to write about the original text, not about the filmed adaptation.

Each essay will be scored holistically. That means that an AP reader will review the essay rather quickly for an overall impression of its content and form. Readers are trained to look for clearly organized, well-developed, and forceful responses that reveal a depth of understanding and insight. Because AP students hope to earn college credit for their efforts, readers also look for prose that is worthy of mature writers. Readers will be most impressed by clarity, coherence, good reasoning, and a writing style that demonstrates—by its diction, voice, syntax, rhythm, and tone—your command of a variety of effective writing techniques. For details on how AP essays are scored, turn to page 45. Also, be sure to read the comments about the sample student essays, pages 49–70.

STRUCTURE OF THE EXAM
(Total time: 3 hours)

Section I (One hour)   55 multiple-choice questions based on
2 or 3 poems and 2 or 3 passages of fiction
45 percent of total score

Section II (Two hours)   3 essays
Essay 1: An analysis of a poem
Essay 2: An analysis of a prose passage from a work of fiction, a letter, or a speech in a play
Essay 3: An analytical essay on a novel or play of your choice
55 percent of total score

USING THIS BOOK TO PREPARE

Most readers of this book are either currently enrolled in an AP English course or about to begin one. If that describes you, this book can accompany you as a friendly and informed companion between now and May, when AP exams are given. Use it as a supplement to class work. Refer to it often as a way to reinforce what you have learned in school. Let it tutor you on matters that you've found elusive or hard to master. You might ask an AP teacher who knows your strengths and weaknesses to recommend which parts of the book to study. Take all the practice tests, of course. They're meant to give you that extra edge that turns a good AP score into a better one.

If you're not taking an AP English course, it's essential to work through the pages of this book from beginning to end. Each part has a distinct role in preparing you to take the exam:

PART 1—Introduces the exam and acquaints you with the types of short-answer and essay questions on the test.
PART 2—Diagnoses the present state of your readiness to take the exam.
PART 3—Expands your ability to read, understand, and analyze poetry.
PART 4—Enhances your skills in reading and writing about fiction and drama.
PART 5—Enables you to evaluate your growth and progress, using model AP exams taken under simulated testing conditions.

Try to build *at least* half an hour of AP prep time into your daily routine. Take the diagnostic test in Part 2 and the model tests in Part 5. Set aside three full hours for each one. By taking all the exams, you'll learn to pace yourself and get to know what to expect on test day. Moreover, you can practice the test-taking tactics described in the pages of this book. It takes stamina to answer several dozen questions about poems and prose passages and then write three essays. So, accustom yourself to extended periods of concentrated work. In a sense, you're like an athlete training for a big competition. The better your condition, the better you're apt to perform.

If AP test day is just around the corner, you obviously won't have the time to study this book from cover to cover. But you can do something. If nothing else, become familiar with the format of the exam. Take as many practice exams as possible. Knowing what to expect on test day reduces anxiety and enhances performance. For instance, you can count on finding an unvarying set of test directions in your exam booklet. Read the directions carefully while taking the practice exams, and follow them to the letter. Once you've taken a couple of exams, the directions are likely become second nature.

Because each section of the AP is timed literally to the second, pacing is critical. By taking practice exams, you can adjust the rate at which you answer the questions and write the essays. With experience you can learn to set a comfortable pace, neither too fast nor too slow. Then, on test day you'll have one less thing to worry about.

TIP

Pacing is critical!

CHAPTER 2

Answering Multiple-Choice Questions

- How to answer questions
- When to guess
- Techniques for reading the passages
- Things to know about poetry questions
- Things to know about fiction questions

Knowing the answers to the multiple-choice questions shows that you've got what it takes to read perceptively and to extract meaning from poems and passages of prose fiction. The selections you'll find on the exam are taken from contemporary literature, as well as from the literature of previous eras. In most cases, the poets and authors are not identified, but the date, which is always given, may drop a hint about the work's historical context. Your knowledge of history isn't being tested, but if a sonnet is dated, say, 1625, you might justifiably surmise that it is a Shakespearean sonnet with a prescribed structure and pattern of rhymes. Likewise, an allusion to a war in a 1920 piece, while not necessarily a reference to World War I, would at least enable you to ignore every war fought since then.

Although the multiple-choice questions are not intended to baffle you, **not everyone who takes the test is expected to answer every question correctly.** Each exam is designed for a range of test-takers. Ninety out of a hundred students may get some questions right, while other questions will probably stump more than half the students taking the exam. This is as it ought to be. If every student earned a perfect score, the AP test would be a test in name only.

Even before you walk into the testing room, you can count on these facts:

1. The test contains poetry and prose passages.
2. Every question has five choices, A–E.
3. The questions are *not* arranged in order of difficulty.
4. The questions generally follow the progress of the poems and passages.
5. You can scribble all over the test booklet, make notes in it, underline, etc.
6. The test directions will be the same as they were on all the practice tests you took, namely,

   > This section consists of selections from literary works and questions on their content, form, and style. After reading each passage or poem, choose the best answer to each question and then fill in the corresponding oval on the answer sheet.

TIP

Memorize test directions so you won't waste precious seconds rereading what you already know.

TACTICS FOR ANSWERING QUESTIONS

The next few pages offer several tried-and-true approaches to answering the questions. Some will work better than others, some contradict each other, some may even be counterintuitive. Nevertheless, try them all to increase your chances of earning a top score on the AP exam. Once you have nailed down the techniques that work best for you, practice them again and again until they become second nature.

Answer the Questions in the Order Presented

Although not everyone agrees (see next tactic, below), you should answer the questions in order. Why? Because working through each question in turn may prepare you to answer later ones. But if you come to a question you really can't answer, don't agonize over it. Just go on to the next one and come back later if you have time. It goes without saying that if you skip a question, you must not bubble in an oval for that question on your answer sheet. (Don't laugh; more than one student has lost track and answered question #12 in the space for #11, etc.) To avoid such a mistake, try this: Write all your answers in the test booklet first. Later transfer them to the answer sheet.

Scan Sections First

When you open your test booklet, scan the test to see what it consists of. Answer the sections of poetry questions first if you're good at poetry. If you're better with prose passages, turn to them first. For each passage or poem, answer those questions you know for sure. Sometimes you'll get a cluster of questions about a single paragraph or stanza. Concentrate on those. It's probably smart to finish all the questions about a poem or passage before going on to the next one, but that's not a hard and fast rule because you may see things with a fresh pair of eyes during a return visit.

Pace Yourself

In one hour you must carefully read four or five passages and poems and answer between 50 and 60 questions. If you spend five minutes reading each passage and poem, you'll have roughly 45 seconds for each question. Every exam contains questions that eat up the clock, especially those that ask you to identify the choice that doesn't apply to the passage or poem (see #3, page 16) and those on which you must pick which of three choices are correct (see #4, page 16). Because these questions are time-consuming, you may wish to save them for last.

Learn to pace yourself by taking the practice tests in this book. Find a quiet place, clear your desk of distractions, and allow yourself exactly one hour to complete the questions. If you run out of time you obviously have to pick up your pace. Perhaps you're reading too slowly (see reading techiques, pages 13–14). Or you may be agonizing too long (60 seconds plus) over hard questions or spending too much time gloating over correct answers.

Don't Know the Answer? Guess!

Each correct answer is worth one point. Your score will be based solely on the number of questions answered correctly. This manner of scoring means that it always pays to guess, even when a question stumps you completely. By guessing at random, you still have a one-in-five chance of getting it right, and by eliminating one or more choices, you dramatically increase the odds of picking the correct answer. In short, DON'T LEAVE BLANKS. ANSWER EVERY QUESTION.

Another piece of folk "wisdom" is that if one choice is longer than the others, that's the one to choose. Don't believe it! Since economy of expression is a virtue in writing test questions as well as in most other places, the shorter choice may just as often be the correct answer. If a question gives you trouble and you can't decide among, say, three choices, common wisdom says that you should go with your initial impulse. Testing experts and psychologists agree that there's a better than average chance of success if you trust your intuition. There are no guarantees, however, because the mind works in so many strange ways that relying on your first choice may not always work.

This above all: Use the process of elimination. AP exam writers often include one choice that is obviously wrong and two others that are moderately far from the mark. Whenever possible, therefore, narrow the five choices to the two that could be correct—one of them almost right, the other unquestionably right. Naturally, you should pick the better of the two, but there's no sure-fire technique for doing that except for a close, perceptive reading of the passage or poem. And to do that nothing beats practice, practice, practice.

Read the Questions Carefully

This piece of advice is self-evident, but in the rush of taking the test it's easy to forget. Pay particular attention to questions that contain the words NOT, LEAST, or EXCEPT (see sample #3, page 16). Answering such questions requires a rapid shift of your thought patterns. Instead of searching a poem or passage for what it says or implies, you must suddenly seek out what it fails to say or imply. Then read every choice, even if you think you've found the answer. After all, choice (B) may be pretty good, but choice (E) may be even better.

Decide on a Reading Technique

The test directions above work for some people, but not necessarily for everyone— including you. As you prepare for the exam, therefore, try to answer the questions in Practice Tests A through D using the various approaches described in the paragraphs below. Although each option carries gains and losses, give each one a chance before deciding which produces the best results for you.

TIP

Answer every question.

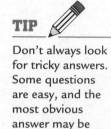

TIP

Don't always look for tricky answers. Some questions are easy, and the most obvious answer may be the correct one.

1. **OPTION A.** Read the poem or passage carefully from start to finish. Don't try to recall every detail. As you read, ask yourself, "What is this poem or passage about?" The answer will often be evident within a few lines. When you have finished, state the point of the poem or passage in your own words. Even if your interpretation is vague, it will give you a starting point for answering the questions. Sometimes the questions themselves will shed light on the point of the poem or passage. Refer to the text as often as you wish while answering the questions.

    This widely used technique takes longer at the start but allows you to make up the time later.

2. **OPTION B.** Skim the poem or passage for its general idea. Read faster than you normally would. At the same time, try to sense what the piece is saying. Read the poem or passage just intently enough to get an impression of what it's about. Don't expect to keep details in mind. Then, as you answer each question, refer to the text.

    This technique saves time at the start and keeps your mind free of needless details. At some point, however, you will be forced to scour the passage for specific answers to the questions.

    Some test takers adopt a variation of Option B. Before reading the passage, they skim the questions for a preview of what to watch for as they read. You might give that technique a try to see if it works for you.

TIP

Don't be tempted to answer a question before reading the whole passage or poem.

3. **OPTION C.** Skim the poem or passage to get its general meaning; then go back and read it carefully. Two readings, one fast and one slow, enable you to grasp the piece better than if you read it only once. During the second reading, confirm that your first impressions were accurate. Then proceed to the questions, referring frequently to the text.

    This technique takes the most time but offers you the firmest grip on the poem or passage.

    Above all, don't even think about answering the questions without first reading the passage or poem at least once from start to finish. Not only will you waste time, but you will be unable to answer questions pertaining to the overall intent or effect of the poem or passage.

Decide What to Do with Your #2 Pencil

During the entire exam you'll have a pencil in your hand. Use it to fill in the ovals on your answer sheet, of course, but also to highlight the key phrases and ideas in poems and passages. When you come to something important, quickly draw a line under it or put a check next to it in the margin. Whatever you do, however, use the pencil sparingly, or you may end up with every line marked or checked. Likewise, feel free to mark up the test questions, underlining key words or striking out obviously incorrect choices. Some people find it useful to write their answer choices next to each question before filling in ovals on the answer sheet.

SAMPLE QUESTIONS ON POETRY

Although many of the poetry questions focus on a small segment of the poem, such as a particular phrase or a pair of lines, you should be familiar with the entire poem when answering the questions.

Sample #1

The poem might best be described as

(A) a recollection of childhood
(B) a series of epiphanies
(C) a touching anecdote
(D) a coming-of-age reminisence
(E) a sentimental journey

To answer this question, read the whole poem and then determine which choice describes it most accurately. Because a few of the choices are similar—(A) and (D), for example—you must choose the *best* description, a judgment that must be based on evidence in the poem, not on your intuition or feelings.

Sample #2

The speaker in the poem views the city primarily in terms of

(A) sounds and smells
(B) colors and shapes
(C) dark and light
(D) textures and patterns
(E) youth and innocence

This question asks you to identify the poem's main images. To choose the best answer, you must inspect every line of the poem, picking out images of sounds, smells, colors, and so forth. Frequency is a good criterion for deciding which images dominate the poem. But not always. If two sorts of images recur about equally, your decision must be based on a more subtle evidence such as the placement of images in the poem. Those that appear in the first and last lines of a stanza will probably stand out from those buried in the middle. Unfortunately, there are no hard and fast rules that apply to every poem. On the test, however, the question is sure to have a reasonably clear-cut answer.

Sample #3

Looking into the dark cave allows the speaker to experience all of the following EXCEPT

(A) a surge of remorse for what he had done
(B) a sudden awareness of his own folly
(C) a rush of anger toward his former companions
(D) pride in overcoming the odds against him
(E) fear of what may be hiding inside the cave

To respond to this question you must read the poem not for what it says but for what it doesn't say. That is, four of the choices make true statements, and the correct answer is the one that states something inaccurate or false. A handful of questions on the exam may be of this type.

Sample #4

The title of the poem suggests that the poem is about

  I. an ancient religious rite
 II. a historic site now overrun by visitors
III. the scene of an unsolved murder

(A) I only
(B) II only
(C) I and II only
(D) II and III only
(E) I, II, and III

Because ambiguity is a cornerstone of literature, you may be asked questions that offer one, two, or three correct choices. On the test, you may find one or two questions in this format. To answer questions formatted in this way, figure out first which of the three choices are valid. Then pick the best answer from the A–E choices. By itself the poem's title may not evoke a complex response, but once you have read the poem, the title may take on far greater significance. Titles are always included on the test and may help you unlock each poem's meaning.

NOTE: Answering this type of question can eat up several minutes. If you're running out of time, move on to simpler types, such as the line-referenced question (See #6 on the next page.) If only seconds remain until time is called, go back to skipped questions and guess at the answer.

Sample #5

The primary rhetorical function of lines 21–23 is to

(A) introduce a digression from the central theme of the poem
(B) extend the metaphor developed in lines 19–20
(C) illustrate the speaker's ambivalence toward the child
(D) contradict a point made previously
(E) develop a theme stated in the first stanza

Although this question relates specifically to lines 21–23, it can't be answered without revisiting the rest of the poem. To determine whether (A) is the best answer, you must reflect on the poem's main theme. Choices (B) and (D) require you to reread material that came before. Choice (C) forces you to assess the speaker's tone or point of view throughout the poem, and (E) obliges you to reread the first stanza.

Not all poetry questions on the exam are strictly interpretive. Some are more objective, calling for straightforward factual answers. Sample questions 6–8 are of this type.

Sample #6

Line 7 includes an example of

(A) hyperbole
(B) oxymoron
(C) allegory
(D) consonance
(E) antithesis

To answer this question you need to be acquainted with rhetorical terms. Then you must be able to identify which of these terms is exemplified in line 7 of the poem. In the Glossary of Literary and Rhetorical Terms on pages 361–370, you'll find a brief definition of each term. For a more thorough discussion of poetic terminology see Part 3.

Sample #7

The form and content of the poem can best be described as that of

(A) an elegy
(B) an ode
(C) a lyrical ballad
(D) a sestina
(E) a sonnet

Helpful Advice

Brush up on your grammar skills *before* the exam.

To answer this question you must know some poetic terminology, more specifically the defining characteristics of an elegy, an ode, and other poetic forms. Part 3 and the Glossary at the end of this book contain the information you need.

Sample #8

Grammatically, the word "demon" (line 14) functions as

(A) the direct object of "eats" (line 12)
(B) an appositive for "underbelly" (line 14)
(C) the subject of "Screams" (line 15)
(D) the direct object of "Screams" (line 15)
(E) the indirect object of "Screams" (line 15)

The test usually contains one question meant to test your knowledge of parts of speech, sentence structure, or standard usage. It may appear as a poetry question or a question on a prose passage. If your grammar skills are rusty, a few hours spent in the company of a basic grammar book prior to the exam may serve you well.

Practice with Poetry

To see how questions apply to a specific poem, carefully read "Sonnet—to Science" by Edgar Allan Poe. Then study the questions. Be sure to read the accompanying comments. They illustrate the kind of analytical thinking that leads to correct answers.

Sonnet—to Science

Science! true daughter of Old Time thou art!
    Who alterest all things with thy peering eyes.
Why preyest thou thus upon the poet's heart,
    Vulture, whose wings are dull realities?

Line
(5)

How should he love thee? or how deem thee wise,
    Who wouldst not leave him in his wandering
To seek for treasure in the jewelled skies,
    Albeit he soared with an undaunted wing?
Hast thou not dragged Diana[1] from her car?

(10)

    And driven the Hamadryad[2] from the wood
To seek a shelter in some happier star?
    Hast thou not torn the Naiad[3] from her flood,
The Elfin[4] from the green grass, and from me
The summer dream beneath the tamarind tree?[5]

(1830)

---

[1] The huntress, a goddess of chastity. Her "car" is the moon.

[2] Wood nymph

[3] Water nymph

[4] Tiny creature residing in flowers

[5] A tropical tree with edible fruit and blossoms used for medicine

1. The speaker's attitude toward science is best described as

 (A) inquisitive
 (B) resentful
 (C) mournful
 (D) indifferent
 (E) antagonistic

Comment: This is an example of the type of bread-and-butter question that appears usually more than once on every test. Read the phrase "speaker's attitude" as a synonym for "speaker's tone." Tone questions are popular on the AP exam because every piece of literature has an identifiable tone, and an analysis of a literary selection would hardly be complete without taking tone into account.

To answer this question, consider the intent of a speaker who laments the effects of science on poetry—a common theme at the dawn of the Darwinian Age (when Poe wrote this sonnet). The speaker asks a series of questions as the poem unfolds, making Choice (A) a feasible answer. But notice that the questions are more accusatory than inquisitive. Each finds fault with science or rational thinking for ravaging the romantic world of the imagination. Choice (C) suggests that poetry has died, an unlikely assertion considering that the poet is actually engaged in writing a poem. Choice (D) is clearly wrong because the speaker mounts a vigorous attack on science. That leaves Choices (B) and (E). *Antagonistic* implies hostility, as though the speaker favors the destruction of science—a totally unrealistic prospect. *Resentful,* on the other hand, is a more moderate feeling and, therefore, best represents the speaker's attitude toward science. The best answer, therefore, is Choice (B).

2. The pronoun "he" in line 5 refers to

 (A) the vulture
 (B) the scientist
 (C) the poet
 (D) God
 (E) science

Comment: Because poets often take liberties with English syntax and disregard conventions of grammar and style, readers are left to puzzle out just what the poet is saying. Poetry questions on the AP test, therefore, sometimes ask you to figure out the intent of certain usages, or in this case, a pronoun reference.

The second quatrain of a sonnet usually starts with a new sentence that may or may not refer directly to something in the first four lines. The antecedent of "he" in line 5 remains ambiguous unless you read on. The images in lines 6–8 reveal that "he" refers to the poet—Choice (C)—a figure who cannot love or respect science because, among other things, it has, like a predatory vulture, snatched away his freedom to wander and "seek for treasure in the jewelled skies."

3. In line 5, "should" is best interpreted as

(A) can
(B) must
(C) is supposed to
(D) may
(E) might

Comment: Because language and usage change constantly, it is hardly a surprise that a poem written nearly two centuries ago will contain diction that, while perfectly proper then, may now sound odd or archaic. The use of "should" in this context is a case in point.

To interpret its meaning you must read the entire sentence in which the word appears (lines 5–8). The sentence is a question in which the speaker asks how he can love something that has restricted his freedom or reined in his imagination. In context, then, "should" is not used in its usual sense, to suggest duty or obligation, but rather to express the conditional. To paraphrase the line loosely: How can you expect me to love you, if you treat me so badly? Choice (A), therefore, is the best answer. All the other choices miss the mark.

4. Which of the following stylistic features most significantly contributes to the poem's unity?

(A) Numerous allusions to folklore and myth
(B) A series of interrogative sentences
(C) An extended metaphor
(D) The use of alliteration
(E) The pattern of end rhymes

TIP

To interpret the meaning of an unfamiliar word, read the entire sentence in which it appears.

Comment: A poem, an essay, a symphony, or any other work of art is unified when all its components—style, subject matter, structure, themes, composition, even its technique—work together to create a harmonious whole. Unity of action, of form, of intent—these, along with dramatic unity, are principles that one might apply to a literary work. The concept of unity in literature is hard to pin down but easy to recognize when absent.

To answer the question, survey the poem for stylistic features listed in Choices (A) through (E). Because the poet used them all, your job is to determine which feature is "most significant" to the poem's unity. Since unity is derived from the overall effect of the work rather than from its individual parts, the best answer is (C), the central metaphor that compares science to a type of vulture. Throughout the poem, the speaker uses words and phrases that suggest the actions of a predatory bird, among them "preyest," "soared," "dragged," and "torn." In comparison to (C), the other choices fail to make the grade.

5. The speaker in the poem suggests all of the following EXCEPT

   (A)   science is responsible for destroying the poet's capacity to dream
   (B)   science fails to value human emotions
   (C)   science reduces everything to observable facts
   (D)   science is the death knell of poetry
   (E)   a function of poetry and of science is to uncover reality

Comment: Four of the five choices restate or paraphrase an idea found in the poem. Your task is to identify the one that doesn't. Choice (A) is suggested by the last two lines of the poem, Choice (B) by the idea that science preys on the poet's heart. Choice (C) is clearly stated in line 2, and Choice (E), while not stated directly, is implied by the notion that science is guided by "dull realities," and that poets find hidden realities in nature—the moon, the sea, the grass, and so forth. Choice (D), the best answer, overstates the influence of science on poetry. While science may diminish poetry, its influence is not fatal. If science had the capacity to kill poetry, this particular poem, among others, would not have been written.

6. Which of the following is the best meaning of the phrase "not leave him" in line 6?

   (A)   Leave him alone
   (B)   Interfere
   (C)   Abandon him
   (D)   Take leave of him
   (E)   Control him

Comment: Because poems often contain nonstandard idiom, AP questions frequently deal with the best paraphrases and interpretations of specific phrases such as this. Usually the answer won't be found in the phrase itself but only in its context. Therefore, think about the overall purpose of the poem. Before you pick an answer, read what precedes and what follows the phrase. Then, substitute each of the choices for the phrase "not leave him."

Characterizing science as a destructive force interested only in cold realities, the speaker finds himself unable to soar in fantasy, sit peacefully dreaming beneath a tree, or, as intimated in lines 6–7, wander in search of inspiring treasures. In other words, science has become the speaker's nemesis. It won't leave him alone to do his thing. Of the choices, only (A) represents what the speaker has in mind.

7. Line 8 ("Albeit . . . wing?") serves primarily to

   (A)   suggest similarities between the speaker and the vulture
   (B)   contrast the poet before and after the coming of science
   (C)   show the magnitude of the poet's imagination
   (D)   reflect the speaker's ambivalence toward the poet
   (E)   undercut the speaker's emotional intensity

Comment: Consider this a "function" question, that is, a question that can be answered only by figuring out not what the line says but its purpose in the poem. Structurally, line 8 is a subordinate clause in which the speaker wonders aloud how he can be expected to do anything but despise the effects of science. In this line, the speaker briefly imagines the way life used to be, when he "soared with an undaunted wing." Looking over the five choices, you'll see that only (B) comes close to describing the function of line 8.

8. Between lines 1–8 and 9–14 there is a shift from

   (A) optimism to pessimism
   (B) emotionalism to rationality
   (C) realism to fantasy
   (D) inquiry to disapproval
   (E) hatred to revulsion

Comment: A point of view—the relation in which a speaker stands to the subject matter—governs the overall character of most poems and other literary works. Speakers, being human, often digress, change their minds, insert asides, apostrophize, or contradict themselves in the middle of whatever they have to say.

Because such a shift takes place within this poem, you are asked to identify the speaker's rhetorical stance toward science both before the shift and after. As a result, you must compare and contrast the speaker's viewpoint in lines 1–8 and in lines 9–14. Eliminate (A) as a possible answer because nowhere does the speaker show an iota of optimism. Choice (E) is not much better because there is hardly a difference between "hatred" and "revulsion." Choice (B) has potential because the speaker's voice is charged with emotion; there's not a hint of greater rationality in the last six lines. If anything, the tone is more antirational than before. With regard to (C), consider that the speaker compares science to a vulture—a poetic conceit inconsistent with a realist's way of thinking. That leaves (D) as the answer. Indeed, in lines 1–8 the speaker spews a series of questions about the harmful effects of science. In the remainder of the poem, the questions become accusatory. They blame science for destroying the sensibilities of poets.

9. The contrast between science and poetry is best illustrated by which pair of phrases?

   (A) "from the wood" (line 10) and "from her car" (line 9)
   (B) "true daughter" (1) and "peering eyes" (2)
   (C) "jewelled skies" (7) and "tamarind tree" (14)
   (D) "undaunted wing" (8) and "happier star" (11)
   (E) "dull realities" (4) and "summer dream" (14)

Comment: To answer this question you might simply try studying the pairs of phrases and picking the one that suggests the conflict that lies at the heart of the poem. Choice (A) hints at a conflict between nature ("wood") and technology ("car") until you remember that the "car" is Diana's chariot, the moon. Choices (B), (C), and (D) contain pairs of phrases that contain no particular contrast. But (E) consists of two contrasting phrases, the first representing the speaker's view of science, the second a metaphor for the the poet's creativity.

10. According to the speaker, the most negative effect of science has been to

    (A) replace emotions with cold, hard objectivity
    (B) change man's perception of the universe
    (C) distort the purposes of scientific investigation
    (D) belittle nonscientists
    (E) convince people to distrust their instincts

Comment: Notice that the question begins with "According to the speaker," a phrase suggesting that the answer will not be found by reading between the lines of the poem but directly in the speaker's words. The phrase "most negative" also obliges you to weigh each effect for its destructiveness. At the same time, you must ascertain that each effect listed in the five choices is mentioned in the poem.

Choice (B) certainly qualifies as a harmful effect but is neither implied nor discussed in the poem. Likewise, there is no evidence of (C) or (D) in the poem. There may be a hint of (E) in the speaker's words but the statement is overgeneralized since the poem focuses on the effects of science on poets and their work. Choice (A), therefore, is the correct answer because the speaker, using a variety of images and ideas, laments the intrusion of science into the life of the imagination. Science, with its dispassionate pursuit of facts, spoils the visions of the creative dreamer, ruins myth, and removes magic from the stars and storied constellations.

11. The speaker alludes to figures from myth and folklore in order to

    (A) symbolize images that have long ignited the imagination of poets
    (B) endow the poem with a classical flavor
    (C) suggest how dramatically science has altered poetry
    (D) heighten the misunderstanding between poets and scientists
    (E) demonstrate the obsolescence of poetry

Comment: Rather than ask you to explain allusions in the poem, this question asks you to identify the reason that Poe included them.

Choice (B) implies that Poe tossed allusions into the poem solely to show off. Choices (C) and (D) restate themes in the poem but in no way account for the speaker's use of allusions. The suggestion that the allusions are meant to illustrate poetry's obsolescence makes Choice (E) an unlikely answer. Choice (A), on the other hand, goes to the heart of the poem's message: Science has brought the poet down to earth and expelled some of the symbolic images that have inspired poets for ages and ages.

SAMPLE QUESTIONS ON PROSE FICTION

Because prose passages on the AP exam are chosen for their intensity of language, you should read them no less carefully than you read poems. In fact, questions on prose passages cover much of the same territory as the poetry questions: sentence structure, the effect of words and phrases in context, major themes, point of view,

TIP

Read prose passages as carefully as you read poems.

and so forth. In addition, they ask about narrative techniques, the interaction of characters, the development of ideas, and numerous other elements of literary analysis.

A review of recent AP exams shows that some topics come up again and again: the tone of the passage, a shift in the speaker's rhetorical stance, the interpretation of a word, phrase, or sentence, the effect or purpose of a figure of speech, and the relationship between sentence structure and meaning. Because passages are usually excerpted from longer works, many exams include a question or two that ask you to make inferences about what may have preceded the events in the passage and what might reasonably follow.

Passages on the exam appear without titles, sources, and authors. Only a date of composition is given, information that may help you answer some of the questions. At the very least, the date may provide a clue to the meaning of an allusion or account for any unusual diction or the quirky style in which the text is written.

The samples below illustrate the types of questions most commonly found on the exam.

Sample #1

Tone

The speaker's tone in the passage can best be described as

(A) satirical
(B) despairing
(C) contemptuous
(D) irreverent
(E) whimsical

TIP

Expect to find several questions about tone on the exam.

Tone is so vital an element in literary analysis that you can depend on seeing three or more tone questions on the exam. Tone questions come in a variety of guises. Some, like this one, are straightforward. Others are couched in words that don't mention tone at all, as in the following:

"In lines 12–15, the speaker's *attitude* toward Hortense can best be described as . . ."
"The speaker's *feelings* about the disaster are suggested by . . ."
"The speaker's *state of mind* is established predominantly by . . ."

The diction may vary, but each italicized word or phrase is a synonym for tone or for the "speaker's rhetorical stance," a term that AP test writers like to use.

When a speaker's tone changes in mid-passage, you may be asked to identify two tones—before and after the change. Not all tone questions are about the entire passage. Some focus on the tone of a word, a phrase, or on any other component of the passage.

Sample #2

Passage as a Whole

The passage as a whole relies on all of the following contrasts EXCEPT

(A) knowledge and ignorance
(B) elegance and bad taste
(C) sanity and madness
(D) urgency and leisure
(E) excitability and apathy

Although you're not likely to be asked about the meaning of the entire passage, some questions, such as this one, can be answered only if you know what the whole passage says. The structure of this question obliges you to search the entire passage for various contrasts. If all goes well, you'll find four of the five listed in (A) through (E). The one you don't find is the answer to the question. You should anticipate two or three questions structured like this one on the exam.

Other questions that require familiarity with the whole passage may be phrased something like:

> "The excerpt is chiefly concerned with a . . ."
> "The change that Lou undergoes in the passage can best be characterized as . . ."
> "By the end of the excerpt, Doc probably believed that Jesse had been . . ."

Sample #3

Making Inferences

The speaker implies in the first paragraph that the narrative preceding the passage most likely included

(A) an altercation in the street
(B) a reunion between two old friends
(C) a description of Venice
(D) a conversation between the shopkeeper and a policeman
(E) the receipt of a shocking letter

Almost certainly you'll be given a question that asks you to infer what might have occurred in the story before the passage begins or to speculate on what events might follow. Clues may appear almost anywhere in the passage. Sometimes before-and-after questions have more to do with style, characterization, setting, tone, or voice than with events in the story. Were a given passage to continue, for example, a tongue-in-cheek narrator would be more likely to say something funny than to tell a sad tale full of teary-eyed sentimentality.

Sample #4

Rhetoric

The phrase "cut her past away" in line 13 does which of the following?

  I. It shifts the tone of the narrative from sentimentality to realism.
 II. It introduces a strain of naturalism into the passage.
III. It foreshadows Mona's momentous decision.

(A) I only
(B) II only
(C) I and II only
(D) II and III only
(E) I, II, and III

On the exam you may expect several questions about the rhetorical function of a word, a phrase, a sentence, or an even lengthier piece of the passage, such as a description of the setting or a character sketch. Asking a question about rhetorical function implies that the author chose language intended to create one or more effects. Your task is to identify those effects. The format of this question indicates that the phrase "cut her past away" may have one, two, or three different functions. To answer questions formatted in this way, it's helpful to determine first which functions apply to the passage and which functions don't. Only then should you look at the A–E choices.

Sample #5

Sentence Structure

In lines 4–8, the major effect of using a series of short compound sentences is to

(A) create tension in the narrative
(B) indicate Mr. Herzog's state of mind
(C) emphasize the narrator's confusion
(D) prepare the reader for the tumultuous events that follow
(E) establish a mood of tranquillity

This question, like others, relates to various effects of sentence structure. Sentence structure always affects meaning, but it may also alter the tone, slow down or speed up the narrative, create suspense, and shape the reader's response in any number of other ways.

Sample #6

Phrases

In the context of the passage, the phrase "remarkably sleek and plump clerks" (line 23) is used as a metaphor for the

(A) indifference of the bureaucracy
(B) stylishness of the downtown area
(C) frenetic activity in the law office
(D) austerity of the courthouse
(E) judge's obsession

This question comes as close to asking you to identify the meaning of a phrase as almost any question you'll find on the exam. Instead of asking you straightforwardly what the phrase means, however, this question is couched in terms of interpreting a metaphor, which, all things considered, is just a sneaky way to assess your comprehension. Other questions meant to check how well you understand pieces of the passage may read as follows:

"Which of the following is the primary meaning of the word 'love' as it is used in line 15?"

"The best paraphrase of the sentence beginning in line 8 is . . . "

"The speaker characterizes a 'farce' (line 19) as all of the following EXCEPT . . . "

"The phrases 'gleamed like an eye below her room' (line 3) and 'rose in the distance like a moon' (line 5) imply a contrast between . . . "

"From the context, the reader can infer that Robbins (line 40) works as a . . . "

Sample #7

Terms

In lines 34–39, the speaker makes use of all of the following EXCEPT

(A) hyperbole
(B) equivocation
(C) dramatic irony
(D) non sequitur
(E) pathos

Two or more questions on the AP exam may test your recognition and understanding of terms common to literary analysis and criticism. No doubt you are already familiar with many of them, but to make sure, study the Glossary at the back of this book.

Sample #8

Characterizations

Victor criticizes his son's performance (lines 37–39) because he

(A) has unrealistic expectations
(B) hopes to make amends for his own failure
(C) wants to comfort Katherine
(D) expects to inspire the boy to try harder
(E) suffers from self-doubt

Because prose fiction passages are often about people, it's almost inevitable that a question or two may relate to characterization, to conflicts between characters, or to the influence of one character on another. In this question you are asked to analyze a character's motives.

Practice with Prose

Carefully read the following passage, an excerpt from the British novel *Moll Flanders* by Daniel Defoe. Then answer the questions. The comments that follow each question explain the reasoning process that led to the correct answers.

> I was very shy of shoplifting, especially among the mercers and drapers,[1] who are a set of fellows that have their eyes very much about them. I made a venture or two among the lace folks and the
>
> *Line* (5) milliners, and particularly at one shop where two young women were newly set up and had not been bred in the trade. There I carried off a piece of bone-lace worth six or seven pounds, and a paper of thread. But this was but once; it was a trick that would not serve again.
>
> It was always reckoned a safe job when we heard of a new shop, (10) and especially when the people were such as were not bred to shops. Such may depend upon it that they will be visited once or twice at their beginning, and they must be very sharp indeed if they can prevent it.
>
> I made another adventure or two after this, but they were but (15) trifles. Nothing considerable offering for a good while, I began to think that I must give over the trade in earnest; but my governess, who was not willing to lose me and expected great things of me, brought me one day into company with a young woman and a fellow that went for her husband, though, as it appeared afterwards, (20) she was not his wife, but they were partners in the trade they carried on, and in something else too. In short, they robbed together, lay together, were taken together, and at last were hanged together.

---

[1] types of fabric and clothing merchants

(25)

(30)

(35)

(40)

(45)

I came into a kind of league with these two by the help of my governess, and they carried me out into three or four adventures where I rather saw them commit some coarse and unhandy robberies in which nothing but a great stock of impudence on their side and gross negligence on the people's side who were robbed could have made them successful. So I resolved from that time forward to be very cautious how I adventured with them; and indeed, when two or three unlucky projects were proposed by them, I declined the offer and persuaded them against it. One time they particularly proposed robbing a watchmaker of three gold watches, which they had eyed in the daytime, and found the place where he laid them. One of them had so many keys of all kinds that he made no question to open the place where the watchmaker had laid them; and so we made a kind of appointment. But when I came to look narrowly into the thing, I found they proposed breaking open the house, and this I would not embark in, so they went without me. They did get into the house by main force and broke up the locked place where the watches were but found but one of the gold watches and a silver one, which they took, and got out of the house again very clear. But the family being alarmed, cried out, "Thieves," and the man was pursued and taken. The young woman had got off, too, but unhappily was stopped at a distance and the watches found upon her. And thus I had a second escape, for they were convicted and both hanged, being old offenders, though but young people. And as I said before that they robbed together, so now they hanged together, and there ended my new partnership.

(1722)

1. The chief contrast made by the speaker in the first paragraph (lines 1–8) can best be described as that between

   (A) males and females
   (B) mercers and drapers
   (C) dishonesty and truthfulness
   (D) danger and safety
   (E) innocence and experience

Comment: The speaker uses the first paragraph to inform the reader about her shoplifting career. We learn that she is "shy" about preying on merchants "that have their eyes very much about them"—that is, shopkeepers who are alert to the threat of shoplifters. But she has had success in places where the shopkeepers are beginners, where they have "not been bred in the trade." In short, (E) is the best answer to the question.

2. In context, the phrase "not bred to shops" (line 10) is best interpreted to mean

   (A) unaccustomed to dealing with customers
   (B) unable to market goods effectively
   (C) unused to operating stores
   (D) not considered skillful salespeople
   (E) unaware of shopping protocol

Comment: This question asks you to figure out the meaning of a phrase that may once have been common in everyday speech but is now all but obsolete. Indeed, the entire passage is packed with usage long out of fashion. What's more, the speaker, an uneducated young woman, uses English that was nonstandard even in her day. The correct answer can nevertheless be found by studying the context in which the phrase occurs.

In line 10 the subject under discussion is shoplifting. In particular, the speaker discusses which shops make the best targets. New shops are "safe" because people unaccustomed to being shopkeepers don't know enough to guard their wares against thieves. Choices (A), (B), (D), and (E) pertain generally to neophyte shopkeepers, but only (C) applies specifically to a trait that would interest a shoplifter. The best interpretation of "not bred to shops," therefore, is "unused to operating stores."

3. Which of the following best describes the function of the statement that "they robbed together, lay together, were taken together, and at last were hanged together" (lines 21–22)?

   (A) It inserts an element of parody into the narrative.
   (B) It exemplifies a lesson with a moral purpose.
   (C) It suggests that the speaker has made an important discovery.
   (D) It serves as a brief introduction to an important episode in the story.
   (E) It lays out facts that symbolize the speaker's tragic life.

Comment: In the third paragraph of the passage, the speaker brings two new characters into her narrative, a young woman and her fellow. In one sentence (lines 21–22) she summarizes their story but provides insufficient details to satisfy the reader's natural curiosity about how the pair met their fate. (D) is the best answer because the speaker follows through with a more detailed account of the couple's misadventure. (A) is not an appropriate answer because the passage contains no evidence that the speaker is ridiculing or imitating another work. Likewise, (B) and (C) are irrelevant choices. Choice (E) inaccurately characterizes the speaker's life and is unrelated to the statement in question.

4. The structure of the sentence beginning in line 23 does which of the following?

   (A) It contradicts assertions made about the young couple in the previous paragraph.
   (B) It reflects the speaker's failure to make her own decisions.
   (C) It implies that the governess can't be trusted.
   (D) It attests to the speaker's ability to accurately assess the character of other people.
   (E) It makes light of the governess's efforts to help the speaker get ahead in her chosen career.

Comment: This question presumes a cause-and-effect relationship between the given sentence and some other aspect of the passage. The particulars of sentence structure actually count for little in working out the answer. What matters more is your ability to understand the meaning of the sentence and determine its role in the passage.

TIP

Remember that every sentence has a distinct function in the passage.

At this point in the passage the speaker disparages her young associates, whose dumb luck rather than skill enabled them to pull off a robbery or two. Because the sentence contradicts nothing that came earlier, eliminate Choice (A). Disregard Choice (B) as well because the speaker's decisiveness is not an issue. Although the sentence vaguely impugns the judgment of the governess, Choice (C) is a stretch, and Choice (E) is irrelevant. Choice (D) correctly identifies the function of the sentence. Indeed, the speaker accurately judges her two colleagues. Her perceptivity is borne out by the couple's misadventures and their death by hanging.

5. In context, the word "impudence" (line 26) is best interpreted to mean

   (A) disrespect
   (B) insolence
   (C) indecency
   (D) shamelessness
   (E) boldness

Comment: If a question asks you to interpret an everyday word such as "impudence," you can be sure that its conventional meaning isn't at issue. Look, therefore, for a secondary or more obscure meaning.

With that principle in mind, survey the five choices and eliminate the two common synonyms of "impudence" found in Choices (A) and (B). According to the speaker, the young couple's "impudence" helped them carry out a few robberies. Since neither "indecency" nor "shamelessness" can be construed as enabling traits of young freebooters, eliminate (C) and (D). That leaves (E), decisively the best answer.

TIP

Pay close attention to questions that include the word EXCEPT.

6. The first three paragraphs suggest that the speaker believes all of the following to be true of shoplifting EXCEPT

    (A) it is more manageable with inexperienced shopkeepers
    (B) it can be a lucrative endeavor
    (C) it will one day lead to her apprehension and punishment
    (D) it is a trade like any other
    (E) it involves a careful selection of prey

Comment: The word EXCEPT is your cue to search through the passage for evidence of each of the five choices. Then select as your answer the item you can't find.

Eliminate (A) because the speaker twice says that she favors plying her trade in the shops of beginners (lines 4–5 *and* lines 9–10). That the work is lucrative—Choice (B)—is implied by lines 5–7. Choice (D) is suggested by the speaker's use of such words as "venture" (line 3), "job" (line 9), and "trade" (line 16), and Choice (E) is discussed in both the first and second paragraphs. Only Choice (C) is missing from the passage. The speaker never discusses the possibility of her own apprehension and punishment.

7. In relating the story of the young couple (lines 23–48) the speaker's attitude toward her two former colleagues might best be described as

    (A) hostile
    (B) scornful
    (C) despicable
    (D) flattering
    (E) generous

Comment: This is a variation of a "tone" question. Read lines 23–48 with your sensors attuned to the speaker's opinion of her two former colleagues.

The fact that she keeps her distance from them (lines 28–31) suggests that the two favorable adjectives—"flattering" (D) and "generous" (E)—should be eliminated. Because there is no evidence of hostility in the speaker's words, eliminate (A). Similarly, because the speaker has no reason to despise the pair, (C) is not a good answer. That leaves (B) as the only choice—a good answer considering the speaker's account of the bungled theft. The fact that the couple's trip to the gallows meant nothing more to the speaker than the end of her partnership, as stated in lines 46–48, indicates that she could never have thought very highly of the unfortunate pair.

8. The speaker in the passage reveals her character primarily through

    (A) her comments and observations
    (B) use of narrative in the first person
    (C) her interaction with others
    (D) physical descriptions
    (E) her use of English idiom

Comment: This question asks you to determine how the author develops the character, a crucial issue in any work of fiction. Because the author uses several techniques, choosing the predominant one is something of a challenge.

Choice (B) could be the correct answer, although a first-person narrative is not necessarily more revealing of a personality than, say, a third-person approach. After all, speakers can lie about themselves and pretend to be different from who they really are. Almost nothing in the passage supports (C) or (D) as the best choice. Choice (E) has some validity because the speaker's use of non-standard English reveals her background. Because the question asks about her *character*, however, (E) fails to hold up as the best answer. Choice (A) is arguably the best choice because the passage consists almost entirely of the speaker's account of her adventures in shoplifting along with thoughts about her anxieties, feelings, and so on. From these comments and observations, readers come to know her.

9. From the statement "I declined the offer and persuaded them against it" (lines 30–31), the reader may infer that

   (A) the speaker plans to reform and go straight
   (B) the young couple's project is destined to fail
   (C) the speaker feels guilty about spurning the young couple
   (D) the speaker has been given good advice by the governess
   (E) the young couple's project requires the speaker's participation

Comment: Like other questions on the AP exam, this one requires you to identify the implications of a particular statement. To the speaker, the words merely report something she did. To a reader in search of meaning behind the meaning, however, the words signify more.

By the time the speaker declines to participate in the couple's questionable ventures, the reader already knows from the previous paragraph that the pair was "taken together, and at last were hanged together" (line 22). The speaker calls their current schemes "unlucky," suggesting that no good could come of them. Consequently (B) is the best answer.

10. Which of the following best describes the speaker's use of language?

   (A) Colloquial and unrefined
   (B) Informative and foul
   (C) Arrogant and self-serving
   (D) Personal and poetic
   (E) Pretentious and pompous

Comment: Had this passage been written recently, its use of language would be idiosyncratic to say the least. But the passage was composed in 1722. Would an eighteenth-century reader have found it equally eccentric? Answering that question puts your "ear" for language to the test.

By considering only the first adjective in each pair, you may quickly dispose of Choices (C) and (E). In no way is the speaker's language either "arrogant" or "pretentious." Now look at the second adjective in the remaining choices. Because there is no evidence of foul or obscene language, eliminate (B). Similarly, disregard (D) because there's hardly a poetic touch in the entire passage. To justify (A) as the only valid choice, consider such usages as "shy of shoplifting" (line 1), and "a fellow that went for her husband" (line 19), colloquial expressions that would not have passed the lips of a well-educated or discriminating speaker.

11. Which of the following characteristics of the speaker does the narrative reveal?

    I. She is self-confident in her work.
    II. She is proud of her ability to size up a situation.
    III. She is optimistic about the future.

    (A) I only
    (B) III only
    (C) I and II only
    (D) II and III only
    (E) I, II, and III

TIP

Some questions put your "ear" for language to the test.

Comment: Although the speaker claims to be "shy" in line 1, she is not timid. Rather, she is cautious—cautious about shoplifting from merchants savvy to the ways of people like herself. Through much of the passage, in fact, she boasts about her good judgment. She chooses victims carefully, stealing only when she knows that she can succeed. She also takes pride in having made the decision not to become involved with a pair of reckless thieves who end up on the gallows. Characteristics I and II, then, are evident in the passage. Because nothing in the story relates to the speaker's future, Choice (C) is the best answer.

Mastering the
Essays

- What you can learn from past exams
- Using your time well
- What AP readers look for
- How essays are scored: what the numbers mean
- Sample student essays on poetry and prose
- What's "free" in a free-response essay

Section II of the AP exam, consisting of three essays to be written in two hours, has a dual purpose. First, it tests your facility with literary analysis, and second, it assesses your ability to write an analytical essay under the pressure of time. Of the two purposes, the first is more important, but frankly it would be hard for you to show off your command of analytical thinking without also being adept at organizing your thoughts and expressing them coherently on paper.

Each essay is written in response to a different question, or "prompt," as test-makers like to call it: one on poetry, one on prose fiction, and one on a novel or play of your choice.

1. **The poetry question.** After reading a poem, you will be asked to write a well-organized essay that discusses how the poet's use of certain poetic techniques helps convey the meaning and effect of the poem. (A variation on this question is an essay on a pair of poems. Another possibility is an essay comparing a poem and a prose passage on the same subject.)

2. **Prose fiction question.** After reading a passage of prose fiction, you will be asked to write a well-organized essay on how the author's use of certain literary techniques helped to convey the contents and effect of the passage.

3. **Free-response question.** You will be asked to write a well-organized essay that discusses a literary issue or concept as it relates to a novel or play of your choice.

NOTE: None of the questions asks you to write a summary of the poem, passage, or work of literature. Your essay should include references to lines, characters, conflicts, incidents, and any other important features. **But the emphasis should be on literary techniques, not on story or plot.** Extensive retelling of what happens in a work wastes time and dilutes the point of your essay. In effect, it almost guarantees a low essay score because it doesn't answer the question.

QUESTIONS FROM PREVIOUS EXAMS

What follows are shortened versions of essay questions given in recent years. Although the types of questions have remained the same, the order of questions 1 and 2 varies. That is, the question on poetry may precede or may follow the question on the prose passage. Invariably, however, the free-response question comes last. In any case, *you may write the essays in any order you choose.*

Because forty minutes is suggested for writing each essay, it is crucial that you apportion your time so that you'll finish all the essays. Guard against getting so wrapped up in the first or second essay that you'll have to rush through the third.

2011

1. Read the poem entitled "The Story" by the contemporary poet Li-Young Lee. Then write an essay analyzing how the poet uses literary devices such as structure and point of view to portray the father-son relationship.

2. In an excerpt from the George Eliot novel *Middlemarch,* the author presents a conversation about family finances between a newly married couple. After reading the passage, write a well-developed essay that analyzes how the couple's relationship is conveyed through the use of such literary techniques as choice of detail and narrative perspective.

3. Identify someone in a novel or play who is affected in a conseqential way by a search for justice. In your essay, analyze the character's understanding of justice and whether he or she successfully achieves it. In your discussion analyze the significance of the search to the work as a whole.

2010

1. After you have carefully read "The Century Quilt," a poem by Marilyn Nelson Waniek, write an essay that analyzes how the poet uses such literary elements as structure, imagery, and tone to develop various meanings that the speaker in the poem ascribes to the quilt.

2. Read a description of Clarence Hervey, a character in *Belinda,* an 1801 novel by Maria Edgeworth. Then write an essay that analyzes how the author develops Hervey's complex character using such literary techniques as tone, point of view, and language.

3. Characters in novels, plays, and epics are sometimes displaced or exiled from home, family, birthplace, or other significant location. Exile can be terrible and sad but also "potent, even enriching," according to the author-scholar Edward Said. Choose a piece of literature in which a character experiences a separation that is both alienating and enriching, and analyze how this experience helps to convey the meaning of the work as a whole.

2009

1. Read a speech from *Henry VIII* by Shakespeare, delivered by Cardinal Wolsey just after he has been fired as the king's close advisor. In your essay, analyze how Wolsey uses allusion, figurative language, and tone to convey his reaction to being suddenly dismissed.
2. The opening of Ann Petry's novel *The Street* (1946) describes a New York neighborhood on a cold, windy November day and introduces the protagonist Lutie Johnson. In an essay, analyze how the author uses such techniques as imagery, personification, and choice of detail to establish Lutie's relationship to the setting.
3. Write an essay about a novel or play in which a symbolic action, event, or object plays a signifigant role or represents something larger than itself. In your essay analyze how the symbol functions and what it says about the characters or themes in the work as a whole.

2008

1. The speakers in two poems—one by Keats, the other by Longfellow—reflect on their accomplishments in life. After reading the pair, write an essay that analyzes the techniques each poet uses to convey his thoughts about his situation.
2. In an excerpt from the 1999 novel *Fasting, Feasting,* by Anita Desai, Arun, an Indian exchange student, goes to the beach with his American host family. After reading the passage, write an essay on the literary devices that Desai uses to capture Arun's experience.
3. Write an essay about a novel or play in which a minor character serves as a "foil," a person whose characteristics serve to intensify the distinctive qualities of the protagonist. In your essay, analyze how the relationship between the two characters helps to convey the meaning of the work.

2007

1. After reading two poems in which an adult speaker addresses a child, write an essay that compares and contrasts the poems and analyzes the literary devices used by the poets to make their point.
2. Read the given passage from *Johnny Got His Gun* by Dalton Trumbo. Then write an essay that analyzes how Trumbo uses such techniques as point of view, syntax, and choice of details to describe the relationship between Joe, the protagonist of the novel, and his father.
3. Write an essay about a novel or play in which the past influences a character's actions, values, or attitudes. Show how the character deals with an aspect of the past and how the character's relationship to the past contributes to the overall meaning of the work.

2006

1. Read the poem "Evening Hawk" by Robert Penn Warren. Then write an essay that analyzes how the poet uses language to describe the scene and convey mood and meaning.

2. After reading an excerpt from *Lady Windermere's Fan*, a play by Oscar Wilde, write an essay that analyzes how the playwright reveals the values of the characters and the nature of their society.
3. Choose a novel or play in which a country setting plays a significant role. Then write an essay that analyzes how the setting functions in the work as a whole.

2005

1. After reading two William Blake poems, each entitled "The Chimney Sweeper," compare and contrast the two poems, taking into account the poetic techniques used in each.
2. After reading a short story by Katherine Brush, write an essay that shows how the author uses literary devices to achieve her purpose.
3. Identify a character in a novel or play who conforms outwardly but questions inwardly. Then write an essay that analyzes how this tension between outward conformity and inward questioning contributes to the meaning of the work.

GUIDELINES FOR WRITING ESSAYS

By this time in your school career, you've probably written reams of essays. Along the way you may have produced exemplary pieces of writing worthy of publication; at other times, you may have written essays fit only for the garbage. Regardless of your essay-writing history, no one expects you to produce three immortal pieces of prose during two hours of the AP exam. Instead, clearly organized, well-developed, and accurately written essays that address the question with insightful interpretations of the text will do. And if your essays also demonstrate a mastery of three fundamental writing goals—clarity, focus, and correctness—they should earn high scores. Why those three?

Essay-Writing Tip

For a top score, make your essays

CLEAR,
FOCUSED,
and
CORRECT

Clarity because your ideas probably need to be clear to you before you can make them clear to others.

Focus because you'll lose your readers if the essay wanders from its main idea.

Correctness because, whether it's fair or not, readers will judge you and your work according to how well you demonstrate the conventions of writing.

This book can't provide a full-scale review of essay-writing, but it can acquaint you with some basic principles to keep in mind as you write your AP essays.

The Writing Process

Because you won't have time to invent a writing process when you take the test, prepare one ahead of time. Try out various processes while writing practice essays, and then stick to the one that helps you work most rapidly and efficiently while producing the best results. In effect, make a plan for what to do during each stage of the writing process.

The first stage, often called *pre-writing*, consists of everything that needs to be done before you actually start writing. During the second stage, *composing*, you choose the words and form the sentences that express your thoughts. And during the final stage, *revising and proofreading*, you polish and refine the text of your essay word by word, making it clear, correct, and graceful. The truth is that these three stages overlap and blend indiscriminately. Writers compose, revise, and proofread simultaneously, they jot down sentences during pre-writing, and even late in the process may weave new ideas into their text. In fact, no stage really ends until the final period of the last sentence is put in place—or until the AP proctor calls "Time!"

Study Each Topic Closely

Start with a meticulous reading of each question. Read it more than once, underscoring key words and ideas. If in doubt read it again because an essay that misses the point of the question gets little or no credit on the exam.

Here is a typical prompt for an essay on a poem or a passage of fiction:

> Read the following poem [or fiction passage] carefully, paying particular attention to the speaker's [or narrator's] emotional vigor. Then write a well-organized essay in which you explain how the poet [or author] conveys not just a literal description of his encounter with a homeless vagrant but a deeper understanding of the whole experience. You may wish to include an analysis of such elements as diction, imagery, metaphor, and form.

The underlined sections lay out the task—to write an essay on how the poet or author conveys emotional vigor on both the literal level and on a deeper psychological or philosophical level.

The phrase "You may wish" indicates that you are being given a suggestion to devote your essay to the four listed elements. Don't be bound by the suggestion—you might do better concentrating on only one or two of the elements while adding others of your own choice. Also, you need not give equal attention to all the elements. Choose one or two to emphasize and discuss the others less fully. In other words, adapt your response to your understanding of the poem or passage. Another point to consider is that choosing relevant elements not listed in the prompt shows a measure of your initiative and insight that could distinguish your essay from others—and perhaps induce the AP reader to add a point or two to your score.

Essay-Writing Tip

AP prompts often give you leeway on what to write about.

A FORTY-MINUTE ESSAY

No one can tell you exactly how much time to devote to each step of the process. What works for you may be different from what works for others. **To do your best, practice writing an essay a day for several days until you get the feel of forty minutes' writing time.** (For topics, use question 3 from each of the previous exams listed on pages 36–38.) Keep track of how much time you spend thinking about the topic, how many minutes you devote to composing the essay, and how long it takes you to proofread and edit. As you practice, adjust the following plan until you get the timing that suits you best.

PRE-WRITING: 5–10 minutes (Add 5 minutes for AP questions containing a poem or passage.)

Reading and analyzing the prompt

Narrowing the topic

Choosing a main idea

Gathering and arranging supporting ideas

COMPOSING: 20–25 minutes

Introducing your thesis

Developing paragraphs

Choosing the best words for meaning and effect

Structuring sentences effectively

Concluding your essay

EDITING AND PROOFREADING: 5–10 minutes

Editing for clarity and coherence

Eliminating excess verbiage

Editing to create interest

Checking for standard usage and mechanical errors, including spelling, punctuation, and capitalization

To make every second count, don't waste time inventing an essay title (your essay doesn't need one). Don't count words, and don't expect to recopy your first draft. Because AP readers understand that your essays are first drafts, feel free to cross out words, or insert words using carets (^). Use neatly-drawn arrows to move blocks of text, as though you were cutting and pasting on a computer screen. If necessary, number the sentences to make clear the order in which they are to be read. You won't be penalized for a sloppy-looking paper. Just make sure that it's readable.

Collect and Organize Ideas

The prompt provides you with the essay's topic—namely, the writer's use of certain elements to create "emotional vigor." Your first task, then, is to locate words, phrases, and ideas that create or even hint at *emotional vigor*. Then arrange whatever you've underlined or circled in a logical, easy-to-follow sequence. Use the order in which they appear in the text, or organize them according to the literary elements you plan to discuss: metaphors in one group, images in a second group, and so on. In effect, prepare a sketchy outline of your essay.

The order of ideas is important. What comes first? Second? Third? The best order is the clearest order, the arrangement that readers can follow with the least effort. The worst plan is the aimless one, the one that presents ideas haphazardly, or in the order they happened to pop into your head.

Try ranking your ideas in the order of importance. Ask, for example, which literary element is most influential in shaping the "emotional vigor" of the poem or passage. Which ranks second? Third? and so on. As you write the essay, save your best evidence for last. Giving it away at the start is self-defeating because everything that follows will be anticlimactic. In other words, work toward your best point, not away from it. An excellent way to plot three good ideas is to lead with your second best, save the best for the end, and sandwich the least powerful idea between the others. This structure recognizes that the end and the beginning of an essay are its most critical parts. A good opening draws the reader in and creates an all-important first impression, but a memorable ending, coming last, is what readers have fresh in their minds when they assign a grade.

TIP

Make a plan for your essay. Decide what to say first, second, third, and so on.

Another effective way to organize an essay in response to a poetry or prose fiction question is to guide the reader line-by-line through the text of the poem or passage. In other words, point out and analyze features of the text in the order they occur. This approach permits you to use an organizing principle virtually handed to you by the author of the text. Moreover, it allows you to begin writing the essay almost immediately, even before you have a firm grasp of the substance and meaning of the entire text.

If you use this method, here's a helpful tip: Leave several blank lines at the top of your paper. Once you've finished writing your analysis, go back to the beginning and add an introduction appropriate to the body of your essay.

Follow the Principles of Good Essay Writing

Let the opening of your essay tell readers what to expect. Get into the meat of your essay quickly. Don't fool around with an opening meant solely to entertain or grab the reader's attention—forty minutes doesn't give you much time for verbal flummery.

Once into your essay, develop your ideas fully with examples and details. Development indicates the depth of your thinking. Each paragraph should have a stated or implied topic sentence, and each sentence should contribute to the development of your main idea. If you can't tell whether all or part of a particular paragraph supports the thesis, trash it or revise it. Be ruthless. Don't fall in love with a particular idea or turn of phrase. Give it the boot if it fails to help you make your case.

Give Your Essay Coherence

Even if all your paragraphs are gems, they must somehow be tied together to give your essay coherence. Transitions, which establish relationships between one thought and the next, will help. Count yourself blessed that English is rich with transitional words and phrases such as *for example.* In addition, there is *in addition, furthermore, likewise, to be sure, accordingly, meanwhile, in other words,* and many, many more. By using transitions, you do your readers a favor. You assure them a smooth trip through your essay. Without transitions, each sentence and paragraph stands like a disconnected link in a chain, causing readers to bump along and lose the point you are trying to make. Although not every sentence requires a transition, three or four sentences in succession without a link of some sort may leave readers doubting that this trip is worth taking.

Avoid Showy Words

Steer clear of fancy, elaborate, and overblown words. This admonition may seem hard to live by when you are trying to impress AP essay readers with your intellect and sophistication. Yet nothing, truly nothing, conveys your erudition better than ideas clearly expressed in ordinary language. AP essay readers are old hands at spotting pretentiousness. You'll get no extra credit for an essay crammed with exotic, multisyllabic words used for no other purpose than to sound exotic and multisyllabic. Likewise, don't drop literary terms into your essay without explaining how they enhance the poem or passage you're analyzing. Some students, thinking that an array of literary terms makes them appear insightful, toss literary words and phrases willy-nilly into each essay. No doubt literary terms are important, but use them only when you have a good reason for doing so. AP readers have coined the derogatory term LitSpeak for essays crowded with pointless literary terms. In short, avoid LitSpeak.

Watch Your Use of Verbs

Being human, AP readers favor those essays that are full of life. To inject life into your writing, pay close attention to your choice of verbs. Verbs, as you know, show action or state of being. *Active* verbs stimulate interest because they perform, stir things up, and move around. They excel all other words in their power to energize sentences and, as a bonus, help you to write more economically. In contrast, *being* verbs such as *is, are, was, were, am, has been, had been,* and *will be* don't do much of anything except connect one thought to another. When used in sentences, each of these being verbs joins a subject to a predicate, and that's all. They act like verbal equal signs, as in "Joanie *is* a genius" (Joanie = genius). Because being verbs (and equal signs) show little life, use active verbs whenever possible.

In addition to generating life, active verbs usually lead to more economical writing. In *Hamlet,* the old windbag Polonius knew what he was talking about when he said "Brevity is the soul of wit." What he meant, in brief, is that Brief is Better. Never use two words when one will do. Readers want to be told quickly and directly what you have to say. They value economy and resent reading more words than necessary. Excess verbiage is a pain in the neck. So cut out unnecessary words.

TIP

Avoid needless words.

Stop! Go back to the last paragraph. Did you notice that the last sentence is redundant? It's short, yes, but it merely adds fat to the paragraph. Sentences, like muscles, should be lean and tight. Because needless words are flabby, trim the fat.

Vary Your Sentences

Use your writing muscles to vary your sentences. It's easy to fall into a rut by repeatedly using the same patterns. Because English is a flexible language, sentences can be endlessly revised until you've got a mix that works. Variety for its own sake, however, is hardly better than assembly-line production of identically structured sentences. So, don't strain for variety. Use it mainly to clarify meaning and emphasize ideas.

In essay writing, declarative sentences usually predominate. But you can create all sorts of fascinating effects with interrogative sentences or even occasional exclamatory and imperative sentences. What's more, you can write sentences interrupted in midstream by a dash—although some people claim that it's not proper to do so in formal prose—and you can use direct and indirect quotations. Again, though, don't deliberately scramble up sentence types just to cook up a sentence potpourri. Be guided always by what seems clearest and by what seems varied enough to hold reader interest.

In addition, pay attention to sentence length. A series of long sentences made up of subordinate clause after subordinate clause and a parade of short sentences make for equally dull reading. A balance is best. Take the trouble to dismantle very long sentences when necessary, and don't hesitate to combine a series of very short ones. But the simplest way to vary sentences is to practice using an array of sentence openings.

Start sentences with:

- prepositional phrases: *In the beginning, From the start, In the first place*
- adverbs and adverbial phrases: *Originally, At first, Initially*
- dependent clauses: *If you follow my lead, When you start with this*
- conjunctions: *And, But, Not only, Either, So, Yet*
- verbal infinitives: *To launch, To take the first step, To get going*
- adjectives and adjective phrases: *Fresh from, Introduced with, Headed by*
- participles: *Leading off, Starting off, Commencing with*
- inversions: *Unique is the essay that begins with . . .*

When you reach the end of each AP essay, you can simply lift your pen off the paper and be done with it. Readers of AP essays, knowing that you've had a time limit, won't penalize you for a brief or even a nonexistent conclusion. But some sort of ending can help readers feel they've arrived somewhere. It pleases both the heart and mind. Let whatever you write as a conclusion spring naturally from the essay's content. Above all, shun summary endings. They insult intelligent readers, who ought to be trusted to remember what you've told them in a few paragraphs of text.

TIP

Avoid summary endings; they insult the reader's intelligence.

Literary Essays: Stylistic Conventions

It's crucial that AP essays follow the customary practices of scholarly writing. You're not expected to produce articles worthy of publication in a professional journal, but your essays should demonstrate that you know the basic conventions of the genre.

TIP

To earn top scores, be sure to follow these 11 stylistic conventions!

1. Use standard English prose, as error-free as you can make it.

2. Place the titles of poems within quotation marks; underline the titles of novels and plays.

3. There is no need to give your essay a title.

4. Discuss poems and passages using the "literary present." In other words, write using present tense verbs. Shift to other tenses only when it is necessary or logical to do so.

5. Refer to the "speaker" or "narrator" of a poem or prose fiction passage, not the "author" because the voice you hear may not be the author's but that of an imaginary spokesperson.

6. If the gender of the speaker is unknown, use either masculine or feminine pronouns—whichever you prefer. Stay away from "he or she," a pedantic and cumbersome usage.

7. Keep yourself in the background. Avoid using "I" unless you absolutely must or if the topic invites you to write from your own observations or experience. Likewise, if you can, avoid addressing the reader as "you." In other words, a detached tone is the most appropriate one, but don't be a slave to it if another will serve you better.

8. When quoting from poems or passages, copy the words and punctuation exactly as they appear in the text. If you must omit anything, indicate the omission with an ellipsis (. . .). Put square brackets [ ] around any words you insert into a quotation. Also, be sure to include line numbers either in parentheses after the quotation or as part of your introduction to the quoted material. If you quote more than one line of a poem, use line breaks ("/") between each line. For example: "Had we but world enough, and time/ This coyness, lady, were no crime" (1–2). Instead of copying long quotations verbatim, save time by using an ellipsis between the first and last words, as in "Had . . . crime."

9. Avoid using a quotation as a sentence all by itself. Rather, introduce the quotation in your own words, as in: *The speaker uses a paradox in line 13 when he says to God, "Except you enthrall me, never shall be free."* Likewise, use quotes only to illustrate what you have explained in your own words or to support what you plan to say.

10. There is no specific length or word count to shoot for. Let your essay be long enough to cover the material and brief enough to remain interesting. An essay of a single paragraph won't develop your ideas sufficiently, and an essay that rambles on page after page will probably lack focus.

11. AP readers know the literature you are writing about. Therefore, it's not necessary to review it for them. Summarize texts only when it's absolutely necessary to explain or clarify an idea. Likewise, since readers know literary terminology, don't waste time explaining or defining technical terms.

HOW ESSAYS ARE SCORED

Essays are scored by highly trained and experienced high school and college English teachers. Each of your essays is scored by a different reader who knows neither your name, school, gender, or anything else about you. Nor does the reader know the score you earned on other essays or on the multiple-choice questions. Some essays are reread by a so-called Table Leader, whose job is to assure that all essays are evaluated fairly and uniformly.

Each essay will receive a grade from 0 (worst) to 9 (best) based on the readers' judgment of the essay as a whole. High scores will be your reward for doing everything well. Exceptionally good writing may compensate for a mediocre analysis and raise the score from, say, a 6 to a 7, but a badly written essay, no matter how insightful, is destined to earn a score no higher than 3. Should the grades assigned by the two evaluators differ by two or more points, the essay will be submitted to a third reader.

Because each question is different, the criteria for evaluating them are different, too. But the descriptions that follow apply generally to the three types of essays found on the exam.

Best Essays: Score 9–8

These well-organized essays address the question astutely. The writer, using relevant and specific references to the text, convincingly develops a valid thesis. Perceptions of the literature are insightful and clearly expressed in language appropriate to literary criticism. The writer may also offer more than a single interpretation of a piece of literature or any of its parts. Although the essays may not be completely error-free, they demonstrate the writer's control of the elements of composition and the craft of analytical writing.

Above-average Essays: Score 7–6

These essays contain a solid, clearly expressed thesis, but the evidence provided for its development and support may fall short of excellence. The analysis of the literature, while thoughtful, may not be thorough or altogether precise. Or the discussion may lack the depth of insight or persuasiveness found in the very best essays. Although the essays give evidence of the student's ability to read and respond sensitively to literature, they are not as mature, sophisticated, and controlled as papers that deserve ratings of 8 or 9.

Mid-range Essays: Score 5

These essays respond to the assignment but offer little more than conventional observations of the literature. Their analysis, while mostly accurate, may suffer from superficiality and a lack of conviction. Support of the thesis may be vague or limited. The text of these essays may accurately convey the students' thoughts but may contain a number of mechanical writing errors, none so severe, however, to obscure meaning.

Lower-half Essays: Score 4–3

Essays in this range often attempt to address the question but do so only marginally, possibly because the writer has either misread the literature or misunderstood the prescribed task. Essays may include a thesis, but supporting material drawn from the text is meager or inexact. As for literary analysis, it is vague and unconvincing, or it may rely largely on paraphrase. The writing in these essays is sufficiently clear to convey meaning, but it may suffer from lack of coherence, weak diction, faulty sentence structure, and a variety of mechanical errors.

Weak Essays: Score 2–1

Failure to respond adequately to the question places an essay into this category. Thus, an essay consisting largely of plot summary may earn a 2. The same applies to essays in which confused or incoherent literary analysis demonstrates the writer's inability to comprehend the literature and to essays that reveal minimal understanding of composition and the conventions of standard written English. Essays that are particularly devoid of content or coherence are scored 1.

Unacceptable Essays: Score 0

No response or a response completely off the topic.

Based on the evaluations of three essays, you will earn a score between 0 and 27 in Section II of the exam. (Let's hope this book will help you skew your score toward the high end of the range.) The College Board won't report that score. Rather, using a complicated formula, it will convert the score to a number on the AP five-point scale. The arithmetic calculations are of no compelling interest to most students, but if you're eager to know, check the "Technical Corner" of the web site: *www.collegeboard.org/ap.*

STUDENT ESSAYS

The Poetry Question

TIP

Your job is to explain how poetic techniques contribute to a poem's meaning

Some poetry questions direct you to discuss a single aspect of the poem such as its themes or its use of imagery. But more often, AP questions ask you to deal with several major elements of the poem and how they relate to each other, or to the meaning, or most often to the overall effect of the poem. In other words, you must explicate the poem—that is, explain how poetic techniques contribute to the poem's meaning.

What follows is an AP-type question on a poem. It is accompanied by responses written by three students—Mark, Tanya, and Clarissa. The essays are typed as written. After reading each essay, jot down your reactions and then compare your impressions with those of a veteran AP reader.

Question: Read the following poem carefully. Then write a well-organized essay in which you analyze how the poet's language, along with such poetic devices as diction, sound, rhyme, and meter, conveys the speaker's attitude toward the taking of human life by hanging.

On Moonlit Heath and Lonesome Bank

On moonlit heath and lonesome bank
  The sheep beside me graze;
And yon the gallows used to clank
  Fast by the four cross ways.

Line
(5) A careless shepherd once would keep
  The flocks by moonlight there,[1]
And high amongst the glimmering sheep
  The dead man stood on air.
They hang us now in Shrewsbury jail:
(10) The whistles blow forlorn,
And trains all night groan on the rail
  To men that die at morn.

There sleeps in Shrewsbury jail to-night,
  Or wakes, as may betide,
(15) A better lad, if things went right,
  Than most that sleep outside.

And naked to the hangman's noose
  The morning clocks will ring
A neck God made for other use
(20) Than strangling with a string.

And sharp the link of life will snap,
  And dead on air will stand
Heels that held up as straight a chap
  As treads upon the land.

(25) So here I'll watch the night and wait
  To see the morning shine,
When he will hear the stroke of eight
  And not the stroke of nine;

And wish my friend as sound a sleep
(30) As lads' I did not know,
That shepherded the moonlit sheep
  A hundred years ago.

        —An excerpt from A. E. Housman,
        "A Shropshire Lad," 1896

---

[1] Poet's footnote: "Hanging in chains was called keeping sheep by moonlight."

Mark's Essay

(Typed as it was written)

By using a large number of contrasting images A.E. Housman's poem "On Moonlit Heath and Lonesome Bank," illustrates the theme that the taking of human life by hanging is a cruel and violent act. In addition, the diction and tone help in making a deeper statement about life and death.

In the first stanza the speaker is on a peaceful moonlit heath among grazing sheep. Being there, where criminals once were hung, provides a contrast between the tranquil scene and violence that took place there. This contrast is emphasized when the peaceful imagery of lines 1 and 2 is broken by the "clank" of chains in line 3. This juxtaposition introduces a kind of duality that dominates the poem and is also reflected in the poet's footnote. To call hanging a man in chains "keeping sheep" is an ironic idea that appears to make the point that the hangmen of the past couldn't face the reality of what they were doing so made up a euphemism for their actions.

In stanza 2, the tranquil image of sheep in the moonlight is set against the eerie image of a hanged man who "stood on air." This contrast has a parallel in the speaker himself. Outwardly he's at peace, but inside he is mentally and emotionally wrought up. His language is plain and casual, but the clash of images implies that the speaker is intensely emotional. However, the reason for this intensity is not explained until the fourth stanza where he explains that a "lad," is waiting to be put to death in Shrewsbury jail. The speaker is disturbed about the impending execution of a boy who doesn't deserve it mainly because he is "better" than "most that sleep outside." (line 16).

Another contrast is set up in the third stanza by explaining that the site of hangings has been switched from the moonlit heath to the Shrewsbury jail. Hangings were once accompanied by the bleating of sheep but are now done where trains groan and whistles "blow forlorn," sounds that make the scene of the hangings even harsher and more grim.

In line 18 the speaker uses a pun on the word "ring." It may seem inappropriate to play word games in a poem about an execution, but since the poem uses many contrasts, the pun is consistent with speaker's double-sided view of the world. Likewise, the word "string" in line 20 is used for "rope," making light of something quite serious. One might argue that the poet used "string" for the sake of the rhyme with "ring," but "string" makes sense when you think of hangings as people "strung up" on the gallows. Therefore, "string" preserves the pattern of duality in the entire poem.

Wherever the hanging takes place—on the heath or at the jail—lines 21–22 return to the grusomeness of the act. The effects are the same regardless of the location—the "dead on air will stand"—an allusion to line 8 ("The dead man stood on air") that helps to unify the poem and supports the speaker's intent to portray hanging as an example of society's sick behavior.

Line 25 returns us to the moonlit heath of line 1, where the speaker will continue his vigil until morning shine. The emphasis on "shine" is poignant since it contrasts with the darkness that the lad must face, both in his last hours on earth and forever after. The casual reference to eight o'clock and nine o'clock signifies the passing of another typical hour, implying that the world goes on even though the lad will not. Incidentally, the speaker himself depends on euphemism here because he cannot face the fact of the lad's hanging. Instead of coming right out and saying that the lad will be executed, he softens the idea by saying "When he will hear the stroke of eight/And not the stroke of nine" (lines 27–28), leaving the reality of what happens unspoken.

In the last stanza the speaker refers to other men who tended sheep in the past. They, too, are dead, like the lad and like he himself will be one day. In a way, he is fatalistically accepts the future that all men face. Saying that we will all die is a fairly trite idea, but if you reconsider the footnote, that keeping sheep means the same as hanging by chains, a shocking element has suddenly been added to the poem. Basically, "keeping sheep" is really just a metaphor for "preparing to die." All of us in a sense are "keeping sheep," although we call it "going to school" or "applying to college," etc.

The subject of the poem is morbid, but Housman won't let the style of writing be morbid. The use of a pun (explained above) and colloquial usage like "lad" and "chap" keeps the tone light, as do the short stanzas, brief lines, and consistent bouncy rhymes. The matter-of-fact informality of a poem that has a ponderous and grim theme give it a wry humor bordering on dark, or black humor, but the contrast between the light style and the dark subject is consistent with the main premise of the poem.

Maybe it is callous to treat death by hanging with a sense of humor. Giving the poet the benefit of the doubt, the subject is terribly painful for the speaker—almost too awful to contemplate. Therefore, he plays down the pain and uses a flippant tone to cover over his deep bitterness and sorrow. He gains artistically by doing that because it makes the impending execution more horrible.

Your impressions: _____

_____

_____

_____

Comment from an AP Reader

Mark: Although the essay is not perfect, its handful of stylistic soft spots (overuse of the verb *explain,* for instance, and writing *hung* instead of *hanged,* and the dubious assertion that Housman uses "black humor") hardly detract from the perceptivity of your discussion of the poem. Your command of the language of literary criticism and analysis is demonstrated throughout the essay. You introduce sophisticated concepts such as the juxtaposition of images and the duality that underlies the structure of the poem.

Your expertise and ambition are apparent from the opening paragraph. Rather than follow the suggestion of the prompt, you focus on imagery. At the same time, however, you manage to work in cogent comments about the poem's tone, diction, sound, and rhyme.

As a writer, you appear committed to using details and incorporating quotations to support ideas. Your thorough dissection of just two words—"ring" and "string"—is impressive, largely because it is rare to find such precise and detailed analyses in AP essays. But more to the point, you avoid being pedantic; your analysis contributes a crucial piece of data in support of the argument that duality exists not only in the poem's content but in the speaker himself. Score: 8

Tanya's Essay

(Typed as it was written)

Housman's poem "On Moonlit Heath and Lonesome Bank" consists of eight separate stanzas telling the story of a man's feelings about the hanging of a boy he knows who is too good to experience such a terrible fate. The man who is the speaker in the poem is a shepherd taking care of his flock of sheep in the moonlight on a heath near a crossroads where "gallows used to clank" (line 3) and people were hung. He is waiting there for the boy to be hung the next morning in Shrewsbury jail.

The feelings of the man are conveyed through the poem's diction, sound, rhyme and meter. He speaks in affectionate terms about the boy, calling him a "lad" (15) and a "friend" (29). He obviously sympathizes with him because he uses phrases to show that the boy was unlucky in life—"if things went right" (15) he wouldn't be waiting to die, because he is "better . . . Than most that sleep outside" (15–16). He also adds that God made the boy's neck "for other use" (19) than having a noose put around it.

The speaker also talks about hanging in diction that indicates how terrible it is. He mentions the "dead man stood on air" (9) meaning swinging from a rope, and "strangling with a string" (20) as the man chokes to death. He uses the word "snap" (21) to create the sound that occurs when the body falls and the neck breaks. Even though he vividly describes hanging with such strong, tactile images, he stays calm about it, waiting patiently until the morning and refers to his friend's death as a sound sleep (29).

So basically, there is an ambiguous tone in the poem, partly violent and gross, partly calm and peaceful. It's like the speaker is sad but since he can't do anything about it he accepts the boy's fate as if it were God's plan.

That sense of a plan is also reflected in the sounds, rhymes and meter of the poem. It is all carefully laid out with a steady rhythm that remains the same from one stanza to the next. Each stanza is four lines. In each, the first and third lines and the second and fourth lines rhyme. There also are many uses of alliteration also. For example in "Fast by the four cross ways" (4) and "Than strangling with a string" (20). The poet also uses sound to support the meaning, as in "snap" (see above) and the onomatopoeia of "whistles blow forlorn" (10) and "trains all night groan" (11).

The kind of laid-back attitude portrayed by the speaker is natural for a shepherd, a man whose life is spent quietly taking care of sheep. An urban person might object to the hanging of the boy, but that is not in the lifestyle of a meek and humble shepherd. He accepts his own fate just as he accepts the fate of the boy.

Your impressions: _____

_____

_____

_____

Comment from an AP Reader

Tanya: Your analysis has a number of virtues, in particular the use of quoted material to illustrate and support assertions about the poem's tone. The point of the essay is clearly stated in the second paragraph, but you follow through with only a partial discussion of each poetic element. You provide examples of sound, but they are tenuously tied to the point you try to make about the speaker's feelings. You properly sense ambiguity in the poem but fail to explain its source with clarity and precision. Your discussion of rhyme and meter has no evident purpose other than to respond to the question. The entire analysis of the poem would have been far richer had you been able to show not only how rhyme and meter contribute to the meaning and effect of the poem, but how the elements work together.

Your use of "hung" instead of "hanged" is jarring, and the repetition of "also" suggests a need for more careful proofreading. Then, too, you might have chosen other words for the colloquialisms "laid back" and "gross." To your credit, you make few other errors in English usage. I only wish that you had more fully fleshed out your ideas. Score: 5

Clarissa's Essay

(Typed as it was written)

A.E. Housman's poem <u>On Moonlit Heath and Lonesome Bank</u> expresses more than just a literal description of a young man's hanging. Using the structure of the poem, and the author's word choice and images, a more profound statement is being made. Since the boy will be put to death in the morning, the author concentrates on his feelings about hanging during the night before.

The poem is separated into eight stanzas. This structure allows Housman to use three stanzas to describe the scene, including the "moonlit heath and lonesome bank" (line 1). In the next five stanzas he tells about the boy, including that he is a good boy who is

"A better lad, if things went right,

Than most that sleep outside."

Then the last stanza returns to the moonlit heath where the poem began.

The authors' word choice also contributes to the deeper message of the poem. He uses certain diction that conveys an opposition to hanging, such as "clank (line 3), naked (line 17), and strangling (line 20)." These words describe hanging as the most brutal, awful way to die. They show him being a sensitive person who shows empathy to the victim of the hanging and tries to convey his feelings about capital punishment in general.

These feelings are conveyed even more by the images that he uses. He talks about the dead man who "stood on air (line 8)", using a visual image, whistles "that blow" (line 10) using sound imagery, and the noose around the "neck made for other use' (line 19), a tactile image. Then, he returns to a visual and sound images associated with the hanging in lines 26–28, where he refers to seeing the "morning shine" and hearing the "stroke of eight/And not the stroke of nine."

Finally, I think Housman was ahead of his time. He wrote the poem in 1896, but his arguments against cruel and unusual punishment are just as important to today's world, especially because DNA testing proves that many innocent men have been executed, or been put in jail, for crimes they didn't perfform. Therefore, the poem is just as relevent today, or maybe even moreso.

Your impressions: _____

_____

_____

_____

Comment from an AP Reader

Clarissa: You are to be commended for writing a five-paragraph essay that includes an introduction, three paragraphs of development, and a conclusion. Beyond the organizational effort, however, I find little to praise. Your main idea—that structure, word choice, and imagery add a measure of profundity to the literal meaning of the poem—could have merit had you provided solid supporting evidence. Citing examples of imagery and listing a few emotionally potent words adds little support to your interpretation of the poem. Basically, you fail to explain how these poetic elements relate to each other or to the speaker's attitude toward hanging. The evidence may hold promise, but it lacks direction and purpose.

The assumption that the "author" is also the speaker in the poem violates a basic principle of literary criticism, and the assertion that Housman objected to capital punishment lacks credibility. Then, too, references to DNA and unjust sentences, while factually correct, step far beyond the bounds of the poem. Although you express yourself clearly, the mechanics of your writing are in dire need of repair. Score: 3

The Prose Fiction Question

Passages used for the prose fiction question usually consist of a one- to two-page excerpt from a novel or short story. Typically, the question relates to the author's narrative techniques. Some questions, however, pertain to character development, others to the use of language. Still others raise issues of structure, tone, theme, or other literary elements.

Most AP students have little difficulty identifying literary techniques. To earn a top essay score, however, requires more than simply naming the ones found in the passage. **You must show how the author uses literary devices to help fulfill the purpose of the passage.** It's one thing to say that a certain phrase is a metaphor. It's quite another to discuss how that metaphor supports the author's intent and contributes to the overall meaning of the passage.

Below is an AP-type question on a passage of fiction from a novel by Charles Dickens. This is followed by three students' essays, typed as they were written in response to the question. Read the essays and record your reactions in the space provided. Then read what a seasoned AP reader said about each essay.

Question: Carefully read the following excerpt from the first chapter of Dickens's novel *Dombey and Son,* in which the title characters are introduced. Observe the author's use of such elements as diction, syntax, figurative language, and tone. Then write an essay that analyzes how the author's use of language creates a vivid portrait of Dombey as a character.

Dombey sat in a corner of the darkened room in the great arm-chair by the bedside, and Son lay tucked up warm in a little basket bedstead, carefully disposed on a low settee immediately in front of the *Line* fire and close to it, as if his constitution were analogous to that of a (5) muffin, and it was essential to toast him brown while he was very new.

Dombey was about eight-and-forty years of age. Son about eight-and-forty minutes. Dombey was rather bald, rather red, and though a handsome well-made man, too stern and pompous in appearance to be prepossessing. Son was very bald, and very red, and though (of (10) course) an undeniably fine infant, somewhat crushed and spotty in his general effect, as yet. On the brow of Dombey, Time and his brother Care had set some marks, as on a tree that was to come down in good time—remorseless twins they are for striding through their human forests, notching as they go—while the countenance of (15) Son was crossed and recrossed with a thousand little creases, which the same deceitful Time would take delight in smoothing out and wearing away with the flat part of his scythe, as preparation of the surface for his deeper operations.

Dombey, exulting in the long-looked-for event, jingled and (20) jingled the heavy gold watch-chain that depended from below his trim blue coat, whereof the buttons sparkled phosphorescently in the feeble rays of the distant fire. Son, with his little fists curled up and clenched, seemed, in his feeble way, to be squaring at existence for having come upon him so unexpectedly.

(25) "The house will once again, Mrs. Dombey," said Mr. Dombey, "be not only in name but in fact Dombey and Son; Dom-bey and Son!"

The words had such a softening influence, that he appended a term of endearment to Mrs. Dombey's name (though not without (30) some hesitation, as being a man but little used to that form of address): and said, "Mrs. Dombey, my—my dear."

A transient flush of faint surprise overspread the sick lady's face as she raised her eyes towards him.

"He will be christened Paul, my—Mrs. Dombey—of course."

(35) She feebly echoed, "Of course," or rather expressed it by the motion of her lips, and closed her eyes again.

"His father's name, Mrs. Dombey, and his grandfather's! I wish his grandfather was alive this day!" And again he said "Dom-bey and Son," in exactly the same tone as before.

(40)   Those three words conveyed the one idea of Mr. Dombey's life. The earth was made for Dombey and Son to trade in, and the sun and moon were made to give them light. Rivers and seas were formed to float their ships; rainbows gave them promise of fair weather; winds blew for or against their enterprises; stars and

(45)   planets circled in their orbits, to preserve inviolate a system of which they were the center. Common abbreviations took new meanings in his eyes, and had sole reference to them: A. D. had no concern with anno Domini, but stood for anno Dombei—and Son.

He had risen, as his father had before him, in the course of life

(50)   and death, from Son to Dombey, and for nearly twenty years had been the sole representative of the firm. Of those years he had been married, ten—married, as some said, to a lady with no heart to give him; whose happiness was in the past, and who was content to bind her broken spirit to the dutiful and meek endurance of the present.

(55)   Such idle talk was little likely to reach the ears of Mr. Dombey, whom it nearly concerned; and probably no one in the world would have received it with such utter incredulity as he, if it had reached him. Dombey and Son had so often dealt in hides, but never in hearts. They left that fancy ware to boys and girls, and boarding-

(60)   schools and books. Mr. Dombey would have reasoned: That a matrimonial alliance with himself *must*, in the nature of things, be gratifying and honourable to any woman of common sense. That the hope of giving birth to a new partner in such a house, could not fail to awaken a glorious and stirring ambition in the breast of the

(65)   least ambitious of her sex. That Mrs. Dombey had entered on that social contract of matrimony: almost necessarily part of a genteel and wealthy station, even without reference to the perpetuation of family firms: with her eyes fully open to these advantages. That Mrs. Dombey had daily practical knowledge of his position in society. That

(70)   Mrs. Dombey had always sat at the head of the table, and done the honours of his house in a remarkably lady-like and becoming manner. That Mrs. Dombey must have been happy. That she couldn't help it.

Maribeth's Essay

(Typed as it was written)

The portrait of Mr. Dombey conveys a vivid impression of a self-important man. He is so wrapped up in himself that on the day of his son's birth his thoughts are not about the little baby but about the importance of the birth to his business. The author Dickens uses several literary devices to create this picture of a totally egotistical character, including sentence structure that emphasizes Dombey's thought processes, diction that exaggerates his lack of human warmth, and figurative language that suggests an obsession with business.

Using parallelism the author gives a physical description of both Dombey and his son. Dombey is 48 years old, bald, red, and too pompous looking to be attractive, the son is 48 minutes old, also bald, red, and "somewhat crushed and spotty." Dombey is also presented as a rigid person by being compared to a tree in the forest. Personifications of Time and Care have left marks on his face just like woodsmen notching trees. Similarly, the baby's skin is filled with "a thousand little wrinkles." This parallelism creates the effect that the son is a like a clone of his father and introduces Dombey's foregone conclusion that the baby will grow up to follow him into the business and carry on the company's name.

That is what pleases Dombey so much about the birth. He repeats the phrase Dombey and Son like a mantra and he exults in pleasure by jingling and jingling his heavy gold watch-chain, a symbol of the wealth he has earned in his business. By using additional figurative language Dickens informs the reader that Dombey is the archetypal business man. "Those three words [Dombey and Son] conveyed the one idea of Mr. Dombey's life." (line 40). In support of that hyperbole, he adds that in Mr. Dombey's view the sun and moon, the rivers and seas, even the whole universe exist only for the sake of the business (lines 41–48). In addition, Dombey translates "anno Domini" into "anno Dombei—and Son" giving it a sacred connotation by alluding to Jesus Christ. In the next line (49) the allusion is strenghtened by saying, "He had risen, as his father had before him. . . ." a clear reference to Jesus.

The only indication of what business Dombey and Son are engaged in comes in line 58. They "dealt in hides, but never in hearts." That's perfect for a man like Dombey, whose is dominated by skin-deep values and qualities. He is presented as incapable of expressing emotion because he has none that don't relate to his business. He is shown struggling to call his wife "my dear." His lack of emotion is further emphasized by the sentence structure in lines 60–72, where reasons why Mr. Dombey married and remained married to Mrs. Dombey are listed. Love had nothing to do with it. Their relationship is based on several reasons listed in a series of clauses beginning with "That," like in the clauses of a legal document.

Dombey's qualities are made known to the reader by his thoughts and actions. As a person, he is a pathetic character who is absorbed by business and his own grotesque self-righteousness. In spite of his flaws, Dickens intends to amuse the reader with this portrait of Dombey. His humerous tone becomes evident in the first paragraph, where he compares the newborn baby to a muffin set by the fire to be toasted. In a way, then Dombey is an object of derision; more a caricature than a character.

Your impressions: _____

_____

_____

Comment from an AP Reader

Maribeth: The essay focuses clearly on Dickens's diverse techniques of character development. Your conclusion that Dombey is more caricature than character comes at the end of an astute and sensitive analysis of the text. My hat is off to you for avoiding the pitfall of paraphrasing or summarizing what happens in the passage. Following the plan laid out in your opening paragraph, you identify several telling examples of diction, sentence structure, and figures of speech that contribute to Dombey's portrait. A couple of spelling miscues, some punctuation errors, and a comma splice mar the essay, but the illuminating and precise explication of the passage is impressive. Few AP essays contain such a variety of accurate and insightful observations. Score: 9

Alfonso's Essay

(Typed as it was written)

It is hard to know whether readers ought to chuckle at the character of Mr. Dombey in the novel <u>Dombey and Son</u>, or to despise him for being a selfish and vulgar egotist. Both qualities can be found in the portrait of him because of Dickens use of language, in particular his diction, syntax, and choice of details.

Looking at Dombey as a comical character, Dickens satirizes his obsession with his family business called Dombey and Son. For years he has been the sole proprieter of the business, yet it was still called Dombey and Son. Finally, he has a newborn son to give legitimacy to the name of the firm. He is thrilled with the idea and says to his wife, "The house will once again, Mrs Dombey, ...be not only in name but in fact Dombey and Son; Dom-bey and Son!" repeating the last name like someone who has fallen in love with it and can't get it out of their mind. All this takes place as he sits in an arm-chair by his wife's bedside less than an hour after the birth of his son, who is lying close to the fireplace for the sake of warmth. Dombey goes overboard about the business in another way, also. Dickens says that those three words (Dombey and Son) "conveyed the one idea of Mr. Dombey's life." His tunnel vision led him to believe that the whole solar system revolved around him and his business, as if Dombey and Son was really Dombey and the Sun. Furthermore, in Dombey's mind, the abbreviation A.D. (anno Domini) stands for "anno Dombei—and Son" according to lines 46 and 47. Obviously, Dickens is exaggerating for comic effect because a man of stature like Dombey could not be a totally out of touch with reality. He can't be insane and also run a good business that owns ships (line 43), be affluent enough to wear a "heavy gold watch-chain" and a trim blue coat with sparkling (gold??) buttons. Furthermore, he believes that Mrs. Dombey married him to be "part of a genteel and wealthy station." (66–67) So, readers could take Dickens creation of Dombey as someone who has many comical aspects to his character.

On the other hand, Dombey displays qualities that are far from funny or admirable. They are repulsive. For example, here is nothing funny about the way he treats his wife. While she is in bed suffering from post partum sickness, he surprises her by calling her "dear" to soften her up for his decision that the baby must be named after him and his grandfather—Paul. It's a fait accompli, and she has no voice in the matter. His insulting attitude toward his wife is more fully illustrated in the final paragraph of the passage where Mrs. Dombey's "broken spirit" is discussed. She is a dutiful and meek wife, but Mr. Dombey would have received such news with "utter incredulity" (line 57) since he practically ignores her and barely acknowledges her as a human being. Instead, he thinks of her as someone has helped by marrying her. In his view, to be married to him is an honor, and gives her social advantages and a higher position in society. And, based on the last lines of the passage, there is no question that a woman with a husband like Mr. Dombey must be happy. She couldn't help it. It's hard to imagine a more obnoxious attitude for a husband to have toward his wife.

This vivid portrait of Dombey is taken from the opening pages of Dickens' novel. Based on what he says, it is a toss-up whether in the rest of the story Dombey will turn out to be a hero or a villain. Probably he'll have elements of both. At this point in writing the novel, maybe Dickens himself didn't know, and so created a character full of ambiguities, like all human beings.

Your impressions: _____

_____

_____

_____

Comment from an AP Reader

Alfonso: Your opening paragraph pays lip service to the AP question. Dickens's diction, syntax, and choice of details, however, are subsumed by your real intent—to explore the two sides of Dombey's character. Whether to laugh at or be repulsed by Dombey constitutes a unique approach to the topic, and the essay masterfully balances the conflicting possibilities. Its conclusion, that Dickens himself may have been unsure, offers intriguing food for thought.

Your writing gives evidence of a sensitive reading of the passage and a grasp of subtleties that elude less perceptive readers. It also reflects your enthusiasm for probing into the text to find supporting details and quotations. Trying to be thorough, however, you devote too much of the essay to recounting and explaining events in the narrative. You might have trusted your readers to be familiar with the text and thus spent more time digging still deeper into the language of the passage. Your own diction, which is generally fresh and spirited, strengthens the overall effect of the essay and nudges the score from a solid 6 to a 7. Score: 7

Maury's Essay

(Typed as it was written)

"Stern and pompous." Those words found in line 8 of the passage from Dombey and Son capture the essence of the title character of the Dickens novel. How Dickens conveys Dombey's stern and pompous personality can be seen in his use of such elements as sentence structure, diction, figurative language, and tone, all of which add to the character portrait of a proud man who takes himself very seriously but is not aware of what a comical image he projects.

As far as sentence structure is concerned, the passage begins with a paragraph made up of one long sentence setting the scene and introducing Mr. Dombey sitting in a great arm chair and his Son lying on a low settee in front of the fire. The next paragraph which begins to tell details starts with two short sentences describing basic similarites and differences between the father and son. The sentences get longer as the paragraph moves on, and the last sentence is a made up of several clauses and side comments, mainly because the subject matter is complex. It explains how "Time and his brother Care" (lines 11–12) have left their marks on Mr. Dombey's brow. This pattern of short sentences for simple ideas and long sentences for more complex ideas continues throughout the passage and comes to an extreem at the end, where between lines 59 and 72, there are six sentences all beginning with the same word—"that."

The diction in the passage is typical of authors that use highly formal language to say simple things but can also use every day words. Therefor, when he says "countenance" for face (line 14) and "appended" for added (line 28), he is showing Dombey's pompousness. Dombey exemplifies sternness in the way he talks to his wife, instead of asking her what she thinks the baby's name should be, he tells her, "He will be christened Paul, . . . of course," obviously, he is not a type of man who will take no for an answer.

Figurative language is not as common as the diction in the passage, but Time and his brother Care are personifications in the second paragraph. Before that, the infant is compared to a muffin. And to illustrate Dombey's sterness, it says that Dombey and Son "often dealt in hides, but never in hearts," a metaphor for feelings.

The tone of the passage is basically a criticism of Dombey. I can find very little complimentary. The only thing that matters to him is Dombey and Son. He has a pompous attitude in thinking that "the sun and moon were made" to give Dombey and Son light and that "rivers and seas were formed to float their ships." It takes alot of chutzpah to think the whole world was made to serve you. Also, his wife doesn't mean anything to him. Her job is to take care of the house and he has done her a favor by marrying her because of the advantages he gave her.

Dombey is one of the most pompous fools in literature.

Your impressions: _____

_____

_____

_____

Comment from an AP Reader

Maury: Your strong feelings about the character of Dombey don't, unfortunately, add up to a strong essay. For one thing, the essay's premise is based on a faulty reading of the passage. The phrase "stern and pompous" pertains to Dombey's appearance, not to his personality, although a case could probably be made for a correlation between the two. The opening paragraph of the essay promises a discussion of four literary elements. Indeed, you dutifully devote a paragraph to each of them, but the discussion pertains only occasionally to Dombey's sternness and pomposity. The longest paragraph in the essay—about sentence structure—accurately describes the author's use of varied sentences but entirely ignores the point of the essay. What's more, you try to show that Dombey's diction reflects pomposity, but as evidence you pick two of the narrator's words, not Dombey's. You recover from this *faux pas,* however, by cogently showing how Dombey bullies his wife.

Although the essay contains numerous writing errors, your analysis of the passage is far from dull. You seem willing to take chances in interpretation and in use of language. How refreshing and rare it is to find the word "chutzpah," for example, in an AP essay. Its use as a synonym for arrogance, however, is slightly off the mark. Too bad that your essay lacks a precise and responsible analysis of the text. But don't despair; your effort is commendable. Score: 3

The Free-Response Question

The prompt for the free-response essay usually starts with a quotation or a broad statement about some aspect of literature. It often relates to the portrayal of character but may also refer to an element of plot or to a theme. Your first task is to pick a novel or play to which the general statement applies. Not every novel or play is an appropriate choice for every question, but the statement will no doubt be broad enough to include a great many of the works you have read and studied in school.

The test always lists twenty or more titles from which to choose. But you may pick your own, provided it is a novel or play "of similar quality" or "comparable literary merit." These phrases generally refer to works taken from the so-called literary canon, works worthy of study and analysis, works that in some way contribute to a mature reader's understanding of life and the human condition. If the novel or play was written before the twentieth century and is still being read or performed on the stage, it would probably pass the test. More recent works that have won Pulitzer Prizes or National Book Awards would also qualify, as would works by highly-regarded contemporary authors such as Saul Bellow, William Trevor, Joyce Carol Oates, and Barbara Kingsolver. On the other hand, books by authors who appear regularly on best-seller lists, such as John Grisham, Jean M. Auel, Mary Higgins Clark, and Stephen King, don't, although one could argue that not all of these authors' books are escapist pulp. No doubt an element of elitism governs the choices, but you probably wouldn't be taking the exam in the first place unless you more or less subscribed to the notion that some books are worthier than others.

Whatever your choice, be sure that you are very familiar with it. The question on the AP exam almost invariably asks you to discuss major events in the story or to write about characters. Therefore, you should know the plot intimately and be able to describe all the major and many of the minor events. You should also know the names and traits of the chief characters. The more you can say about the setting, the structure of the work, major themes, and the author's narrative techniques, the more you'll be able to demonstrate the depth of your reading and analytical skills. **Above all, be conversant with the meaning of the work as a whole. That is, you should have a firm grasp of the author's main points.**

Remember that your essay will be evaluated by literate readers familiar with the work you choose. This may work either for you or against you. An informed reader could give you the benefit of the doubt if something you write is fuzzy or unclear. But a reader who knows the work well may also penalize you for inaccuracies or omissions. Just because AP readers cannot have read every novel or play ever published, don't be tempted to choose a very obscure title. Or even worse, don't invent one on the spot (don't laugh; it's been tried); it could work against you.

Because there is no way to predict the question you'll be asked, you should prepare an assortment of titles, some of which are reviewed in Part 4. Also, some works are so rich that they can be used for a broad range of questions. *Hamlet* may be one such work, along with *Great Expectations, Heart of Darkness, Wuthering Heights, Invisible Man,* and *The Great Gatsby.* Knowing these works cold would be good preparation for answering just about any question the AP examiners could devise. For more titles, check the College Board's *101 Great Books for College-bound Readers* at *www.collegeboard.com.*

To give you an idea of how various titles could be used on topics from recent AP exams, the entries below suggest numerous possibilities taken from AP reading lists used in schools throughout the country. This is a limited list. No doubt you can probably add many other equally appropriate titles. Use the blank spaces to suggest titles of your own.

TIP

For the free-response essay, pick a work you know very well.

Topic: A character opposed to or alienated from society

Carol Kennicott finds little joy in small-town life in *Main Street.*

Stephen Dedalus defies tradition to become a writer in *A Portrait of the Artist as a Young Man.*

Holden Caulfield is repelled by society's hypocrisy and the compromises of adulthood in *The Catcher in the Rye.*

Joseph K in *The Trial,* when faced with incomprehensible accusations, discovers that he is truly alone in a world.

John Grady, a boy from Texas, can't adapt to Mexican culture in *All the Pretty Horses.*

_____

_____

_____

Topic: A character investigates a mystery

> Oedipus uncovers the truth about his birth and destiny in *Oedipus Rex*.
>
> Hamlet hopes to learn the truth about the death of his father in *Hamlet*.
>
> Marlow attempts to unlock the mystery of Kurtz in *Heart of Darkness*.
>
> Jaffrey in *The House of the Seven Gables* seeks the vanished deeds to the house.
>
> Several narrators search for the thief of a cursed jewel in *The Moonstone*.

_____

_____

_____

Topic: An ending with spiritual reassessment or moral reconciliation

> Jim in *Lord Jim* makes up for an act of cowardice.
>
> Wrongfully accused of murder, Jefferson in *A Lesson Before Dying* understands the simple heroism of resisting the inevitable.
>
> Death creates an atmosphere of wonder and awe for the grieving characters in *A Death in the Family*.
>
> Weak-willed and profligate, Father Mendez dies a Christ-like death to atone for his shortcomings in *The Power and the Glory*.
>
> Becoming increasingly isolated and paranoid, Solness in *The Master Builder* finds that the enemy to his peace lies not outside himself but within.

_____

_____

_____

Topic: Suspenseful mental or psychological events

> Othello is driven mad with jealousy by Iago's diabolical mind games in *Othello*.
>
> Mrs. Pontelier in *The Awakening* suffers egregiously for betraying her family.
>
> Captain Ahab in *Moby Dick* struggles against what he believes are malevolent forces in nature.
>
> Defeated by a business rival, Michael Henchard pursues self-destructive revenge in *The Mayor of Casterbridge*.

Clarissa Dalloway and Septimus Smith lead seemingly separate but psychologically interconnected lives in *Mrs. Dalloway.*

Topic: A significant social event

The ghost of Banquo shows up at Macbeth's banquet in *Macbeth.*

Romeo and Juliet meet and fall in love at the Capulets' ball in *Romeo and Juliet.*

During wedding festivities, Frankie in *Member of the Wedding* discovers a future different from the one she expected.

At a stag party for white men the protagonist of *Invisible Man* begins to understand his station in life.

In *One Flew Over the Cuckoo's Nest,* McMurphy throws a wild party with dire consequences for some of the guests.

Topic: A character faces a dilemma created by competing forces

Frederick Henry in *A Farewell to Arms* volunteers to fight in the war but considers desertion after becoming disillusioned.

George in *Of Mice and Men* must decide whether to kill Lennie or let him be arrested and tried for murder.

The title character in *Ethan Frome* is caught between his marriage to a shrewish, sickly wife and his infatuation for a sweet young woman.

Obsessed with a desire for vengeance against her husband, the title character in *Medea* ignores law, culture, and her motherly instincts.

Arkady in *Fathers and Sons* is drawn to the progressive manners and attitudes of his friend Bazarov, but conventionality holds him back.

Topic: A character harboring an important secret

> Emma's secret discontent with her marriage ripens her for adulterous relationships in *Madame Bovary.*
>
> Rochester in *Jane Eyre* cannot escape the mysterious disappearance of his wife.
>
> Blanche in *A Streetcar Named Desire* conceals a sordid past.
>
> A secret affair with Hester in *The Scarlet Letter* gnaws at Dimmesdale, who finds himself unable to make peace with himself or God.
>
> Henry Fleming in *The Red Badge of Courage* knows that his award for valor was earned by fear of showing fear in battle.

Topic: The effect of a minor or absent character on the protagonist

> Ben in *Death of a Salesman* both inspires and plagues Willie Loman.
>
> An unknown benefactor enables Pip to succeed in *Great Expectations.*
>
> Tom in *The Glass Menagerie* follows in the footsteps of his absent father.
>
> The memory of Ben in *Look Homeward, Angel* inspires Eugene to break away from his overbearing family.
>
> Young Vladimir in *First Love* is tormented by an unknown rival for the affections of flirtatious Zinaida.

Topic: A victim of prejudice

> In *Native Son,* the young black man, Bigger Thomas, faces a future without hope.
>
> The Okies in *The Grapes of Wrath* encounter abuse and oppression in California.
>
> In *The Fixer,* Yakov Bok is wrongfully accused of a crime solely because he is a Jew.
>
> At the trial of Kabio Miyamoto in *Snow Falling on Cedars,* bigotry left over from the war influences the proceedings.

In *Cry, the Beloved Country,* Stephen Kumalo and his son Absolom struggle against the injustices of South African apartheid.

_____

_____

_____

Topic: A character overcoming odds to succeed

Beset with poverty, crime, and despair, Jurgis in *The Jungle* finds a refuge in socialism.

The title character in *Jasmine* heroically casts off her poverty-ridden background in India to become a liberated American woman.

Pursued by the law for stealing a loaf of bread, Jean Valjean in *Les Misérables* redeems himself by helping downtrodden members of society.

Yuri in *Dr. Zhivago* preserves his identity in the face of revolution and a reign of terror meant to obliterate men's individuality.

Self-discipline enables the title character in *One Day in the Life of Ivan Denisovich* to endure ten years of harsh imprisonment in a Soviet labor camp.

_____

_____

_____

Topic: A rebel at odds with society

Anna in *Anna Karenina* pays with her life for transgressing the hypocritical moral codes of her society.

Julien, a woodcutter's son in *The Red and the Black,* aims to make it big in the upper class but is vigorously rebuffed.

John Proctor in *The Crucible* keeps his good name but is put to death by society for challenging its authority.

Lily Bart in *The House of Mirth* is shunned by a society that rejects rebellious, iconoclastic women.

Huck in *Huckleberry Finn* undertakes a voyage of discovery in a hostile world he cannot understand.

_____

_____

_____

Questions and Student Essays

What follows is a free-response question and three student essays. After reading each essay, write your comments in the space provided, and then see what an AP evaluator thought.

Question: In literature, characters often find themselves torn by conflicting loyalties. In such cases, loyalty to friends or family or society may contend with such competing forces as morality, law, or personal conviction. When they face such dilemmas, characters often reveal their true nature not only to readers but also to themselves.

Choose a novel or play of literary merit in which a major character encounters a conflict of loyalties, and in a well-organized essay, explain the conflict, how the character responds, and how the resolution of the conflict contributes to the meaning of the work as a whole. Please do not merely summarize the plot.

Feel free to select from the list below, or you may choose another work of comparable literary merit appropriate to the topic. Please do not write about a short story, poem, film, or work of non-fiction.

An American Tragedy	*One Flew Over the Cuckoo's Nest*
The Age of Innocence	*Othello*
As I Lay Dying	*Père Goriot*
Beloved	*The Picture of Dorian Gray*
Crime and Punishment	*The Portrait of a Lady*
A Doll's House	*Pride and Prejudice*
Ethan Frome	*Romeo and Juliet*
Great Expectations	*The Remains of the Day*
The Great Gatsby	*The Scarlet Letter*
Heart of Darkness	*A Streetcar Named Desire*
Miss Lonelyhearts	*Tess of the d'Urbervilles*
Madame Bovary	*Waiting for Godot*

Pat's Essay

(Typed as it was written)

<u>Montana, 1948</u> is coming-of-age novel by Larry Watson. It tells the story of Wesley Hayden, the sheriff in Bentrock, a small town in rural Montana. He is facing a dilemma of whether to investigate rumors that that the doctor in the town, Dr. Frank Hayden, has sexually molested Native-American women and girls while performing medical examinations. Ordinarily, this would not be a problem, but in this case the doctor happens to be Wesley's brother. The situation is made worse by the fact that Frank is a well-loved war hero and the Haydens are the leading family in the town. Also, Wesley is kind of a bigot and neither likes nor trusts Indians, so he is torn about following up on their accusations. His wife, Gail, applies some pressure on him. She expects him to do his duty, partly because it's his job and partly because a Sioux girl, Marie Little Soldier, is a loyal live-in housekeeper in their home and claim that Dr. Frank has molested her. She and the other victims have said nothing in public because of prejudice against Indians. They figured no one would believe their allegations, anyway.

The story is told through the eyes of twelve-year old David, the son of Wesley and Gail. David doesn't understand what is going on, but as the story develops, he overhears conversations, observes the actions of his parents, and more or less figures it out. He is actually drawn into the action by chance because he sees Frank enter their house when no one is home but Marie, who is sick in bed. That afternoon, Marie is found dead, and David has a dilemma that parallels his father's dilemma. Should he tell what he saw or should he keep it to himself. All his life he has admired his Uncle Frank and he now realizes that he has witnessed something that might destroy him and his family. Finally, he tells his father, which makes the conflict inside Wesley even more intense. His brother may be more than a rapist; he may also be a murderer.

It is then that the true character of Wesley emerges. He could look the other way and let Frank go free, since no one knows anything except his deputy, who is completely loyal to him. Wesley's father, the former sheriff, wants him to let Frank go, and sends four men to try and help Frank escape from Wesley's basement where he is temporarily incarcerated. Meanwhile, Gail is beginning to change her mind because he sees how the arrest is ruining her family life. When Wesley sees how little remorse Frank has over what he has done, however, he decides to resolve his dilemma by turning the case over to the prosecuting attorney of the county. He feels that the rules of society must be obeyed because they are more important than family ties. This realization is motivated partly by his own relationship with his father. Since old Mr. Hayden loves and favors Frank far more than Wesley, Wesley could be motivated by a desire for revenge against Frank for being the favorite son. In explaining his decision, Wesley tells his wife that a man must be guided by moral absolutes. He could not live with himself if he looked away, so Frank must be prosecuted and pay for his crimes.

The night before he is supposed to be turned in, Frank slits his wrists in the basement. To save the family name, Wesley says his death was an accident. But the family breaks apart anyway because old Mr. Hayden can't forgive Wesley for arresting Frank in the first place, and Frank's widow holds Wesley responsble for her husband's death.

This resolution relates closely to the novel's meaning as a whole because it is really the story of an important incident in David's boyhood. As a result of seeing how his family and others reacted to a tense situation, he grows up quickly. Before, he is just a little kid. Whenever his parents need to talk seriously, they send him to his room or concoct an errand for him. By the end, he has seen and learned so much about adult behavior that his innocence is lost. He is completely aware of adult hypocrisy and how adults hold grudges and make self-serving decisions. In an epilogue, David has grown up to be a history teacher. He admits that he is a cynic about what he teaches. After seeing how his father wavered about what to do and then swept the truth under the rug after Frank's death, David has no faith in the rule of law. He never tells his students that history contains stories about sexual abuse, murder, and suicide solves problem. Following in the footsteps of his father, he only pretends to tell the truth.

Your impressions: _____

_____

_____

_____

Comment from an AP Reader

Pat: Your gift for writing is obvious from the start. The novel that you chose to write about is an elegant choice for this essay, for conflicting loyalties is precisely its major theme. Your essay's praiseworthy introduction specifically lays out Wesley's dilemma. That you find a parallel between Wesley's quandary and David's adds a subtle dimension to the analysis of the story. Too bad, however, that you fail to capitalize on your insight, for David's decision to tell his father what he had seen marks a turning point in his youth. A child no longer, he has suddenly in effect become responsible for his uncle's fate.

The essay concentrates on the dynamics within the Hayden family. Yet you assert that the novel is really about an important incident in David's life. Given more time than forty minutes, I suspect that you might have refocused the essay on David. But why quibble? You deserves a pat on the back for displaying a firm grasp of the novel and writing an essay worth celebrating. Score: 9

Sasha's Essay

(Typed as it was written)

Tom Joad, the protagonist of John Steinbeck's Grapes of Wrath, is an tough ex-con just released on parole from an Oklahoma state penitentiary. He killed a man in a fight after the man accosted him with a knife. Self-defense was the defense at the trial, but he was ruled guilty. His conviction was unfair, but he had no choice and went to prison for five years of his sentence before being let out. The provisions of his parole are he has to stay out of trouble, required to obey the law, and required to remain inside Oklahoma. Upon his release, he intends to follow the provisions fully and he makes his way home to find his family.

At the farm, it is abandoned. A former neighbor Muley Graves tells Tom about the banks that owned the land in this part of Oklahoma which have kicked sharecroppers out of their houses and off their farms because they have been unable to grow enough crops as a result of the drought that has caused the Dust Bowl in that part of the country in the 1930s. The Joads, evicted from the land that they have lived on for centuries, have joined a mass migration westward along Route 66 to California where they think they can find jobs and created a new and happy life.

His family situation gives Tom a dilemma. Should he follow the rules of his parole, or should he take his chances and go with his family to California? Since he had unjustly been convicted of killing a man in self-defense, he has no allegiance to the government or its legal system. He also sees that the government has ignored his family just when they need protection from the money-hungry banks that kicked them off the land. Therefore, he decides that his family needs him in California more than the government needs him in Oklahoma. Loyalty to his family is far more important.

This turns out to be ironic. When they finally make it to California, he and the Joads are treated like "damn Okies," meaning lower than low. They are unwanted vagrants. One night Tom gets into a fight with an abusive deputy sheriff, killing him. All of a sudden he is made a fugitive. As a hunted man, he is danger to his family, who might be punished by never finding work again if they were caught harboring a cop-killer. To protect and save his family, he decides to leave them.

Tom's loyalty to his family shows that he is man willing to sacrifice himself for others, a decision is closely tied to the underlying base of the whole story. Steinbeck's book is socialist slant to it, telling a story with a message of how through collective action, oppression, and exploitation can be overcome. One man alone, or even one family alone doesn't have the power to resist the rich and powerful land owners from taking advantage of poor people like the Joads and thousands of others by paying them paltry wages and knowing that if they protest working for low wages there will always be others who will work for even less. Only by joining together, by organizing unions, and striking against the owners and thus letting the fruit wither and spoil on the trees, will the workers be able to survive and create respectable decent lives.

After the killing of the deputy, Tom would like to stay with his folks and help them, but he can't. When he leaves, he has the intentions of preaching like Preacher Casey did earlier. Casey believing that society was not made up of many individual souls but consisted of one great big "over-soul." Tom expects to finish the work Casey began by organizing the little people, getting them together to fight against the bosses, because he knows that in collectivization is where success lies. One he leaves on his mission, he leaves the book but his message stays behind to inspire his family to keep on going, to fight for a decent living and join with others to overcome poverty and exploitation. He is a symbol for "we, the people," as Ma says when Tom leaves. Just as Tom first got into trouble by defending himself from a knife attack, he wants the little people to defend themselves by fighting back against the owners of the farms and orchards of California.

Your impressions: _____

_____

_____

_____

Comment from an AP Reader

Sasha: Tom Joad isn't the most obvious candidate for a character torn between conflicting loyalties. After all, when faced with the choice of remaining with a family that needs him or following the provisions of his parole, his folks win hands down. Yet you clearly explain Tom's decision and its aftermath, paying particular attention to his transformation from hard-boiled ex-con to a self-sacrificing spokesman for the little people. Showing that Tom's actions represent Steinbeck's purpose and predilections reveals considerable insight. Where your essay falters is in its sometimes verbose and awkward expression and perhaps its overabundant recapitulation of the plot. Score: 7

Chris's Essay

(Typed as it was written)

Plays and novels often contain a character who is torn apart of conflicting loyalties, which conflict between what his family wants and what they feel they must do to lead a life that is self-satisfied. This case happens in "The Glass Managerie" the play by Arthur Miller in which Tom, the son in the Wingfeld family is pulled in two conflicting directions. He loves his younger sister, Laura, but despises for his single mother who was abandon by her husband, a "telephone man falling in love with long distance." Tom also hates his job and home life, in particular the constant nagging by his mother Amanda Wingfeld and can't wait to escape them both. He's looking for adventure, like his father did so he goes to the movies almost every night to have vicarious adventures. He also gets drunk to escape his drab life. His mother, of course wants Tom to support her and Laura and she pleads with Tom not to run away mainly because Laura is sickly and an introvert. She is so bashful that she won't go to secretarial school. Instead, she wanders around town when her mother thinks she's taking typing classes. At home, she plays with her collection of glass animals which is her way of escaping from reality. Then Amanda finds out that Laura is a truant from school and is very upset.

More upset comes after Tom agrees to stay around at least until Laura finds a man to marry. One day he invites a friend Jim from work to dinner and to meet Laura. Amanda is excited and practically redecorates the apartment to impress Jim, the one and only "gentleman caller" Laura ever had. Amanda uses her stories of gentlemen callers when she was growing up in the South. She naturally regrets winding up with the husband who ran off. Telling stories about her younger days as a southern bell is like her fantasy life and gives her a way to escape from her troubles.

Amanda fantasizes that Jim is going to be the family savior. He will marry Laura and free Amanda of life burdens. Then Tom can do whatever he wants and go wherever he wants to go. Only it turns out that Jim is engaged to be married. Laura is crushed, and Amanda goes ballistic at Tom. She yells at him and calls him names. Tom refuses to take it any more. He talks back to his mother and decides then and there that he's outta there, and he goes off by himself to join the marines and wander the earth in search of adventure.

He returns on stage as the narrator of the play and speaks to the audience and Laura, telling her that he couldn't help himself by running away and telling her that he still loves her in spite of it all.

Your impressions: _____

_____

_____

_____

Comment from an AP Reader

Chris: It's a stretch to consider this essay an adequate response to the question. Putting aside your mistaken attribution of *The Glass Menagerie* to Arthur Miller, there is regrettably little in the essay that deals directly with conflicting forces that weigh either on Tom or on any other character. Your essay holds promise at the start but soon evolves into little more than a synopsis of the play, with an emphasis on how the characters contrive to escape from unendurable lives. Your awareness that Tom functions as the narrator suggests that you've seen or read the play and perhaps been present when it was discussed in class, but from the experience you seem to have carried away little more than superficialities. The diction and writing style fall short of AP standards, and there is little in the essay to suggest that you are sufficiently acquainted with anything but the most elementary principles of literary criticism and analysis. I'm sorry to tell you that your essay cannot earn more than a minimal score. Score: 2

PART 2

DIAGNOSTIC TEST

Diagnostic Test

> • Taking a full-length AP exam
> • Finding the *best* answers
> • Checking your answers
>
> • How to score your own essays
> • What the numbers tell you
> • Calculating your AP test score

INTRODUCTION

This self-assessment is similar in length and format to the AP exam. Use it to determine your readiness to take the actual exam, administered in May of each year.

Take this test as though it were the real thing. Set aside three hours at a time you are wide awake and your mind is fresh. Remove all distractions, sharpen your pencil, read the directions, and go to work.

Allow yourself one hour to answer the multiple-choice questions. Use the answer sheet provided. At the end of the hour take a five-minute break and then respond to the essay questions. Write your essays on standard 8-1/2 × 11 composition paper, the approximate size of an official AP essay response sheet. Write your essays as clearly and legibly as possible with a pen, preferably in dark blue or black ink. Allow yourself approximately 40 minutes for each question. Keep in mind that quality is more important than quantity.

Scoring the Diagnostic Test

When you have finished, check your answers with the Answer Key on page 99. Then read the Answer Explanations. Spend some time analyzing your wrong answers. Try to identify the reason you missed each question: Did you misinterpret the question? Was your choice too specific or too general? Did you misread the passage or poem? Did you base your answer on the wrong material? Did you jump to a conclusion that led you astray? Knowing why you stumbled can help you avoid similar errors on future tests.

At the same time, don't ignore the items you got right. You may discover a helpful pointer or two.

Although it is hard to evaluate your own essays, don't shy away from trying. Let the essays cool for a while—maybe even for a day or two—and then, insofar as possible, reread them with an open mind and a fresh pair of eyes. Rate your essays using the Self-Scoring Guide on page 110.

Finally, using data from the Answer Key and the Self-Scoring Guide, calculate the score you earned on this test.

Answer Sheet
DIAGNOSTIC TEST

Section I

1 Ⓐ Ⓑ Ⓒ Ⓓ Ⓔ	16 Ⓐ Ⓑ Ⓒ Ⓓ Ⓔ	31 Ⓐ Ⓑ Ⓒ Ⓓ Ⓔ	46 Ⓐ Ⓑ Ⓒ Ⓓ Ⓔ
2 Ⓐ Ⓑ Ⓒ Ⓓ Ⓔ	17 Ⓐ Ⓑ Ⓒ Ⓓ Ⓔ	32 Ⓐ Ⓑ Ⓒ Ⓓ Ⓔ	47 Ⓐ Ⓑ Ⓒ Ⓓ Ⓔ
3 Ⓐ Ⓑ Ⓒ Ⓓ Ⓔ	18 Ⓐ Ⓑ Ⓒ Ⓓ Ⓔ	33 Ⓐ Ⓑ Ⓒ Ⓓ Ⓔ	48 Ⓐ Ⓑ Ⓒ Ⓓ Ⓔ
4 Ⓐ Ⓑ Ⓒ Ⓓ Ⓔ	19 Ⓐ Ⓑ Ⓒ Ⓓ Ⓔ	34 Ⓐ Ⓑ Ⓒ Ⓓ Ⓔ	49 Ⓐ Ⓑ Ⓒ Ⓓ Ⓔ
5 Ⓐ Ⓑ Ⓒ Ⓓ Ⓔ	20 Ⓐ Ⓑ Ⓒ Ⓓ Ⓔ	35 Ⓐ Ⓑ Ⓒ Ⓓ Ⓔ	50 Ⓐ Ⓑ Ⓒ Ⓓ Ⓔ
6 Ⓐ Ⓑ Ⓒ Ⓓ Ⓔ	21 Ⓐ Ⓑ Ⓒ Ⓓ Ⓔ	36 Ⓐ Ⓑ Ⓒ Ⓓ Ⓔ	51 Ⓐ Ⓑ Ⓒ Ⓓ Ⓔ
7 Ⓐ Ⓑ Ⓒ Ⓓ Ⓔ	22 Ⓐ Ⓑ Ⓒ Ⓓ Ⓔ	37 Ⓐ Ⓑ Ⓒ Ⓓ Ⓔ	52 Ⓐ Ⓑ Ⓒ Ⓓ Ⓔ
8 Ⓐ Ⓑ Ⓒ Ⓓ Ⓔ	23 Ⓐ Ⓑ Ⓒ Ⓓ Ⓔ	38 Ⓐ Ⓑ Ⓒ Ⓓ Ⓔ	53 Ⓐ Ⓑ Ⓒ Ⓓ Ⓔ
9 Ⓐ Ⓑ Ⓒ Ⓓ Ⓔ	24 Ⓐ Ⓑ Ⓒ Ⓓ Ⓔ	39 Ⓐ Ⓑ Ⓒ Ⓓ Ⓔ	54 Ⓐ Ⓑ Ⓒ Ⓓ Ⓔ
10 Ⓐ Ⓑ Ⓒ Ⓓ Ⓔ	25 Ⓐ Ⓑ Ⓒ Ⓓ Ⓔ	40 Ⓐ Ⓑ Ⓒ Ⓓ Ⓔ	55 Ⓐ Ⓑ Ⓒ Ⓓ Ⓔ
11 Ⓐ Ⓑ Ⓒ Ⓓ Ⓔ	26 Ⓐ Ⓑ Ⓒ Ⓓ Ⓔ	41 Ⓐ Ⓑ Ⓒ Ⓓ Ⓔ	
12 Ⓐ Ⓑ Ⓒ Ⓓ Ⓔ	27 Ⓐ Ⓑ Ⓒ Ⓓ Ⓔ	42 Ⓐ Ⓑ Ⓒ Ⓓ Ⓔ	
13 Ⓐ Ⓑ Ⓒ Ⓓ Ⓔ	28 Ⓐ Ⓑ Ⓒ Ⓓ Ⓔ	43 Ⓐ Ⓑ Ⓒ Ⓓ Ⓔ	
14 Ⓐ Ⓑ Ⓒ Ⓓ Ⓔ	29 Ⓐ Ⓑ Ⓒ Ⓓ Ⓔ	44 Ⓐ Ⓑ Ⓒ Ⓓ Ⓔ	
15 Ⓐ Ⓑ Ⓒ Ⓓ Ⓔ	30 Ⓐ Ⓑ Ⓒ Ⓓ Ⓔ	45 Ⓐ Ⓑ Ⓒ Ⓓ Ⓔ	

SECTION I

Multiple-choice Questions

TIME—1 HOUR

Instructions: This section of the exam consists of selections from literary works and questions on their content, form, and style. After reading each passage and poem, choose the best answer to each question and then fill in the corresponding oval on the answer sheet.

Questions 1–11. Read the following passage carefully before you decide on your answers to the questions.

The very old couple, of whom everyone at the beach is so highly aware, seem themselves to notice no one else at all. Tall and thin, she almost as tall as he, they are probably somewhere in their eighties.
Line They walk rather slowly, and can be seen, from time to time, to stop
(5) and rest, staring out to sea, or to some private distance of their own. Their postures, always, are arrestingly, regally erect; it is this that catches so much attention, as well as their general air of distinction, and of what is either disdain or a total lack of interest in other people.

Their clothes are the whitest at the beach; in the ferocious
(10) Mexican sun of that resort they both wear large hats, hers lacy, his a classic panama.

They look like movie stars, or even royalty, and for all anyone knows they are, deposed monarchs from one of the smaller European countries, world-wanderers.

(15) Because there is not much to do at that resort, almost nothing but walking and swimming, reading or whatever social activities one can devise, most people stay for fairly short periods of time. Also, it is relatively expensive. The Chicago people, who have come as a group, will be there for exactly ten days. The couple who have the room
(20) just next door to that of the distinguished couple will be there for only a week—a week literally stolen, since he is married to someone else, in Santa Barbara, and is supposed to be at a sales conference, in Puerto Rico.

But the old people seem to have been there forever, and the others
(25) imagine that they will stay on and on, at least for the length of the winter.

And while everyone else can be seen, from time to time, to wonder what to do next—the Chicago people, apparently committed to unity of action, were heard arguing in the dining room over
(30) whether, or when, to rent a boat for deep-sea fishing—the two old people have a clear, unwavering schedule of their own. After breakfast, to which they come quite late, as they do to all meals, they sit

(35) out on their small porch for a couple of hours. The girl in the room next door, who is named Amanda Evers, is passionately curious about them, and she tries to look through the filagree[1] of concrete that separates the two porches. But she discovers nothing. (She is in fact too curious about too many people; her lover, Richard Paxon, has told her so. Curiosity contributes to the general confusion of her life.) The old man reads his newspapers, a Mexico City *News* that he

(40) has delivered to his table each morning, at breakfast, and sometimes he seems to be writing letters—or perhaps he keeps a journal? The woman does not read the paper; she seems to be doing nothing at all—a thing Amanda, who is restlessly energetic, cannot imagine. (Amanda manages a travel agency, in Santa Cruz, California; she

(45) often considers other careers.)

The arrival of the elderly couple, down at the beach, at almost precisely noon each day, is much noticed; it is when they look, perhaps, most splendid. In trim dark bathing suits, over which they both wear white shirts, in their hats and large dark glasses, advancing on their

(50) ancient legs, they are as elegant as tropical birds—and a striking contrast to everyone else on the beach, many of whom wear bright colors. One such woman in the Chicago group has a pea-green caftan[2] that literally hurts Amanda's eyes.

The old people sit each day under the same small thatched shelter,

(55) a little apart from the others, at the end of the line. After a while they will rise and begin one of their long, deliberate walks, the length of the beach and back. Then, returned to their shelter, in a slow and careful way they divest themselves of the shirts, the hats and glasses; they walk down to the edge of the water, and slowly, majestically,

(60) they enter the lapping small green waves. After a not quite total immersion, they return to the shelter, to rest. Even in such apparent repose, however, they both have a look of attentiveness. They seem highly conscious of each moment, and very likely they are.

(1981)

---

[1] web-like design
[2] a loose ankle-length garment

1. The narrator's attitude toward the old couple is chiefly one of

   (A) tenderness and affection
   (B) admiration and wonder
   (C) hidden envy
   (D) exaggerated praise
   (E) disguised contempt

2. The narrator's use of the phrase "private distance of their own" (line 5) does which of the following?

   (A) It confirms that the man and woman want to be left alone.
   (B) It suggests that the couple harbors a dark secret of some kind.
   (C) It raises suspicions about the couple's deteriorating mental condition.
   (D) It implies that the couple leads a boring life.
   (E) It heightens the intrigue surrounding the couple.

3. In context, the word "arrestingly" (line 6) is best interpreted to mean

   (A) attractively
   (B) strikingly
   (C) worthy of attention
   (D) hard to describe
   (E) out of style

4. At the beginning of the passage (lines 1–14), the old couple are characterized mainly by the speaker's description of

   (A) their age
   (B) what others say about them
   (C) their appearance
   (D) their feelings
   (E) their actions

5. The shift in the narrator's rhetorical stance that occurs from the third paragraph (lines 12–14) to the next paragraph (lines 15–23) can best be described as one from

   (A) generalized to specific
   (B) speculative to factual
   (C) meandering to interpretive
   (D) enthusiastic to indifferent
   (E) realistic to exaggerated

6. The structure of the sentence in lines 27–31 does which of the following?

   (A) It exaggerates the crankiness of the people from Chicago.
   (B) It offers the narrator an opportunity to ridicule the Chicago group.
   (C) It implies that old people are usually more set in their ways than young people.
   (D) It emphasizes the contrast between the group from Chicago and the elderly couple.
   (E) It uses a specific example to illustrate a general statement made in the previous paragraph (lines 24–26).

7. The parenthetical comment in lines 36–39 can be considered ironical for which of the following reasons?

   (A) The narrator has been spying on Amanda.
   (B) The narrator has overheard Richard Paxon berating Amanda.
   (C) Amanda herself is a subject of the narrator's curiosity.
   (D) The narrator is no less curious about other people than Amanda.
   (E) A sense of "general confusion" (line 38) also characterizes the narrator's life.

8. The narrator of the passage can best be described as a person who

   (A) takes pleasure in people-watching
   (B) readily gives advice to others
   (C) has been vacationing at the beach for many years
   (D) considers wealth a status symbol
   (E) gladly participates in the activities offered by the resort

9. In context, the narrator's simile "as elegant as tropical birds" (line 50) serves primarily to

   (A) reiterate the couple's distinctive and distinguished appearance
   (B) provide fodder for gossip among the resort's other guests
   (C) suggest the couple's exotic taste in clothing
   (D) reinforce the idea stated earlier (line 12) that the couple look like movie stars
   (E) emphasize how closely the man and woman resemble each other

10. Amanda most likely serves as the narrator's source of information based on all of the following facts EXCEPT

   (A) the resort is expensive (lines 17–18)
   (B) an adulterous affair is going on in the room next to that of the old couple (lines 19–22)
   (C) Amanda has been accused of being too nosy (lines 36–39)
   (D) Amanda works as a travel agent in California (line 44)
   (E) The caftan of one of the other guests hurts Amanda's eyes (lines 52–53)

11. The last two sentences of the passage ("Even . . . they are") suggest that the narrator

   (A) thinks that the elderly man and woman are attempting to enjoy their lives to the fullest possible extent
   (B) believes that the couple may soon be leaving the resort
   (C) may doubt the authenticity of the couple's public image
   (D) suspects that the couple may be anxious about maintaining their privacy
   (E) assumes that wealthy people can never be fully at ease

Questions 12–23. Read the following poem carefully before you decide on your answers to the questions.

In Your Mind

The other country, is it anticipated or half-remembered?
Its language is muffled by the rain which falls all afternoon
one autumn in England, and in your mind
Line   you put aside your work and head for the airport
(5)   with a credit card and a warm coat you will leave
on the plane. The past fades like newsprint in the sun.

You know people there. Their faces are photographs
on the wrong side of your eyes. A beautiful boy
in the bar on the harbour serves you a drink – what? –
(10)   asks you if men could possibly land on the moon.
A moon like an orange drawn by a child. No.
Never. You watch it peel itself into the sea.

Sleep. The rasp of carpentry wakes you. On the wall,
a painting lost for thirty years renders the room yours.
(15)   *Of course.* You go to your job, right at the old hotel, left,
then left again. You love this job. Apt sounds
mark the passing of the hours. Seagulls. Bells. A flute
practising scales. You swap a coin for a fish on the way home.

Then suddenly you are lost but not lost, dawdling
(20)   on the blue bridge, watching six swans vanish
under your feet. The certainty of place turns on the lights
all over town, turns up the scent on the air. For a moment
you are there, in the other country, knowing its name.
And then a desk. A newspaper. A window. English rain.

(1990)

12. In line 1, the speaker is doing which of the following?

   (A) Introducing an ambiguity that lingers throughout the poem
   (B) Creating suspense that builds to a climax at the end of the poem
   (C) Maintaining her distance from the events described in the poem
   (D) Establishing that the speaker is not the same person whose experiences
       are recounted in the poem
   (E) Asking a hypothetical question

13. References to rain near the beginning of the poem (lines 2–3) and again at the end (line 24) do all of the following EXCEPT

    (A) provide a contrast between England and the "other country"
    (B) suggest the fleeting nature of the speaker's imaginary journey
    (C) separate the daydream from reality
    (D) emphasize that rain has an allegorical meaning
    (E) reiterate that rain has served as a stimulus for the speaker's escape

14. Which of the following best explains why the speaker chose this particular "country" as her destination?

    (A) She used to live and work there.
    (B) Someone who had gone there recommended it to her.
    (C) She is fluent in the language spoken there.
    (D) The choice was made intuitively, without thinking about it.
    (E) Friends who live there invited her to visit.

15. Which of the following describes the primary purpose of the simile "The past fades like newsprint in the sun" (line 6)?

    (A) To comment on the insignificance of the news published every day
    (B) To create a poetic balance with images of rain earlier in the poem
    (C) To illustrate metaphorically the transitory nature of memory
    (D) To suggest that the speaker is of a certain advanced age
    (E) To indicate the speaker's attitude toward office work

16. Which of the following best paraphrases the meaning of "photographs/on the wrong side of your eyes" (lines 7–8)?

    (A) photographs that are out of focus
    (B) images that can only be remembered or imagined
    (C) photographs that all look alike
    (D) pictures that have been forgotten
    (E) ghostly images

17. The mood of the poem can best be described as

    (A) cynical
    (B) passionate
    (C) enchanted
    (D) visionary
    (E) pedantic

18. In lines 7–23, the speaker's emotional state can best be described as

    (A) refreshed and pleased
    (B) relieved and self-satisfied
    (C) excited and childish
    (D) nostalgic and energized
    (E) cautious and amused

19. The image of a "moon like an orange drawn by a child" (line 11) serves primarily to

    (A) indicate that the speaker lacks sophisticated tastes
    (B) emphasize the primitive, unspoiled character of the setting
    (C) illustrate the depth of the speaker's imagination
    (D) suggest the age of the boy serving drinks in the bar
    (E) reflect the speaker's newfound frame of mind

20. In context, "lost" (line 14) means

    (A) misplaced
    (B) aimless
    (C) forgotten
    (D) deprived
    (E) bewildered

21. In line 19, "lost but not lost" is meant to imply the speaker's feeling of

    (A) alienation
    (B) panic about returning home
    (C) going around in circles
    (D) being lost in thought but not in body
    (E) knowing where she is but not why

22. The "other country" referred to in lines 1 and 23 can best be described as

    (A) a glamorous but isolated vacation spot on the ocean
    (B) a small seacoast town in a warm climate
    (C) a remote desert island in the tropics
    (D) a ranch on a mountain overlooking the sea
    (E) a beach resort popular with English-speaking tourists

23. Which of the following best describes the effect of the structure of line 24?

    (A) It undercuts the rhythm used throughout the poem.
    (B) It suggests that the speaker intends to quit her job.
    (C) It comments on the futility of escaping from the circumstances of one's life.
    (D) It illustrates the speaker's sudden change of heart.
    (E) It signifies the speaker's abrupt return to reality.

Questions 24–34. Read the following passage carefully before you decide on your answers to the questions.

New York seemed not so much awakening as turning over in its bed. Pallid men rushed by, pinching together their coat-collars; a great swarm of tired, magpie girls from a department-store crowded *Line* along with shrieks of strident laughter, three to an umbrella; a squad (5) of marching policemen passed, already miraculously protected by oilskin capes.

The rain gave Amory a feeling of detachment, and the numerous unpleasant aspects of city life without money occurred to him in threatening procession. There was the ghastly, stinking crush of the (10) subway—the car cards thrusting themselves at one, leering out like dull bores who grab your arm with another story; the querulous worry as to whether some one isn't leaning on you; a man deciding not to give his seat to a woman, hating her for it; the woman hating him for not doing it; at worst a squalid phantasmagoria of breath, (15) and old cloth on human bodies and the smells of the food men ate— at best just people—too hot or too cold, tired, worried.

He pictured the rooms where these people lived—where the patterns of the blistered wall-papers were heavy reiterated sunflowers on green and yellow backgrounds, where there were tin bathtubs and (20) gloomy hallways and verdureless, unnamable spaces in back of the buildings; where even love dressed as seduction—a sordid murder around the corner, illicit motherhood in the flat above. And always there was the economical stuffiness of indoor winter, and the long summers, nightmares of perspiration between sticky enveloping (25) walls ... dirty restaurants where careless, tired people helped themselves to sugar with their own used coffee-spoons, leaving hard brown deposits in the bowl.

It was not so bad where there were only men or else only women; it was when they were vilely herded that it all seemed so rotten. It (30) was some shame that women gave off at having men see them tired and poor—it was some disgust that men had for women who were tired and poor. It was dirtier than any battle-field he had seen, harder to contemplate than any actual hardship moulded of mire and sweat and danger, it was an atmosphere wherein birth and marriage and (35) death were loathsome, secret things.

He remembered one day in the subway when a delivery boy had brought in a great funeral wreath of fresh flowers, how the smell of it had suddenly cleared the air and given every one in the car a momentary glow.

(40) "I detest poor people," thought Amory suddenly. "I hate them for being poor. Poverty may have been beautiful once, but it's rotten now. It's the ugliest thing in the world. It's essentially cleaner to be corrupt and rich than it is to be innocent and poor."

He seemed to see again a figure whose significance had once
(45) impressed him—a well-dressed young man gazing from a club
window on Fifth Avenue and saying something to his companion
with a look of utter disgust. Probably, thought Amory, what he said
was: "My God! Aren't people horrible!"

Never before in his life had Amory considered poor people. He
(50) thought cynically how completely he was lacking in all human sympathy. O. Henry had found in these people romance, pathos, love,
hate—Amory saw only coarseness, physical filth, and stupidity. He
made no self-accusations: never any more did he reproach himself for
feelings that were natural and sincere. He accepted all his reactions as
(55) a part of him, unchangeable, unmoral. This problem of poverty
transformed, magnified, attached to some grander, more dignified
attitude might some day even be his problem; at present it roused
only his profound distaste.

(1920)

24. The first paragraph differs from the remaining paragraphs in the passage
in that

(A) it is metaphorical rather than realistic
(B) it consists mostly of the narrator's observations
(C) it includes details that only an omniscient narrator would know
(D) it is written from Amory's point of view
(E) it contains few visual images

25. As described in the passage, Amory's distaste for the city is based primarily
on its

(A) poverty-stricken neighborhoods
(B) oppressive crowds
(C) bleak appearance
(D) noise pollution
(E) unsanitary conditions

26. Describing the rooms occupied by subway riders (lines 17–22), the narrator uses a series of parallel clauses primarily to

(A) intensify the wretched conditions in which the people live
(B) comment on Amory's moral superiority
(C) shock readers into a state of disbelief that such conditions actually exist
(D) justify Amory's attitude, stated in line 52, that poor people are coarse
and stupid
(E) suggest the need to eliminate poverty

27. Amory's attitude toward poverty-stricken people might best be described as

    (A) totally indifferent
    (B) bitterly sarcastic
    (C) genuinely unsettled
    (D) mildly sympathetic
    (E) utterly contemptuous

28. The use of the phrase "some shame that women gave off" in line 30 indicates that Amory

    (A) thinks that women want the approval of men more than they want the approval of other women
    (B) believes that women are more emotional than men
    (C) judges poor women more harshly than he judges poor men
    (D) has met and talked with a number of women about their feelings regarding poverty
    (E) fears poor women more than he fears poor men

29. The effect of the funeral wreath on the subway passengers (lines 36–39) might best be characterized as an example of

    (A) a paradox
    (B) whimsy
    (C) hyperbole
    (D) irony
    (E) synecdoche

30. The narrator's tone in the passage can best be described as

    (A) frivolous
    (B) self-centered
    (C) detached
    (D) overconfident
    (E) critical

31. In the passage, Amory attributes to poverty all of the following conditions EXCEPT

    (A) crowds of vile people on the subway
    (B) seedy, foul-smelling living quarters
    (C) unsanitary eating places
    (D) the scorn of those who are not poor
    (E) people's sense of hopelessness about escaping poverty

32. The last paragraph of the passage (lines 49–58) indicates that the speaker believes which of the following to be true of Amory?

    (A) Amory is conscience-stricken by the depth of his negative attitude toward poor people.
    (B) Amory's ambition is to write books and stories about the poor.
    (C) Amory is not bothered by his own prejudices and misanthropic thoughts.
    (D) Until recently, Amory has led a sheltered life.
    (E) Amory aims to be rich and well-dressed some day.

33. In context, the narrator's allusion to O. Henry (line 51) serves primarily to

    (A) imply that O. Henry is some kind of hero to the impoverished residents of New York
    (B) contrast two different sets of feelings about New York's poor people
    (C) exaggerate the intensity of Amory's prejudices
    (D) suggest that in the future Amory should adopt O. Henry as a role model
    (E) convince readers that Amory is a social misfit

34. The contents of lines 55–58 suggest that this passage most probably precedes an account of

    (A) how Amory changes his opinions about the poor
    (B) Amory's efforts to become wealthy
    (C) a turn of events in which Amory becomes friendly with poor people
    (D) Amory's attempts to help society solve the problem of poverty
    (E) circumstances that reinforce Amory's lack of human sympathy

Questions 35–45. Read the following poem carefully before you decide on your answers to the questions.

A Litany

    Ring out your bells, let mourning shows be spread:
    For Love is dead.
        All Love is dead, infected
Line With plague of deep disdain;
(5)   Worth, as nought worth, rejected,
    And Faith fair scorn doth gain.
        From so ungrateful fancy,[1]
        From such female franzy,[2]

---

[1] love
[2] frenzy

From them that use men thus,

(10)   Good Lord, deliver us!

Weep, neighbors, weep! do you not hear it said

That Love is dead?

His death-bed, peacock's folly;

His winding-sheet is shame;

(15)   His will, false-seeming holy;

His sole executor, blame.

From so ungrateful fancy,

From such a female franzy,

From them that use men thus,

(20)   Good Lord, deliver us!

Let dirge[3] be sung and trentrals[4] rightly read,

For Love is dead.

Sir Wrong his tomb ordaineth[5]

My mistress Marble-heart,

(25)   Which epitaph containeth,

"Her eyes were once his dart."

From so ungrateful fancy

From such a female franzy,

From them that use men thus,

(30)   Good Lord, deliver us!

Alas, I lie, rage hath this error bred;

Love is not dead.

Love is not dead, but sleepeth

In her unmatchéd mind,

(35)   Where she his counsel keepeth,

Till due desert she find.

Therefore from so vile fancy,

To call such wit a franzy,

Who Love can temper thus,

(40)   Good Lord, deliver us!

—Sir Philip Sidney, c. 1580

---

[3]song for the dead

[4]thirty Roman Catholic masses for the dead

[5]solemnly declares

35. Which of the following events most likely preceded the writing of the poem?

    (A) The speaker's lover passed away.

    (B) A mass was held at the church.

    (C) The speaker was cast aside by his lover.

    (D) The speaker had a dispute with his neighbors.

    (E) The speaker attended a graveside funeral service.

36. The emotional effect of the first stanza (lines 1–10) is achieved mainly by

    (A) use of hyperbole
    (B) use of alliteration
    (C) use of a concluding couplet
    (D) a long first line followed by a terse second line
    (E) a metaphor comparing love with the plague

37. One effect of lines 5–6 is to emphasize the speakers's sense of

    (A) pity
    (B) modesty
    (C) regret
    (D) loyalty
    (E) powerlessness

38. What feeling does the speaker convey in lines 11–12?

    (A) Self-righteousness
    (B) Isolation and resentment
    (C) Wrath and guile
    (D) Panic and terror
    (E) Reverence and respect for God

39. Which two lines come closest to stating the same idea?

    (A) Lines 1 and 10
    (B) Lines 1 and 21
    (C) Lines 3 and 9
    (D) Lines 3 and 14
    (E) Lines 31 and 33

40. The last four lines of stanzas 1, 2, and 3 can best be paraphrased as

    (A) "Lord, let other women be more grateful for my affection"
    (B) "Lord, save me from ungrateful, irrational women"
    (C) "Lord, spare men the emotional turmoil brought on by women"
    (D) "Lord, why must women be so heartless?"
    (E) "Lord, I am suffering; please don't let me fall in love again"

41. The most unconventional and idiosyncratic aspect of the poem is its

    (A) rhymes
    (B) meter and rhythm
    (C) spelling
    (D) syntax
    (E) figurative language

42. Lines 37–40 imply all of the following about the speaker EXCEPT that he

    (A) regrets reacting so hysterically
    (B) is never likely to fall in love again
    (C) recognizes that his love for the lady was flawed
    (D) mistook uncontrollable passion for love
    (E) hopes never to make the same mistake again

43. Which images are most extensively used in the poem?

    (A) Those pertinent to disorder and chaos
    (B) Those relevant to male-female relationships
    (C) Those alluding to death and dying
    (D) Those relating to religious rituals
    (E) Those concerning love and romance

44. Which of the following marks a turning point in the speaker's tone?

    (A) "And Faith fair scorn doth gain" (line 6)
    (B) "Weep, neighbors, weep!" (line 11)
    (C) "His sole executor, blame" (line 16)
    (D) "'Her eyes were once his dart'" (line 26)
    (E) "Love is not dead" (line 32)

45. The poem is best described as

    (A) a lyric on the death of love
    (B) a polemic on women's fickleness
    (C) an allegory about a man's self-discovery
    (D) a ballad about love's hardships
    (E) an ironic ode to a heartless woman

Questions 46–54. Read the following passage carefully before you decide on your answers to the questions.

> The schoolmaster sat in his homely dwelling attached to the
> school, both being modern erections; and he looked across the way
> at the old house in which his teacher Sue had a lodging. The
> *Line* arrangement had been concluded very quickly. A pupil-teacher who
> (5) was to have been transferred to Mr. Phillotson's school had failed
> him, and Sue had been taken as stop-gap. All such provisional
> arrangements as these could only last till the next annual visit of
> H.M. Inspector, whose approval was necessary to make them perma-
> nent. Having taught for some two years in London, though she had
> (10) abandoned the vocation of late, Miss Bridehead was not exactly a
> novice, and Phillotson thought there would be no difficulty in
> retaining her services, which he already wished to do, though she had

only been with him three or four weeks. He had found her quite as
bright as Jude had described her; and what master-tradesman does
(15) not wish to keep an apprentice who saves him half his labour?

It was a little over half-past eight o'clock in the morning and he
was waiting to see her cross the road to the school, when he would
follow. At twenty minutes to nine she did cross, a light hat tossed on
her head; and he watched her as a curiosity. A new emanation, which
(20) had nothing to do with her skill as a teacher, seemed to surround her
this morning. He went to the school also, and Sue remained governing her class at the other end of the room, all day under his eye. She
certainly was an excellent teacher.

It was part of his duty to give her private lessons in the evening,
(25) and some article in the Code made it necessary that a respectable,
elderly woman should be present at these lessons when the teacher
and the taught were of different sexes. Richard Phillotson thought of
the absurdity of the regulation in this case, when he was old enough
to be the girl's father; but he faithfully acted up to it; and sat down
(30) with her in a room where Mrs. Hawes, the widow at whose house
Sue lodged, occupied herself with sewing. The regulation was,
indeed, not easy to evade, for there was no other sitting-room in
the dwelling.

Sometimes as she figured—it was arithmetic that they were
(35) working at—she would involuntarily glance up with a little inquiring
smile at him, as if she assumed that, being the master, he must perceive all that was passing in her brain, as right or wrong. Phillotson
was not really thinking of the arithmetic at all, but of her, in a novel
way which somehow seemed strange to him as preceptor. Perhaps
(40) she knew he was thinking of her thus.

(1895)

46. Between the first and second sentences of the passage there is a shift from

   (A) a tone of humility to a tone of pride
   (B) melodrama to exposition
   (C) inner thoughts to physical action
   (D) present events to recalled events
   (E) speculation to reality

47. The characteristic referred to in line 14—that Miss Bridehead was "quite as bright" as she'd been described—is reinforced most strongly by which of the following phrases?

    (A) "not exactly a novice" (lines 10–11)
    (B) "an apprentice who saves him half his labour" (line 15)
    (C) "a new emanation . . . seemed to surround her" (lines 19–20)
    (D) "certainly was an excellent teacher" (line 23)
    (E) "Perhaps she knew he was thinking of her thus" (line 40)

48. The speaker in the passage uses the rhetorical question in lines 14–15 primarily to

    (A) support Phillotson's decision to keep Sue on his teaching staff
    (B) provide evidence to win the approval of H.M. Inspector, referred to in line 8
    (C) suggest that Phillotson has grown tired of his job
    (D) introduce an account of Sue's efficiency as a teacher
    (E) indicate that Phillotson thinks his job of schoolmaster is no different from that of a factory foreman

49. The characteristics of Sue conveyed by the phrase "a light hat tossed on her head" (lines 18–19) are best described as

    (A) impulsiveness and impatience
    (B) distraction and absent-mindedness
    (C) excitement and charisma
    (D) recklessness and indifference
    (E) youth and self-confidence

50. In context, the phrase "new emanation" (line 19) is meant to imply that

    (A) the schoolmaster is an extremely perceptive person
    (B) Phillotson appreciates Sue for more than her teaching ability
    (C) Sue has become more sociable during her time at the school
    (D) the teacher is very young—barely out of her teens
    (E) the schoolmaster is concerned that Sue will be late for class

51. The verb "governing" (lines 21–22) serves primarily to

    (A) suggest that Sue maintains order and effectively presides over her class
    (B) indicate that Sue is a strict and demanding teacher
    (C) give readers an unfavorable impression of Sue's teaching style
    (D) show that Sue possesses qualities at odds with those established in the previous paragraph
    (E) reflect an attitude of ambivalence on the part of Phillotson

52. The description of Phillotson throughout the passage has the primary effect of

    (A) creating doubt about the man's personal integrity
    (B) alerting readers to several problems typically faced by schoolmasters
    (C) reflecting the intensity of the speaker's admiration for dedicated schoolmasters
    (D) portraying him as a conscientious schoolmaster with a human frailty
    (E) revealing Phillotson's fanaticism about making his school a first-rate institution

53. The third paragraph (lines 24–33) provides evidence that the speaker believes which of the following about Phillotson?

    (A) He takes great pleasure in instructing young teachers at the school.
    (B) Although he abides by the rules of the school, he doesn't agree with them.
    (C) He has a reputation of someone attracted to women.
    (D) He believes in the equality of the sexes.
    (E) Through his past efforts, the school enjoys a homely atmosphere.

54. In which of the following ways does the phrase "as if she assumed that" (line 36) function in the last paragraph?

    (A) It reveals that Sue suspects Phillotson of harboring unprofessional thoughts about her.
    (B) It is a sign of Sue's weakness in arithmetic.
    (C) It indicates that Sue is trying to flirt with Phillotson.
    (D) It ridicules Sue for being excessively naive.
    (E) It suggests the degree of Sue's respect for Phillotson.

55. From the statement "Phillotson was not really thinking of the arithmetic at all, but of her" (lines 37–38), the reader may infer that

    (A) a theme dealing with youth and age has been introduced by the story's narrator
    (B) subtle irony is an integral part of the story
    (C) an element of romantic love may soon enter the story
    (D) Phillotson thinks privately that arithmetic lessons are a waste of time
    (E) Phillotson is determined to help Sue succeed as a teacher

SECTION II

Essay Questions

TIME—2 HOURS

Suggested time for each essay—40 minutes
Each essay counts as one-third of the total essay section score

Instructions: This section of the exam consists of three questions that require responses in essay form. You may write the essays in any order you wish and return to work on a completed essay if time permits. Although it is suggested that you spend roughly 40 minutes on each essay, you may apportion your time as you see fit.

Each essay will be evaluated according to its clarity, effectiveness in dealing with the topic, and the overall quality of your writing. If you have the time, go over each essay, checking its punctuation, spelling, and diction. Unless plenty of time remains, try to avoid major revisions. In the end, the quality of each essay counts more than its length.

For Question 3, please choose a novel or play of at least the same literary merit as the works you have been assigned in your AP English course.

Essays should be written in pen, preferably with black or dark blue ink. Use lined paper and write as legibly as you can. Do not skip lines. Cross out any errors you make. Feel free to make notes and plan your essay on a piece of scrap paper. Please number your essays and begin each one on a new sheet of paper. Good luck.

ESSAY QUESTION 1

The following two poems are about lost love. Read them carefully and write a well-organized essay in which you contrast the two speakers' responses to their losses. You may consider such elements as diction, tone, imagery, and structure.

Time Does Not Bring Relief

Time does not bring relief; you all have lied
    Who told me time would ease me of my pain!
I miss him in the weeping of the rain;
Line   I want him at the shrinking of the tide;
(5)   The old snows melt from every mountain-side,
    And last year's smoke in every lane;
    But last year's bitter loving must remain
Heaped on my heart, and my old thoughts abide!

There are a hundred places where I fear
(10)   To go,—so with his memory they brim!
And entering with some relief some quiet place
Where never fell his foot or shone his face
I say, "There is no memory of him here!"
     And so stand stricken, so remembering him!

—Edna St. Vincent Millay (1917)

Gouge, Adze, Rasp, Hammer[1]

So this is what it's like when love
leaves, and one is disappointed
that the body and mind continue to exist,

Line   exacting payment from each other,
(5)   engaging in stale rituals of desire,
and it would seem the best use of one's time

is not to stand for hours outside
her darkened house, drenched and chilled,
blinking into the slanting rain.

(10)   So this is what it's like to have to
practice amiability and learn
to say the orchard looks grand this evening

as the sun slips behind scumbled clouds
and the pears, mellowed to a golden-green,
(15)   glow like flames among the boughs.

It is now one claims there is comfort
in the constancy of nature, in the wind's way
of snatching dogwood blossoms from their branches,

scattering them in the dirt, in the slug's
(20)   sure, slow arrival to nowhere.
It is now one makes a show of praise

for the lilac that strains so hard to win
attention to its sweet inscrutability,
when one admires instead the lowly

---

[1]All are hand tools used in carpentry

(25)   gouge, adze, rasp, hammer—
fire-forged, blunt syllabled things,
unthought-of until a need exists:

a groove chiseled to a fixed width,
a roof sloped just so. it is now
(30)   one knows what it is to envy

the rivet, wrench, vise – whatever
works unburdened by memory and sight,
while high above the damp fields

flocks of swallows roil and dip
(35)   and streams churn, thick with leaping salmon,
and the bee advances on the rose.

—Chris Forhan (2003)

ESSAY QUESTION 2

Read the following passage from William Faulkner's story "Dry September." Then write a careful analysis of how the narrator characterizes the life of Minnie Cooper from her girlhood to adulthood. You may choose whichever literary devices (for example, tone, selection of detail, syntax, point of view) you find most significant.

      She was thirty-eight or thirty-nine. She lived in a small frame house with her invalid mother and a thin, unflagging aunt, where each morning between ten and eleven she would appear on the porch
Line in a lace-trimmed boudoir cap, to sit swinging in the porch swing
(5) until noon. After dinner she lay down a while, until the afternoon began to cool. Then, in one of the three or four new voile[1] dresses which she had each summer, she would go downtown to spend the afternoon in the stores with the other ladies, where they would handle the goods and haggle over the prices in cold, immediate
(10) voices, without any intention of buying.
      She was of comfortable people—not the best in Jefferson, but good people enough—and she was still on the slender side of ordinary looking, with a bright, faintly-haggard manner and dress. When she was young she had a slender, nervous body and a sort of hard
(15) vivacity which had enabled her for a time to ride upon the crest of

_____
[1]made of sheer silk or cotton

the town's social life as exemplified by the high school party and church social period of her contemporaries while still children enough to be un-classconscious.

(20) She was the last to realize that she was losing ground; that those among whom she had been a little bit brighter and louder flame than any other were beginning to learn the pleasure of snobbery—male— and retaliation—female. That was when her face began to wear that bright, haggard look. She still carried it to parties on shadowy porticoes and summer lawns, like a mask or a flag, with that bafflement of (25) furious repudiation of truth in her eyes. One evening at a party she heard a boy and two girls, all schoolmates, talking. She never accepted another invitation.

She watched the girls with whom she had grown up as they married and got homes and children, but no man ever called on her (30) steadily until the children of the other girls had been calling her "aunty" for several years, the while their mothers told them in bright voices how popular Aunt Minnie had been as a girl. Then the town began seeing her driving on Sunday afternoons with the cashier in the bank. He was a widower of about forty—a high- (35) colored man, smelling always faintly of the barber shop or of whiskey. He owned he first automobile in town, a red runabout; Minnie had the first motoring bonnet and veil the town ever saw. Then the town began to say: "Poor Minnie." "But she is old enough to take care of herself," others said. That was when she began to (40) ask her old schoolmates that their children call her "cousin" instead of "aunty."

It was twelve years now since she had been relegated into adultery by public opinion, and eight years since the cashier had gone to a Memphis bank, returning for one day each Christmas, which he (45) spent at an annual bachelors' party at a hunting club on the river. From behind their curtains the neighbors would see the party pass, and during the over-the-way Christmas day visiting they would tell her about him, about how well he looked, and how they heard that he was prospering in the city, watching with bright, secret eyes her (50) haggard, bright face. Usually by that hour there would be a scent of whiskey on her breath. It was supplied her by a youth, a clerk at the soda fountain: "Sure, I buy it for the old gal. I reckon she's entitled to a little fun."

Her mother kept to her room altogether now; the gaunt aunt that (55) ran the house. Against that background Minnie's bright dresses, her idle and empty days, had a quality of furious unreality. She went out in the evenings only with women now, neighbors, to moving pictures. Each afternoon she dressed in one of the new dresses and went downtown alone, where her young "cousins" were already strolling in (60) the late afternoons with their delicate, silken heads and thin,

awkward arms and conscious hips, clinging to one another or shriek-
ing and giggling with paired boys in the soda fountain when she
passed and went on along the serried store fronts, in the doors of
which the sitting and lounging men did not even follow her with
(65)   their eyes any more.

(1930)

ESSAY QUESTION 3

Authors frequently people their works with characters who are dissatisfied with the
circumstances of their lives. Such characters want to change the conditions in which
they find themselves, but for one reason or other they don't, or can't do so—at least
not right away.

Choose a play or novel in which a character is unhappily trapped in "what is" and
has, at least temporarily, shut the door to the surprises and opportunities of "what
could be." Then write an essay that analyzes how the plight of the character contributes to the meaning of the work as a whole.

The work may come from the following list, or you may choose another play or
novel of equivalent merit. Please avoid plot summaries, and don't pick a short story,
poem, film, or work of nonfiction.

The Adventures of Huckleberry Finn	*Go Tell It on the Mountain*
A Doll's House	*Great Expectations*
Ah! Wilderness	*Hedda Gabler*
All My Sons	*King Lear*
An Enemy of the People	*Madame Bovary*
Anna Karenina	*Middlemarch*
Antigone	*Main Street*
As You Like It	*Obasan*
David Copperfield	*One Day in the Life of Ivan Denisovich*
Death of a Salesman	*The Scarlet Letter*
Ethan Frome	*The Seagull*
Fahrenheit 451	*Washington Square*
Fathers and Sons	*Who's Afraid of Virginia Woolf?*
The Fountainhead	*Winesburg, Ohio*

Answer Key
DIAGNOSTIC TEST

Section I

1. B	16. B	31. E	46. D
2. E	17. D	32. C	47. D
3. B	18. A	33. B	48. A
4. C	19. B	34. A	49. E
5. B	20. C	35. C	50. B
6. D	21. D	36. A	51. A
7. D	22. B	37. E	52. D
8. A	23. E	38. B	53. B
9. A	24. B	39. B	54. E
10. A	25. E	40. C	55. C
11. C	26. A	41. D	
12. A	27. E	42. B	
13. D	28. A	43. C	
14. A	29. D	44. E	
15. C	30. C	45. A	

SUMMARY OF ANSWERS IN SECTION I MULTIPLE-CHOICE

Number of correct answers _____

Use this information when you calculate your score on this examination.
See page 113.

ANSWER EXPLANATIONS

Section I

1. **(B)** The narrator is impressed with the couple's distinctive appearance and refined behavior, especially in contrast to those of other guests at the resort. Because the narrator's observations are made from a distance and never through conversation or face-to-face contact, the couple remains something of a mystery throughout the passage.

2. **(E)** The narrator is puzzled by the elderly couple. The phrase "private distance of their own" adds another dimension to their aura of mystery. Of the other choices, only (A) may have some validity, but the couple's aloofness is established by the narrator's observation, stated in the first sentence, that the couple seemed to take no notice of anyone else at the beach.

3. **(B)** The word "arrestingly" is used to describe the distinctive posture of the old couple. Their carriage is strikingly regal, so erect that the startled people cannot help looking at the elderly pair. This definition of "arrestingly" is reinforced by the clause, "it is this that catches so much attention" (lines 6–7).

4. **(C)** Aside from a brief description of the couple's slow gait, the opening lines dwell chiefly on their clothes and overall bearing. Other information, such as their age and their actions, is of secondary importance in the first three paragraphs of the passage.

5. **(B)** In the third paragraph, the narrator offers theories about the identity of the elderly couple. The next paragraph contains a factual description of the resort and a detailed account of some of its visitors.

6. **(D)** By placing a description of the Chicago contingent in the same sentence with the statement that the aged couple "have a clear, unwavering schedule of their own," the narrator heightens the contrast between the group and the couple.

7. **(D)** The comment is somewhat critical of Amanda's inquisitiveness. Yet, the narrator's tendency to mind other people's business is even more pronounced than Amanda's. It is ironic that the narrator appears to be unaware that he/she is even more preoccupied with other people's private lives than Amanda. Nothing in the passage suggests the validity of the other choices.

8. **(A)** Most of the passage is devoted to the narrator's observations of people at the resort. The narrator not only observes people very carefully but somehow acquires details about their personal lives.

9. **(A)** Typically, tropical birds sport bright colors, but ironically this description emphasizes the opposite: the couple's subdued dark and light attire, which contrasts with the brightly colored glitzy clothes worn by other guests. The couple's bathing suits are "trim;" another guest wears a caftan, a baggy, loosely fitting garment. Although the phrase "ancient legs" (line 50) suggests both the spindly legs of water birds and the thin, pasty legs of the elderly, the couple, according to the narrator, still maintain an aura of grace and elegance.

10. **(A)** The nature of the personal and sometimes intimate details contained in all the choices but (A) suggests that Amanda has been talking to the narrator about herself.

11. **(C)** The last sentences suggest that the narrator has somehow come to wonder whether the couple's image is too studied, too well-rehearsed, too perfect to be real. Early in the passage, the narrator says that the couple projected an image of "either disdain or a total lack of interest in other people" (line 8), but now, the couple's aura of aloofness has weakened. Even in "apparent repose," they seem tense, "highly conscious of each moment."

12. **(A)** In line 1 the speaker questions the nature of her thoughts about the "other country." Are her thoughts rooted in past reality—i.e., as "half-remembered" images—or are they imagined—i.e., anticipated visions? As the poem proceeds, we find that the speaker's perplexity is rooted neither in vague recollection nor in anticipation of the future. Rather, it is brought about by an ambiguous combination of both. (C) deserves consideration as the answer because it names a possible effect created by the speaker's uncertainty about what is real and what is imagined. But precise details later in the poem cast aside the notion that the speaker is removed or disconnected from events in the poem. (E) is wrong because the question is not hypothetical. That is, it doesn't propose a theory or condition that requires some sort of proof.

13. **(D)** The references to rain provide a frame for the poem. Like all flights of fancy, this one ends where it begins—in the rain. Also, the dreary images of rain in England contrast starkly with the beauty of the other country. The presence of rain can also explain the appeal of escaping to a warm, romantic place by the sea. In the context of the poem, the rain symbolizes the bleakness of England, but it has no allegorical overtones, making (D) the correct answer.

14. **(A)** The third stanza provides evidence that the speaker has been in this country before: She occupies the same room, and in her mind she can still navigate the streets to her old job at the hotel. Even the sounds of seagulls, bells, and a flute are familiar to her.

15 **(C)** The simile is meant to echo the question asked in line 1: Is the other country "anticipated or half remembered?" Before heading for the airport, the speaker looks forward to revisiting a place only half-remembered. In short, her recollections have faded "like newsprint in the sun." Thoughts of her work and the dreary English weather are soon replaced by newly revived images of the other country. (A) and (E) don't apply because the speaker says nothing about the news or about office work. (B) correctly points out the juxtapostition of rain and sun, but in terms of the entire poem, the contrast, while poetically noteworthy, is relatively insignificant.

16. **(B)** Images of the other country exist not in front of the speaker's eyes, but inside her head. (A) has possibilities as the correct answer because the phrase "out of focus" can be taken to mean "vaguely remembered." But (B) is a more literal interpretation and therefore a better answer.

17. **(D)** As the title "In Your Mind" suggests, the story takes place inside a person's head. In effect, a person imagines escaping to a place (and, perhaps, a time) more agreeable than dreary, rain-soaked England in the fall. (B) is partly true because of the speaker's intense feelings for "the other country," but by far the primary mood of the poem is visionary.

18. **(A)** In contrast to the discontent implied by dreary, rain-soaked England (lines 2–6), during her imaginary journey, the speaker seems relieved to be away from her desk. Her responses to the sights and sounds of the "other country" suggest that she's been revived, even rejuvenated, by the change of scene.

19. **(B)** The moon in a child's picture, drawn with an untrained hand, is likely be a crude representation of the real thing. In the poem, the speaker implies that the setting, like the drawing, is simple and far removed from reality. Hence also, the verbal exchange about men landing on the moon. Why the transplanted character denies the possibility of men on the moon is a puzzle. Perhaps she prefers not to let the outside world intrude upon the boy's innocent conception of the world.

20. **(C)** Waking up in her room, the speaker has been transported into the past and suddenly recognizes the painting on the wall, an object that she hasn't thought of in thirty years. Her startling rediscovery of the painting is made dramatic by the italicized exclamation "*Of course*" (line 15).

21. **(D)** The speaker finds herself dawdling on "the blue bridge," a familiar landmark to her. In her mind, however, she continues to be lost in her daydream about a far-away place.

22. **(B)** Evidence in the poem indicates that the setting is close to the sea, a place with seagulls (line 17), a place where you can watch the moon drop below the horizon of the sea (line 12). Details such as the "rasp of carpentry" (line 13), the "flute practicing scales" (lines 17–18), and the practice of swapping a "coin for a fish on the way home" (line 18) all suggest the intimacy of a small town or village. That drinks are served by a "beautiful boy" rather than by an adult also contributes to the picture of a low-key, quiet place. Leaving a warm coat on the plane (lines 5–6), in effect, says that you're headed to a destination where heavy clothing isn't needed.

23. **(E)** The terse phrases of the last line, coming after a far longer and complete sentence in lines 22–23, jolt the speaker (as well as the reader) back to reality. In addition, the images contained in the last line recall the conditions in the first stanza that prompted the speaker's escape in the first place. (C) may be implied by the entire poem, but (E) is a better answer because it focuses directly on the last line.

24. **(B)** Except for the impressionistic idea of its first sentence, the paragraph consists of the narrator's description of people on a New York street. (A) cannot be correct because the paragraph's details are realistic rather than metaphorical. (C) is wrong because the details of the scene can be observed

by anyone, not just by an omniscient narrator. (D) is a poor choice because the paragraph is the only one in the passage not written from Amory's point of view. (E) is not a valid answer because most of the images in the paragraph are visual.

25. **(E)** The passage contains several references to Amory's aversion to dirt and to the lack of cleanliness, as well as to the foul odors of people and food. Less pronounced, but still evident, are Amory's views of "gloomy hallways" and "verdureless" backyards (line 20). By contrast, Amory remembers one instance when a "wreath of fresh flowers" provided a "momentary glow" in a subway car (lines 37–39). If you chose (A), you may have been misled by the expression *poverty-stricken*. Amory detested poverty-stricken people, but the passage refers hardly at all to their neighborhoods.

26. **(A)** The narrator piles details one on top of the other, listing one miserable feature after the next. The cumulative effect of this barrage is to paint a striking portrait of dismal, almost inhuman living conditions.

27. **(E)** Nothing says it better than Amory's thoughts in lines 40–41: "I detest poor people . . . I hate them for being poor."

28. **(A)** The paragraph beginning in line 28 discusses Amory's perception of poor people: Women feel less ashamed of their poverty in the company of women than in the company of men. In other words, Amory thinks that in the presence of men, women want to make a favorable impression.

29. **(D)** The incident is ironic because the wreath of fresh flowers, commemorating someone's death, "cleared the air and [had] given every one in the car a momentary glow." From others' grief, in other words, came a moment of joy. (A) comes close to an alternative answer because the flowers contrast with the stale air of the subway. But there's nothing inherently paradoxical— that is, self-contradictory—about the funeral wreath.

30. **(C)** Except for the first paragraph, in which the narrator observes the people of the city, the passage is generally an in-depth report of Amory's attitudes and feelings. The narrator has no particular bias for or against Amory but just states the facts. (E) might be a tempting answer because of Amory's overall negativity, but again, the narrator just tells it as it is, in an impartial, detached manner. Choices (A), (B), and (D) do not apply.

31. **(E)** Choice (A) is discussed at length in the second paragraph (lines 7–16). As for (B), Amory envisions the squalid living conditions in lines 17–27. Choice (C) is mentioned in lines 25–27, and (D) is implied by the incident described in lines 44–48. No mention is made in the passage of people's pessimism about lifting themselves out of poverty.

32. **(C)** Lines 53–55 summarize Amory's attitude toward himself: Amory appears to be unwilling or unable to change his own feelings and reactions toward the poor. Although he recognizes his rancorous and malevolent views, he's not inclined to moderate them.

33. **(B)** By mentioning O. Henry, the narrator juxtaposes Amory's lack of sympathy toward poor people against O. Henry's humanistic and charitable feelings about New York's poor.

34. **(A)** The speaker implies that poverty might some day be Amory's problem. It would be presumptuous to infer from that that Amory himself will fall into poverty, but because in lines 57–58 the speaker plainly states that Amory despises poverty "*at present,*" it's not unreasonable to assume that somehow Amory's attitude will change. Therefore, (A) is the best choice.

35. **(C)** The speaker's anguish responds to rejection by the woman he loves. That's why he cries out "Love is dead."

36. **(A)** The speaker exaggerates the intensity of his dismay by stating, "*All* Love is dead," when the truth is that only he has lost his love. In effect, he views his private misfortune as a public disaster. The poet uses the devices named in the other choices (B)–(E), but none of them conveys the speaker's passion as vividly as his use of hyperbole.

37. **(E)** In the face of his lady's disdain, the speaker feels impotent. His "worth" was considered worthless (line 5), and his faithfulness to her earned only her scorn (line 6). Is it any wonder that he feels impotent? (C) doubtlessly describes the speaker's general feelings, but (E) is a more precise answer.

38. **(B)** Expecting his neighbors to have heard the news that love is dead, the speaker is vexed by their indifference and insists that it's about time that they mourn with him.

39. **(B)** Line 1 calls for the church to ring its bells and otherwise go into mourning mode in order to spread the word that a death has occurred. Likewise, line 21 asks the church to hold services that include the singing of dirges and the saying of masses for the dead. Thematically, many of the other pairs of sentences relate to the main topic of the poem, but their meanings do not resemble each other.

40. **(C)** The refrain is a short prayer asking God to "deliver"—that is, to remove from his life both "ungrateful fancy" (unrequited or unappreciated love) and "female franzy," an ambiguous phrase that refers to women who behave as though they've lost their minds as well as to the irrational habit of men to be in love with women.

41. **(D)** The poem contains some enigmatic sentence structure. For example, customary word order is reversed in line 35: "Where she his counsel keepeth." The poem also contains elliptical constructions, as in lines 23–26, that may be paraphrased as follows: "Sir Wrong solemnly declares that my mistress's Marble-heart is love's tomb, on which the epitaph says 'His mistress's eyes once sent him love darts.'"

42. **(B)** The speaker has not permanently discarded love, but he'll steer clear of the kind of insane passion that ruled him during his recent experience.

43. **(C)** Images and words related to death and dying pervade the poem, including "death-bed," "winding-sheet, and "tomb." Religious references such as "dirge" and "tentrals" relate to services for the dead.

44. **(E)** Through the third stanza, the speaker is beside himself with woe over losing his love. Then he suddenly comes to his senses. Love had not fled, after all. It had merely been put on hold.

45. **(A)** The poem exemplifies a lyric poem—a highly personal expression of emotion by a single speaker.

46. **(D)** Except for the first sentence of the paragraph, the narration consists of the schoolmaster's thoughts about the teacher Sue—how she came to be hired, her past experience, and how she has fared as a teacher since her arrival. The first sentence is written in the simple past tense. All the other sentences use the past perfect tense, indicating that the action occurred prior to the events being described.

47. **(D)** Although "bright" has several different meanings, in this context it refers to the intelligence that Miss Bridehead manifests as a teacher. Therefore (D), the only choice related to Miss Bridehead's teaching ability, supports the notion that she is "bright."

48. **(A)** The question is meant to explain Phillotson's rationale. To him, it makes perfect sense to retain Sue as a teacher. She is an excellent worker and has lightened his burden by half. The other choices are inferences that may have some validity, but there's little evidence in the passage to support them.

49. **(E)** That she "tossed" a light hat onto her head conveys a sense of Sue's free-and-easy disposition. A less self-assured older woman in a new job would probably dress more carefully and be more mindful of her appearance. (D) has some validity because Sue's casual way of wearing a hat can certainly be interpreted as evidence of her indifference about her appearance, but it's a stretch to consider it a sign of recklessness.

50. **(B)** Taken literally, "emanation" refers to an emission of a thing or quality. That is, a person's appearance can radiate any number of qualities—dignity, intelligence, style, mystery, and countless others. Precisely what Sue emanates is left unsaid, but Phillotson's reaction suggests that the young woman has somehow aroused his interest in ways beyond her teaching ability.

51. **(A)** Phillotson's observation that Sue is an "excellent teacher" (line 23) supports the use of "governing" to mean that Sue is in charge and in full control of her class throughout the day. In other words, she does all that Phillotson expects of a good teacher. (B) may well characterize the teaching style that Phillotson favors, but the passage fails to mention it.

52. **(D)** Much of the passage shows Phillotson doing his job, especially working out the details of Sue's employment and figuring out ways to retain her on his staff. At the same time, however, the passage contains more than a strong

hint that Phillotson has extracurricular feelings that even he thinks are "strange" (line 39). (A) overstates Phillotson's failing. Unprofessional feelings for Sue don't attest to a lack of integrity but to the presence of ordinary human emotions.

53. **(B)** Phillotson thinks it's absurd to require the presence of a "respectable, elderly woman" when he gives private lessons to Sue (line 28), but as the schoolmaster he is obliged to follow the school's Code.

54. **(E)** If Sue assumes that Phillotson can read her mind, she must have more faith in him than he deserves. Her glances up at him suggest a misplaced and naïve trust—like the trust of an innocent child for the word of an adult. The phrase "as if," of course, indicates that the narrator is interpreting Sue's behavior, not describing it as fact.

55. **(C)** Phillotson seems distracted by Sue. Precisely why or how is not made clear, but his reaction "seemed strange to him as preceptor." The last sentence of the passage implies that Phillotson has begun to wonder whether Sue senses his interest in her. Also, considering Phillotson's reaction earlier in the passage as he watches Sue cross the road (lines 17–18), it appears that she has triggered some unexpected feelings in the schoolmaster.

Section II

Although answers to essay questions will vary greatly, the following descriptions suggest an approach to each question and contain ideas that could be used in a response. Perhaps your essay contains many of the same ideas. If not, don't be alarmed. Your ideas may be at least as valid as those presented here.

Note: Don't mistake these descriptions for complete essays; essays written for the exam should be full-length, well organized, and fully developed. For an overview of how essays are graded, turn to "How Essays Are Scored," on page 45.

ESSAY QUESTION 1

Both poems are about the suffering that almost always follows the loss of love. One speaker is a woman, the other a man, but both endure intense emotional pain and both seek ways to relieve it.

Neither poem explains the circumstances that tore the lovers apart. But the speaker in "Time Does Not Bring Relief" refers to "last year's bitter loving" (line 7), a phrase implying that some sort of conflict preceded the break-up. The speaker in "Gouge, Adze, Rasp, Hammer," on the other hand, does not divulge the reason he stands pining in the rain for hours outside the darkened house of his beloved (lines 6–9).

"Time Does Not Bring Relief" is a Shakespearean sonnet, an interesting choice for a speaker beset by emotional turmoil. Instead of emoting wildly, she expresses feelings circumspectly, using the rhythm, rhyme scheme, and prescribed structure of a sonnet. The form, perhaps, provides a kind of anchor for her, something solid and dependable, something more substantial than the love she has lost.

In the first quatrain, the speaker describes her state of heart and mind: Above all, she feels betrayed by those who told her that time would ease her pain. Relying on images of water—"the weeping of the rain," which parallels her tears, and "the tide," suggesting regular daily bouts of sorrow—she remains as bereft as ever over her loss.

The second quatrain conveys the duration of the speaker's anguish. Images of nature mark the passage of time. She alludes to "The old snows," which have now melted, and to "last year's leaves," which have fallen, been raked up, and burned. In short, nature goes through its cycles while she is stuck with memories of "bitter loving" and burdened with the same "old thoughts" heaped on her heart.

The sestet asserts that the speaker's torment won't go away, or, at any rate, it won't go away soon. Wherever she goes, even to places with no connection to her former love, she cannot purge him from her mind. In the poem's last line, overwhelmed with frustration, she exclaims her desperation: "And so stand stricken, so remembering him."

The forlorn lover in "Gouge, Adze, Rasp, Hammer" is no less distressed, but the poem, written in free verse, is more casual and conversational: "So this is what it's like when love/leaves," he comments in the first stanza. And again later: "So this is what it's like to have to/practice amiability"—perhaps a reference to finding himself socially obliged to be rational on the outside while his emotions are seething inside.

This poem also uses images of nature, but for different purposes and effects than those in "Time. . . ." Here, the speaker thinks he is supposed to find comfort in the "constancy of nature" (line 17) because nature, unlike love, follows set patterns, such as "the wind's way of snatching dogwood blossoms from their branches" (lines 17–18). But in the end, nature fails him. In effect, the speaker is like the slug (lines 19–20), going "nowhere."

So he turns for relief to "fire-forged, blunt-syllabled things" (line 26). Indeed, the very names of tools—gouge, adze, rasp, hammer—are hard and solid, like the objects themselves. In stark contrast to abstractions like love and beauty in nature, tools are tangible. They can be held and do what the hand bids them. For the speaker, they provide an escape from pain. After all, "the rivet, wrench, vise" have no feelings, no "memory and sight" (lines 31–32)—qualities that someone in emotional anguish might envy. But the speaker's escape is temporary, for the last lines of the poem return to nature, although the images are different from those that came before. Earlier, the speaker talks mostly of trees and clouds and blossoms. Here, he talks of active things—birds that "roil and dip," salmon that leap, a bee advancing on a rose. The change in images implies a change in the speaker's disposition, no doubt encouraged by the brief encounter with his tools. In effect, his recovery from lost love seems to have begun.

ESSAY QUESTION 2

This passage is about Minnie Cooper, a forlorn, isolated, and somewhat enigmatic figure. In creating Minnie's portrait, the narrator chooses details that emphasize her drab existence, especially during her adulthood: She lives "in a small frame house with her invalid mother and a thin, unflagging aunt" (lines 1–2), and the days of her life follow an aimless routine that includes swinging on the porch, napping, and rummaging through shops in her town with no intention of buying anything.

In her youth, however, she showed promise: She had "vivacity" (line 15), she partied with her friends, and she is described as having been a "brighter and louder flame" than the other girls her age (line 20). But somehow—and we are never told exactly why—Minnie's flame went out, and her prospects for an active and agreeable life faded away. The narrator explains only nebulously the cause of Minnie's decline, one reason being "the bafflement of furious repudiation of truth in her eyes" (lines 24–25). We are also told that once at a party Minnie overheard a conversation between her schoolmates and after that never accepted another invitation. But we are left in the dark about what was said.

In fact, the narrator—no doubt deliberately—leaves us with many unanswered questions about Minnie. Uncertainty is created not only by his choice of details but also by his detached and passionless tone. We never hear Minnie speak. Nor do we know her feelings about anything except her wish to be called "cousin" instead of "aunty" by the children of her former schoolmates, implying that she has grown touchy about her advancing age. What we learn about Minnie comes mostly via the townspeople of Jefferson, whose eyebrows are raised, for example, when she is seen driving around on Sunday afternoons with the bank cashier. The observers assume, of course, that she is involved in an adulterous relationship. But because they don't really know her, no one can say for sure. They, like readers of the passage, remain in the dark.

Not even the narrator knows all there is to know about Minnie. He's uncertain, for example, whether she's thirty-eight or thirty-nine (line 1). Physical descriptions of Minnie are ambiguous. We are told that Minnie's manner and dress were "bright" and "faintly-haggard" (line 13), her face began to wear a "bright haggard look" (lines 22–23). Bright *and* haggard? His oxymoron leaves us slightly unsure of what she really looks like. Considering Minnie's colorless personality, there is an implied paradox, too, in her "bright dresses" (line 55) and the fact that she rode around town in a "red runabout." Furthermore, the narrator says that Minnie's "idle and empty days" have a quality of "furious unreality" (line 56)—another apparent contradiction, because idle and empty days, by definition, lack fury or passion of any sort. In effect, the passage presents Minnie as a remote and elusive figure. She wanders ghost-like through life, a notion supported by the concluding statement that "lounging men did not even follow her with their eyes any more."

ESSAY QUESTION 3

Each of the works discussed briefly below contains material appropriate to answering the question.

Ethan Frome

In the small and grim New England village of Starkfield, Ethan Frome, a sawmill owner and the title character of Edith Wharton's novel, leads an isolated and lonely life. Trapped in both a failing lumber business and a marriage with a hypochondriacal and tyrannical wife, Zeena, Ethan thinks about how things might have been different, but he's unable to escape from or change his circumstances. The time is winter, when the land, symbolic of Ethan's life, is cold, dark, and dead. When Zeena's cheerful young cousin Mattie comes to live with them as a housekeeper, however, Ethan is consumed by romantic thoughts of Mattie, all the while feeling guilty as well as terrified that Zeena will somehow realize his secret passions. When Zeena decides that Mattie must be let go—they can no longer afford to pay her—the tragedy of Ethan's story is compounded. Desperate to escape, he tries to kill himself and Mattie in a sledding accident. But they survive and Mattie, now a demanding invalid, resides permanently in the Fromes' house, burdening Ethan with the care of two sickly women, suggesting that there is no real escape, except death perhaps, from one's burdens.

One Day in the Life of Ivan Denisovich

By definition, prison limits opportunities for changing the circumstances of one's life. The title character in *One Day in the Life of Ivan Denisovich* by Alexander Solzhenitzn is confined in a Siberian labor camp for ten years. Escape is out of the question; so in order to survive, he adapts, making every effort to conform and remain anonymous. He obeys every rule and does nothing to call attention to himself. Yet, during every waking moment he remains alert to opportunities to stay a little warmer, to gain an extra bite of food, to preserve his strength—anything to avoid the despair that has beaten down a number of his fellow prisoners. His perseverance makes a statement not only about Ivan as an individual, but about man's noble character and the will to survive.

Death of a Salesman

Willie Loman in Arthur Miller's *Death of a Salesman* epitomizes a man trapped in the circumstances of his life. For years he has pursued an idealized vision of the American dream. But his dream has been tarnished by his small and rundown home, his old car in need of repairs, and his two disappointing sons, Biff and Hap. Now, nearing the end of his career, Willie has seen his sales slump to zero. Moreover, a personal mantra that he has depended on—namely, the importance of being "well-liked" by others—has turned out to be dross. Looking back in pain and frustration, Willie realizes that he's wasted much of his life chasing a mirage. One last time, desperate for relief, he counts on Biff, one of his ne'er-do-well sons, to land a respectable job. But his hopes are a delusion. In the end, Willie, intent on helping Biff succeed with life insurance money, commits suicide. Miller's play is an indictment of false values, and Willie is an unwitting emblem of their tragic and destructive influence on American society.

SELF-SCORING GUIDE FOR THE DIAGNOSTIC TEST
Scoring Section 2 ESSAYS

After referring to "How Essays Are Scored," on page 43 of this book, use this guide to help you evaluate each essay. Do your best to evaluate your performance in each category by using the criteria spelled out below. Because it is hard to achieve objectivity when assessing your own writing, you may improve the validity of your score by having a trusted and well-informed friend or experienced teacher read and rate your essay.

On the Rating Chart that follows, enter a number (from 1 to 6) that you think represents your level of performance in each category (A–F).

Category A: OVERALL PURPOSE/MAIN IDEA
>   6 clearly establishes and cogently defines an insightful purpose
>   5 clearly establishes and generally defines an appropriate purpose
>   4 identifies and defines an appropriate purpose
>   3 identifies and develops a mostly appropriate purpose
>   2 attempts to identify but falls short of defining a clear purpose
>   1 fails to identify the purpose of the essay

Category B: HANDLING OF THE PROMPT
>   6 clearly and completely addresses and directly answers each part of the prompt
>   5 directly addresses and answers each part of the prompt
>   4 answers each part of the prompt directly or indirectly
>   3 answers most parts of the prompt directly or indirectly
>   2 fails to address important parts of the prompt directly or indirectly
>   1 does not address the prompt or misinterprets requirements of the prompt

Category C: ORGANIZATION AND DEVELOPMENT
>   6 insightfully organizes sequence of ideas according to the purpose of the essay; presents a cogent analysis using fully-developed, coherent paragraphs
>   5 organizes material clearly and develops ideas with generally insightful evidence in unified paragraphs
>   4 organizes conventional evidence or commentary in appropriate but perfunctorily arranged, formulaic paragraphs
>   3 organizes material with little relation to the point or purpose of the essay; develops ideas adequately but with occasional irrelevancies
>   2 organizes weak material in a confusing manner; generally ignores appropriate paragraph development
>   1 lacks discernible organization; ignores relevant development of ideas

Category D: SENTENCE STRUCTURE

    6 uses clear, precise, and appropriately varied sentences to convey meaning and create effects

    5 uses clear sentences with appropriately varied structures to create interest

    4 consists of mostly clear sentences with some structural variety

    3 contains minor sentence errors and little sentence variety

    2 includes sentence errors that sometimes interfere with meaning

    1 contains serious sentence errors that obscure meaning

Category E: USE OF LANGUAGE

    6 uses precise and effective vocabulary extremely well-suited to the subject and the audience

    5 contains vocabulary that clearly and accurately convey meaning

    4 uses conventional but generally correct and appropriate vocabulary

    3 uses ordinary vocabulary with some errors in diction or idiom

    2 contains awkward word choices and frequent errors in diction or idiom

    1 uses words that often obscure meaning

Category F: GRAMMAR AND USAGE

    6 avoids all or virtually all grammar and usage errors

    5 includes occasional minor errors in standard English grammar and usage

    4 uses standard English grammar and usage but with several minor errors in standard English

    3 contains errors in standard English grammar and usage that occasionally obscure meaning

    2 contains errors in standard English grammar and usage that frequently obscure meaning

    1 contains several major errors in standard English grammar and usage that block meaning

RATING CHART

RATING CHART			
Rate your essay:	Essay 1	Essay 2	Essay 3
Overall Purpose/Main Idea	_____	_____	_____
Handling of the Prompt	_____	_____	_____
Organization and Development	_____	_____	_____
Sentence Structure	_____	_____	_____
Use of Language	_____	_____	_____
Grammar and Usage	_____	_____	_____
Composite Scores (Sum of each column)	_____	_____	_____

By using the following chart, in which composite scores are converted to the 9-point AP rating scale, you may determine the final score for each essay:

Composite Score	AP Essay Score
33–36	9
29–32	8
25–28	7
21–24	6
18–20	5
15–17	4
10–14	3
7–9	2
6 or below	1

AP Essay Scores   Essay 1 _____   Essay 2 _____   Essay 3 _____

TEST SCORE WORKSHEET

Calculating Your AP Score on the Diagnostic Test

The scores you have earned on the multiple-choice and essay sections of the exam may now be converted to the AP 5-point scale by doing the following calculations:

I. Determine your score for Section I (Multiple-Choice)

Step A: Number of correct answers _____

Step B: Multiply the figure in Step A by 1.2272 to find your Multiple-Choice Score _____ . (Do not round)

II. Determine your score for Section II (Essays)[1]

Step A: Enter your score for Essay 1 (out of 9) _____

Step B: Enter your score for Essay 2 (out of 9) _____

Step C: Enter your score for Essay 3 (out of 9) _____

Step D: Add the figures in Steps A, B, and C _____

Step E: Multiply the figure in Step D by 3.0556 _____ (Do not round). This is your Essay Score.

III. Determine Your Total Score

Add the scores for I and II to find your composite score _____ .

(Round to the nearest whole number)

To convert your composite score to the AP 5-point scale, use the chart below. The range of scores only approximates what you would earn on the actual test because the exact figures may vary from test to test. Be aware, therefore, that your score on this test, as well as on other tests in this book, may differ slightly from your score on an actual AP exam.

Composite Score	AP Grade
114–150	5
98–113	4
81–97	3
53–80	2
0–52	1

---

[1]After the AP exam, essays are judged in relation to other essays written on the same topic at the same time. Therefore, the score you assign yourself for an essay may not be the same as the score you would earn on an actual exam.

PART 3

POETRY

What You Need to Know About Poetry

CHAPTER 4

- 10 questions that crack open any poem
- The poet's vocabulary
- What to listen for in a poem
- Types of poetry: how to tell an epic from an elegy
- Discussions of popular AP poems

POETRY OVERVIEW

Whether you abhor poetry or eat it for breakfast, whether you think poetry is cool or hot, scintillating or dull—none of that really matters on the AP exam. When you take the test, you'll be handed two or maybe three poems accompanied by roughly twenty-five multiple-choice questions. In addition, you'll be asked to write an essay that analyzes one or more additional poems. If poetry is in your blood, you'll probably deal deftly with the poetry sections of the exam. However, if poetry is something you can live without, this chapter may not change your attitude, but it can prepare you to score high in the poetry sections of the exam.

What You Won't See on the Exam

Before reviewing what you need to know, let's quickly dispense with what you can do without. Rest assured that you won't be asked to identify the title of any poems or recall facts about a poet's life. Nor will you need to dredge up information concerning the history of poetry or expound on the various schools of poetic criticism that have long flourished in academia. Because highly technical aspects of poetry are generally off limits on the exam, you won't be expected to have mastered the intricacies of poetic metrics and its baffling vocabulary—although it could be advantageous to know both the meaning of such terms as *iambic pentameter* and *dactyl* and the function of a poetic *foot*. Also, because the AP exam will never ask you to expound on the esoterica of versification, rhyme, and the multitude of poetic forms, you won't need to know more than the rudiments of each.

Most literate people would probably argue that poetry should be read for pleasure. The poems on the AP exam, however, are not put there for your enjoyment or appreciation. With luck you may enjoy reading them, but you needn't praise their artistry or revel in their emotion. Your task will be more mundane—to read each poem, figure out its meaning, examine its structure, and analyze the effects of poetic techniques that the poet brought to bear. In short, you'll pore over the anatomy of each poem and respond to the questions. In Section I, the multiple-choice questions themselves will steer you through the poems, pointing out important features. In Section II, you're left to find and discuss them on your own.

What You Need to Know

You are expected to have a reasonably firm grasp of poetic structure, form, sound, and the other elements that give poetry the power to move, entertain, and enlighten. To put it plainly, you should be able to answer the question *How does a poem convey meaning?* In your English classes these past years, while studying the fundamentals of diction, metaphor, rhyme, and the other components of poetry, chances are you've been developing the background and acquiring the know-how to answer that question insightfully.

HOW TO READ A POEM

Ideally, poems should be read aloud. Poetry, after all, is an oral art akin to music. Its sounds, rhythms, and rhymes are meant to be heard. Regrettably, you can't read a poem out loud during the AP exam or an irate proctor will haul you away. So you'll have to settle for the next best thing: Read it aloud to yourself—a paradox, to be sure, but also a piece of advice that means reading it slowly, pronouncing each word in your mind's ear, skipping not a single syllable or mark of punctuation, paying attention to built-in pauses and to line and stanza breaks. In short, listen to yourself reciting the poem.

TIP

Read a poem several times to unlock its meanings.

Easier said than done? Perhaps, because the poems pitched to you during the exam are a world away from "Roses are Red/Violets are Blue" or "Casey at the Bat"—ditties that may share the name *poem* with "In Memorium" and "The Lovesong of J. Alfred Prufrock" but can't compare in artistry or in the authentic expression of human experience. Because poems on the exam tend to be far from transparent, plan to read them two or three times. With each reading, a poem should start to reveal its meanings.

Before you begin to read a poem, think about the possible meaning of its title. The title may contain just the clue needed to crack open the world within the poem. After reading the poem, think about the title again. Very possibly, its meaning will have been expanded in ways you couldn't have imagined before.

As you read, avoid pausing at the end of every line; unnecessary pauses create a choppy effect that obscures meaning. Rather, pause where punctuation, if any, indicates that a pause is needed.

Reading poetry well is a skill like any other, and the more you practice, the better you'll get. That's why the best thing you can do to prepare for the exam is to read scores of poems—many more than appear in this book. For each one, have a go at answering the ten generic questions that follow:

1. **Who is talking?**

   What can you tell about the speaker's age, gender, station in life, opinions, and feelings? What, if anything, does the poem reveal about the speaker's character?

   Some speakers take on a distinct personality. The speaker in Andrew Marvell's "To His Coy Mistress," for example, is urgently "on the make," citing reasons his sweetheart should go to bed with him. Other speakers simply reflect on a theme; in e. e. cummings's "in just," the speaker pays tribute to the coming of spring. Aside from that, we learn nothing of his character. Likewise, the speaker in "Pied Beauty" by Gerard Manley Hopkins meditates on the magnificent colors, shapes, and textures of God's creations. Beyond that, there's little to say about him or her.

   TIP

   Read the title first and speculate on what the poem might be about.

2. **To whom is the speaker talking?**

   To the reader only? To someone else? If so, to whom, and what is the listener's relationship to the speaker?

   Some poems, such as Shelley's "Ozymandias," are addressed only to the reader. Others, such as Blake's "A Cradle Song," are directed at a third person but focus so intently on the subject of the poem that they reveal nothing about the speaker's connection to his audience. Still others are dramatic monologues—poems that resemble a speech in a play. In such monologues speakers address a specific person and often respond to the listener's unspoken reactions. Matthew Arnold's "Dover Beach" and Tennyson's "Ulysses" are examples.

3. **What is the dramatic context of the poem?**

   Is there a reason or occasion for the poem? Is there any evidence of a setting, a time, place, season, or situation?

   For lyric poems the answer will most likely be *no* to those questions. Narrative poems, dramatic monologues, ballads, and other poems that tell or imply stories often provide background that helps to shape the poem's effect and meaning. Frost's *"Out, Out—"* takes place on a farm during wood-cutting season. In Coleridge's "Rime of the Ancient Mariner," the speaker tells the story to guests at a wedding reception.

4. **What happens during the poem?**

   Is there a conflict? If an event occurs, is it in the past or the present? Is it external or internal? Why is it important to the speaker or to a character in the poem? From what perspective does the speaker describe events: as an omniscient narrator? as a participant? as an observer? Poems often begin in one place and end in another. So, look for shifts in the speaker's insights or understanding of the experience.

   The speaker in "The Twa Corbies," who happens to overhear two ravens talking about their next meal, has no vested interest in the conversation. In Wordsworth's "Composed upon Westminster Bridge," however, the speaker expresses his great affection for the city of London. Lyric poems, such as Keats's "Ode on a Grecian Urn," refer to no particular events, although it seems likely that the speaker is at that moment scrutinizing an ancient urn.

TIP

See page 157 for a list of adjectives that can help you identify the tone of many poems.

5. **What motivates the speaker to speak now, in the tone he/she uses?**
Does the speaker evince an attitude or bias regarding the subject matter of the poem? What imagery, diction, figures of speech, and choice of details contribute to the speaker's tone? Does the speaker use comparisons made via metaphors, similes, personification, or metonymy? Do you see any shifts in tone or perspective? Any contradictions?

To understand a poem you must understand its tone. The tone of William Blake's "The Tyger" has long puzzled and intrigued readers. To this day, therefore, more than two centuries after it was written, the poem remains an enigma. In contrast, there's nothing elusive about the tone of "Counting-Out Rhyme" by Edna St. Vincent Millay and "Jabberwocky" by Lewis Carroll. Both poems are intended solely to entertain readers with collections of playful sounds. The types of poems you've studied in class, as well as those that typically show up on AP tests, fall somewhere between those two extremes. For instance, the topic of Shakespeare's sonnet #33, "When to the Sessions of Sweet Silent Thought," is friendship. The speaker reflects on how the presence of his "dear friend" soothes his troubled spirit.

The Beauty of Paraphrasing

Perhaps the best way to crack open a poem's meaning is to write a paraphrase. Putting into your own words line-by-line exactly what takes place in the poem can be eye-opening. It can transform a vague impression into a clear and firm grasp of the poet's intent, particularly if your paraphrase contains the same number of sentences as the poem itself. Students report that paraphrasing poems often clears away the fog. Try it!

6. **How does the language of the poem contribute to its meaning?**
Is there anything distinctive about the poem's diction? Does the poet repeat words, sounds, phrases, and ideas? If so, to what purpose and effect? Which figures of speech and images are particularly potent? Do alliteration, assonance, consonance play a role in the poem?

Since words are the lifeblood of poetry, look hard and long at the poem's language, especially at the connotations of words. Think of Macbeth's powerful words as he ponders his life: "Life's but a walking shadow . . . full of sound and fury, signifying nothing." Or consider a challenging poem like "Thirteen Ways of Looking at a Blackbird," in which Wallace Stevens embodies meaning in a series of intense, compact, and suggestive images. William Butler Yeats, spellbound by a fiercely independent woman, fills his love poem "No Second Troy" with language that alludes to Ireland's quest for freedom from England. Indeed, good poets bind language and meaning so tightly that altering a syllable would damage the poem's integrity.

7. **How is the poem organized?**

Does it adhere to a closed form, such as a sonnet or villanelle? Or does it take liberties? Is it free form? Is it grammatical? Is the poem constructed with complete sentences? With phrases? With a mixture of usages? Does the poet use stanzas? Lines of different lengths? Changes in sound or diction? Are the form and meaning of the poem related in some way? Does the ending contain some sort of resolution? How does organization, including syntax, contribute to the poem's meaning and effect?

The fourteen-line structure of the sonnet used by Shakespeare, Milton, Browning, and countless others has come to be considered the embodiment of human thought, just as the limerick seems just pithy enough to convey a whimsical idea with cleverly crafted rhymes. On the other hand, a more free-flowing organization is appropriate for "Ode to the Confederate Dead" by Allen Tate, a poem that takes place in the mind of a person wandering among the headstones in a Confederate cemetery and pondering the meaning of the soldiers' sacrifice.

8. **Do patterns of rhyme and rhythm contribute to the meaning and effect of the poem?**

How does rhyme function in the poem? Are there patterns of sound that help to convey meaning or create effects? What does the meter contribute to the poem's meaning?

Rhyme and rhythm that distract from the sense of a poem is a common flaw of second-rate poems. Thus, critics scorn Tennyson's "Charge of the Light Brigade" for its thundering hoof beats and repetitive rhymes that make the poem easy to remember but hard to take seriously. In high-quality poems, rhyme and meter are more than decorative features. They are a medium that subtlely enhances meaning and effect. Frequent shifts of meter in Shelley's "Ode to the West Wind," for example, suggest the wildness of the wind itself.

9. **What themes does the poem contain?**

Are themes stated or are they implied? Can you make a generalization about life or human nature from the poem? In short, what idea is the poet communicating to the reader?

Poetic motifs are often vividly suggested or even stated outright. Anarchy, for instance, is evoked by a series of brief statements in William Butler Yeats' "The Second Coming": "The falcon cannot hear the falconer;/Things fall apart; the center cannot hold;/Mere anarchy is loosed upon the world."

Themes, on the other hand, are rarely articulated. Instead, they must be inferred from the text. Sometimes a theme practically jumps off the page, as in the antiwar poems of Wilfred Owen (e.g., "Anthem for Doomed Youth"). In other poems, themes are less accessible. For example, "The Red Wheelbarrow" by William Carlos Williams consists of three visual images preceded by the words "so much depends/upon"—an altogether sparse amount of evidence from which to identify a theme. Yet it's sufficient. Williams's poem is about writing poetry. For him poems start with visual cues like "a red wheel /barrow" and "white/chickens."

10. **What was your initial response to the poem?**
Did the poem speak to you? Touch you? Leave you cold? Confuse you? Anger you? Blow your mind? Cause you to text a friend?

More important, did your response change after reading the poem a second, third, or even a fourth time?

These ten meaty questions are far too many to keep in mind all at once. But they'll give you enough information to take a stab at putting poems into your own words. A reasonably accurate paraphrase is a sure sign that you've conquered a poem—that you've found its essence. And you can depend on the ten questions to sink in as you use them repeatedly while prepping for the AP exam.

First, however, find a poetry anthology such as *The Book of Living Verse* edited by Louis Untermeyer or *The Norton Anthology of Poetry*. Each contains a variety of poems—old, new, easy, hard, long, short. Taking your time, read a poem and run through the list of questions. Then read another and answer the questions again. Then read a few more, and then still more. Repeat the routine the following day and again the day after. Read whenever you have a few spare moments—while waiting for the bus, having coffee, standing in the cafeteria line. Gradually, the questions will sink in, and as you continue to read poems, you'll start reading all poems more deeply. For every poem you read deeply, you'll learn something about reading the next one. In time it will become second nature to read poetry perceptively. Not that you'll breeze through every poem you encounter, but you will have at your command a number of strategies for insightfully drawing out a poem's effects and meanings.

To start you off, here is a Walt Whitman poem followed by the ten questions and some possible answers.

When I Heard the Learn'd Astronomer

When I heard the learn'd astronomer;
When the proofs, the figures, were ranged in columns before me,
When I was shown the charts and the diagrams, to add, divide,
Line   and measure them,
(5)   When I, sitting, heard the astronomer, where he lectured with
      much applause in the lecture-room,
How soon, unaccountable, I became tired and sick,
Till, rising and gliding out, I wander'd off by myself,
In the mystical moist night-air, and from time to time,
(10)   Look'd up in perfect silence at the stars.

(1865)

1. **Who is talking?**
The speaker may be a student or perhaps the poet himself. In either case, he is someone who attends lectures and has no stomach for pedantry. Before the lecture ends, he stalks out of the room repulsed by both the astronomer's presentation and the audience's response.

2. **To whom is the speaker talking?**
   He is talking to the reader and also to himself, perhaps to justify or make sense of his impulsiveness.

3. **What is the background of the poem?**
   The speaker attends a lecture on the heavens given by a learned astronomer.

4. **What happens during the poem?**
   Hard facts and mathematical problems dominate the astronomer's presentation. Disappointed in both the lecture and the audience's receptivity to it, the speaker leaves the lecture hall. Outside, as if awestruck, he occasionally looks up at the stars, saying nothing.

5. **What motivates the speaker to speak now, in the tone he/she does?**
   The speaker distances himself from the lecturer's scholarly, scientific perspective in favor of a more personal one. In fact, he appears to disavow science by assuming an almost disdainful, holier-than-thou attitude toward the astronomer. He also objects to the audience, whose applause pays unwarranted homage to the learned lecturer.

6. **How does the language of the poem contribute to its meaning?**
   The "facts" of astronomy are represented by a barrage of hard, clipped words: "proofs," "figures," "charts," "diagrams." The repeated use of "When" at the beginning of successive clauses suggests the astronomer's plodding delivery as well as an absence of concern for anything other than getting the facts across to his audience. The repetition of "lecture" (line 6) further emphasizes the spiritlessness of the astronomer's presentation.

   In contrast, the speaker's view of the stars is couched in poetic language including such sound-rich phrases as "off by myself,/In the mystical moist night-air."

   In the last line the speaker feasts his eyes on stars "in perfect silence," suggesting that words are not only unnecessary but inadequate to describe the mystery of what he observes. The speaker's silence also contrasts with both the lecture and the applause it elicited.

7. **How is the poem organized?**
   The poem is structured like a short story with a beginning (lines 1–4), middle (5–8), and end (9–10). The lecture serves as the stimulus for the speaker's response and his escape from the lecture room. The episode is resolved as the speaker looks up at the stars in silence. All parts of the poem work together to tell a brief anecdote and to convey the speaker's disapproval of both the astronomer's approach to his subject and the audience's reaction.

8. **Do patterns of rhyme and rhythm contribute to the meaning and effect of the poem?**
   As an example of "free verse," the poem ignores customary patterns of meter or rhyme. It creates its effect via the words, images, subtle variations in

rhythm and length of the lines. The account of the lecture, for example, consists of lengthy, prosaic lines. Only at the end does the speaker's poetic voice reassert itself. For a poem about a person who rejects conventionality, free verse seems an appropriate choice.

9. **What themes does the poem contain?**

The speaker, a romantic, seems to believe that rationality robs nature of beauty and mystery. As someone with an antiscientific bent, he prefers to contemplate the stars in silence. On one level, the speaker's silence is literal, but it also implies a sense of isolation. While others in the audience applaud the astronomer, the speaker disapprovingly slinks out of the room to commune with the stars. Ironically, his silence is a sham because it is trumpeted loud and clear by this poem.

10. **What was your initial response to the poem?**

The answer to this question will vary from reader to reader.

PRACTICE IN READING POEMS

For practice in reading and dissecting poems, answer the questions accompanying each of the following three selections. Write your responses in the spaces provided, and compare your answers to those on pages 131–137.

POEM A

A Poison Tree

I was angry with my friend:
I told my wrath, my wrath did end.
I was angry with my foe:
Line   I told it not, my wrath did grow.

(5)   And I watered it in fears
Night and morning with my tears,
And I sunned it with smiles
And with soft deceitful wiles.

And it grew both day and night,
(10)   Til it bore an apple bright,
And my foe beheld it shine,
And he knew that it was mine—

And into my garden stole
When the night had veiled the pole;
(15)   In the morning, glad, I see
My foe outstretched beneath the tree.

(1794)

1. *Who is talking?*

_____

_____

_____

2. *To whom is the speaker talking?*

_____

_____

_____

3. *What is the dramatic context of the poem?*

_____

_____

_____

4. *What happens during the poem?*

_____

_____

_____

5. *What motivates the speaker to speak now, in the tone he/she uses?*

_____

_____

_____

6. *How does the language of the poem contribute to its meaning?*

_____

_____

_____

7. *How is the poem organized?*

_____

_____

_____

8. *Do patterns of rhyme and rhythm contribute to the meaning and effect of the poem?*

_____

_____

_____

9. *What themes does the poem contain?*

_____

_____

_____

10. *What was your initial response to the poem?*

_____

_____

_____

POEM B

A Solitary Reaper

       Behold her, single in the field,
       Yon solitary highland lass!
       Reaping and singing by herself;
Line   Stop here, or gently pass!
(5)   Alone she cuts and binds the grain,
       And sings a melancholy strain;
       O listen! for the vale profound
       Is overflowing with the sound.

       No Nightingale did ever chaunt
(10)   More welcome notes to weary bands
       Of travelers in some shady haunt,
       Among Arabian sands:
       A voice so thrilling ne'er was heard
       In spring-time from the cuckoo-bird,
(15)   Breaking the silence of the seas
       Among the farthest Hebrides.

       Will no one tell me what she sings?—
       Perhaps the plaintive numbers flow
       For old, unhappy, far-off things,
(20)   And battles long ago:

Or is it some more humble lay,
Familiar matter of to-day?
Some natural sorrow, loss, or pain,
That has been, and may be again?

(25)   Whate'er the theme, the Maiden sang
As if her song could have no ending;
I saw her singing at her work,
And o'er the sickle bending;—
I listen'd, motionless and still;
(30)   And, as I mounted up the hill
The music in my heart I bore,
Long after it was heard no more.

(1805)

1. *Who is talking?*

_____

_____

_____

2. *To whom is the speaker talking?*

_____

_____

_____

3. *What is the dramatic context of the poem?*

_____

_____

_____

4. *What happens during the poem?*

_____

_____

_____

5. *What motivates the speaker to speak now, in the tone he/she uses?*

_____

_____

_____

6. *How does the language of the poem contribute to its meaning?*

_____

_____

_____

7. *How is the poem organized?*

_____

_____

_____

8. *Do patterns of rhyme and rhythm contribute to the meaning and effect of the poem?*

_____

_____

_____

9. *What themes does the poem contain?*

_____

_____

_____

10. *What was your initial response to the poem?*

_____

_____

_____

Poem C

The Cambridge Ladies

the Cambridge ladies who live in furnished souls
are unbeautiful and have comfortable minds
(also, with the church's protestant blessings

Line   daughters, unscented shapeless spirited)
(5)   they believe in Christ and Longfellow, both dead,
are invariably interested in so many things—
at the present writing one still finds
delighted fingers knitting for the is it Poles?
perhaps. While permanent faces coyly bandy

(10)   scandal of Mrs. N and Professor D
. . . . the Cambridge ladies do not care, above
Cambridge if sometimes in its box of
sky lavender and cornerless, the
moon rattles like a fragment of angry candy

(1923)

1. *Who is talking?*

_____

_____

_____

2. *To whom is the speaker talking?*

_____

_____

_____

3. *What is the dramatic context of the poem?*

_____

_____

_____

4. *What happens during the poem?*

_____

_____

_____

5. *What motivates the speaker to speak now, in the tone he/she uses?*

_____

_____

_____

6. *How does the language of the poem contribute to its meaning?*

_____

_____

_____

7. *How is the poem organized?*

_____

_____

_____

8. *Do patterns of rhyme and rhythm contribute to the meaning and effect of the poem?*

_____

_____

_____

9. *What themes does the poem contain?*

_____

_____

_____

10. *What was your initial response to the poem?*

_____

_____

_____

Answers to Practice Questions

Some questions invite interpretation. Therefore, don't expect your answers to be precisely the same as those below. If any of your responses differ markedly from these, however, be sure that you can defend your position with specific evidence drawn from the poem.

POEM A: "A POISON TREE" BY WILLIAM BLAKE

1. *Who is talking?* The speaker could be the poet himself, but when you consider his depravity, the speaker is more likely an invention of the poet's imagination.

2. *To whom is the speaker talking?* First and foremost, he addresses the reader. His self-incriminating revelations suggest that he may be seeking forgiveness from some sort of father confessor. Either way, he has taken the audience into his confidence.

3. *What is the dramatic context of the poem?* For an unspecified reason the speaker has been miffed by both a friend and a foe. He makes peace with the friend but not with the foe.

4. *What happens during the poem?* The speaker comes to terms with his friend. But with respect to his foe, he keeps rage bottled up inside where it festers and grows into an obsession to kill. While feigning friendship, he hatches a plot to tempt his foe into stealing and eating a poison apple. The sight of his foe's corpse sprawled beneath the apple tree gladdens the speaker's heart.

5. *What motivates the speaker to speak now, in the tone he/she uses?* The speaker describes two contrasting relationships, one with a friend, the other with a foe. In explaining the latter, he takes pride in how he disposed of his enemy through guile and deceit. Lacking a trace of remorse, he appears unaware of his own malevolence.

6. *How does the language of the poem contribute to its meaning?* Simple and straightforward language, the kind that a friend might use to talk about everyday events, dominates the poem. An off-handed expression of deceit disguises the speaker's diabolical nature. The incongruity between his language and the subject matter underscores his callousness. The speaker's joy after killing his foe adds still another dimension to his diabolical nature. Nothing the speaker says contains the slightest hint that he wants sympathy or deserves redemption. In that sense, he is no less a victim of evil impulses than his unfortunate foe.

   In relating his experience, the speaker alludes to an "apple" and a "garden," words that call to mind the biblical story of man's fall from innocence. The speaker tempts his foe just as Satan tempted Adam and Eve to eat the forbidden fruit.

7. *How is the poem organized?* Each stanza adds another dimension to the speaker's self-portrait. First the speaker represents himself as someone capable of both good and evil. But in the lines that follow, he flaunts only his maliciousness. At the end of the third stanza, the speaker briefly turns his

attention to his foe's behavior, and in the last line we are shown the speaker at the height of his wantonness, rejoicing at the consequences of his efforts.

8. *Do patterns of rhyme and rhythm contribute to the meaning and effect of the poem?* The poem's regular rhymes and steady, singsongy rhythm disguise its dark subject matter and imply the speaker's insensitivity to his own wickedness. Indeed, the incongruity between the speaker's message and the means by which it is delivered heightens the poem's emotional impact.

   Lines 1 and 3, in which the speaker expresses his anger, are trochaic. Lines 2 and 4, which tell of the speaker's action, are iambic, a sequence that sets up a brief dialogue between feelings and action. The only other all-iambic line is the last line, in which the speaker celebrates his deadly achievement. The change in rhythm intensifies the climax of the poem by setting it apart from the other lines in the stanza.

9. *What themes does the poem contain?* Biblical overtones expand the poem's meaning. By tempting an innocent to eat a poison apple, the speaker takes on Satan-like characteristics. At the same time, the speaker plays God by taking another's life. Paradoxically, then, he is an amalgam of evil and good, as he himself suggests early in the poem. Thereby, he represents humankind both before and after the fall from innocence.

   An altogether different interpretation is that the poem may be little more than a recipe for vengeance or a warning to readers against the dangers of insincerity.

10. *What was your initial response to the poem?* The answer will vary from reader to reader.

POEM B: "A SOLITARY REAPER" BY WILLIAM WORDSWORTH

1. *Who is talking?* The speaker is a traveler on horseback passing by a field in the highlands. He is deeply moved by the singing of a country lass harvesting grain. His blasé allusions to far-off places (Arabia and the Hebrides) suggest he is well traveled, perhaps even weary of his aimless roaming across deserts and oceans. As the poem begins, he is ready to be awakened to more profound aspects of both himself and the human condition.

2. *To whom is the speaker talking?* Unable to contain himself, the speaker must tell someone—the reader in this case—about the singing he heard in the highlands.

3. *What is the dramatic context of the poem?* Because the lass "cuts and binds the grain" (line 5), it is harvest time, presumably the late summer or fall.

4. *What happens during the poem?* Passing a field, a traveler hears a song being sung by a solitary peasant girl harvesting grain. Deciding to stop and listen rather than continue on his way, the speaker is struck by the beauty of the song. He compares it to other beautiful sounds—the song of a nightingale and the song of a cuckoo-bird. The speaker begins to muse on the possible meaning of the song but can discern only its sorrowful tone. Finally, he rides away haunted by the music he has heard.

5. *What motivates the speaker to speak now, in the tone he/she uses?* The speaker tries to determine why he has been deeply touched by the melancholy strains of the girl's song. Recognizing only the song's plaintiveness (line 18) and its "sorrow, loss, or pain" (line 23), he carries the music away with him, harboring sorrow in his heart, even long after he can no longer hear the notes (line 32). His reaction seems to be a kind of epiphany, as though he has been suddenly awakened to his inner self and now understands the sorrows of others.

6. *How does the language of the poem contribute to its meaning?* Two exclamations (in lines 1–2 and in line 4) not only add drama to the opening of the poem but suggest that the speaker has been suddenly energized by the sound of the girl's singing. How deeply he has been affected, however, is not made clear until the third and fourth stanzas. By emphasizing solitude ("single in the field," "singing by herself," "alone she cuts . . ."), the speaker visually and emotionally keeps the girl at a distance, but by the end of the poem, she and her song have sunk into his soul. This shift from outside to inside begins with the word "melancholy" (line 6) and accelerates during the third stanza, nudged along by the girl's "plaintive," and "unhappy" song.

   The poem's diction, like the peasant girl of the title, is generally plain and simple, but in the second stanza the speaker's words turn more exotic and fanciful: "chaunt," "shady haunt," "Arabian sands"—words and phrases befitting the stanza's more imaginative subject matter.

   The use of the past tense in the last stanza signals the climax of the poem. The fading image of the girl contrasts to her song, which shall never end. The concluding lines show the traveler altered by his brief encounter with a mythic, symbolic figure. The music has awakened him to the universality of human woe, an artifact of which is now lodged in his heart.

   The final couplet contains the simplest language in the poem. Almost entirely monosyllabic, it captures the essence of the speaker's transformation. His discovery that sorrow is a common aspect of everyday experience is conveyed in common, everyday words. Containing sounds that echo the sense, the words repeat a long *o* (b*o*re, l*o*ng, m*o*re) that resonates with the girl's music and reiterates the set of *o*-sounds that simulate the girl's song in lines 7–8. As the traveler continues on his way, a series of mellow *m*-sounds capture his subdued mood.

   Calling the girl a "reaper" is an irony. Yes, she reaps grain, but the word is commonly associated with "grim reaper," the proverbial personification of death. Here, of course, the reaper is a young lass, a life-affirming figure, not a spectre of death. With her song, she unwittingly lays to rest some of the speaker's encrusted attitudes and endows him with new life, or at least with a new vision of the world.

7. *How is the poem organized?* Initially, the speaker confronts melancholy singing that sweeps through the valley. Next, he compares the music to the call of birds in far-off places, using images that awaken his desire to understand the meaning of the melody. Recognizing that sorrow can "have no ending" (line 26), he continues on his way with the music buried deep in his

heart. All told, then, the poem begins with the speaker's external, sensual response to the music, goes on to explore his intellectual reactions, and concludes with a deeply felt self-realization.

These events, which occur at a confluence of two different worlds—that of a simple peasant girl and that of a worldly and superficially successful traveler—reflect the poem's symmetry. Each of four eight-line stanzas is composed of two quatrains, each devoted to a different aspect of the traveler's experience. The first four lines of the poem, for example, show what the man sees, the second four tell what he hears. This arrangement parallels the dramatic structure, for the poem is an account of a man's transformation. Before the change, he is an aimless, world-weary traveler. Afterwards, having realized not only that sorrow pervades the world but that he must share in that sorrow, he has become enlightened.

8. *Do patterns of rhyme and rhythm contribute to the meaning and effect of the poem?* Rhyme and meter support the poem's basic symmetry. The second and third stanzas contain identical rhyme schemes: *a-b-a-b-c-c-d-d*. The others differ only in the third line, an exception that softens the effects of a consistent and assertive rhyme. The pairs of rhyming couplets that end each stanza serve as a kind of coda that creates a climactic emotional surge.

Most lines are written in iambic tetrameter, a rhythm akin to everyday speech and appropriate to a poem about an ordinary country girl singing in the fields. With the occasional intrusion of dactyls such as *reaping* (line 3) and *breaking* (line 15), a rhythmic tension is created, a tension that reflects the state of the speaker's emotions. In addition, there are pauses, or caesuras, in mid-line, as in "Behold her" (line 1) and "Stop here" (line 4), suggestive of the pause taken by the traveler on his journey.

9. *What themes does the poem contain?* Two related themes—solitude and melancholy—dominate the poem. The first is introduced by the title and by such references to the girl's isolation as "singing by herself" (line 3). From solitude it is a short step to melancholy, and the speaker dwells on images of sadness and sorrow. While these themes are used to describe the girl and her song, the speaker, too, is a solitary figure, who, by listening to the music, becomes attuned to the melancholy nature of life.

While these themes help to establish the mood of the poem, the third stanza, consisting largely of a series of questions, holds the key to the poem's most important theme. Lines 21–24 ask what amounts to a rhetorical question about the nature of sorrow: Is it something that "has been, and may be again?" In a flash, the speaker realizes that sadness and pain "have no ending" (line 26). That is to say, suffering is part of the human nature. As he rides off, the traveler understands that private, internal events attest far more vividly to a man's humanity than such superficial experiences as globetrotting.

10. *What was your initial response to the poem?* This answer will vary from reader to reader.

POEM C: "THE CAMBRIDGE LADIES" BY E. E. CUMMINGS

1. *Who is talking?* The speaker is either the poet or a spokesman for the poet. The phrase "at the present writing" (line 7) suggests that the speaker may be a journalist or a researcher-type preparing a sociological article or exposé.

2. *To whom is the speaker talking?* To the reader.

3. *What is the dramatic context of the poem?* Evidently, the speaker has had occasion to observe or to talk with this group of women he deprecatingly calls the "Cambridge ladies." Lacking individuality, they are given a collective persona that serves as an easy target for satire.

4. *What happens during the poem?* The speaker paints an unflattering portrait of the ladies' values, manners, and characteristics. He comments directly or indirectly on their hypocrisy, their conventional minds, their shallowness and superficiality. He also targets their banal efforts to help others, their tendency to gossip, and their mindless indifference to everything but keeping up appearances.

    Of all their faults, hypocrisy may arguably be the most egregious. The ladies pretend to be Protestants (note the lowercase *p*, implying the ladies' hollow piety). They act in un-Christianlike ways, unaware of their mean-spiritedness as they gossip "coyly" about the scandalous behavior of Mrs. N and Professor D, presumably two of their Cambridge neighbors. Also, because it is fashionable to do so, they "believe" in Christ and Longfellow, a pairing that both demeans Christ and elevates Longfellow. Regardless, the speaker pointedly declares them "both dead," not unlike the ladies' adherence to Christ's teachings and their comprehension of Longfellow's poetry. The ladies voluntarily knit for "is it the Poles?/perhaps." But their altruism is a sham, done to impress others rather than to help the needy.

5. *What motivates the speaker to speak now, in the tone he/she uses?* The speaker intends to mock the women using satire and in-your-face sarcasm. Ultra-cynical, even destructive, he endows the ladies with not a single redeeming quality. In the last four lines, the speaker turns indignant, condemning the group for not caring about anything except their social standing. Even the moon, a symbol rich in meaning for people everywhere, means nothing to them. They view it as a piece of candy rattling around in a mostly empty (like the ladies themselves) lavender box.

6. *How does the language of the poem contribute to its meaning?* The language of the poem is off-beat. It takes liberties with syntax (". . . one still finds/delighted fingers knitting for the is it Poles?"), punctuation ("unscented shapeless spirited"), capitalization ("protestant"), and diction ("unbeautiful"). The quirkiness of the language stands in stark contrast to the ladies, who revere conventionality.

    The phrase "furnished souls" (line 1), implying that the ladies are virtual automatons, introduces a concept built up and reinforced throughout the poem. The women possess "comfortable minds," that never question, think, or probe. Absent an imagination or dreams, and lacking both creativity and curiosity, they have been programmed by their provincial society to go to church, knit, and talk about other people. Meanwhile, they wear "permanent faces" and never consider what their various activities add up to. In effect, they are the living dead, a notion that gives ironic overtones to the verb "live" in line 1.

Occasional fragments of conversation reveal still more about the ladies. Their claim to be "interested in so many things" (line 6) reflects their pedantry. The phrase "knitting for the is it Poles?" (line 8) indicates that their volunteer work is nothing more than a perfunctory duty.

7. *How is the poem organized?* In order to mock the ladies, the poet contrives an organization that mimics but fails to follow the conventions of the traditional sonnet. Like a sonnet, "The Cambridge Ladies" contains fourteen lines, but it ignores the customary arrangement of ideas. Very loosely, however, the initial eight lines (the octave) present a spuriously objective account of the ladies, while the last six lines (the sestet) are overtly judgmental. In fact, the speaker's undisguised scorn emerges in the final four lines.

Structurally, the poem, which begins with a general description of the ladies, becomes increasingly specific. Sweeping generalities in the first lines evolve into examples of the ladies' behavior, which abruptly give way to the speaker's perception of what goes on—or more accurately, what fails to go on—inside the ladies' heads.

8. *Do patterns of rhyme and rhythm contribute to the meaning and effect of the poem?* Playful patterns of rhyme and rhythm help cast the ladies in a comic light. There are no rhymes in the first six lines, but lines 7 and 8 rhyme with lines 2 and 1 respectively. The poet has rhymed the last six lines *g-g-f-f-g-g*, but in each couplet an unstressed syllable is paired with a stressed one, as in "bandy" and "Professor D." Instead of employing consistent end rhymes, then, the poet scatters internal rhymes throughout, relying on, among other techniques, alliteration and assonance. Line 6, for example, contains four instances of "in": "*in*variably *in*terested *in* so many th*in*gs—." Line 9 contains two words beginning with "per," and ends with a pair of similar words, "coyly bandy." In line 10, the consonants *n* and *d* in "scandal" are echoed in the names of "Mrs. N and Professor D." And in the poem's final line, the "rattle" of the moon is onomatopoetically represented by "a fragment of angry candy."

The poem's rhythms are equally capricious. Five-foot lines prevail, but the final quatrain contains two four-foot lines and a culminating six-footer. In other words, the poem is a kind of mischievous romp of sound and rhythm, its eccentricities contrasting vividly with its subject.

9. *What themes does the poem contain?* The main theme is the conventionality of the Cambridge ladies, whose lives follow a preordained pattern. Each of the ladies' flaws and foibles becomes a mini-theme in the poem. Thus, the allusion to Christ and Longfellow suggests that the ladies' values are skewed toward the dead, implying further that the ladies themselves are emotionally and intellectually insensible.

10. *What was your initial response to the poem?* This answer will vary from reader to reader.

WHAT TO LISTEN FOR IN POETRY

Here is a fact you *don't* need to know for the AP exam: Every pattern of rhyme and rhythm has a name.

Here's another fact, one that you *should* know for the exam: What is important in analyzing poems is not the names of various patterns of rhyme and rhythm, but that rhyme and rhythm contribute to the meaning and effect of a poem. If you can tell a slant rhyme from a spondee, more power to you, but what counts on the exam is your ability to describe the function of slant rhyme in a particular place or to explain the effect of a given spondee.

Because a feature of any good poem is unity, its sounds cannot be separated from its themes, structure, imagery, and so forth. That's why rhyme, rhythm, the use of repetition, and each of several other sound-related techniques are more than abstractions. They are integral to a poem's totality.

Rhyme

Rhyme is perhaps the most easily recognized characteristic of poetry, particularly *end rhyme,* the repetition of identical sounds at the end of successive lines, as illustrated by this excerpt from W. H. Auden's "It's No Use Raising a Shout":

> A long time ago I told my *mother*
> I was leaving home to find *another:*
> I never answered her *letter*
> But I never found a *better*
> Here am I, here are *you:*
> But what does it mean? What are we going to *do?*

Equally vivid end rhymes may occur in alternating lines, as in this fragment of Lord Byron's "She Walks in Beauty":

> She walks in beauty like the *night*
> Of cloudless climes and starry *skies*
> And all that's best of dark and *bright*
> Meet in her aspect and her *eyes:*

Another common rhyming pattern consists of end rhymes in only the second and fourth lines of a four-line stanza, illustrated in the anonymously written "The Dying Airman":

> Take the cylinders out of my kidneys,
> The connecting-rod out of my *brain,*
> Take the cam-shaft out of my backbone,
> And assemble the engine *again.*

Study Tip

In poetry, the "sound must seem an echo to the sense."

—Alexander Pope, "An Essay on Criticism"

TYPES OF RHYMES

Customarily, rhyme is produced by one syllable words (*fat/cat*) or by the final syllables of multisyllabic words (*prevail/entail; disclosure/composure*).

Sounds that are close but not exact duplicates of one another are called, among other things, *slant* rhymes, *off* rhymes, and *near* rhymes (*seen/been; ill/all; summer/somewhere*). A major function of slant rhymes is to help avoid the monotony of repetitious conventional rhyme. The slant offers a change of pace, a small but welcome deviation, as in the concluding lines of this fragment from F. T. Prince's "To a Friend on His Marriage":

> A beautiful girl said something in your praise.
> And either because in a hundred ways
> I had heard of her great worth and had no *doubt*
> To find her lovelier than I *thought*
> And found her also cleverer, or *because*
> Although she had known you well it *was* . . .

Sometimes, an individual line of poetry contains two or more words that rhyme. Examples of such an *internal rhyme* are found in Tennyson's "Blow, Bugle, Blow":

> The splendour *falls* on castle *walls*
> And snowy summits old in story:
> The long light *shakes* across the *lakes*
> And the wild cataract leaps in glory.

Poets may include internal rhymes for emphasis or additional unity. If used excessively, however, internal rhymes could create monotony rather than interest.

RHYME SCHEME

A rhyme scheme is the pattern of rhyming words within a given stanza or poem. For convenience, each similar end rhyme is usually identified with a letter of the alphabet, here illustrated by Francis Cornford's "The Watch":

> I wakened on my hot, hard bed,   *a*
> Upon the pillow lay my head;   *a*
> Beneath the pillow I could hear   *b*
> My little watch was ticking clear.   *b*
> I thought the throbbing of it went   *c*
> Like my continual discontent,   *c*
> I thought it said in every tick: *d*
> I am so sick, so sick, so sick;   *d*
> O death, come quick, come quick, come quick,   *d*
> Come quick, come quick, come quick, come quick.   *d*

This shorthand technique applies to rhymes in any poem. The rhyme scheme of "It's No Use Raising a Shout" is simply *a-a-b-b-c-c;* of "She Walks in Beauty": *a-b-a-b;* and of "The Dying Airman": *a-b-c-b.* On the AP exam, you are not likely to be asked about rhyme scheme unless it is germane to the effect or meaning of a particular poem. "The Watch," though hardly more than fluff, illustrates how rhyme can support and enhance meaning. By ending the poem with four rhyming lines, the speaker simulates the relentless and repetitive ticking of a mechanical timepiece.

Lines that come in pairs *(couplet)* often rhyme, as do three lines, or *triplets* (or *tercets*) as in Tennyson's "The Eagle":

> He clasps the crag with crooked *hands*;
> Close to the sun in lonely *lands*,
> Ringed with the azure world he *stands*, . . .

It's easy to locate triplets in a poem. More of a challenge is to figure out why Tennyson used three consecutive rhymes. That is, what purpose is served by the repetition?

Here are two possibilities, both related to the sound of the words. Perhaps you can discern others.

1. The broad *a* sound in the rhymed words (*hands, lands, stands*) echoes the same broad *a* sound elsewhere in the poem (*clasp, crag, azure*), in effect, unifying the three lines through assonance.
2. The triple *a* sound may suggest the *aah-aah-aah* of the eagle's cry. Ornithologists are known to record the eagle's call in various ways—*ka-ka-ka, we-aaaaa, we-aaaaa, we-aaaaa,* for example—but what they all have in common is a broad *a*.

In a distinct group of four lines, called a quatrain, rhymes can vary enormously from a-a-a-a to a-b-a-b, a-b-c-b, and so on. And in stanzas of a greater number of lines, rhyming possibilities are virtually endless.

On the AP exam you're not likely to be required to describe the rhyme scheme or distinguish one type of rhyme from another, but when you write your essay on a given poem, it may be useful to discuss rhymes that contribute to the poem's meaning or effect.

Onomatopoeia

Using *onomatopoeia*, words that virtually replicate sound, poets often create vivid effects. Is there a more expressive word than *moan*, for example, to make the sound of . . . well, a moan? Likewise, *murmur* resembles the sound of a murmur. And numerous other words, too—*boom, buzz, clang, crack,* and so on—all echo their sense. Because sound can cause words to crawl or race, flow smoothly or stumble along, express beauty or ugliness, poets often choose words according to the effects they wish to create. Meaning ordinarily takes precedence over sound, but an astutely picked onomatopoetic word may add both sense and sensuality to an image or phrase, as in these lines by W. H. Auden:

> And the fenders grind and heave,
> And the derricks clack and grate, as the tackle hooks the crate,
> And the fall-ropes whine through the sheave . . .

Alexander Pope, in this verse from "An Essay on Criticism," encapsulates the use of onomatopoeia and other sounds in poetry:

> 'Tis not enough no harshness gives offense,
> The sound must seem an echo to the sense:
> Soft is the strain when Zephyr gently blows,
> And smooth stream in smoother numbers flows;
> But when the loud surges lash the sounding shore,
> The hoarse, rough verse should like the torrent roar:
> When Ajax strives some rock's vast weight to throw,
> The line too labors, and the words move slow;

THE USE OF REPETITION

Other sound-related poetic techniques, more subtle than onomatopoeia, are those that involve repetition through alliteration, assonance, and consonance.

Alliteration

Alliteration is the repetition of initial sounds in words and syllables. Sometimes such repetition is merely ornamental, but skillful poets use it to intensify effects, add weight to an idea, and in the process make the verse easier to remember.

From Gerard Manley Hopkins's "Spring" come these lines emphasizing not only the beauty of the season but also the sound of spring, especially the alliterative *l*-sound (*long, lovely, lush,* and more), suggesting the la-la-la sound of music or in this case the song of the thrush.

> Nothing is so beautiful as spring—
> When weeds, in wheels, shoot long and lovely and lush;
> Thrush's eggs look little low heavens, and thrush
> Through the echoing timber does so rinse and wring
> The ear, it strikes like lightning to hear him sing;

Overused, alliteration sounds silly, as in this deliberately exaggerated excerpt from Shakespeare's *A Midsummer Night's Dream*:

> Whereat, with blade, with bloody blameful blade,
> He bravely broach'd his boiling bloody breast;

Assonance

Assonance is the repetition of similar vowel sounds. It is generally ornamental, but because it can also create a near, or slant, rhyme, it may engender subtle poetic effects. Such rhymes include *earth* and *hearth, willow* and *yellow, peer* and *fur, little* and *beetle*.

Wilfred Owen relies heavily on assonance in the opening stanza of "Futility," a poem about a soldier severely wounded in World War I:

> Move him into the sun—
> Gently its touch awoke him once,
> At home, whispering of fields unsown.
> *Line* Always it woke him, even in France,
> *(5)* Until this morning and this snow.
> If anything might rouse him now
> The kind old sun will know.

The word "touch" in the second line is in assonance with "sun" (lines 1 and 7) and to "unsown," "once," and "Until." Also the "*o*" in "awoke" (line 2) is echoed in "unsown," "woke," "snow," "old," and "know." Similar sounds that course steadily through these lines contrast subtly to the condition of the wounded soldier—alive at the start but now dead. This juxtaposition deepens the overall meaning of the poem and offers the reader a thought to reflect upon. The sun, an emblem of consistency—hence the same sound over and over—is an enduring force of nature. The soldier, in contrast, is a transient. Like all humans, he briefly walks the earth and then is gone.

Assonance is rarely as obvious as alliteration, but vowel sounds that resonate throughout a poem contribute a melodic effect and subtlely bind the lines to each other. Also, assonance combined with alliteration may produce engaging rhymes, such as "blossom" and "bosom" in these two lines from "Patterns" by Amy Lowell:

> For the lime-tree is in blossom
> And one small flower has dropped upon my bosom.

Similarly, observe the assonantal rhymes in lines 2 and 4 of this stanza from "Captain Carpenter" by John Crowe Ransom:

> Captain Carpenter mounted up one day
> And rode straight way into a stranger rogue
> That looked unchristian but be that as it may
> The Captain did not wait upon prologue.

The repetitious "o" sound suggests the rolling movement of the captain's mount, but the off-rhyme of *rogue* and *prologue* is more closely tied to the meaning of the verse. Captain Carpenter, we are told, encounters a rogue and does "not wait for prologue." That is, he forgoes the niceties that usually occur when two people meet each other. The captain's instantaneous action—whatever it may be—is unorthodox. It's a little off, just like the two words that don't quite rhyme.

Consonance

Consonance is the repetition of consonants appearing within a line or at the end of words. In combination with certain vowels, a series of similar sounds creates subtle harmonies. A few examples are *odds* and *ends*, "*struts* and *frets*" (Shakespeare), and the "*d*" and "*l*" sounds in this couplet from Gerard Manley Hopkins's "God's Grandeur":

> And all is seared with trade; bleared smeared with toil;
> And wears man's smudge and shares man's smell: the soil

Because the technique sometimes goes by such names as *dissonance, half rhyme,* and *oblique rhyme,* it creates considerable confusion among students of poetry. Not to fret, however. The odds are one in a million that you'd be asked about consonance on the AP exam.

Meter and Rhythm

Patterns of rhythm in poetry are based on *meter,* a word synonymous with "measure." Using the poetic *foot* as the unit of measurement, the meter of any line of poetry can be analyzed according to the number and arrangement of its stressed and unstressed syllables. Poetic *feet* may consist of two syllables (disyllabic) or three syllables (trisyllabic), and have names based on the order in which the syllables appear.

KINDS OF POETIC FEET

TIP

Want your essay to stand out? Explain how meter affects the poem's meaning

In analyzing meter, a vertical slash (/) is used to separate poetic feet. A ∪ represents an unstressed syllable, and a – stands for a stressed syllable.

- An *iamb* (∪ –) is a two-syllable foot, the first syllable unstressed, the second stressed. All of the following words are *iambic:* re-spect, ex-tent, e-nough, at-tack, mis-judge. In a line of poetry, however, the syllables of a multisyllabic word may belong to different feet, as in:

    From eve/ry room / descends/ the pain/ted face.

- A *trochee* (– ∪) is a two-syllable foot, the first syllable stressed, the second unstressed. The following words are *trochaic:* mit-ten, gun-shot, cryp-tic, aud-it, ap-ple. In a poem, two syllables of the same word may fall into different feet. In the couplet below *re/ceive* is such a word.

    Johnny/ Jones is/ laid to/ rest
    Earth re/ceive an/ honored/ guest;

- A *spondee* (– –) is a two-syllable foot consisting of two equally stressed syllables. Spondees are often found at the end of a poetic lines, as in:

    High on the shore sat the great god Pan.

- A *dactyl* (– ∪∪) is a three-syllable foot composed of a stressed syllable and two unstressed ones, as in pos-sib-le, crock-e-ry, crim-i-nal, trav-el-er. The following line contains three dactyls:

    Red were her/ lips as the / berry that/ grows. . .

- An *anapest* (∪∪ –) is a three-syllable foot containing two unstressed syllables followed by a stressed one, as in ling-er-ie, pal-is-ade, le-mon-ade, reg-u-late. All six feet in this line are anapests:

    At the top/ of the mount/ ain were ap/ ples, the big/ gest that ev/ er were seen/

To help you remember the names and structure of poetic feet, here is a mnemonic device[1] using women's names:

> *Irene* in an iamb.
> *Tanya* is a trochee
> *Sue-Ann* is a spondee
> *Deborah* is a dactyl
> *Antoinette* is an anapest

[1]Contributed by English teacher Marti Kirschbaum, Falls Church, Virginia.

Roughly 90 percent of poems in English use the iamb as the basic metrical unit, most probably because it closely resembles the rhythm of the English language. On the AP exam you'll never be asked directly to name the characteristics of poetic feet, but you can do yourself a favor by habitually scanning the poems you read. If you're good at *scansion*, the process of analyzing meter—or, at least, sensitive to its effects—you can wow AP essay readers by explaining how meter contributes to the poem's meaning, structure, tone, and effect. Hordes of students can dutifully label metrical techniques, but only an elite few can explain why poets use them.

Say, for instance, that you're analyzing Robert Frost's familiar poem "Stopping by Woods on a Snowy Evening" (1923), reproduced here:

> Whose woods these are I think I know,
> His house is in the village though;
> He will not see me stopping here
> To watch his woods fill up with snow.
>
> My little horse must think it queer
> To stop without a farmhouse near
> Between the woods and frozen lake
> The darkest evening of the year.
>
> He gives his harness bells a shake
> To ask if there is some mistake.
> The only other sound's the sweep
> Of easy wind and downy flake.
>
> The woods are lovely, dark, and deep,
> But I have promises to keep,
> And miles to go before I sleep,
> And miles to go before I sleep.

In your essay you've discussed the speaker's isolation and his contemplative tone. You've also pointed out images of a falling snow and noted that the silence of the setting is emphasized by Frost's use of sibilant sounds, as in "The only other sound's the sweep/Of easy wind . . ." Perhaps you've also observed that the rhyme scheme repeats itself from stanza to stanza and the meter is made up of nonstop iambs from beginning to end. This combination of regular rhyme and rhythm produces a kind of drowsy, almost hypnotic effect that befits the mysterious ambiguity and dream-like texture of the entire poem. Frost's poem can be interpreted literally, of course. But its "dark, and deep" overtones that seem to relate to dreams, sleep, and ultimately, death are supported by the poet's suggestive use of meter.

Chaucer, Shakespeare, Marlowe, Milton—these and many other poets knew that iambic pentameter (that is, iambs in five-foot lines) creates a natural, easy-flowing effect. To emphasize an image or idea, however, poets often insert other rhythmic units into their verses. The initial syllables found in trochees and dactyls, for example, create a forceful effect, not unlike a sudden drumbeat in a piece of music.

A case in point is Wordsworth's "Composed Upon Westminster Bridge," in which the speaker describes the view as he approaches the city of Westminster:

> This city now doth, like a garment wear
> The beauty of the morning; silent, bare
> Ships, towers, domes, theaters, and temples lie
> Open unto the fields and to the sky;
> All bright and shining in the smokeless air. . . .

This verse, cast largely in iambic meter, takes an abrupt turn in the third line with a series of trochees and spondees. This rhythmic switch reflects the poet's intent—to contrast serene open fields with man-made structures silhouetted against the sky.

While scanning poems, be aware of *elisions,* or unstressed syllables omitted for the sake of meter. Functioning as ordinary contractions, most elisions turn two-syllable words into words of a single syllable, as in *o'er* (over), *ne'er* (never), and *'ere* (before). Also note that poems often plod along monotonously like *Mary Had a Little Lamb* if they contained only one metric pattern. Attempting to animate their verse, poets often shift from one foot to another, thereby simulating the rhythms of speech. Rhythmic shifts also permit poets to pause, add asides, express emotions, speed up, slow down—in other words, give verse a human voice. Poets sometimes interweave a second rhythm, just as a musician may add counterpoint to a melody. If the poetic rhythms are too complex, however, or if they change too rapidly, the poem may end up sounding more like prose than poetry. In any case, don't get frustrated while scanning poems. Stay cool. Scansion is far from a precise science.

> **Pointer**
>
> Scansion is not a precise science.

Caesura and Enjambment

Some lines of poetry call for internal pauses, called *caesura,* that are usually indicated by a period, a semicolon, a dash, or other mark of punctuation. Such pauses mimic human speech, as in the first and third lines of this excerpt from James Stephens's "What Thomas An Buile Said in a Pub":

> I saw God. Do you doubt it?
>   Do you dare to doubt it?
> I saw the Almighty Man. His hand
>
> *Line*   Was resting on a mountain, and
> *(5)*   He looked upon the World and all about it:
> I saw Him plainer than you see me now,
>   You mustn't doubt it.

Punctuation at the end of lines 1, 2, 5, and 6 also cues the reader to pause briefly before going on. Lines containing these so-called *end-stops* contrast with *enjambed* lines (3 and 4). *Enjambment,* often called *run-on,* is indicated by an absence of punctuation and eliminates the need to pause. Sentence structure most often determines enjambment, but a poet may deliberately use it to let words tumble uncontrollably perhaps to suggest the speaker's emotional state, as in Thomas An Buile's insistence that he saw God.

Still other effects can be achieved by changing the lengths of various lines. In *Dr. Faustus,* for example, Christopher Marlowe breaks up lines 3, 4, 5, and 6 with caesura and varies the accents to convey the speaker's lust for the beautiful Helen of Troy:

> Was this the face that launched a thousand ships,
> And burnt the topless towers of Ilium? —
> Sweet Helen, make me immortal with a kiss, —
Line　Her lips suck forth my soul; see, where it flies!
(5)　Come, Helen, come, give me my soul again.
> Here will I dwell, for heaven is in these lips,
> And all is dross that is not Helena.

Free Verse

As the name suggests, free verse ignores conventions of meter and rhythm. Poems in free verse may derive their effects from subtle variations of cadence, irregular length of line, and recurring imagery. Sound patterns such as alliteration, assonance, internal rhyme, and even a scattering of end-rhymes may also compensate for the absence of regular meter.

The following excerpt from Amy Lowell's "Lilacs" uses line breaks as a means to create rhetorical effect:

> Lilacs,
> False blue,
> White,
> Purple,
> Color of lilac,
> Your great puffs of flowers
> Are everywhere in this my New England.

Almost every line is an image that comes to a dead stop. Each stands more or less alone and receives equivalent emphasis.

Blank Verse

Unlike free verse, blank verse—sometimes called unrhymed verse—incorporates conventional meter. It is often associated with the verse patterns in most of Shakespeare's plays and in Milton's *Paradise Lost,* a sample of which follows:

> The sun was sunk, and after him the star
> Of Hesperus, whose office is to bring
> Twilight upon the Earth, short arbiter
Line　'Twixt day and night, and now from end to end
(5)　Night's hemisphere had veiled the horizon round,
> When Satan, who late fled before the threats
> Of Gabriel out of Eden, now improved
> In meditated fraud and malice, bent
> On man's destruction, maugre, what might hap
(10)　Of heavier on himself, fearless returned.

Notice that even without rhyme, Milton controls the texture of the verse with meter (iambic pentameter) and with alliteration (lines 1, 9–10), personification (2–3), and allusion (2, 6, 7). Perhaps you can detect additional poetic devices.

Stanzas

Foremost among structural patterns in poetry is the *stanza*, grouped lines of verse that serve as a poem's building blocks. Ordinarily, the structure of the first stanza sets the pattern for those that follow. If it consists of four lines, five feet per line, and a particular rhyme scheme, those characteristics, perhaps with minor variations, will usually be maintained throughout the poem.

Variations between stanzas often enlarge a poem's meaning, but word-for-word repetition may have the same effect. Stanzas are described by the number of lines they contain: *couplet* (two lines), *tercet*—also called *terza rima* (three), *quatrain, cinquain, sestet,* and so on. In many poems, stanzas end with a *refrain* of lines or phrases, a pattern probably left over from the days when poetry was sung. Refrains, while often decorative, can also unify a poem or reiterate the poem's main theme.

THE LANGUAGE OF POETRY

Diction—the poet's choice of words—is the living force of poetry. The words of a good poem carry meaning on both a literal and an abstract level. Literal meaning is what people agree a word stands for.

Take, for instance, the everyday word *square*, the name of a four-sided polygon with 90-degree corners and equal sides. *Square* also stands for an open space in the middle of town, a kind of dance, a roofer's unit of measurement, and much more. A good dictionary may contain a dozen or more definitions, or denotative meanings, of the word. But all the definitions become useless when *square* is used as an adjective describing a person. Suddenly, *square* becomes an abstraction, connoting a respectable, law-abiding, tradition-bound personality. It may also evoke images of a stick-in-the-mud, old-fashioned, totally un-cool, nerdy individual—perhaps someone like you back in third grade. In short, *square*, along with countless other words, teems with meaning and when used in a poem may carry a good deal of weight.

Not only does the poet's choice of words provide clues to the speaker's values, attitude, personality, and intent. It may also reveal the speaker's background, education, time of life, gender, and more. On an elemental level, then, in diction lies the essence of poetry.

Think of a poem as you would a painting. Even the most realistic painting doesn't recreate or record reality. By selecting colors, devising shape, creating a composition, and applying paint in various ways, an artist interprets the subject, thereby expanding its meaning. Likewise, poets amplify the meaning of their works by choosing words that can be understood both on and below the surface.

Thinking About Diction

In this poem by Emily Dickinson, observe how diction amplifies meaning far beyond its literal level:

There Is No Frigate Like a Book

There is no frigate like a book
　To take us lands away,
Nor any coursers like a page
　Of prancing poetry.
This traverse may the poorest take
　Without oppress of toll;
How frugal is the chariot
　That bears the human soul.

(c. 1875–1880)

On the literal level, Dickinson compares reading books to traveling—hardly a unique idea. Her choice of conveyances, however, endows the poem with power. Instead of settling for ships and horses and coaches, the common forms of transportation in her day, she uses "frigate" and "coursers" and "chariot," words that conjure up images of romance and adventure, the very things readers often find in books.

But the poem contains still deeper dimensions. Notice the diction in the last four lines: "poorest," "oppress of toll," "frugal"—all money-related words meant to suggest the pecuniary benefits of vicarious travel. Finally, the speaker's reference to the "human soul" takes the poem to still another level of meaning. Although books are cheap, they excite and broaden our vision. Indeed, they possess enough power to alter our very nature.

"There Is No Frigate Like a Book" reaches far greater depths than you might have guessed after one reading. The fact is that ambiguities keep most poems from revealing all they have to give during an initial encounter. By reading the same poems over and over, however, you create opportunities to mine profound and rewarding treasures lurking below the surface.

It is often said that poetry is written in a double language. One language turns on the intellect; the other fires up emotions and the imagination. Driven by the power of suggestion and the allure of ambiguity, poetry speaks in two tongues, evinced by its ample use of figurative language.

> **Study Tip**
>
> By reading a poem over and over, you'll find its treasures lurking below the surface.

Figurative Language

When a poet wrote, "The road is a ribbon of moonlight," he neither told the truth nor lied. Rather, he made a comparison that gives the reader an artistic representation of the truth.

Comparisons, in fact, serve as the foundation of several figures of speech, or *tropes,* as they are sometimes called, especially the metaphor, the simile, and the symbol.

METAPHORS AND SIMILES

Foremost among figures of speech are the metaphor and the simile, each an effective means to describe one thing in terms of another. It may seem odd to say one thing when you mean another, but metaphors and similes are meant to communicate complex ideas in understandable, concrete terms. Besides, they often pump life into notions that might otherwise be a bore.

In such metaphors as "the lake was a quicksilver mirror," and "the girl wafted into the room," resemblances between disparate things are implied (lake/mirror, girl/air-borne object). A simile makes the comparison more explicit by using *like* or *as:* "the lake was *like* a quicksilver mirror;" "the girl wafted into the room *like* a feather." Because similes merely join two disparate ideas or images, they are generally less fertile than metaphors, which can evoke additional and fresh shades of meaning.

Most simple metaphors and similes are easily understood. It's no stretch to imagine what Robert Burns had in mind when he compared his love to "a red, red rose." Why Robert Frost chose to compare drops of snowmelt in the sun to "silver lizards" is equally apparent. But metaphors that invite several interpretations require more effort. "He has wild stag's feet" suggests speed and grace, but also daring and the spirit of adventure. Shakespeare's "All the world's a stage" conjures up any number of possible implications, among them man's pretentiousness and the unreality of the world. In "The Love Song of J. Alfred Prufrock," T. S. Eliot writes "When the evening is spread out against the sky/ Like a patient etherized upon a table." The comparison may be striking but its meaning hardly jumps off the page. Once you read further into the poem, however, the simile not only makes sense but opens a window to the speaker's soul.

Metaphors and Similes on the AP Exam

On the AP exam you may well find yourself dealing with a slew of metaphors and similes in both the multiple-choice section and the essay. You'll not only be asked to recognize such figures of speech but to interpret or explain their meaning. Especially in the essay, you may wish to discuss why a poet included a particular simile or how a metaphor serves as an organic element in the poem. Or you may comment on how a certain trope contributes to the poem's structure, theme, or tone. **Keep in mind that simply identifying a metaphor or simile usually won't be enough. What matters is your ability to analyze and explain its function.**

Some poems contain an array of similes and metaphors. On occasion, a single metaphor is developed at length—hence, the name *extended metaphor*. Sustaining a metaphor gives the poet an opportunity to dig deeply into apt and meaningful resemblances between literal and figurative meanings, as illustrated in "Uphill," Christina Rossetti's poem in which the speaker uses a "day's journey" as a metaphor for approaching death.

> Does the road wind uphill all the way?
> Yes, to the very end.
> Will the day's journey take the whole long day?
> From morn to night my friend.

Line
(5)   But is there for the night a resting place?
> A roof for when the slow dark hours begin.
> May not the darkness hide it from my face?
> You cannot miss that inn.

> Shall I meet other wayfarers at night?
(10)   Those who have gone before.

Essay Writing Tip

Identifying a poetic figure of speech is only half the job. The other half is explaining its function in the poem.

Then must I knock, or call when just in sight?
They will not keep you standing at that door.

Shall I find comfort, travel-sore and weak?
Of labour you shall find the sum.

(15)   Will there be beds for me and all who seek?
Yea, beds for all who come.

(1858)

The questioner in the poem seeks to learn what lies ahead in her journey. Her respondent assures her that she needn't worry. All will be well, for many others have gone before (line 10). No one who shows up at death's door will be turned away (line 12), and "beds"—i.e., graves—are plentiful (lines 15–16). Although the traveler seems to fret about the journey itself, her anxiety implies more profound misgivings, perhaps apprehension about the slumber that precedes salvation and entry into Heaven.

While preparing for the AP exam, you might look up other poems using extended metaphors, among them "Because I Could Not Stop for Death" by Emily Dickinson and "A Hillside Thaw" by Robert Frost. Notice that a sustained comparison works best when it is appropriate to the subject matter of the poem and to the poet's tone. A metaphor must also seem natural and unforced, as though the comparison it makes were virtually inevitable.

Because metaphors and similes are widely used not only in poetry but in prose and everyday speech, many of them have lost their original freshness and have become clichés. In addition, metaphors roll off tongues so readily and mindlessly that *mixed metaphors,* that is, usages that leap to two or more illogical, inconsistent, often grotesque resemblances, have become bred in the bones of the common herd—if you'll pardon the expression.

Sensitive to the pervasiveness of trite metaphors in love poetry, Shakespeare wrote "My Mistress' Eyes Are Nothing Like the Sun," a sonnet that parodies the emptiness of conventional declarations of love, particularly those that compare a person with beauties found in nature: eyes like stars, cheeks like roses, lips like cherries. Naturally, Shakespeare alludes to metaphors current in the seventeenth century, equivalents of today's assertions of love, such as "Oh, babe, you're my everything," "Loving you is my dream come true," "My love is deep as the ocean and high as the sky," "You're my future, you're my past,/Loving you is all I ask, honey, yeah, yeah, yeah," and countless others.

As you read the sonnet, underline everything that strikes you as an allusion to hackneyed poetic expressions of love.

My mistress' eyes are nothing like the sun;
Coral is far more read than her lips' red:
If snow be white, why then her breasts are dun;[1]
If hairs be wires, black wires grow on her head.
I have seen roses damasked,[2] red and white,

---

[1] brownish-gray
[2] of different colors

> But no such roses see I in her cheeks;
> And in some perfumes is there more delight
> Than in the breath that from my mistress reeks.
> I love to hear her speak, yet well I know
> That music hath a far more pleasing sound:
> I grant I never saw a goddess go,—
> My mistress, when she walks, treads on the ground.
>   And yet, by heaven, I think my love as rare
>   As any she belied with false compare.

Notice how the concluding couplet, the speaker's sincere expression of love, sends the poem in a new direction.

SYMBOL

A symbol is a figure of speech that communicates a second meaning along with its literal meaning. To put it another way, a symbol represents itself as well as something other than itself. Take, for example an ordinary roadside marker. Literally it is a piece of sheet metal mounted on a pole. But it also stands as a warning to drivers to slow down for the slippery pavement or the curve ahead.

A traffic sign, because it conveys a single meaning, is one of the simpler symbols. But others, like the American flag, can stimulate all kinds of responses, some alike, some contradictory. To many Americans, the flag symbolizes a country that stretches from sea to shining sea, one nation indivisible . . . and all that. But even to the most ardent patriot, the flag may also evoke dismay over some harmful or destructive governmental policy or practice. And to an anti-American, the Stars and Stripes can symbolize everything evil in the world. In short, some symbols acquire a multitude of meanings, some widely shared, others idiosyncratic, some contradictory, some conflicted, some ambivalent. In effect, a symbol, like a rock dropped into a pond, can send ripples in all directions.

A symbol that seems simple at the beginning of a poem may brim with meaning at the end. Consider the albatross in Coleridge's "Rime of the Ancient Mariner" as a case in point. A mere bird, the albatross symbolizes nature at the start. As the narrative develops, it acquires additional meanings: torment, guilt, terror, the abandonment of humane values, and the Mariner's fall from grace. The slaying of the albatross is a symbolic event that gradually transforms Coleridge's literary ballad about an ocean voyage into a soul's journey through a purgatory of horrors. No wonder that in everyday parlance *albatross* has been given a bad rap and has become synonymous with an unwanted burden or a pain in the neck.

TIP

Figure out how symbols contribute to a poem's meaning and effect.

Symbol Hunting on the AP

On the AP test, you won't go symbol-hunting for its own sake. Instead, you should be prepared to determine how symbols contribute to a poem's meaning and effect. Start with the assumption that poets have reasons for including symbols in their work. The more integrated the symbol, the better, especially if it is bound tightly to the poem's main theme.

A powerful symbol stands at the heart of the William Blake poem "The Sick Rose." Without it, in fact, there would be no poem at all.

The Sick Rose

O Rose, thou art sick!
The invisible worm
That flies in the night,
In the howling storm,

Has found out thy bed
Of crimson joy,
And his dark secret love
Does thy life destroy.

(1794)

For over two centuries this poem has intrigued readers. In poetry, as well as in song and fiction, a rose has long stood as a symbol for love and passion. Reading the poem, you must ask what force (here called an "invisible worm") flies in the night and can sicken, and ultimately destroy, love? (*Worm* is an apt choice, isn't it, since a worm can sap the life out of a rose.) But what unseen, intangible power can drain the life out of love? Boredom? Maybe. Complacency? Perhaps. Jealousy? Aha, that must be it. Jealousy (a "dark secret love") has stealthily crept into the rose's bed and snatched away the love residing there.

In "Sea-Shell Murmurs" by Eugene Lee-Hamilton (1845–1907), the sounds of the ocean that we pretend to hear echoing in seashells become symbolic of another common self-deception, the expectation of a life after death:

The hollow sea-shell which for years hath stood
 On dusty shelves, when held against the ear
 Proclaims its stormy parent; and we hear
The faint far murmur of the breaking flood.

We hear the sea. The sea? It is the blood
 In our own veins, impetuous and near,
 And pulses keeping pace with hope and fear
And with our feelings' every shifting mood.

Lo, in my heart I hear, as in a shell,
 The murmur of a world beyond the grave
Distinct, distinct, though faint and far it be.

Thou fool; this echo is a cheat as well,—
 The hum of earthly instincts; and we crave
A world unreal as the shell-heard sea.

(c. 1890)

IMAGE

Images are words and phrases that refer to something that can be seen, heard, tasted, smelled, or touched. In other words, an image is a figure of speech evocative of the senses. From John Masefield's "The West Wind" comes the following stanza invoking at least three of the five senses:

> It's a warm wind, the west wind, full of birds' cries;
> I never hear the west wind but tears are in my eyes.
> For it comes from the west lands, the old brown hills,
> And April's in the west wind, and daffodils.

In Louise Bogan's "Putting to Sea," an image-filled stanza reads this way:

> Motion beneath us, fixity above.
> O, but you should rejoice! The course we steer
> Points to a beach bright to the rocks with love,
> Where, in hot calms, blades clatter on the ear;

Imagery often helps to establish the tone and meaning of a poem. Because images are usually quite literal and concrete, regardless of their connotative values, they differ markedly from symbols.

PERSONIFICATION

First cousin to metaphor, personification occurs when the poet assigns human characteristics to a nonhuman object or to an abstraction such as love, death, envy, victory, and so on.
In "Rime of the Ancient Mariner," Coleridge personifies the sun:

> The sun came up upon the left,
> Out of the sea came he!

Emily Dickinson not only endows insects with human personalities but gives them the ability to read and write:

> Bee, I'm expecting you!
> Was saying yesterday
> To somebody you know
> That you were due.
>
> The frogs got home last week,
> Are settled and at work,
> Birds mostly back,
> The clover warm and thick.
>
> You'll get my letter by
> The seventeenth; reply,
> Or better, be with me.
> Yours,
>   Fly.

Shakespeare personifies confusion when he has Macbeth say: "Confusion now hath made his masterpiece." And the speaker in e. e. cummings's "Gee I Like to Think of Dead" endows several objects with human characteristics:

>   every
>   old thing falls in rosebugs and jacknives and kittens and
>   pennies they all sit there looking at each other having the
>   fastest time because they've never met before

Poets' fondness for personification derives from the human tendency to ascribe human qualities to nonhuman objects. We project our emotions onto pets and other animals, we refer to cars and boats as "she," and assign human names to hurricanes. Through personification we breathe life into what might otherwise be lifeless and bestow on nonhuman objects a personality, willpower, the ability to think and feel and act in every way like a human being. While stimulating our imaginations, personification often surprises us with insights.

METONYMY

A headline writer who says "White House Plans New Tax Cuts" uses **metonymy, a figure of speech that substitutes a word or phrase that relates to a thing for the thing itself.** In other words, the phrase "White House" stands not for the mansion on Pennsylvania Avenue but for its current occupants. The writer used one name with the intention that another be understood.

Shakespeare did it too: In saying "The crown will find an heir" he substituted "crown" for "king." In Housman's "Is My Team Ploughing?" the speaker says "leather" when he means "a football":

>   Is football playing
>   Along the river shore,
>   With lads to chase the leather,
>   Now I stand up no more?

Although metonymy resembles metaphor, it implies both a literal meaning and something else. But unlike metaphor, it narrows rather than expands meaning. Yet, an aptly conceived metonymy is a treat. With a single word or phrase, the poet opens readers' eyes and stimulates their imagination.

SYNECDOCHE

Synecdoche resembles metonymy so closely that differentiating them is akin to splitting hairs. Although you probably won't be asked to distinguish between them on the AP exam, keep in mind that **a synecdoche substitutes a part for a whole.** When, say, a rock climber credits her partner for "saving my skin," that's synecdoche. So is the word "hands" for workers, and the phrases "18-wheeler" for truck and "talking head" for TV commentator. The word "summers" in "She was a lass of twenty summers" is also synecdoche because the summer is part of a year. William Cowper uses synecdoche by substituting "wave" for "sea" in these lines:

>   Toll for the brave!
>   The brave that are no more,
>   All sunk beneath the wave . . .

In *Henry VI*, Shakespeare wrote "neck" as a synecdoche for "person," a particularly apt usage considering his subsequent reference to "yoke":

> Yield not thy neck
> To fortune's yoke, but let thy dauntless mind
> Still ride in triumph over all mischance.

Effective use of synecdoche can add a delightful and surprising aesthetic dimension to a poem.

ALLUSION

TIP

Allusions are drawn from literature, history, the arts, even from pop culture.

An allusion is a historical, literary, or cultural reference to a person, a place, or event. A well-chosen allusion can be enormously suggestive and richly symbolic, but only if the reader understands it. An allusion to Waterloo will be lost on someone clueless about Napoleon. On the other hand, an informed reader will make the connection between Waterloo and the notion of ultimate defeat and downfall. Because allusions can be drawn from anywhere, readiness to recognize them depends on familiarity with history, literature (especially mythology and the Bible), the arts, and one's general fund of knowledge.

On the AP exam, instead of simply recognizing the source of an allusion, it may be more important for you to grasp its intent. For example, the title of Robert Frost's poem *"Out, Out—"* alludes to bitter words ("Out, out, brief candle," etc.) spoken by Macbeth following the untimely death of his wife. The poem's title prepares you for its subject matter: the death of a small boy. More importantly, though, Macbeth's words resonate through the poem's themes: the uncertainty of life, the waste of human potential, and the tragedy of a life suddenly snuffed out.

In *Doctor Faustus,* Christopher Marlowe asks:

> Was this the face that launched a thousand ships.
> And burnt the topless towers of Ilium?

This allusion contains a wealth of suggestiveness to one who knows the story of Helen and the fall of Troy. In a few words, Marlowe conveys the passion implicit in the tale of a woman whose beauty almost led to the destruction of a civilization.

ALLEGORY

An allegory is a story or vignette that, like a metaphor, has both a literal and a figurative meaning. Many allegories use concrete images or characters to represent abstract ideas. To keep readers from missing the point, characters may actually bear the names of the ideas they stand for. For example, Good Deeds, Knowledge, Beauty, and Discretion are names in the *Dramatis Personae* of *Everyman,* a sixteenth-century allegorical play in verse by an anonymous author. Other famous allegories include Spenser's "The Faerie Queen" and Tennyson's "Idylls of the King."

OXYMORON

An oxymoron is a phrase that seems self-contradictory or incompatible with reality: *eloquent silence, jumbo shrimp, free gift.* While oxymorons may be used just for fun, they are more frequently employed to suggest ambiguity or to develop a theme.

PARADOX

A paradox is an apparently self-contradictory statement that under scrutiny makes perfect sense. It has the same effect as an oxymoron. Note the paradoxical quality of Hamlet's statement, "I must be cruel only to be kind," or Wallace Stevens's assertions in "Thirteen Ways of Looking at a Blackbird":

> It was evening all afternoon.
> It was snowing
> And it was going to snow.

Paradoxically, oxymorons and paradoxes contain both absurdity and truth at the same time. They invite the reader of a poem to cast aside conventional responses in favor of more whimsical interpretations. If you find an oxymoron or paradox in a poem on the AP exam, start looking for the presence of subtexts and implied meanings.

UNDERSTATEMENT

Understatement is a principal source of power in poetry. Think of Richard Cory, the eponymous character of Edwin Arlington Robinson's famous poem. Because no reason is given to explain why Cory put a bullet through his head, we are left to imagine the demons that drove him to it. Robinson, letting the action speak for itself, evidently understood the impact of understatement.

Another form of understatement is saying less than one means or using restraint in ironic contrast to what might be said. The speaker in "The Sum" by Paul Lawrence Dunbar, for example, attempts to capture several of life's momentous events in a brief phrase or two:

> A little dreaming by the way,
> A little toiling day by day;
> A little pain, a little strife
> A little joy,—and that is life.
>
> A little short-lived summer's morn,
> When joy seems all so newly born,
> When one day's sky is blue above,
> And one bird sings—and that is love.
>
> A little sickening of the years,
> The tribute of a few hot tears
> Two folded hands, and failing breath,
> And peace at last,—and that is death.
>
> Just dreaming, loving, dying so,
> The actors in the drama go—
> A flitting picture on a wall,
> Love, Death, the themes; but is that all?

One might argue that Dunbar's poem, with its singsongy rhythm and rhymes, trivializes life, but that may be just the point. Implying that we tend to exaggerate the gravity of everyday human experiences, the speaker aims to take a larger view—to be more circumspect. Yet, in the last line, he questions his own judgment, or at least allows that he could be understating the significance of life's defining themes.

LITOTES

A teacher responding to your English essay by commenting "Not at all bad" is using **litotes, a form of understatement in which a positive fact is stated by denying a negative one.** You might retort with another litotes: "You are not a bad teacher."

In the funeral oration of *Julius Caesar,* Marc Antony uses litotes in "Not that I loved Caesar less . . ." The effect is to draw a sharp contrast with the second half of the statement, "but that I loved Rome more."

Writing about his birthday in "Anniversary," poet John Wain writes:

> As a little scarlet howling mammal,
> Crumpled and unformed, I depended entirely on someone
> Not very different from what I am to-day.

In the third line, the speaker makes the point that someone—presumably his mother—was much the same as he is today, but the sentiment, more emphatically expressed via litotes, is stated as a denial of its opposite.

HYPERBOLE OR OVERSTATEMENT

Hyperbole is an exaggeration, a useful device for poets to intensify emotions, values, physical features, the weather, or virtually anything. W. H. Auden's "As I Walked Out One Evening" includes this hyperbolic declaration of love:

> I'll love you, dear, I'll love you
> Till China and Africa meet,
> And the river jumps over the mountain
> And the salmon sing in the street.

Macbeth, having murdered Duncan, uses hyperbole to express the horror he feels:

> Will all great Neptune's ocean wash this blood
> Clean from my hand? No. This my hand will rather
> The multitudinous seas incarnadine,
> Making the green one red.

Here's a hyperbole found in Carl Sandburg's poem "The People, Yes" that pokes fun at a very boring place:

> "It's a slow burg—I spent a couple of weeks there one day."

Tone

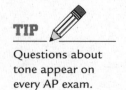

TIP

Questions about tone appear on every AP exam.

Tone is the poet's or speaker's attitude toward the subject of the poem, toward the reader, or toward himself. Because tone derives from the sum total of the emotional and intellectual effects of a poem, comprehending the tone almost guarantees that you comprehend the whole thing. **Tone carries so much weight in poetry explication, in fact, that it's virtually impossible to take the AP exam without having to deal with it, either in the multiple-choice questions or as a topic to discuss in an essay.**

A single tone prevails in most poems, but a poet can't be stopped from changing his mind or altering the thrust of a poem in midstream. Therefore, the tone of many poems is multidimensional. This is as it should be. After all, feelings consist of an amalgam of impulses and reactions, sometimes ambivalent or contradictory.

What follows is an assortment of adjectives that might be used to describe the tone of various poems. No doubt you could expand the list many times over and perhaps cite examples from the repertoire of poems that you know well.

> brash, jovial, dour, playful, intimate, earnest, whimsical, grave, comic, urbane, fanciful, affected, rhapsodic, resigned, devotional, eulogistic, intemperate, fervent, elegiac, tender, sardonic, cynical, nostalgic, indignant, flippant, meditative, didactic, bitter, wry, sentimental, patronizing, extravagant

TIP

To signify tone, use adjectives such as those listed on the left.

Identifying Tone

Because you can't hear the actual voice of the speaker in a poem, your interpretation of tone is a matter of using the evidence offered by the poem itself. Sometimes tone is found in figures of speech, at other times through rhymes and rhythms. Diction and word sounds may also help you identify the tone of a poem. Unfortunately, there is no universal formula on which to rely. Because it takes the interaction of several ingredients, from imagery to structure, to create the tone of a poem, a thorough analysis works best to nail it down.

Using the following poem by Robert Browning, try your hand in determining tone:

Meeting at Night

> The grey sea and the long black land;
> And the yellow half-moon large and low;
> And the startled little waves that leap
>
> *Line*   In fiery ringlets from their sleep,
> *(5)*   As I gain the cove with a pushing prow,
> And quench its speed i' the slushy sand.
>
> Then a mile of warm sea-scented beach;
> Three fields to cross till a farm appears;
> A tap at the pane, the quick sharp scratch
> *(10)*   And blue spurt of a lighted match,
> And a voice less loud, through its joys and fears,
> Than the two hearts beating each to each!

Before deciding on the tone of "Meeting at Night," consider what happens in the poem: Night has fallen. The speaker, apparently a romantic youth, is rushing to a tryst with his ladylove. The route, first on the water, then across the land, is long. Arriving outside her window, he taps on the glass, then enters her room where the lovers fall into an embrace.

Using a series of sensual images, the poet tracks the young man's progress toward his destination and puts into words his growing eagerness to get there. The images ("grey sea and the long black land") reflect the young man's state of mind as he starts on his journey. Soon, in accord with his increasing desire, the images brighten: "yellow half-moon," "fiery ringlets." Finally, a "blue spurt of a lighted match" marks the climactic meeting of the two lovers.

The first stanza, in which the young man rows slowly to a distant beach, consists almost entirely of watery images. Just like the "startled little waves" awakening from their sleep, the young man's hormonal juices begin to flow. As his anticipation grows, the journey, as well as the poem, speeds up. In two lines (7 and 8) he races across a mile-wide beach and traverses three fields. In rapid succession, a tap on the window and a burst of light bring the journey to a swift end. Abruptly, all motion ceases. Movement gives way to the two lovers' pounding hearts, the repetition of "each" vaguely simulating the sound of their heartbeats.

Diction throughout the poem underscores the speaker's fervor. The repeated use of "and" at the beginning of lines 2, 3, 6, 10, and 11 resounds with breathlessness. In lines 7 and 8 the words flow one into the other. Only in line 9 is there a caesura that briefly slows down the verbal deluge and prepares the reader for the young man's arrival in his lover's arms.

If the tone of "Meeting at Night" were to be reduced to a single word, *breathless* is a good choice. Throughout his journey, the speaker is portrayed as someone beside himself with love, and panting with desire to reach his lover's arms.

From a speaker consumed by love, let's turn to one who sees the world from an entirely different perspective. Read Arthur Hugh Clough's "The Latest Decalogue."

The Latest Decalogue[1]

Thou shalt have one God only; who
Would be at the expense of two?
No graven images may be
Line Worshipped, except the currency.
(5) Swear not at all; for, for thy curse
Thine enemy is none the worse.
At church on Sunday to attend
Will serve to keep the world thy friend.
Honour thy parents; that is, all
(10) From whom advancement may befall.
Thou shalt not kill; but need'st not strive
Officiously to keep alive.
Do not adultery commit;
Advantage rarely comes of it:
(15) Thou shalt not steal; an empty feat,
When it's so lucrative to cheat.
Bear not false witness; let the lie
Have time on its own wings to fly.
Thou shalt not covet, but tradition
(20) Approves all forms of competition.

(1862)

---

[1]The Ten Commandments

The speaker in this poem is complaining about the morality of his time. He could have written a straightforward verse criticizing man's indifference to biblical teachings, but chose instead to express his disapproval through irony.

Even the title is ironic because the Ten Commandments are supposed to be a permanent, binding set of rules. To call them the "latest" suggests that modern men, while paying lip service to the word of God, adapt the rules for their convenience.

The poem devotes two lines, or two rhyming couplets, to each of the ten commandments ("Thou shalt not kill," "Thou shalt not steal," etc.). Each commandment is undercut by a remark meant to show why its principle conflicts with the interests and values of contemporary society. In lines 19–20 ("Thou shalt not covet, but tradition/Approves all forms of competition") the speaker cynically declares that society's business has made quaint and obsolete what once was a guiding principle of moral behavior. Man's pursuit of money has forced each commandment to be cast aside or amended. Materialism is man's new religion. By implication, man worships Mammon (the god of money) instead of God, and the speaker doesn't like it.

IRONY

Irony comes in many forms, from a chem teacher's sarcastic "Good work!" on a quiz you've flunked to an ironic twist of fate, such as the urban legend of the man who missed an airplane that crashed shortly after takeoff but was killed on the highway during his drive home from the airport. A poet making use of irony is free to use any form, of course, but verbal irony is what poets seem to favor.

Basically verbal irony is an implied contrast between what exists and what might be. Users of irony don't expect their words to be taken at face value. Rather, they hope that a reader will see the reality behind their pose. On the surface a poem may sound grave, but in actuality, the speaker may be poking fun at, say, a particular human foible or frailty. While ridiculing hypocrisy, for example, the speaker may sound objective and emotionally uninvolved, but intense concern may underlie his criticism. He may, in fact, feel so passionate or distraught about his topic that rather than face it head on, he prefers to express his views indirectly, via irony, thereby heightening the impact on the reader.

In the poem "A Mirage" by W.S. Gilbert, the speaker, addressing a man she loves, idealizes the pleasures of matrimony. Her visions of a happy marriage include:

> *Upon thy breast/My loving head would rest.*
> *This heart of mine/Would be one heart with thine.*
> *Our lives would be a song/No grief, no wrong.*

The concluding couplet of the poem—*But then, unhappily/I'm not thy bride!*—reveals, however, that the entire poem is little more than an ironic fantasy, an exercise in wishful thinking.

POETIC STYLES AND FORMS

Below you will find a compilation of poetic terms that you should know for the AP exam. Although you won't be asked specifically to identify a sonnet or a villanelle or a dramatic monologue, knowing the basic characteristics of these and other poetic forms could give you a leg up in answering multiple-choice questions. As for writing an essay on poetry, a familiarity with basic terminology can give you a head start and as a bonus save you considerable time—time that could be spent polishing your essay instead of painstakingly describing a form that can be identified with a single word or phrase.

Narrative Poem

True to its name, **a narrative poem tells part or all of a story.** It adheres to no prescribed form, and while it may contain lyrical and descriptive passages, its primary purpose is to tell a tale. Epics such as *Gilgamesh, The Odyssey,* and *Sir Gawain and the Green Knight* are narrative poems, each about a heroic adventurer. While some narrative poems are book-length epics, others may be just a few lines, such as this one by Herman Melville:

The Figure Head

The *Charles-and-Emma* seaward sped.
(Named from the carven pair at prow)
He so smart, and a curly head,
She tricked forth as a bride knows how:
    Pretty stem for the port, I trow!

But iron-rust and alum-spray
And chafing gear, and sun and dew
Vexed this lad and lassie gay,
Tears in their eyes, salt tears nor few;
    And the hug relaxed with the failing glue.

But came in end a dismal night,
With creaking beams and ribs that groan,
A black lee-shore and waters white:
Dropped on the reef, the pair lie prone:
    O, the breakers dance, but the winds they moan!

(1888)

In three brief stanzas the speaker relates the story of the *Charles-and-Emma,* a sailing ship with a striking wood carving—an attractive bride and groom clinging to each other—at its prow. In time, the figures deteriorate, the glue that binds them dissolves, and the ship is wrecked. The pair ends up on a reef battered by water and wind. The tale is simple, but its subtext suggests the inevitable erosion of youth, love, and life.

Lyric Poem

Sonnets, elegies, odes, villanelles—these and many other poetic forms are lyric. In fact, any poem that is neither dramatic nor narrative is lyric. **Lyric poems express an individual's thoughts and emotions.** They can be mystical, didactic, satirical, reflective, mournful; the possibilities are endless.

What follows is a brief Robert Herrick lyric that may at first seem like a public-service message about fire but is actually an emotion-laden statement by a speaker in some serious love-related trouble:

The Scare-Fire[1]

Water, water I desire,
Here's a house of flesh on fire;
Ope' the fountains and the springs,
And come all to bucketings.
What ye cannot quench, pull down,
Spoil a house to save a town:
Better 'tis that one should fall,
Than by one to hazard all.

(1648)

---

[1]A sudden conflagration

Another lyric poem, this one by Marianne Moore, conveys the speaker's feelings about the subject of this chapter. Once you've read it, please return to the poem's first four words and ask yourself whether Moore meant them to be taken seriously.

Poetry

I, too, dislike it: there are things that are important beyond all this fiddle.
Reading it, however, with a perfect contempt for it, one discovers in
it after all, a place for the genuine.
Line   Hands that can grasp, eyes
(5)   that can dilate, hair that can rise
if it must, these things are important not because a

high-sounding interpretation can be put upon them but because they are
useful. When they become so derivative as to become unintelligible,
the same thing may be said for all of us, that we
(10)   do not admire what
we cannot understand: the bat
holding on upside down or in quest of something to

eat, elephants pushing, a wild horse taking a roll, a tireless wolf under
a tree, the immovable critic twitching his skin like a horse that feels
   a flea, the base—

(15)   ball fan, the statistician—
   nor is it valid
      to discriminate against "business documents and

school books"[1]; all these phenomena are important. One must make a
   distinction
however: when dragged into prominence by half poets, the result is
   not poetry,

(20)   nor till the poets among us can be
      "literalists of
         the imagination"[2]—above
            insolence and triviality and can present

for inspection, "imaginary gardens with real toads in them," shall we have
(25)   it. In the meantime, if you demand on the one hand,
      the raw material of poetry in
         all its rawness and
            that which is on the other hand
               genuine, you are interested in poetry.

(1921)

---

[1] Poet's note from Tolstoy's journal: "Where the boundary between prose and poetry lies,
   I shall never be able to understand. . . . Poetry is verse: prose is not verse. Or else poetry
   is everything with the exception of business documents and school books."
[2] Yeats said of Blake, "He was a too literal realist of the imagination."

The speaker, presumably the poet, doesn't dislike poetry at all. Rather, she takes
a dim view of poems that can't be understood. In lines 2–8, she acknowledges that
poems can be "useful," but not until line 24 is usefulness defined as a poetic quality
that enables readers to see "'imaginary gardens with real toads in them.'"

In writing this lyric about poetry, Moore relies on rather prosaic language. Were
the text reformatted as a prose passage, a reader probably couldn't tell it was orig-
inially a poem. The piece appears to be almost antipoetic not only in its sentiment
but in its free verse style. Moore ignores many features of conventional poetry: it
has no rhymes, no discernible rhythm, no end-stops. But to avoid formlessness, she
divides the poem into stanzas and for no reason other than perhaps to assert her
individuality uses nineteen syllables for the first line of each one.

Based on "Poetry," how do you regard Moore as a poet? Is she a "half poet,"
alluded to in the fourth stanza, or is she one of the "literalists of the imagination"
(lines 21–22)?

Metaphysical Poetry

The word "metaphysical" describes the lyric poems of certain seventeenth-century men—Donne, Marvell, Herbert, and others—who, like poet-psychologists, were fond of writing highly intellectual and philosophical verses on the nature of thought and feeling. Their work, which also concerns ethics, religion, and love, blends emotion with intellectual ingenuity in a manner that modern readers often find far-fetched if not downright obscure. To illustrate, here are two short poems by Richard Crashaw about "Infant Martyrs," an allusion that Crashaw's biblically literate audience would instantly have understood even without benefit of a footnote.

TIP 🖉

All metaphysical poetry is lyrical, but lyric poetry is not all metaphysical.

To the Infant Martyrs[1]

Go, smiling souls, your new-built ages break,
In heaven you'll learn to sing, ere here to speak
Nor let the milky fonts that bathe your thirst
          Be your delay;
The place that calls you hence is, at the worst,
          Milk all the way.

Upon the Infant Martyrs

To see both blended in one flood,
The mothers' milk, the children's blood,
Make me doubt[2] if heaven will gather
Roses hence, or lilies rather.

(1646)

---

[1] The Holy Innocents, the newborns of Bethlehem murdered by Herod in a vain attempt to destroy the one who, according to prophesy, would grow up to be the ruler of Israel.
[2] wonder

Although written separately, the two poems complement each other. The first addresses the dead children with words of solace and comfort. The second laments the children's murder.

Romantic Poetry

In everyday usage, romances are love poems, verses that declare poets' feelings for their sweethearts. In literary parlance, however, romances are carefully structured metrical poems that originated in medieval France and told stories of chivalrous knights undertaking perilous journeys often to rescue damsels in distress.

Romantic poetry refers to the literary movement that peaked in England during the nineteenth century. Wordsworth, Coleridge, Keats, Shelley, and Byron are often linked as the five luminaries of the romantic period (some scholars add Tennyson to make it six), but their differences are no less pronounced than their similarities. In general, their work constitutes a protest against the classic formalism that had long pervaded poetry. Therefore, their poems tend to focus on inner experience and feelings, including dreams and the subconscious. Their work also deals with cultures of nonclassic lands: with nature, particularly in its wilder moods, with exotic pleasures, with the supernatural, and with Christianity and transcendentalism. Above all, romantic poetry lionizes the individual hero, often a young man consumed by melancholy and ennui or a firebrand rebelling against traditional society. The poetry itself reflects individuality. It breaks with convention and rules in favor of spontaneity and lyricism. Much of it is ponderously dreamy and given to reverie and reflection.

The following excerpt taken from Wordsworth's "Lines Composed a Few Miles Above Tintern Abbey" provides a glimpse of the kinds of moods and subjects that inspired not only Wordsworth but a vast number of his contemporaries:

> And now, with gleam of half-extinguished thought,
> With many recognitions dim and faint,
> And somewhat of a sad perplexity,
> The picture of the mind revives again:
> While here I stand, not only with the sense
> Of present pleasure, but with pleasing thoughts
> That in this moment there is life and food
> For future years. And so I dare to hope,
> Though changed, no doubt, from what I was when first
> I came among these hills; when like a roe
> I bounded o'er the mountains, by the sides
> Of the deep rivers, and the lonely streams,
> Wherever nature led—more like a man
> Flying from something that he dreads, than one
> Who sought the thing he loved. For nature then
> (The coarser pleasures of my boyish days,
> And their glad animal movements all gone by)
> To me was all in all.

The speaker has returned to the country after a long absence and reflects on his now-vanished youth. Notice his idealization of nature and trancelike occupation with himself. In the next sentence of the poem, the speaker says, "I cannot paint/What then I was," suggesting, perhaps disingenuously, that he lacks the skill with words to accurately portray himself. Rather, he offers a representation of himself and his feelings as he would like them to have been.

Ballad

Originally sung, folk ballads tell engrossing stories about life, death, heroism, and, as in "The Twa* Corbies," love, murder, and betrayal:

The Twa Corbies

As I was walking all alane,[1]	[1]alone
I heard two corbies[2] making a mane;[3]	[2]two ravens; [3]moan
The tane[4] unto t'other say,	[4]one
"Where sall be gang[5] and dine today?"	[5]shall we go
"In behint yon auld fail dyke,[6]	[6]old turf wall
I wot[7] there lies a new-slain knight;	[7]know
And naebody kens[8] that he lies there,	[8]knows
But his hawk, his hound, and his lady fair.	
"His hound is to the hunting gane,	
His hawk to fetch the wild-fowl hame,	
His lady ta'en another mate	
So we may mak our dinner sweet.	
"Ye'll sit on his white hause-bane,[9]	[9]neck bone
And I'll pick out his bonny blue een;[10]	[10]eyes
Wi ae[11] lock o' his gowden hair	[11]With one
We'll theek[12] our nest when it grows bare.	[12]thatch
"Mony a one for him makes mane,	
But nane shall ken where he is gane;	
O'er his white banes when they are bare,	
The wind sall blaw for evermair."	

—Anon

————————
*Ancient Scottish for "two"

The ravens in this ballad haven't a clue that they are telling us a tale of adultery and murder. They just have their eyes on a tasty meal.

The original authors of folk ballads remain anonymous, but literary ballads have known authors whose works may echo if not imitate the style and character of folk ballads. Coleridge's "Rime of the Ancient Mariner" is an example.

Couplet

A couplet is made up of two rhymed lines, usually in the same meter, but not always, as illustrated by this two-line, slant-rhymed poem by Ezra Pound:

In a Station of the Metro

The apparition of these faces in the crowd;
Petals on a wet, black bough.

(1916)

Couplets rarely stand by themselves as complete poems. Rather, they are the building blocks of much longer works.

Heroic couplets, so called from their use in epics or heroic poetry, express a complete thought, with the second line often reinforcing the first. Because of this completeness, the couplet is said to be *closed* or *end-stopped.*

What follows is an excerpt from Alexander Pope's "Rape of the Lock." Belinda, the young heroine of the poem, has just been awakened by her personal maid and is about to have her makeup applied:

> And now, unveiled, the toilet stands displayed,
> Each silver vase in mystic order laid.
> First, robed in white, the nymph intent adores,
> *Line* With head uncovered, the cosmetic powers.
> *(5)* A heavenly image in the glass appears;
> To that she bends, to that her eyes she rears.
> The inferior priestess, at her altar's side,
> Trembling begins the sacred rites of pride.
> Unnumbered treasures ope and once, and here
> *(10)* The various offerings of the world appear.

(1712)

To avoid the monotony of regular rhymes and end-stopped lines, Pope varies his couplets with off-rhymes (lines 3–4) and enjambment (lines 9–10). He also breaks the steady rhythm of iambic pentameter with a short caesura in line 3. If you have been struck by the incongruity between the heroic tone of this excerpt and the triviality of its subject matter, that is just the point. "The Rape of the Lock" is a *mock epic.*

Dramatic Monologue

A dramatic monologue is a poem spoken by one person to a listener who may influence the speaker with a look or an action but says nothing. Although dramatic monologues differ from internal monologues and soliloquies, they can be equally effective in revealing the character of the speaker.

Robert Browning's dramatic monologues serve as models of the genre, including the one that follows:

My Last Duchess[1]

Ferrara

> That's my last duchess painted on the wall,
> Looking as if she were alive. I call
> That piece a wonder, now; Frà Pandolf's hands
> *Line* Worked busily a day, and there she stands.
> *(5)* Will't please you to sit and look at her? I said

---

[1]The poem, set in Ferrara during the Renaissance, is meant to reflect values and attitudes of the time. Names do not refer to specific people but to types.

"Frà Pandolf" by design, for never read
Strangers like you that pictured countenance,
The depth and passion of its earnest glance,
But to myself they turned (since none puts you by

(10)   The curtain I have drawn for you, but I)
And seemed as they would ask me, if they durst,
How such a glance came there; so, not the first
Are you to turn and ask thus. Sir, 'twas not
Her husband's presence only, called that spot

(15)   Of joy into the Duchess' cheek: perhaps
Frà Pandolf chanced to say "Her mantle laps
Over my lady's wrist too much," or "Paint
Must never hope to reproduce the faint
Half-flush that dies along her throat." Such stuff

(20)   Was courtesy, she thought, and cause enough
For calling up that spot of joy. She had
A heart—how shall I say?—too soon made glad,
Too easily impressed; she liked whate'er
She looked on, and her looks went everywhere.

(25)   Sir, 'twas all one! My favor at her breast,
The dropping of the daylight in the west,
The bough of cherries some officious fool
Broke in the orchard for her, the white mule
She rode with round the terrace—all and each

(30)   Would draw from her alike the approving speech,
Or blush, at least. She thanked men—good! but thanked
Somehow—I know not how—as if she ranked
My gift of a nine-hundred-years-old name
With anybody's gift. Who'd stoop to blame

(35)   This sort of trifling? Even had you skill
In speech—(which I have not)—to make your will
Quite clear to such a one, and say, "Just this
Or that in you disgusts me; here you miss,
Or there exceed the mark"—and if she let

(40)   Herself be lessoned so, nor plainly set
Her wits to yours, forsooth, and made excuse,
—E'en then would be some stooping; and I choose
Never to stoop. Oh, sir, she smiled, no doubt,
Whene'er I passed her; but who passed without

(45)   Much the same smile? This grew; I gave commands;
Then all smiles stopped together. There she stands
As if alive. Will't please you rise? We'll meet
The company below, then. I repeat,
The Count your master's known munificence

(50)   Is ample warrant that no just pretense
Of mine dowry will be disallowed;

Tip

As the duke talks
we see that he's
a jealous and
possessive
husband.

> Though his fair daughter's self, as I avowed
> At starting, is my object. Nay, we'll go
> Together down, sir. Notice Neptune, though,
> *(55)* Which Claus of Innsbruck cast in bronze for me!

(1849)

In this monologue the Duke of Ferrara takes pains to impress the envoy of an unnamed count whose daughter he wishes to marry. The duke escorts the gentleman around his villa, pointing out the artwork, dropping names, and bragging about his aristocratic lineage. But mostly he talks about the duchess. Listening to the duke's account of his late wife, we gain entrance into his mind and discover that he is a jealous, possessive, and relentless martinet.

The use of heroic couplets in iambic pentameter—used in much heroic or epic poetry in English—attests to both the duke's pretentiousness and his overblown self-esteem. Using a consistent rhyme scheme (a-a-b-b, etc.) he flaunts his facile tongue, and thereby undermines his disingenuous claim that he lacks skill in speech (lines 34–35). Intent on pumping himself up, the duke unwittingly lays bare his faults and foibles. Several instances of enjambment reveal an inability to reign in his emotions. His effort to flatter the envoy by saying that "none puts you by/The curtain I have drawn for you, but I," (lines 9–10) rings hollow.

When the envoy questions the unusual look on the subject's face, the duke can hardly contain himself. He enthusiastically explains how "such a glance" (line 12) may have come to her face and why a "spot/Of joy" (lines 14–15)—i.e., a blush—adorned her cheek. As usual, his words are boastful and self-serving. Giving himself at least some of the credit for exciting his wife's emotions, he says, "'twas not/Her husband's presence only, called that spot/Of joy into the Duchess' cheek" (lines 13–15). But more to the point, the duke answers the envoy's question by elaborating on his wife's defective character. She was easily flattered by the artist's offhand remarks, he says, and "had/A heart—how shall I say?—too soon made glad,/Too easily impressed" (lines 21–23). In other words, she was gullible, naïve, and unduly susceptible to the attentions of other men.

On the surface, the question, "how shall I say?" appears once again to reflect the duke's false modesty. But it also hints that the duke believed his wife to have been a flirt, a temptress, maybe even a slut. Hoping to pass himself off as a refined gentleman, however, the duke feigns an inability to express such an indelicate idea.

Similarly, in line 32, the duke inserts an offhand "I know not how," referring to the ways in which his wife thanked men for the gifts they gave to her. Here, the duke plays the role of the innocent, possibly the cuckolded, husband, suggesting to the envoy that he had been wronged by this woman. Even worse, according the duke, she lacked the decency to appreciate the most valuable thing he could give her, the noble and glorious gift of a "nine-hundred-years-old name" (line 33). To her, the title of "duchess" was no more important than a mule ride "round the terrace" (line 29).

At first, the duke's litany of his late wife's shortcomings seems like a spontaneous outpouring of grievances. By the time he is finished, however, it's clear that the duke has been trying all along to justify his ill feelings toward the duchess. Although he stops short of explaining how his late wife met her end, he is so convinced of his own rectitude that he recklessly hints that his "commands" (line 45) may have led to her demise. The envoy sees through the duke's lies and hypocrisy and attempts to take his leave (lines 53–54). Suspecting that the man will render an unfavorable report to his master, the duke in the last two lines of the poem shows off still more of his art collection and drops still another name ("Claus of Innsbruck")—a last-ditch effort to win him over.

Elegy

An elegy, sometimes called a *dirge*, is a poem of mourning and meditation, usually about the death of a person but occasionally about other losses, such as lost love, lost strength, lost youth. Considering their subject matter, elegies are typically solemn and dignified.

The following elegy by the American author Ambrose Bierce, laments the death of President Ulysses S. Grant in 1885. Grant had made a name for himself as the victorious commanding general of the Union forces in the Civil War. As an eighteen-year-old, Bierce fought under Grant but left the army embittered, disillusioned, and virulently opposed to war. Twenty years later, however, he paid a prayerful tribute to his fallen leader:

The Death of Grant

FATHER! whose hard and cruel law
Is part of thy compassion's plan,
Thy works presumptuously we scan
For what the prophets say they saw.

Line
(5)   Unbidden still, the awful slope
Walling us in, we climb to gain
Assurance of the shining plain
That faith has certified to hope.

In vain: beyond the circling hill
(10)   The shadow and the cloud abide;
Subdue the doubt, our spirits guide
To trust the Record and be still;

To trust it loyally as he
Who, heedful of his high design,
(15)   Ne'er raised a seeking eye to thine,
But wrought thy will unconsciously,

Disputing not of chance or fate,
Not questioning of cause or creed:
For anything but duty's deed
(20) To simply wise, too humbly great.

The cannon syllabled his name;
His shadow shifted o'er the land,
Portentous, as at his command
Successive cities sprang to flame!

(25) He fringed the continent with fire,
The rivers ran in lines of light!
Thy will be done on earth—if right
Or wrong he cared not to inquire.

His was the heavy hand, and his
(30) The service of the despot blade;
His the soft answer that allayed
War's giant animosities.

Let us have peace: our clouded eyes
Fill, Father, with another light,
(35) That we may see with clearer sight
Thy servant's soul in Paradise.

At the start, the speaker addresses the Divinity. He declares his faith and trust in Him. Although grieved by Grant's death, he won't presume to fathom God's "hard and cruel law." Instead, he prays for the strength to remain faithful, hoping that, in spite of the "shadow and the cloud" that now hang over him, a "shining plain" (presumably a place in heaven) awaits those who subdue their doubt, keep quiet, and trust "the Record" (line 12) of God's ultimate goodness.

Having affirmed his faith, the speaker turns his attention to Grant, who rose above the doubts and concerns that beset ordinary mortals. Unlike the speaker, Grant sought no help from God, for he was blessed with godlike qualities and seemed divinely inspired to carry out God's will "unconsciously" (line 16). Accordingly, Grant, in the name of peace, plunged confidently into violent war ("The cannon syllabled his name;/His shadow shifted o'er the land/. . .He fringed the continent with fire,/The rivers ran in lines of light!"). Ever devoted to his "high design" (line 14), Grant never swerved from his duty, never wondered whether he did right or wrong, and by literally sticking to his guns, "allayed/War's giant animosities."

In the last stanza the speaker renews a prayerful attitude, beseeching God—as Grant never could or would—to give the general's soul a place in Paradise.

Limerick

Not considered a serious form of poetry, the **limerick is one of the most popular lighter forms.** Its simplicity—five lines built on two rhymes with the third and fourth lines shorter than the others—may explain why it is easy to recite and remember. Limericks often surprise readers with a curious rhyme or a pun in the last line, like this one by the ubiquitous Anon:

> There was a young fellow named Hall,
> Who fell in the spring in the fall;
>   'Twould have been a sad thing
>   If he'd died in the spring,
> But he didn't—he died in the fall.

Ode

An ode, an ancient form of poetic song, is a celebratory poem. Highly lyrical or profoundly philosophical, odes pay homage to whatever the poet may hold dear— another person, a place, an object, an abstract idea.

Among the most widely read odes in English are Wordsworth's "Intimations of Immortality from Recollections of Early Childhood," and Keats's "Ode on a Grecian Urn" and "Ode to a Nightingale." All employ an essentially uniform stanza throughout, as in the following ode by Alexander Pope:

Ode on Solitude

> Happy the man whose wish and care
> A few paternal acres bound,
> Content to breathe his native air,
>   In his own ground.
>
> Whose herds with milk, whose fields with bread,
> Whose flocks supply him with attire,
> Whose trees in summer yield him shade,
>   In winter fire.
>
> Blest, who can unconcernedly find
> Hours, days, and years slide soft away,
> In health of body, peace of mind
>   Quiet by day,
>
> Sound sleep by night; study and ease,
> Together mixed; sweet recreation;
> And innocence, which most does please
>   With mediation.

Thus let me live, unseen, unknown;
　Thus unlamented let me die;
Steal from the world, and not a stone
　　Tell where I lie.

(c. 1709)

Any reader who ever longed to be left alone or wished to step away from the frenetic pace of modern life can appreciate Pope's heartfelt sentiment. The regular and consistent rhymes and rhythm, along with the plain diction and use of mellow sounds endow the poem with qualities commonly found in a pastoral or a lullaby.

SONNET

Sonnets come in many guises, but virtually all are fourteen-line lyric poems expressing one main thought or sentiment in iambic pentameter. The subject matter of sonnets ranges from love to politics. Any subject is fair game.

The *Italian sonnet,* developed by Petrarch and sometimes called the Petrarchan sonnet, is divided into two discrete units: an *octave,* consisting of the first eight lines rhymed *a-b-b-a a-b-b-a,* and a *sestet*—the remaining six lines frequently but not always rhymed *c-d-c-d-c-d* or *c-d-e-c-d-e.* The rhyme scheme usually corresponds with the progress of thought. In other words, the poet uses the octave to present a problem, question, story, or idea. The sestet resolves, contrasts with, or comments on the contents of the octave.

A twentieth-century example of an Italian sonnet is the following poem, entitled "Sonnet," by Edna St. Vincent Millay:

Time, that renews the tissues of this frame,
That built the child and hardened the soft bone,
Taught him to wail, to blink, to walk alone,
Stare, question, wonder, give the world a name,
Forget the watery darkness whence he came,
Attends no less the boy to manhood grown,
Brings him new raiment, strips him of his own:
All skins are shed at length, remorse, even shame.

Such hope is mine, if this indeed be true,
I dread no more the first white in my hair,
Or even age itself, the easy shoe,
The cane, the wrinkled hands, the special chair:
Time, doing this to me, may alter too
My anguish, into something I can bear.

In this sonnet, the octave describes the generalized effects of time on a boy growing to manhood. Over time, the child develops physically, of course, but he also becomes a different person intellectually and emotionally. The final six lines, the sestet, express the speaker's hope that the description presented by the octave is valid. The speaker not only has lost her fear of time's ravages—the white hair, the wrinkled hands, etc.—but embraces the passage of time because, as stated in the last pair of lines, time may finally relieve her unbearable anguish.

Millay's sonnet conforms precisely to the Italian form, but if truth be told, nothing in sonnet-writing, except perhaps its fourteen-line length, is truly fixed. Variations abound, especially in rhyme schemes and in sestets, which can be either more or less emotionally charged than the octave. This kind of malleability, in fact, may explain why poets have repeatedly been drawn to the form. It's irresistible.

Here is another example, this one by John Milton. How closely does it follow the Italian model?

On His Blindness[1]

When I consider how my light is spent
Ere half my days, in this dark world and wide,
And that one talent which is death to hide

Line   Lodged with me useless, though my soul more bent
(5)   To serve therewith my Maker, and present
My true account, lest he returning chide;
"Doth God exact day-labor, light denied?"
I fondly[2] ask: but Patience to prevent
That murmur, soon replies, "God doth not need
(10)   Either man's work or his own gifts; who best
Bear his mild yoke, they serve him best. His state
Is kingly. Thousands at his bidding speed
And post o'er land and ocean without rest:
They also serve who only stand and wait."

(1652)

---

[1] By 1651, at age 43, Milton had completely lost his sight.
[2] foolishly

Early in Milton's sonnet, the speaker, presumably the poet himself, reflects on his untimely loss of sight. Being unable to see is devastating, but being unable to write is tantamount to death, and because his soul demands that he serve God by using his writing talents, he despairs over being deficient in the eyes of God. (Milton is alluding to the biblical parable of the talents in the book of *Matthew,* in which a servant is cast "into outer darkness" as punishment for burying his one God-given talent.) In an instant of spiritual blindness paralleling his physical blindness, the speaker verges on asking his "Maker" whether as a blind man, he is expected to continue doing God's work. Patience, personified, holds the speaker back, assuring him that those who bear their burdens in silence serve God best. Besides, God has legions to do His bidding. Comforting the speaker still further, Patience affirms that "They also serve who only stand and wait."

"On His Blindness" adheres to the rhyme scheme of the Italian sonnet but ignores the customary break between the octave and sestet. Having already begun a response to the concerns expressed in the opening lines, Milton uses enjambment at the end of line 8. He also deviates from the Italian pattern by embedding a short but independent sentence into the sestet (lines 11–12). Thus, "On His Blindness" borders on the traditional Italian form but doesn't quite make it. Milton's variation, used frequently by other poets, is called, as you might expect, the *Miltonian sonnet.*

The structure of the *English,* or *Shakespearean,* sonnet differs still more from the Italian form. Instead of an octave and sestet as its basic building blocks, it consists of three quatrains and a climactic couplet with a new rhyme. Its typical rhyme scheme is *a-b-a-b-c-d-c-d-e-f-e-f-g-g,* a pattern that obliges the poet to look for seven different rhyming pairs. Since Shakespeare's time poets have changed and adapted the form to suit themselves. They've shortened or lengthened lines and occasionally scrapped iambic pentameter in favor of some other meter.

The following sonnet by Shakespeare, however, follows to the letter the form that bears his name. Three discrete quatrains end with periods. A concluding couplet clinches the poem's theme. Every line is five feet, or ten syllables long. Each rhyme is exact—no slant rhymes in sight. In other words, Shakespeare plays it straight in this sonnet, shunning deviations that could distract readers from enjoying his intricate word play.

Sonnet 138

When my love swears that she is made of truth,
I do believe her, though I know she lies,
That she might think me some untutored youth,
Line Unlearnéd in the world's false subtleties.
(5) Thus vainly thinking that she thinks me young,
Although she knows my days are past the best,
Simply I credit her false-speaking tongue:
On both sides thus is simple truth suppressed.
But wherefore says she not she is unjust?
(10) And wherefore say not I that I am old?
Oh, love's best habit is in seeming trust,
And age in love loves not to have years told.
Therefore I lie with her and she with me,
And in our faults by lies we flattered be.

VILLANELLE

A villanelle is a nineteen-line poem with five three-line stanzas and a concluding quatrain. It is usually light in tone and is based on only two rhymes. Here is a villanelle by W. E. Henley about villanelles:

Villanelle

A dainty thing's the Villanelle.
Sly, musical, a jewel in rhyme,
It serves its purpose passing well.

Line   A double-clappered silver bell
(5)   That must be made to clink and chime,
A dainty thing's the Villanelle.

And if you wish to flute a spell,
Or ask a meeting 'neath the lime,
It serves its purpose passing well.

(10)   You must not ask of it the spell,
Of organs grandiose and sublime—
A dainty thing's the Villanelle.

And filled with sweetness, as a shell
Is filled with sound, and launched in time,
(15)   It serves its purpose passing well.

Still fair to see and good to smell
As in the quaintness of its prime,
A dainty thing's the Villanelle.
It serves its purpose passing well.

If you don't already know it, find and read Dylan Thomas's "Do Not Go Gentle into That Good Night." It's probably the best-known villanelle in modern English.

PART 4

FICTION AND DRAMA

CHAPTER 5

Literature

- Reading with head *and* heart
- Unlocking fictional worlds
- What's more important, stories or plots?
- Meeting fictional characters
- Why readers keep turning pages
- How authors cast their spell

- Disassembling a book and putting it back together
- The language of literature
- Six popular AP novels by Austen, Joyce, Ellison, and others
- Essay ideas for novels and plays

FICTION ON THE EXAM

The AP exam asks more questions about fiction than about any other genre. Two of the essay questions and at least half of the multiple-choice questions involve passages of fiction. Most passages come from novels and short stories. The multiple-choice questions range from broad to narrow—from the meaning of the passage to the use of a single word or phrase. You may be asked about themes, structure, character, setting, tone, purpose, language. Virtually every aspect of the passage is fair game for the multiple-choice questions.

In the essay section the passage of fiction will be an excerpt from a longer work. After reading the passage, you are expected to write a well-organized analytical essay. In most cases, the question will suggest a focus for your essay—usually such elements as tone, imagery, use of language, choice of details, and so on. Your analysis should show how such elements are used to contribute to the meaning or effect of the passage.

The open-ended essay question tells you to choose a novel or a play to write about. Although novels and plays are drastically different creatures, the question makes no distinction between them. Both are "works of literature," with such common characteristics as plot, structure, conflict, settings, themes, major and minor characters, and some sort of resolution.

The present chapter reviews some of the major elements of fiction and drama. It also suggests several essay topics appropriate to literary works often used in AP English classes.

TIP

In your essay, be sure to show how literary elements contribute to the meaning or effect of the passage.

RESPONDING TO LITERATURE

As an AP English student you are expected to respond to a short story, a play, or a novel with something more substantial than "It's good," or "I didn't like it." Not that a snap judgment about a piece of literature is wrong, but you might render the same verdict about a song by Beyoncé or a dish of pudding. A piece of literature on which an author toiled, sometimes for years, deserves more than a simple thumbs up or thumbs down. The next several pages explain and illustrate what thoughtful people think about when they read fiction or go to the theater. By studying this material, your repertoire of responses to literature should grow broader. As you prepare for the AP English exam, that's a goal worth striving for.

INITIAL RESPONSES

Typically, an initial response to a work of literature comes from the heart rather than the head. Readers may be struck by the beauty of the language, stirred by an author's passion, or thrilled by the intensity of a scene or situation. Sometimes readers identify with a place or character, or a story is so engagingly told that they lose themselves in the work and must exert some effort to jolt themselves back into reality. Do you recall the gripping scene early in Herman Hesse's *Siddhartha* when the young Siddhartha, hoping to exact his father's permission to leave home to join the wandering Samanas, stands waiting silently all through the night? Siddhartha's vigil proves to his father how desperately his son wishes to leave. Whether you empathize with the young man on the verge of adulthood or feel pity for his anxious father who wants to protect his only son from harm, or even if you don't take sides at all, it's hard to resist being caught up in the timeless and universal conflict between generations that the incident epitomizes.

No doubt you can think of other scenes in books that for a time drew you away from the world of reality. During those moments you literally gave yourself up to the world of fiction.

How, you might ask, does a work elicit such a hypnotic response? The answer, of course, lies partly within you. As a reader, you are willing to surrender yourself to the world created by the author. More specifically, you are stimulated by esthetic and psychological forces that a skillful author marshals through use of language, style, form, rhythmic patterns, allusions, figurative expression, and much, much more.

Basically the intensity of an emotional response to a piece of literature is measured by how thoroughly you become immersed in it. When you give yourself completely, you tend to like, even to love, the work. When you can't get into it, or the work holds you at arm's length, your response will be unfavorable or, at best, indifferent.

> **Reminder**
>
> First responses to literature come from your heart, not your head.

Plot

The words *plot* and *story* are often used interchangeably, as though they were synonymns. Literary experts, however, like to distinguish between the two. By *story* they mean the narrative—the unfolding of events that concludes on the last page and makes the question *What happens next?* irrelevant.

When they talk of *plot*, on the other hand, they mean the story *plus* the complex interconnections between events. When a plot "thickens," events of the story become more intricate. Conflicts develop, characters face new dilemmas, a resolution grows farther away and harder to discern.

Think, for instance, of Steinbeck's *Of Mice and Men*, the tale of George, an itinerant farmhand, and his dull-witted sidekick Lennie. Toward the end of the novel, an event occurs that leads to the dénouement, or climax, of the story. Lennie, unable to control his brute strength, has accidentally broken the neck of a woman who had playfully flirted with him. As a posse hunts for the killer, George must decide what to do with Lennie, who is unaware that he has erred. George could let Lennie be caught and hanged for murder, or he could destroy Lennie himself, thereby sparing his longtime companion much pain and confusion. Those events comprise the *story*. The *plot*, however, teems with nuances about George and Lennie's interdependence. Lennie trusts George implicitly. Should George betray that trust? Is George's obligation to Lennie greater than his obligation to society and the rule of law? George's dilemma brims with moral, emotional, psychological, social, and legal implications.

COMPONENTS OF A PLOT

Some readers regard plot as the most compelling component in a work of fiction. It's a thing that they expect to find when they sit down to read. It keeps them turning the pages. In one form or other the plot they encounter can be charted roughly as follows:

> **Reminder**
>
> The "plot" is one thing; the "story" is something else.

- *Exposition:* Acquaints readers with the setting of the story (time and place) and introduces the characters.
- *Conflict:* The primary obstacle that prevents the protagonist (main character) from reaching his or her goal. The most common conflicts are man vs. man, man vs. nature, man vs. society, and man vs. himself.
- *Rising action:* The complications that develop and prolong the central conflict.
- *Climax:* The point of greatest tension in a story; the point of no return.
- *Falling action:* The result of the conflict.
- *Dénouement:* A resolution that ties up loose ends.

Although the concept of plot connotes a formal, relatively inflexible structure, not unlike that of a sonnet or a five-act play, few plots follow this formula to the letter. Variations abound, but almost always, the conflict raises interest and keeps readers engrossed because they want to know how it turns out.

Conflict

The conflict, or problem, serves as the backbone of the story and means basically that two forces of relatively equal strength are at odds with each other. The struggle may be internal and consist of a dilemma that offers a choice between two equally desirable or undesirable alternatives. Whatever the choices, undesirable alternatives are infinitely superior for heightening drama. Trivial or frivolous choices are . . . well, trivial and frivolous. But forcing a character to choose the lesser of two significant evils—as George does when he shoots Lennie in the head, or as Othello does when he smothers Desdemona, or as Sidney Carton does when he steps up to the guillotine—builds tension, magnifies pathos, and reveals the true nature of the chooser as nothing else can.

Tying Everything Together

A good plot should also be unified. That is, everything in the story, from conflict to character, from theme to point of view, is related to the story's basic purpose or effect. Any event that fails to follow plausibly from preceding developments dilutes the effectiveness of the plot. Stories needn't be told chronologically, but harmony must exist between the unfurling of events and the meaning and intent of the narrative. Authors who want to create suspense almost always organize the action more or less chronologically. Before the twentieth century, except for inserting occasional flashbacks to fill in background, novelists rarely structured plots in any other way. But over time, authors experimented wildly and often rearranged time beyond recognition. James Joyce, among others, devised plots in which past, present, and future exist simultaneously, as they do in a person's thoughts. Today, a narrative that adheres faithfully to a chronological time sequence is considered almost quaint.

Finally, to fully understand the meaning of a novel or play, you must read it to the end. Because an AP essay question may ask you to discuss how the plot of a novel or play relates to the meaning of the whole work, don't even think of writing about a work you haven't read to its conclusion. A story in which the protagonist emerges victorious—call it a "Hollywood ending"—says one thing. A tragic ending says something else. A story that ends with a tainted victory expresses still another meaning, as does a story in which the conflict remains wholly or partly unresolved. In fact, final paragraphs and sentences, like aphorisms, may contain a world of profundity, or at least provide closure by giving you the literary equivalent of a party favor, a thought to carry away. Recall how Fitzgerald ends *The Great Gatsby*: "So we beat on, boats against the current, borne back ceaselessly into the past"—fourteen pithy words that sum up Nick's experience. (Nick, along with Gatsby, longed for a better, simpler, and nobler time. Nick knows the past cannot be reclaimed but he can't stop trying.) Or consider how the last two sentences of *Huckleberry Finn* capture the very essence of young Huck: "But I reckon I got to light out for the territory ahead of the rest, because Aunt Sally she's going to adopt me and civilize me, and I can't stand it. I been there before."

Here is something for you to try: Reread the last page of any novel you've read. See if your memory isn't jogged and if you are not inspired to think about the meaning of the work as a whole.

Reminder

Endings matter in novels and plays.

TIP

Last pages often provide clues to the author's purpose.

MINI-WORKOUT ON PLOT

Instructions: Think about a novel or play you've read recently. Then name the ten most important events in the plot. Remember to include moments of conflict, the climax of the story, and the dénouement, if any. If possible, compare your answers with those of a friend who has read the same work.

Title and author: _____

1. _____

2. _____

3. _____

4. _____

5. _____

6. _____

7. _____

8. _____

9. _____

10. _____

Setting

Like strangers arriving in a town for the first time, readers try to get their bearings when they enter a fictional world. They want to know almost immediately where they are, what kind of place it is, and what sort of people they should expect to meet. Broadly speaking, they need to make sense of the "world of the work" in which they find themselves, and from the first page seek information about the community, its customs, beliefs, and values.

UNDERSTANDING THE "WORLD OF THE WORK"

Using a profusion of details, some of which may at first strike you as trivial and unnecessary, authors often present a full-blown portrait of a society to their readers.

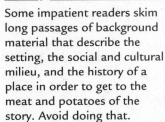

TIP

Some impatient readers skim long passages of background material that describe the setting, the social and cultural milieu, and the history of a place in order to get to the meat and potatoes of the story. Avoid doing that.

In *War and Peace*, Tolstoy, never one to skimp on words, piles facts on facts and details on details to help readers understand what it meant to be a Russian noble at the time of Napoleon's ill-fated attempt to conquer Russia in the early 1800s. Likewise, James Baldwin in *Go Tell It on the Mountain* creates a kaleidoscope of life in Harlem of the 1930s. The tale of 14-year-old John Grimes illustrates the conseqences of racial bigotry and poverty. It reveals the long-lasting and debilitating effects of slavery and the disappointments and frustrations of Southern blacks transplanted to a Northern slum. Most of all, it shows the people's dependence on both the Bible and the evangelical church to provide comfort and to give meaning to an existence that would otherwise be utterly bleak. And William Faulkner, in his fourteen Yoknapatawpha novels and many stories, creates a fictional county in northern Mississippi with a long social history, a culture, and a population of 6,298 whites and 9,313 blacks.

Some novels won't let you escape the social setting. What would *Pride and Prejudice* be if you ignored the social customs that govern the behavior of the Bennet family and their circle of friends and relatives? In some novels such as Virginia Woolf's *Mrs. Dalloway*, the social setting *is* the book. We are shown a segment of 1920s London society through the eyes of the title character as she prepares for a party that she will host that evening. Mrs. D's thoughts during the day and the gathering itself capture the entire lives of several middle-aged characters, most of whom have outlived the possibilities of their youth. The lively, glittering party portrays a social reality poised on the brink of its own demise. As we are drawn to the bittersweet quality of the people who fill the room, we also cringe at their capacity for shallowness and insensitivity.

Because surroundings profoundly influence the thoughts, emotions, and actions of the characters, a place can be as significant to a story as any of the people in it. If you accustom yourself to carefully reading the descriptions of setting and other background matters, your experience with the book will be that much richer, and you will soon grow aware of the reasons for the selection of details.

As you read a work of literature and become involved in its world, you can hardly avoid making judgments about it. When you enter the world of Franz Kafka's *The Castle*, for example, you are suddenly transported to a weirdly illogical place where the individual struggles against elusive and anonymous powers. As someone accustomed to a degree of freedom and autonomy, you are likely to be repelled by the world Kafka has created. Yet, you read on because the story of "K," the novel's protagonist, resonates with you and perhaps causes you to reflect on the pathos of a place where human isolation is the norm and an individual's quest for freedom and responsibility never succeeds. Certainly you wouldn't choose to live in a world such as Kafka's. In fact, you couldn't even if you wanted to. His world doesn't exist except in the pages of his novel, but in spite of knowing that fact, readers suspend their disbelief, even their rationality at times, and go along with the illusion. Thus, the worlds of Oedipus's Thebes, Hamlet's Elsinore,

Worth Knowing

In a story, the setting can be as significant as a character.

Ethan Frome's Starkfield, and Madame Bovary's Rouen seem as real to readers as their own home towns—more real, perhaps, because the folks next door, not to mention members of your own family, can be forever strangers.

The conclusions that readers draw about the world of the work usually are the most enduring. Readers may soon forget the names of characters, subplots, elements of form and structure, and twists and turns of the story. What remains in memory is that which gives a piece of literature its general identity. Thus, the world of Hemingway's *The Sun Also Rises* is the American expatriate subculture drifting through Europe after World War I. The world of Dickens's *A Tale of Two Cities* is London and Paris during the time of the French Revolution and the Reign of Terror. Flaubert's *Madame Bovary* is a stark and scathing portrait of nineteenth-century France.

MINI-WORKOUT ON SETTING

Instructions: Choose two works of literature you've read recently in which the setting plays a significant part. For each novel, list ways in which the setting contributes to its meaning or effect.

A: _____

_____

_____

_____

_____

_____

B: _____

_____

_____

_____

_____

_____

Character

What attracts most readers to a story, novel, or play is usually its cast of characters. After all, literature is about people, and in literature you meet such interesting and unusual types, from monsters to heroes, from losers to people you'd die to know in real life. Unless you are a self-centered, antisocial, reclusive egomaniac, you probably have an abiding curiosity about other people—how they live, what they think, and most of all, what they are like. That may explain why so much of one's daily conversation and thinking is about other people, and also why character analysis is often thought to be the most agreeable aspect of literary criticism.

RESPONDING TO CHARACTERS

Reminder

Fictional settings can be as real as your own home town.

In books, characters' innermost lives are often revealed as they rarely are in life. You are privy to others' desires and dreams and to secrets that would be virtually impossible to know if the character actually existed. In *Moby Dick*, for instance, you learn in the very first paragraph that Ishmael is subject to bouts of depression, that he follows funerals, pauses in front of coffin warehouses, and has a hard time resisting the urge to knock people's hats off. You learn too that "whenever it is a damp, drizzly November" in Ishmael's soul, he casts off his anger and spleen by going to the ocean and boarding a ship to see "the watery part of the world." Were Ishmael a fellow you just met on a bus, how long would it take to learn so many intimate facts about him?

At the start of *Crime and Punishment*, you learn that the protagonist, Raskolnikov, is a "crushingly poor" student, that he is frightened by his landlady, to whom he owes money, and that he's got murder on his mind. In fact, when you meet him, he's going out to rehearse the murder he soon expects to commit. Because would-be killers usually don't advertise their intentions, you know something about Raskolnikov that would never be revealed to you in real life.

TIP

In literature, characters' private thoughts are revealed as they rarely are in life.

On the other hand, in a work of literature not everything about a character is presented. You see only that portion of a person the author chooses to show. This is necessary because people are multidimensional, and there are countless elements of a character's behavior, speech, emotional life, and personality that don't fit the author's purpose. To include what Romeo liked to eat for breakfast or how often Richard III took a bath might thrill a gossip-hound but would only befuddle Shakespeare's aims. Even though you see only part of a character, selected elements can provide a reasonably accurate picture of the whole person. Thus, you can easily speculate that, given the choice of staying home and reading a book on Friday night or going bowling with the gang, a character like Elizabeth Bennet in *Pride and Prejudice* would sit in the parlor and read, while Randall McMurphy in *One Flew Over the Cuckoo's Nest* would end up at Bowl-o-Rama.

Because they have been shaped by the customs, beliefs, and values of their time and place, characters in books shed light on the world of the work and may reveal aspects of their society that might otherwise remain hidden. For example, Macbeth first resists murdering the king because Duncan is his overnight guest at Inverness. Macbeth's thoughts reveal the sanctity of the relationship between a monarch and his subjects as well as his particular responsibility to keep his guests safe from harm.

Knowing that by murdering Duncan, Macbeth violates a "double trust," you can more fully understand why guilt drives him to ruin later in the play. In *A Tale of Two Cities*, the actions of memorable Madame Defarge embody the anger and resentment of the French lower classes against the aristocracy at the time of the Revolution. In Richard Wright's novel, *Native Son*, Bigger Thomas, for all practical purposes, represents the victimization of blacks in America during the 1950s. Such characters, while having distinctive and discrete personalities, also represent their time and place.

In any work of literature, you are likely to meet an assortment of minor characters who show up once or twice in a play or novel, help to move the story along, or add a bit of local color to the world of the work. They are not throwaway characters. Pay attention to them, especially when they touch the lives of the main cast of characters. In Steinbeck's *The Grapes of Wrath*, the Joad family, en route to California, meets scores of minor characters, among them a one-eyed junk dealer, portrayed as a pathetic and defeated loser whose chief joy in life is to feel sorry for himself. Why give the man more than a glance? On the surface, he is just another hapless victim of the Depression and Dust Bowl of the 1930s. His presence in the book, however, serves another function: to contrast vividly with Tom Joad, whose troubles are no less burdensome than the junk dealer's. Yet Tom won't be defeated. He endures, and when you consider how easy it was succumb to self-pity, Tom's fortitude is all the more impressive.

Fully comprehending literary characters takes time and vision. Examine not only their individual personalities but their relationships with one another and their behavior in response to the demands of the community. Like a detective, seek motives for their actions. Ask how they see themselves and how they are seen by others, and try to determine how the narrator or author wishes you to see them.

In general, look for information about characters in three main places.

1. **What the author or narrator tells you.** What you learn about a character is determined, of course, by what the author wishes to tell you. Thus, the author wields great power in influencing your attitude toward a character. In *Crime and Punishment*, Dostoevsky describes the old pawnbroker this way: "She was a tiny dried-up scrap of a creature, about sixty years old, with sharp, malicious little eyes and a small sharp nose. . . Her fair hair, just beginning to go grey, was thick with grease. A strip of flannel was twisted round her long thin neck, which was wrinkled and yellow like a hen's legs . . . ." Perhaps you'll agree that Dostoevsky was trying to stack the cards against the old lady. He seems to want the reader to feel repulsed by her appearance, just as Raskolnikov is, and to feel, as Raskolnikov and others do, that her death will be no great loss to society. Descriptions such as that of the pawnbroker not only help to define characters but sometimes provide clues to the author's overall purpose. In part, *Crime and Punishment* attacks the nihilists of mid-nineteenth-century Russia, who rejected all traditional moral values. To Dostoevsky, a nihilist had no right to take another's life, even if the victim were a wretched old hag.

2. **What other characters say.** When information comes from other characters, you must be more circumspect and be prepared to read between the lines. Don't accept the information at face value, not at the outset, at least. Like people in real life, characters in literature have hidden motives, vested interests, propensities to distort the truth or to exaggerate—all qualities that keep them from describing others with complete accuracy and objectivity. After you're familiar with an informant's background and personality, you'll then be in a somewhat better position to judge the validity of the information given to you. Better still, try to define the relationship between the speaker and the character about whom he or she is talking, as well as the dynamics between speaker and listener. Each relationship may subtly alter what the speaker says. When, for instance, Mr. Collins in *Pride and Prejudice* first describes his patroness, Lady Catherine de Bourgh, in a letter to the Bennets, you might believe that the lady has a kind heart. After meeting Mr. Collins in person, however, and hearing from Jane Austen that he is "not a sensible man," but rather a "mixture of pride and obsequiousness, self-importance and humility," your preconception of Lady Catherine's bounty must be cast aside. Why does Mr. Collins present Lady Catherine as an exalted figure when, in fact, she is a rancorous shrew? In the answer lies a clue to Mr. Collins's personality and values. Consider also the works of Joseph Conrad. Does Marlow's view of Jim in *Lord Jim* and of Kurtz in *Heart of Darkness* coincide with the actual characters? Or is Marlow's vision slightly blurry? If Marlow is not seeing Jim and Kurtz clearly, why not?

3. **What characters say and how they act.** The words and actions of characters are probably the surest indicators of who they truly are. Nevertheless, proceed cautiously in making definitive character analyses because fictional people, like those in real life, often lie, put on airs, wear masks, and disguise their true nature in countless other ways. Stories told in first person can be particularly deceptive because narrators will often select very carefully what to reveal about themselves. At the beginning, any judgments you make should be extremely tentative. Through much of *Huckleberry Finn*, Huck, the narrator, calls himself "ornery" and "low down." In other words, he doesn't think much of himself because no one has ever thought much of him. By the end of the book, though, you realize that Huck has many admirable qualities—basic kindness, loyalty, love of life, and a well-tuned sense of right and wrong. In short, don't be swayed by everything that characters say about themselves. Only after reading the last page should you feel reasonably sure that you fully grasp what makes a character tick.

    Whether the old observation that "actions speak louder than words" applies to analysis of characters in literature is a question worth pondering. Do actions or do words provide more helpful clues? Hamlet has customarily been seen as confused and contemplative. In soliloquies and speeches, he grieves at his own inability to act decisively. Yet, as the play goes on, Hamlet adopts an "antic disposition," writes some lines for the traveling players, kills Polonius, plots against Rosencrantz and Guildenstern, fights Laertes, and more. He may be more of a man of action than he claims to be.

> **Reminder**
>
> Don't believe everything that characters say about themselves.

The Narrator

When analyzing a character it is equally important to take into account who is telling the story. The narrator or speaker will deeply affect your perceptions. In the short story by Willa Cather, "Paul's Case," Paul, a troublesome teenager, is someone people loved to hate. Had the tale of his adventures been told from his own viewpoint, however, he might have explained and justified his delinquent behavior, causing you to judge him less harshly. But had his bitterly disappointed father told the story, Paul would probably lack a single redeeming trait. Since Cather assumes the role of omniscient narrator, you get all the facts about Paul but no cues as to the way you should feel about the facts. Therefore, your attitude toward Paul is likely to fall somewhere between scorn and pity.

The Antagonist and Protagonist

Of all the characters in a play, novel or story, those that require the most careful scrutiny are the protagonist and the antagonist. The protagonist particularly deserves your attention because that person very often bears messages from the author. Consider such characters as King Lear, Elizabeth Bennet (*Pride and Prejudice*), and Lieutenant Frederic Henry (*A Farewell to Arms*). Lear's division of his kingdom unleashes the forces that lead ultimately to the catastrophic ending of the play. Shakespeare uses Lear to show the consequences of upsetting the natural order that Elizabethans held dear. Through Elizabeth Bennet, Jane Austen comments on issues of marriage and the burdens borne by single women in the polite society of her time, and Lieutenant Henry's life and experience vividly illustrate the loss of innocence and the disillusionment that Hemingway means to convey in his story of love and death in World War I.

Usually it's quite clear who the protagonist is in a work of fiction. Occasionally, however, especially when the conflict pits two equally "good" forces against each other, or when two appealing personalities clash, it is not so easy. Generally a case can be made for either character. Is it Phaedra or Hippolytus who is the protagonist of Euripides' *Hippolytus*? Is it Antigone or Creon who is the protagonist of Sophocles' *Antigone*? Who is the protagonist of Conrad's *Heart of Darkness*? Is it Marlow, the narrator, who receives from Kurtz's experience a revelation of the potential for evil in man? Or is it Kurtz, who is destroyed by the consequences of living in the tropics and acquiring supreme power over the natives of the region?

Identifying the true protagonist is not necessarily a critical issue, but it often forces you to think deeply about the characters, events, and themes in a work of literature. In that sense, it is a valuable exercise in literary analysis. Similarly, the identity of the antagonist, the force that opposes the protagonist, is worth pondering. Antagonists range from individual adversaries, who for various reasons seek to thwart the protagonist, to inner psychological demons that threaten or even destroy him. Consider Akaky Akakievich, the protagonist of Gogol's "The Overcoat." He falls prey to his associates at work, to the Russian bureaucracy, to the frigid St. Petersburg winter, and to the muggers who steal the coat. All seem to conspire to defeat Akaky, but he is really brought down by an internal nemesis, his inability to cope with the slings and arrows of workaday life. The protagonist of Eugene O'Neill's play The *Emperor Jones* is pursued through the jungle by rebel tribesmen who seek to dethrone him, but it

 TIP

Conflict between or within characters often reveals the essential meaning of a work.

remains unclear whether he is finally subdued by the hunters or by the accumulated horrors of his life that appear in his mind's eye as he tries to avoid capture. Hamlet must overcome the thinking that "puzzles the will" before he can move to avenge the murder of his father. Othello falls prey to jealousy, the "green-eyed monster." In both *Hamlet* and *Othello*, the protagonists face physical adversaries (Claudius, among others, and Iago), but the main sources of their tragedies lie within themselves.

In many works, protagonists encounter forces that are other than human. Nature and God can also deal a cruel hand. The central conflicts in Ole Rolvaag's *Giants in the Earth*, Willa Cather's *My Antonia*, and Pearl Buck's *The Good Earth* find humans struggling against nature. Per Hansa, the Shimerda family, and Wang Lung face unrelenting hardships while scraping a living from the land or trying to survive in the face of nature's freakish, seemingly antagonistic, behavior. Opposition from the gods often comes in the form of fate that, for good or ill, determines human destiny. In the works of Thomas Hardy, fate invariably shapes the lives of the characters. Tess, the protagonist of *Tess of the d'Urbervilles*, no matter how hard she tries to pick herself up from despair experiences one setback after another. Her destiny is to suffer and die. Fate plays a crucial role in classical Greek drama. Oedipus, Antigone, Agamemnon, Clytemnestra, and Orestes cannot avert the disasters that the oracles decree for them. Like Hamlet, Othello, and King Lear, they also suffer from a personal flaw that to a large extent contributes to their fate.

Themes

Economic, social, and political forces also serve as the grist of literature. How people cope with poverty and hunger, oppression and greed, is the theme of works like John Steinbeck's *The Grapes of Wrath*, Emile Zola's *Germinal*, and Upton Sinclair's *The Jungle*. How people of color respond to prejudice and alienation is dealt with in novels like Ralph Ellison's *Invisible Man*, Toni Morrison's *Beloved*, and David Guterson's *Snow Falling on Cedars*. The laws and institutions that a society establishes to maintain order sometimes produce injustice that overwhelms innocent members of the society. Such situations occur in John Galsworthy's *Justice*, Victor Hugo's *Les Miserables*, and Theodore Dreiser's *An American Tragedy*. Frequently also, idealists—those who see flaws in society and try to fix them—run headlong into the opposition of vested interests who want to preserve the status quo. Such confrontations are the stuff of Henrik Ibsen's *An Enemy of the People*, George Bernard Shaw's *Saint Joan*, and Ernest Hemingway's *For Whom the Bell Tolls*.

Worth Knowing
The struggle between the protagonist and the antagonist keeps readers turning pages.

In the end, the crux of a work of literature, and the very reason you are apt to keep reading, is the struggle between the protagonist and the antagonist. A story ends in either victory or defeat, but it could just as well end in a stalemate. Victory leads most often to a happy ending, defeat to a tragic one, although many works end ambiguously by balancing a bit of both. With the human condition being so subtle and the human personality so complex, it is not surprising that what sometimes appears as disaster may be a triumph, particularly when an assertion of moral force accompanies the fall or when the protagonist's collapse is accompanied by the promise of a resurrection of good. As *Wuthering Heights* draws to a close, for instance, Heathcliff's fury is spent.

Heathcliff joins his beloved Catherine in death, and the tempests subside. Young Catherine and Hareton now can find tranquility in a world cleansed of the passionate extremes of love and hate. Oedipus blinds himself after he discovers the truth about the murder of Laius. The act, however, restores clarity to his vision of himself. Yes, he was wronged by the casual and wanton actions of the gods, but he sees clearly that his quest for power and his arrogance have caused his downfall. He paid the price of thinking that he was an equal of the gods. In disaster he finds the peace that had eluded him throughout his life.

MINI-WORKOUT ON CHARACTER

Part 1

Instructions: For two works of literature you have read recently, identify the protagonist and the antagonist. Describe the nature of their conflict, how it affects their behavior, and what its resolution, if any, contributes to the overall meaning of the book.

A: _____

_____

_____

_____

_____

B: _____

_____

_____

_____

_____

Part 2

Instructions: Choose a memorable character of a novel or play you've read recently and analyze the techniques used by the author to present that character to the reader.

_____

_____

_____

_____

_____

Narrative Voice or Point of View

Every piece of literature has a narrator or speaker. In non-fiction, it is the author's voice you hear. But in fiction and poetry the identity of the narrator may not be so apparent. It takes practice to examine the language and imagery, the characters and conflicts, the themes and plots—virtually every aspect of a literary work—to discover whether the narrator or speaker is the author, someone assigned to speak for the author, or an invented voice whose beliefs and values differ from the author's.

HEARING THE VOICE OF THE AUTHOR

Gustave Flaubert uses *Madame Bovary*, in part, to express his disapproval of the treatment of women in France in the 1850s. Moreover, the novel's focus on Emma's inner life—her memories, dreams, and fantasies—might very well reflect Flaubert's own obsessions with love, sexuality, and art. Because straight-laced Germans of the early 1900s spurned romantic writers, Herman Hesse wrote the novel *Steppenwolf* to tell the reading public of his displeasure about how artists and intellectuals felt ostracized. Some critics consider *The Grapes of Wrath* a piece of literary propaganda that Steinbeck wrote to espouse his socialist views. *Women in Love* by D. H. Lawrence has a pervasive note of gloom that undoubtedly reflects the author's response to World War I. Novels like *Johnny Got His Gun* by Dalton Trumbo and *All Quiet on the Western Front* by Erich Maria Remarque are statements that passionately convey their authors' antiwar positions.

FIRST-PERSON NARRATION

When a story is told in first person, the narrator may or may not represent the author's views. The narrator in "Family Happiness," a story by Tolstoy, is Masha, an innocent young woman from the country who falls in love with and marries an older man. Masha is swept up by the social whirl when her new husband introduces her to big city life. In every way, she's a world apart from Tolstoy himself, who was well over fifty and firmly entrenched in his country estate when he wrote the story. In *Wuthering Heights*, several narrators, including Lockwood, Catherine, Ellen Dean, Heathcliff, and Isabella, tell the story. None of them speaks for Emily Brontë, the author. Nick Carraway narrates *The Great Gatsby*, but he is not F. Scott Fitzgerald, although they both came from Minnesota and attended Ivy League colleges. (If anything, Jay Gatsby is more like Fitzgerald.) Similarly, David Copperfield is not Charles Dickens, nor is Ishmael Herman Melville in *Moby Dick*, although some parallels exist between the lives of the characters and the lives of the authors. Poetry offers the same kinds of ambiguities as prose fiction. Shakespeare's sonnets are assumed to express the poet's love for the so-called dark lady, but you can't be sure. The poems of the romantics (Wordsworth, Keats, Shelley, and Coleridge) seem also to have been written straight from the heart, but there are exceptions. One certainty, however, is that in dramatic monologues, such as "My Last Duchess" by Robert Browning, the speaker is always someone other than the poet. In drama, except when a playwright deliberately uses a narrator, as in *Our Town* and *A Man for All Seasons*, there seems to be no omniscient narrator, although one or more characters in a play may very well represent and express the author's views.

Reminder

A first-person narrator may or may not represent the author's views.

THIRD-PERSON NARRATION

Third-person narrators are sometimes trickier to pin down, for authors often invent voices completely different from their own. The narrator may be the author, but often is not, and there is a danger of misinterpretation in ascribing to the author the views and attitudes of the narrator. Would it be fair to say that the author of *Studs Lonigan*, James T. Farrell, is anti-Catholic or anti-Irish because he presents a critical portrait of Irish-Catholic life in Chicago? Is Philip Roth of *Goodbye, Columbus* fame antisemitic because so many of the Jewish characters in his novels behave badly? Are James Joyce's views of Catholicism in *A Portrait of the Artist as a Young Man* the same as those of his protagonist Stephen Dedalus? Contrary to what many readers think, Jonathan Swift, the author of *Gulliver's Travels*, did not accept entirely the beliefs by which the Houyhnhnms governed their lives. Nor did Voltaire, who wrote *Candide*, find perfection and the answer to the ills of mankind in the values of El Dorado.

OMNISCIENT NARRATION

Omniscient narrators complicate the task even more because they move in and out of characters' minds, know everything about everybody and may even pause occasionally to editorialize on the story. In order to thoughtfully judge the psychological and social connection between authors and narrators, study carefully the manner in which narrators tell the story and the range and completeness of their knowledge of characters and events. Do they know all about the characters' lives and background? Who is their source? Do they know what characters are thinking and dreaming? Are they privy to confidential information? Is the narrator a character in the story or just an observer? Answers to such questions help to unravel the tone of a story. Edith Wharton's *Ethan Frome* is narrated by a young man who hears the story from Ethan himself twenty-four years after the events occurred. Since memory is highly selective, readers should not unquestioningly accept everything in the account of Ethan's love affair with Mattie Silver as the absolute truth. Similarly, because *First Love* by Ivan Turgenev is a story of sixteen-year-old Vladimir's first brush with love told by Vladimir in middle age, distortions and half-truths are bound to occur.

MINI-WORKOUT ON NARRATIVE VOICE

Instructions: Choose a novel or play you've read recently and analyze how the story is told. From whose point of view is the story told? Does the narrator play a part in the telling of the story? What evidence, if any, exists to suggest that the narrator expresses views that reflect or are different from those of the author or playwright?

_____

_____

_____

_____

_____

Structure

Although it is often said that literature imitates life, it doesn't. Authors select experiences from the vast context of life and redesign them to suit their purposes. They abstract life and give it a form and a semblance of order rarely found in the chaotic universe in which we lead our lives. The result is often a unified and coherent literary work. All its parts—the world of the work, the action, the characters, the theme, the language, the imagery—combine to produce a pleasing artistic structure.

RESPONDING TO THE ART OF LITERATURE

As a student of literature, you should know how individual elements work together to create a sense of unity in a novel, story or play. If you focus on only one element (the characters, for example), you'd find yourself in the position of the blind man and the elephant, using only a small piece of evidence to generalize about the whole thing. How organic unity is achieved isn't always easy to pin down. Yet you know it when you see it and miss it when it's absent. No one says, "Okay, I'm going to read this book for its organic unity." Rather, a reader's intuition or sense of harmony and balance will serve as a guide. You know that neon lights don't belong in a cathedral, nor a rumble seat on a sleek new Porsche. Likewise, an incongruous turn of events, trite ideas, senseless sequences, a character's inconsistent or impossible behavior, figurative language that seems forced, snatches of dialogue that are stylized and artificial, as well as many other writing sins tend to tear organic unity apart.

Unity

Unity is achieved partly through the structure of a work. For instance, a sonnet usually consists of two parts. The first part, the octave, develops a question, a story, or an idea. The second section, the sestet, offers an answer, a comment, or a proposition. If either part were missing or out of sync with the other, the coherence and unity of the piece would be lost. Similarly, plays are often constructed like a pyramid, the moment of their greatest tension at the apex. A play with a too early climax would flop. Because novels are often long and far-ranging, discovering their structure takes time and practice.

One simply structured work is Conrad's "The Secret Sharer." Like its style of writing, the tale is straightforward, with no shifts in time and space. The story's structure consists simply of a character's movement from ignorance to knowledge. By the end of the story, the young captain knows himself more thoroughly. As a consequence, he is a better leader than he was at the start. You'll find a more complex structure in *The Great Gatsby*. Fitzgerald begins the story in the present, using the first three chapters to describe the novel's four main locales: Daisy's house, the valley of ashes, New York City, and Gatsby's house. The plot of the novel is developed in the next several chapters. Only toward the middle of the book, when he is pretty sure that the reader will be curious about the enigmatic Gatsby, does Fitzgerald begin to tell the story of Gatsby's past. In the climactic last chapter, the past and the present come together. This design seems to suit the novel perfectly because Fitzgerald reveals information as Nick Carraway acquires it, in bits and pieces over a period of time. As the story nears its climax, the reader learns more and more about Gatsby so that by the end, Gatsby's motivation and behavior are thoroughly understandable. The technique that Fitzgerald employs—first-person narrative combined with gradual revelation of the past—works well and endows the novel with unity and coherence.

The unifying structure of Joyce's *A Portrait of the Artist as a Young Man* invites several interpretations, the simplest being that each of the book's five chapters represents a stage in Stephen Dedalus's growth from childhood to maturity. The book has also been thought to have a three-part structure that reflects the three phases of Stephen's increasing self-awareness. An alternate view is that the book is structured as a series of rhythmic waves. Each chapter moves from a trough of Stephen's self-doubt to a peak of triumph. Since the action rises slowly, only to fall at the start of the next chapter, the pattern has also been likened to the myth of Daedalus, Stephen's mythic namesake. Each chapter recounts Stephen's attempt to break away, and at each chapter's end, he breaks another link in the chain that binds him to his

Reminder

Individual elements work together to create unity in a novel or play.

roots. Finally, at the book's climax, Stephen leaves for good. Whether he will succeed in the world like Daedalus or fall like Icarus remains unclear.

MINI-WORKOUT ON STRUCTURE

Instructions: Examine a novel or play you know well and describe its structure or shape. In what ways, if any, does the structure contribute to the work's themes, characters, or overall meaning?

_____

_____

_____

_____

_____

Storytelling Techniques

Because there are innumerable ways to tell a tale, no one method is superior to another. What counts is whether the manner of storytelling fits the point and purpose of the story being told. The most elementary way, of course, is chronological. What happens first is told first, what happens next is told next, and so on. Children's stories are usually told chronologically, as are picaresque novels like Cervantes's *Don Quixote* and Henry Fielding's *Tom Jones*, in which a central character undergoes numerous adventures, one after another. Most chronological works include references to the past, often to give readers background to comprehend what comes next. For example, Homer's *The Odyssey* begins with Telemachus's decision to journey forth to seek news of his absentee father. Why the young man undertakes the search is not made clear until Homer goes back in time to tell the story of Odysseus's adventures after the Trojan War. In almost all of Shakespeare's plays, as well as in dramas by Ibsen and others, early dialogue informs the audience of the events that occurred before the curtain rose.

A backward look can also provide a window into a character. When Billy Budd, the title character of Melville's story, is impressed into His Majesty's navy, the captain of Billy's ship explains to the British lieutenant (and to the reader) that Billy is no ordinary sailor. He's "the best man . . . the jewel of 'em," the crewmember whose presence turned the ship from a "rat-pit of quarrels" to a place of peace and good will. This description accounts for Billy's subsequent actions and makes his tragic fate all the more poignant. Then, too, Jay Gatsby is a more intriguing char-

Reminder

The manner of storytelling must fit the point and purpose of the work.

acter because we are told that long ago he may have been not only a crook, a boot-legger, and a companion of criminals, but also a German spy and a killer. Similarly, in *Candide*, characters frequently stop to relate tales of their past misfortunes. Still other stories, such as Melville's "Bartleby the Scrivener" and Turgenev's "First Love," begin with a narrator in the present recalling events of long ago, another popular storytelling device.

Different Voices

Conrad's *Lord Jim*, Faulkner's *As I Lay Dying*, and Toni Morrison's *Beloved* use another narrative technique for relating the story. Events are recounted by multiple voices that move forward and backward in time. Because the voices change repeatedly, we are told of the same events again and again, but each time from a different perspective. In *Beloved*, for example, we hear of Paul D's arrival in Cincinnati related first from Denver's point of view, then later by Sethe and then by Paul D. Some readers react negatively to this kind of storytelling, claiming that it's too repetitious and confusing, or that the author's virtuosity as an artist seems to overshadow the point of the book itself. To a point, such responses may be valid. (Certainly they're valid for those readers.) On the other hand, life is often like a Gordion knot: disorderly, chaotic, and too complex to unravel easily, and in order to be faithful to reality, stories should not oversimplify human experience.

Connections to Real Life

Clearly, a piece of literature need not be realistic to reflect real life. Even the most improbable stories can mirror reality. Think of the fantastical occurrences in works by authors from Hawthorne to Hesse, the absurdist plays of Ionesco, Albee, and Becket, and the remarkable story by Nikolai Gogol, "The Nose," in which a man discovers one morning that his nose has vanished from his face, only to have it show up in the breakfast muffin of his barber, who lives across town. Literature is filled with unnatural events and supernatural beings. The story of Hamlet is launched by the appearance of a ghost, the setting of *Beloved* is haunted by the spirit of a dead child, and Gulliver for a time is taken prisoner by a horde of people no taller than his thumb. Does this mean that Shakespeare, Morrison, and Swift and their fellow authors have a distorted sense of reality? No, it means that they give expression to reality rather than recreate it. Having apprehended reality, authors transmute it and give it a shape and a clarity by focusing on meticulously selected elements that depict their vision sharply and truthfully. Artistic license permits authors to shuffle sequences, omit or enlarge happenings, change and combine characters, spin the world in any way they like.

But there are limits. Unless there is an artistic reason for doing so, they should not introduce implausible psychological distortions in human response or behavior. If an incident could not happen in any world, real or imagined, or if a character with a certain personality acts inconsistently, or if historical anomalies creep into the work (e.g., the use of jet planes in World War II) the author may well have betrayed the truth, misrepresented reality, and written a flawed work—but not always.

TIP

Many authors give expression to reality instead of re-creating it.

Before you can respond somewhat intelligently to a work of literature, therefore, it helps to be a little dry behind the ears, that is, to have tasted a little bit of life, either in person or vicariously. If you didn't know anything about individual freedom, for example, reading Kafka's *The Castle* would be a totally meaningless exercise, or if you had no understanding of religion, it would be pointless to read, say, *A Portrait of the Artist as a Young Man.* In other words, responses to books involve assessing how effectively authors have remolded the raw material of life into works of art. It takes a passion for real life to react passionately to the life in books. You can't be out to lunch and also appreciate good literature.

MINI-WORKOUT ON STORYTELLING

Instructions: Choose a novel or play you've read recently and analyze the sequence in which the story unfolds. If the sequence is other than chronological, how would you describe it? Does the sequence of events contribute to the work's themes or its overall meaning?

_____

_____

_____

_____

_____

Writing Style

The feature of a work of literature that you're apt to notice first is writing style. After a few paragraphs you'll know whether the language is poetic or plain, flowery or simple, lofty or down-to-earth, figurative or literal. Almost from the outset you can tell whether the narrator is humorous or serious, bitter or cheerful, proud or humble, hard-boiled or romantic. Sentence length and structure, word choice, figures of speech, allusions, use of dialogue—with all of these the author establishes a mood and tone. **More important than simply recognizing the components of a writer's style is determining whether the language is appropriate for the purpose of the work and assessing whether the language contributes to the work's impact on the reader.** These decisions cannot be made until you've read most of the work. Hemingway's distinctive style of writing is a case in point. You probably know that Hemingway wrote simple, spare, journalistic prose, full of sensory detail. In a way, his style resembles his characters—tough, terse, and not given to wearing emotions on their sleeves. Frederic Henry, the protagonist in *A Farewell to Arms,* distrusts abstract concepts like *patriotism* and *honor*. His wound in battle has nothing to do with bravery or glory. His leg hurts; that's all that matters. Hemingway's writing has a hard edge to it. Using short, concrete, tangible words and phrases (a glass of wine, hot bath, soft bed) rather than multisyllabic, abstract words, he captures the more-or-less macho personalities of men and women caught up in the conflicts of war, the bull ring, the sea, and the big game hunt.

James Joyce's style is a world away from Hemingway's. Using all the resources of the English language, Joyce sets a mood, creates a tone, and captures the essence of the characters. In *A Portrait of the Artist as a Young Man*, he portrays Stephen Dedalus and his world by taking liberties with language that might give an English teacher fits. He coins words, expands meanings, plays with rhythms and sounds, spells whimsically, ignores punctuation when it suits him, and pours his thoughts into streams of consciousness, apparently not giving a hoot whether the reader will understand or not. Much of the language is meant to suggest the confused state of young Stephen's emotions, the boy's inner turmoil. The style changes with Stephen's age, starting with the short, choppy sentences of a tot, and developing complexity as Stephen grows to manhood. In his inimitable way, Joyce integrates language with the meaning and purpose of his novel.

Dealing with Life's Unpleasantries

At some point you'll probably run into authors who employ a style at odds with the content of the work. For example, murder and suicide are pretty grim topics. Yet they can be given a light touch or written about in poetic language of great beauty. Likewise, violent and painful death can be described with the detachment of a scientist taking lab notes; and an everyday occurrence like spreading cream cheese on a bagel can be related in ornate, bombastic, grandiloquent words. Such oppositions between language and content or between style or form and content are called *tensions*, created for a humorous, satirical, or in some cases, a bitterly ironic effect. When Jonathan Swift, in "A Modest Proposal," advances the idea of eating babies to put an end to lower-class starvation, he uses a no-nonsense, objective style of writing. The contrast between the horror of his culinary idea and its cool, impersonal presentation makes the piece one of the most enduring satirical essays ever written. In his many stories and novels, Franz Kafka records bizarre and frightening experiences—for one, a man wakes up one morning to discover he's been turned into a cockroach—in simple, direct, deceptively innocent language. Alexander Pope's poem "The Rape of the Lock" focuses on an attractive young woman about to have a lock of hair snipped from her head. Written in the style of a grand epic worthy of Homer or Virgil, the piece is known aptly as a "mock" epic. By using inflated language, Pope has trivialized (i.e., mocked) the event.

> **Definition**
>
> Conflicts between style and content are called *tensions*.

Figurative Language

By definition, figurative language expresses ideas in other than their literal sense. Meaning derives from likenesses—not visual likenesses necessarily, but from those that represent reality on more than one level of reference at the same time. To take an obvious and mundane example, think of the American flag. On one level the flag is nothing but a piece of fabric. On a figurative level, though, it represents America and, depending on the observer, can mean almost anything. To a patriot, the flag is likely to stand for, or symbolize—among many other things—the values and principles of freedom and democracy. To an anti-American terrorist, it has the opposite effect; it represents a range of hateful evils.

Authors get lots of mileage by using symbol, metaphor, metonymy, allusion, simile, personification, and any number of other figures of speech. (See the Glossary of Literary and Rhetorical Terms, page 361, for definitions and some examples.) In poetry as well as prose, nothing enriches and broadens meaning like fresh and original figures of speech, and readers who are aware of them will be treated to understandings, appreciations, and delights beyond imagining.

A metaphor such as "All the world's a stage," for example, evokes the thought that our lives are fleeting dramas, that life from birth to death is a performance that succeeds or fails according to our skill as actors. The parallels can be extended much farther. By thinking of what it takes to mount a play from its birth to final curtain, and thinking then of what it takes to make a life, the power of Shakespeare's metaphor is bound to become obvious. Metonymy, the use of a closely related idea for the idea itself, is also a comparison. In the phrase "The pen is mightier than the sword," pen stands for the writer, sword for the warrior. The sentiment (that a writer wields more power with words than a warrior with arms) is conveyed vividly and is actually a living example of its meaning.

> **Reminder**
>
> Figures of speech enrich and broaden meaning.

Use of Metaphors

A modern work rooted in a biblical tale or in ancient Greek myth or drama can be viewed as a metaphor for its source. *East of Eden* by John Steinbeck, for one, is a modern adaptation of the story of Cain and his brother Abel. *The Grapes of Wrath* has numerous parallels to the Old Testament's account of the Israelites' search for the promised land. In reading modern literature, you can hardly go far without running into Christ-like figures, people who sacrifice themselves to save others from death or indignity, like Sonia in *Crime and Punishment*, McMurphy in *One Flew Over the Cuckoo's Nest*, and the hero of *The Informer* by Liam O'Flaherty. No doubt you can think of stories and novels in which a parent, acceding to a higher moral duty, gives up a child. Chances are those works are metaphors for the story of Abraham's obedience to God's command to sacrifice his son Isaac. If you have read tales of children defying their parents, it's likely that they are metaphorical adaptations of the parable of the prodigal son.

Greek myth and drama have also served as the source of modern works. A story in which a child slays a parent alludes metaphorically to Oedipus. Antigone's compulsion to bury her brother in defiance of the law serves as the basis for works in which family loyalty takes precedence over loyalty to the state. Much of Clytemnestra is to be found in such modern characters as Ibsen's Hedda Gabler. James Joyce's mammoth novel *Ulysses* is a latter-day transmutation of *The Odyssey*, in which the hero, instead of wandering around the waters and isles of the ancient Mediterranean, roams the streets and sites of modern Dublin.

Finally, consider the metonymic significance of certain literary characters; Arthur Miller's Willy Loman (*Death of a Salesman*) as the modern worker lost in changing economic times; Kafka's Joseph K. (*The Trial*) as the modern citizen lost in the bureaucratic maze; Beckett's Didi and Gogo (*Waiting for Godot*) as modern man lost in a meaningless existence.

MINI-WORKOUT ON FIGURATIVE LANGUAGE

Instructions: Pick up a novel or play you're familiar with and reread half a dozen pages chosen at random. Identify figurative language used in those pages. Name the figures of speech and analyze what they contribute to the meaning or effect of the particular scenes or events in which they appear. Consider whether they affect such matters as tone, theme, development of character, or the meaning of the work as a whole.

Novel: _____

_____

_____

_____

_____

Theme

Authors write novels and shorter works to inform, entertain, or enlighten readers. But the best of them also convey ideas they want to pass along to readers about the state of society, the plight of the world, or any aspect of the human condition they have on their minds. When Melville's *Moby Dick* was first published, critics dismissed it as a story about whaling. Over time, though, readers began to see that Melville's book had things to say beyond its "story." What seemed a realistic account of a whaling voyage was also an allegorical exploration of the conflict between man and his fate, the nature of good and evil, and the consequences of a man's obsession. In other words, underneath the story lay profound philosophical themes.

Because a theme is an *idea* that the author wants to explore and communicate, it should not be confused with the subject matter of the work. For example, the subject of Toni Morrison's *Beloved* is slavery, but its theme is what Morrison has to say about slavery. Even though the story is set in 1873, a decade after slavery was declared illegal in the United States, Morrison's premise is that time cannot separate former slaves from the horror of their experiences nor undo its effects. Sethe, the main character, in fact, wears permanent scars of slavery on her back, and she is perpetually deluged with nightmarish visions of Sweet Home, the plantation on which she had been enslaved.

Similarly, the subject of *War and Peace* is what the title indicates, but Tolstoy's themes reflect his thinking about how men find purpose in their lives. The nihilist Andrei, one of the primary characters, despairs of identifying a purpose until, ironically, he lies on his deathbed after suffering a wound in combat. Pierre, whose experiences on the field of battle and on the home front make up the bulk of the novel, is moved by an out-of-the-ordinary belief in life's possibilities. In the clash of life and death, he discovers reasons for carrying on. In fact, all the important characters in the novel are to some degree engaged in a quest for happiness and for the satisfaction of knowing that their days on earth will add up to something more than a shapeless gray blur.

Definition

A theme is an idea that the author wants to explore and communicate.

Themes vs. Morals

Generally, themes express big ideas, too sweeping and elusive to summarize in just a catch phrase or two. Attaching a label such as "man's inhumanity to man" or "the triumph of good over evil" may be a convenient way to identify a theme, but it usually fails to do justice to the author's vision. Besides, themes are often multidimensional, too complex to be readily pigeonholed.

That's one reason that a theme should not be confused with the *moral* of a story. A moral such as *Hard work pays off* is a platitude unambiguously conveyed, for example, by the famous fable of the ant and the grasshopper. Although a serious piece of literature may deal with issues of rectitude and virtue, by and large it isn't going to preach at you. Nor will it contain a theme quite so obvious and banal as that in Aesop's story. Knowing that art is a faithful mirror of what goes on in the human psyche and that human experience is too complex to be reduced to a Sunday-school maxim, good authors devise themes that reflect reality as they see it.

No thoughtful novelist would propose that a given generalization is always true; rather, it may be true only under certain conditions. For example, the sentiment that hard work pays off won't apply to a frail old man with a heart condition and a long driveway to shovel after a blizzard. In addition, themes are often ambiguous and subject to modification. Good is never totally good, nor evil totally evil. Even such personifications of depravity like Iago and Lady Macbeth have a redeeming quality or two. Because a theme won't apply to everyone at all times, it must be tempered to take into account the rich variation that makes up the world.

Authors rarely state their themes outright. Rather they communicate themes through plot, character, setting, point of view, symbols, language, and all other basic literary elements. A several-hundred page novel may contain scores of characters, descriptive passages, background material, and long chains of events, some more significant than others. Drawing a theme out of such a work takes practice, patience, and insight. It requires a knack for finding meaning under the surface of things, for weaving a single impression out of a series of diverse episodes, and conferring a sense of wholeness and integrity on what initially may seem fragmented and chaotic. Clues are there, but they must be found and interpreted.

A work of fiction is not a math problem for which there is only one correct answer. Different readers have different responses. Authors select and arrange material to express certain themes. Your interpretation may coincide with the

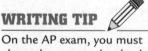

TIP

Some AP exam questions ask you to write about the interrelationship between theme and other aspects of a novel.

WRITING TIP

On the AP exam, you must always be prepared to back up your opinions with specific references to the plot, characters, language, setting, and so forth. If your interpretation of a novel is contradicted by details in the story, back off, reconsider, and change course.

author's intent or it may be far afield. Either way it is neither wrong nor right. Rather, because literary criticism isn't a free-for-all, the validity of your interpretation depends on the evidence that can be drawn from the text to support your views.

MINI-WORKOUT ON THEME

Instructions: Choose a novel or play you've read recently. Interpret the work for its major themes. For each theme you identify, note the evidence you can find to support your interpretation.

Major theme #1: _____

Evidence: _____

_____

_____

Major theme #2: _____

Evidence: _____

_____

_____

Major theme #3: _____

Evidence: _____

_____

_____

Canonical Literature vs. Popular Fiction

The presence of significant themes in literature—at least in the kind of literature usually studied in AP classes—separates so-called literary classics from escapist potboilers that keep readers entertained but have little enduring value. To be sure, the lines between "classic" and "pop," or "pulp," fiction, are not always apparent. But one distinct difference is that high-quality works offer readers ideas to think about while pop fiction ordinarily emphasizes plot above all else. People read novels by John Grisham and Tom Clancy, for instance, mainly to find out what happens. Does the hero win the girl? Who has sex with whom? How is the villain defeated?. . . and so on. These are all titillating questions, but they lack the power to lift readers out of themselves, stimulate readers' imagination, or provide anything resembling an intellectual or transcendent experience.

To be fair, some authors of pop fiction infuse themes into their works, but the themes are generally mundane, unambiguous, or both. Stephen King's novels and stories are known for recurring themes that pertain to frightening and malevolent forces abroad in the land. Although King introduces themes into his riveting plots, literary scholars refuse to take his work seriously. Why this is so raises questions about the nature of literature.

Truly, there is no litmus test to determine whether a work is "literary" or pulp. The literary canon (novels and plays deemed worthy of study in AP classes and elsewhere) is always in flux. Authors come and go based on many factors. Sinclair Lewis, author of *Main Street, Babbitt*, and many other novels, was awarded a Nobel Prize for Literature in 1930. Afterward, he fell from grace, but early in the twenty-first century enjoyed a partial rebirth in literary circles after a reappraisal of his work in a well-received biography by Richard R. Lingeman. For decades, *The Awakening* by Kate Chopin was regarded as a pop novel. With the advent of feminism in the 1960s, however, it was rediscovered and made part of the canon.

Writing About Selected Novels

The novel you choose to write about in response to the third essay question on the exam will depend mostly on the nature of the question. But many novels read widely in AP English classes offer material that would be excellent for many different topics.

ANALYSES OF SELECTED NOVELS

In the next section of this book you will find discussions of several novels often studied in AP English classes. All of the titles, representing a cross section of works from the literary canon, are suitable for the free-response essay (Question #3) that you must write on the exam.

Pride and Prejudice by Jane Austen

Pride and Prejudice is one of the most popular works read in AP English classes. What makes it endure is not its humorous portrait of an obsolete society, although it unquestionably contains much to make readers laugh out loud. Rather, the book lives on because Austen's subject is basic to human experience. Yes, the process of courtship and marriage has changed since the early 1800s, but the emotions surrounding the search for a partner and falling in love remain the same.

Most of the novel takes place in Hertfordshire, an area of small villages and large estates outside of London. It tells the story of the Bennets, a family with a problem. Because Mr. and Mrs. Bennet have five daughters and no sons, their estate, Longbourn, is "entailed," which means that, upon Mr. Bennet's death, Longbourn will be inherited by his closest male relative, a distant cousin. Therefore, it's crucial for the daughters, whose ages range from sixteen to twenty-three, to find good, preferably wealthy, husbands. How some of the Bennet girls go hunting for a mate is the subject of the novel.

Pride and Prejudice is applicable to any number of essay questions, including those relating to 1) family conflict, 2) social stratification, 3) the conflict between reason and passion, 4) the hazards of first impressions, and 5) the dimensions of satire.

You might also base an essay on the following topic, given on a previous AP exam:

Choose a novel that includes a wedding, funeral, party, or other social event. Show how the event contributes to the meaning of the work as a whole.

Crime and Punishment by Fyodor Dostoevsky

Written in the mid-1860s, *Crime and Punishment* is a murder story, but not a *who-dunit*. Rather, it is a psychological account of a crime. Decades before Freud and other analysts of the human psyche, Dostoevsky studied the depths of the criminal mind and in doing so raised big moral and social questions about values, fate, and the human condition, all ageless issues for readers to ponder and, as luck would have it, to write about on AP English exams.

Use *Crime and Punishment* as the subject for an essay on 1) a character in conflict with himself, 2) fate vs. free will, 3) the effects of poverty, 4) sin and redemption, 5) the power of dreams, 6) man's depravity, 7) moral ambiguities, and many other topics, including this one paraphrased from a previous AP exam:

Write an essay about a novel that ends with some kind of "spiritual reassessment or moral reconciliation." Identify the reassessment or reconciliation, and explain its significance to the work as a whole.

A Portrait of the Artist as a Young Man by James Joyce

Neither all fact nor all fiction, *A Portrait of the Artist* fuses the two. In recounting his first twenty years, James Joyce calls himself Stephen Dedalus and chronicles the emotional and intellectual adventures that shaped his personality and molded his values. The novel—although it's also an autobiography—details the social milieu and psychological factors that drove the young protagonist, a sensitive and thoughtful boy, to look inward, to turn away from his family and church, and ultimately to leave Ireland to become a writer.

You should find *A Portrait of the Artist as a Young Man* applicable for an essay on any of the following: 1) psychological realism, 2) a misunderstood rebel, 3) the power of religion, 4) father-son relationships, and 5) a young man's sexuality.
   Or try this topic from a previous AP exam:

Write an essay about a novel that contains a character who is alienated from a culture or society because of gender, race, class, or creed. Show how that character's alienation reveals the values and assumptions of that culture or society.

Their Eyes Were Watching God by Zora Neale Hurston

Black culture pervades the story of *Their Eyes Were Watching God*. It shapes the characters, provides the setting, plots the events, and determines the language in the novel. But unlike many other mid-twentieth-century black authors, Zora Neale Hurston never intended to use her art as a form of social protest. She says more about the reality of black women's lives than about the problems of racial prejudice. Her book, in essence, recounts the quest of Janie Crawford to find a voice and create a meaningful life—a theme that transcends time, place, race, and gender.

Use *Their Eyes Were Watching God* as the subject for an essay on 1) a hero's search for identity, 2) gender roles, 3) the influence of nature on men's lives, 4) the effects of prejudice, 5) the power of words, and 6) a protagonist at odds with the established culture.

Hurston's book would also be a good choice for writing a response to the following question from a previous AP exam:

Write an essay on a novel that contains the investigation of a crime and the trial of the accused. Show how these events contribute to the development of a character, a theme, or to the meaning of the work as a whole.

Invisible Man by Ralph Ellison

Invisible Man tells the story of a young black man's struggle to find his identity in mid-twentieth-century America. Published during the heyday of racial segregation, the novel documents some of the effects of discrimination during the 1940s. The race riot near the end of the book is based on events in Harlem in 1943. It also anticipates the turmoil that rocked many American cities during the Civil Rights movement in the late 1950s and the 1960s.

Use *Invisible Man* as the subject for an essay on 1) a character alienated from society, 2) a character's loss of innocence, 3) a character torn between conflicting forces, 4) the influence of an absent character on the protagonist, and 5) the significance of a particular social event on the meaning of the work.

An essay on *Invisible Man* can also be written in response to the following question from a previous AP exam:

Write an essay about a novel in which a tragic figure functions as an instrument of suffering of others. Explain how the suffering brought upon others contributes to the tragic vision of the work as a whole.

All the Pretty Horses by Cormac McCarthy

All the Pretty Horses is a coming-of-age story about love—love of nature, love of life, love of freedom, and also romantic love. It's also about friendship, loyalty, and inescapable evil. En route to adulthood, John Grady, from whose point of view the story is told, emerges as warrior-hero. While in Mexico, he is beset by antiheroic, self-destructive traits such as stubbornness, pride, and naïveté. Yet, after enduring a series of harrowing life-changing moments, John Grady achieves an adult awareness. By the time he returns to Texas, he has recognized just who he is and what he might expect to be for the rest of his life.

Use *All the Pretty Horses* as the subject for an essay on 1) coming of age, 2) a fall from innocence, 3) the clash of cultures, 4) friendship and loyalty, 5) a young protagonist at odds with an established culture, and 6) a hero's quest.

An essay might also be written in response to the following:

Write an essay about a novel in which a conflict between free will and fate plays a significant role. In your essay, explain the conflict, how it is resolved, and what its resolution contributes to the work as a whole.

DRAMA ON THE EXAM

For the third essay of Section 2 on the exam, you are offered the option of choosing either a novel or a play as your subject.

Chances are that if you choose to write about a play on the AP exam it will be one you have read and studied. Having done so, you will probably know that reading a play is a far different experience from reading a novel. The vast majority of plays are more compact than novels, and unless you stop now and then to reflect on what you've read, can be finished more quickly.

Some novelists, particularly those using an omniscient narrator, fill their work with more facts and details than any reader can remember. A novel may contain scores of chapters, hundreds of scenes, numerous narrative passages, page after page of description, and more. Playwrights, on the other hand, work within stricter constraints: a few acts (five in a Shakespearean play; fewer in most modern works), at most, a handful scenes per act, and that's it.

Although some playwrights meticulously describe sets, music, costumes, lighting, and the appearance of characters, dialogue is the primary means of communication. Behind the relatively few things a character says and does there is a whole universe to which we are not privy. Good playwrights, however, will give us glimpses of the unknowable. To do so, they must exclude everything that is not essential, leaving the audience of readers (or viewers) to infer what has been left out. As a consequence, whatever a good playwright puts into a drama has a peculiar prominence. Nothing may be taken for granted. In a well-crafted play, that which appears in the text is like the visible part of an iceberg. The bulk of it remains hidden below the surface.

Like readers of fiction, readers of plays draw inferences about the meaning of the work from the words on the page. In effect, the author or playwright speaks directly to the reader. On stage the dynamic is far different. A third party, the actor, functions as a go-between, an interpreter of the writer's words and ideas. Then, too, a character seen through the personality of one actor may be vastly different from the same character rendered by a second actor and still more different from the character you meet on the printed page. What's more, an actor's portrayal may change from one performance to the next, depending on his mood, the interplay of other actors, the personality of the audience, the lighting, and a host of other variables. Add to that the influence of a director and the character we see on stage may be virtually unrecognizable from the person we know only through words we have read.

WRITING ABOUT SELECTED PLAYS

If you choose to write an essay on a play, consider one of the four plays listed below. Each offers rich material that can be used to respond to a variety of question.

Medea by Euripides

First presented in 431 B.C., *Medea* shows the effects of a powerful love gone bad. The title character is a strange, barbaric princess and sorceress, hideously repellent and totally fascinating at the same time. The mother of two young boys, she's not your everyday soccer mom.

Before the play opens, her husband Jason has betrayed her, and Medea lusts for revenge. As the play unfolds, her passions run shockingly amok. Whether Euripides condones her fury or condemns it remains uncertain. While reading the text or attending a performance of *Medea*, you'll have to make up your own mind, just as audiences have done for the past 2,500 years.

> Use *Medea* as the subject for an essay on how extremes of human passion (love, hatred, vengeance) can overwhelm reason, law, culture, self-esteem, and basic human instincts. An essay on the play might also discuss issues of family loyalty, physical and/or psychological violence, and the eternal conflict between men and women.

Hedda Gabler by Henrik Ibsen

Hedda Gabler Tesman engages in a private struggle against the stifling conventions of the bourgeois world in which she is trapped. At age twenty-nine, in anguish, she discerns nothing ahead but years of dullness and boredom.

Hedda's problems, however, are not initiated by the forces of an indifferent society. Rather, she is wracked with torment from within. She can't cope with the emptiness of her existence and as a result lashes out against others and finally against herself. In short, the play *Hedda Gabler* is the portrait of a woman's psychological turmoil.

Written in 1890, *Hedda Gabler* broke fresh ground for the playwright Henrik Ibsen. For the first time a female protagonist suffers frustrations that had previously been consigned to Ibsen's male characters. Vivid insights into Hedda's agonized personality constitute the purpose and meaning of the play.

> Use *Hedda Gabler* as the subject for an essay on the psychological make up of a character who is part victim, part victimizer. Other topics germane to the play include 1) the vagaries of love, 2) a protagonist seemingly devoid of redeeming virtues, 3) the nature of power, and 4) the age-old conflict between individualism and conformity.

A Streetcar Named Desire
by Tennessee Williams

Produced on Broadway in 1947, *A Streetcar Named Desire* captured the Critics' Circle Award, won the Pulitzer Prize, and vaulted Tennessee Williams into the front rank of twentieth-century American playwrights.

Williams found the stuff of *Streetcar* in the agonies of his own life. Places where he had lived became settings, plots were drawn from life's experiences. He barely disguised his parents, his sister, and himself when he cast them as characters on the stage. If you combine Williams's mother, a genteel and prudish southern lady, with his fragile sister Rose, you get Blanche Dubois, the central character in *Streetcar*. Stanley Kowalski, Blanche's nemesis, is a brute like Williams's father. When Stanley clashes with Blanche, the fireworks come straight out of brutal, pitched battles that Williams witnessed at home. Few artists have ever left behind a more personal and intense legacy.

Use *A Streetcar Named Desire* as the subject for an essay on 1) the pangs of loneliness, 2) the triumph of savagery over civility, 3) illusion vs. reality, or 4) various forms of love. In addition, any of the main characters would serve as the subject for a case study of irrational behavior.

Oleanna
by David Mamet

Oleanna, first produced in 1992 and later made into a movie, takes place at an unnamed university. It has a cast of two, a female student named Carol and her male professor, John, who teaches a course in education. Others play roles, too—but we neither see nor hear them. The entire play is set in John's office, where Carol and John meet on three different occasions perhaps a week or two apart. Their dialogue and interaction comprise the sum and substance of the play.

A play with only two characters and a single set may sound rather static, maybe even dull. But it's nothing of the kind. *Oleanna* always gets audiences and readers buzzing, feeling tense, shocked, stirred up. AP teachers report that few works of literature generate livelier discussion and controversy in their classes than *Oleanna*. Why? Well, you'll see after viewing or reading David Mamet's play.

Use *Oleanna* as the subject for an essay on 1) problems of communication between people, 2) characters in conflict with each other, 3) the perils of relying on first impressions, 4) a work of literature that reflects the values and mores of its time.

An essay on *Oleanna* can also be written in response to the following question adapted from a previous AP exam: Write an essay about a play in which a character faces competing desires, ambitions, or influences. Identify the conflicting forces and explain how the conflict illuminates the work as a whole.

PART 5

PRACTICE TESTS

Answer Sheet
PRACTICE TEST 1

Section I

1 Ⓐ Ⓑ Ⓒ Ⓓ Ⓔ   16 Ⓐ Ⓑ Ⓒ Ⓓ Ⓔ   31 Ⓐ Ⓑ Ⓒ Ⓓ Ⓔ   46 Ⓐ Ⓑ Ⓒ Ⓓ Ⓔ
2 Ⓐ Ⓑ Ⓒ Ⓓ Ⓔ   17 Ⓐ Ⓑ Ⓒ Ⓓ Ⓔ   32 Ⓐ Ⓑ Ⓒ Ⓓ Ⓔ   47 Ⓐ Ⓑ Ⓒ Ⓓ Ⓔ
3 Ⓐ Ⓑ Ⓒ Ⓓ Ⓔ   18 Ⓐ Ⓑ Ⓒ Ⓓ Ⓔ   33 Ⓐ Ⓑ Ⓒ Ⓓ Ⓔ   48 Ⓐ Ⓑ Ⓒ Ⓓ Ⓔ
4 Ⓐ Ⓑ Ⓒ Ⓓ Ⓔ   19 Ⓐ Ⓑ Ⓒ Ⓓ Ⓔ   34 Ⓐ Ⓑ Ⓒ Ⓓ Ⓔ   49 Ⓐ Ⓑ Ⓒ Ⓓ Ⓔ
5 Ⓐ Ⓑ Ⓒ Ⓓ Ⓔ   20 Ⓐ Ⓑ Ⓒ Ⓓ Ⓔ   35 Ⓐ Ⓑ Ⓒ Ⓓ Ⓔ   50 Ⓐ Ⓑ Ⓒ Ⓓ Ⓔ
6 Ⓐ Ⓑ Ⓒ Ⓓ Ⓔ   21 Ⓐ Ⓑ Ⓒ Ⓓ Ⓔ   36 Ⓐ Ⓑ Ⓒ Ⓓ Ⓔ   51 Ⓐ Ⓑ Ⓒ Ⓓ Ⓔ
7 Ⓐ Ⓑ Ⓒ Ⓓ Ⓔ   22 Ⓐ Ⓑ Ⓒ Ⓓ Ⓔ   37 Ⓐ Ⓑ Ⓒ Ⓓ Ⓔ   52 Ⓐ Ⓑ Ⓒ Ⓓ Ⓔ
8 Ⓐ Ⓑ Ⓒ Ⓓ Ⓔ   23 Ⓐ Ⓑ Ⓒ Ⓓ Ⓔ   38 Ⓐ Ⓑ Ⓒ Ⓓ Ⓔ   53 Ⓐ Ⓑ Ⓒ Ⓓ Ⓔ
9 Ⓐ Ⓑ Ⓒ Ⓓ Ⓔ   24 Ⓐ Ⓑ Ⓒ Ⓓ Ⓔ   39 Ⓐ Ⓑ Ⓒ Ⓓ Ⓔ   54 Ⓐ Ⓑ Ⓒ Ⓓ Ⓔ
10 Ⓐ Ⓑ Ⓒ Ⓓ Ⓔ   25 Ⓐ Ⓑ Ⓒ Ⓓ Ⓔ   40 Ⓐ Ⓑ Ⓒ Ⓓ Ⓔ   55 Ⓐ Ⓑ Ⓒ Ⓓ Ⓔ
11 Ⓐ Ⓑ Ⓒ Ⓓ Ⓔ   26 Ⓐ Ⓑ Ⓒ Ⓓ Ⓔ   41 Ⓐ Ⓑ Ⓒ Ⓓ Ⓔ
12 Ⓐ Ⓑ Ⓒ Ⓓ Ⓔ   27 Ⓐ Ⓑ Ⓒ Ⓓ Ⓔ   42 Ⓐ Ⓑ Ⓒ Ⓓ Ⓔ
13 Ⓐ Ⓑ Ⓒ Ⓓ Ⓔ   28 Ⓐ Ⓑ Ⓒ Ⓓ Ⓔ   43 Ⓐ Ⓑ Ⓒ Ⓓ Ⓔ
14 Ⓐ Ⓑ Ⓒ Ⓓ Ⓔ   29 Ⓐ Ⓑ Ⓒ Ⓓ Ⓔ   44 Ⓐ Ⓑ Ⓒ Ⓓ Ⓔ
15 Ⓐ Ⓑ Ⓒ Ⓓ Ⓔ   30 Ⓐ Ⓑ Ⓒ Ⓓ Ⓔ   45 Ⓐ Ⓑ Ⓒ Ⓓ Ⓔ

SECTION I

Multiple-choice Questions

TIME—1 HOUR

Percent of total grade on the exam: 45 percent

Instructions: This section of the exam consists of selections from literary works and questions on their content, form, and style. After reading each passage and poem, choose the best answer to each question and then fill in the corresponding oval on the answer sheet.

Questions 1–15. Read the following passage carefully before you decide on your answers to the questions.

The sun (for he keeps very good hours at this time of the year) had been some time retired to rest when Sophia arose greatly refreshed by her sleep, which, short as it was, nothing but her
Line extreme fatigue could have occasioned; for though she had told her
(5) maid and, perhaps herself too that she was perfectly easy when she left Upton, yet it is certain her mind was a little affected with that malady which is attended with all the restless symptoms of a fever and is, perhaps, the very distemper which physicians mean (if they mean anything) by the fever of the spirits.

(10) Mrs. Fitzpatrick likewise left her bed at the same time and, having summoned her maid, immediately dressed herself. She was really a very pretty woman and, had she been in any other company but that of Sophia, might have been thought beautiful, but when Mrs. Honour of her own accord attended (for her mistress would not
(15) suffer her to be waked) and had equipped our heroine, the charms of Mrs. Fitzpatrick, who had performed the office of the morning star and had preceded greater glories, shared the fate of that star and were totally eclipsed the moment those glories shone forth.

Perhaps Sophia never looked more beautiful than she did at this
(20) instant. We ought not therefore to condemn the maid of the inn for her hyperbole, who when she descended after having lighted a fire declared, and ratified it with an oath, that if ever there was an angel upon the earth, she was now above-stairs.

Sophia had acquainted her cousin with her design to go to
(25) London, and Mrs. Fitzpatrick had agreed to accompany her; for the arrival of her husband at Upton had put an end to her design of going to Bath or to her aunt Western. They had therefore no sooner finished their tea than Sophia proposed to set out, the moon then shining extremely bright, and as for the frost, she defied it; nor had
(30) she any of those apprehensions which many young ladies would have felt at travelling by night, for she had, as we have before observed,

some little degree of natural courage, and this her present sensations, which bordered somewhat on despair, greatly increased. Besides, as she had already travelled twice with safety by the light of the moon, *(35)* she was the better emboldened to trust it a third time.

The disposition of Mrs. Fitzpatrick was more timorous; for though the greater terrors had conquered the less, and the presence of her husband had driven her away at so unseasonable an hour from Upton, yet being now arrived at a place where she thought herself *(40)* safe from his pursuit, these lesser terrors of I know not what operated so strongly that she earnestly entreated her cousin to stay till the next morning and not expose herself to the dangers of travelling by night.

Sophia, who was yielding to an excess, when she could neither laugh nor reason her cousin out of the apprehensions, at last gave *(45)* way to them. Perhaps, indeed, had she known of her father's arrival in Upton, it might have been more difficult to have persuaded her, for as to Jones, she had, I am afraid, no greater horror at the thoughts of being overtaken by him; nay, to confess the truth, I believe she rather wished than feared it, though I might honestly *(50)* enough have concealed this wish from the reader, as it was one of those secret, spontaneous emotions of the soul to which the reason is often a stranger.

When our young ladies had determined to remain all that evening in their inn, they were attended by the landlady, who desired to know *(55)* what their ladyships would be pleased to eat. Such charms were there in the voice, in the manner, and in the affable deportment of Sophia that she ravished the landlady to the highest degree, and that good woman, concluding that she had attended Jenny Cameron,[1] became in a moment a staunch Jacobite and wished heartily well to the Young *(60)* Pretender's cause from the great sweetness and affability with which she had been treated by his supposed mistress.

(1749)

[1]The legendary mistress of Scotland's Bonnie Prince Charlie, who led the Jacobite rebellion against England in 1745 and pretended to (i.e., claimed) Great Britain's throne.

1. The opening paragraph suggests that this passage was most probably preceded by

    (A) a sleepless night
    (B) a dispute with "Jones"
    (C) an upsetting incident
    (D) a doctor's visit
    (E) an unidentified illness

2. The narrator's parenthetical remark, "if they mean anything," (lines 8–9) can best be described as a comment on

(A) the pretentiousness of doctors
(B) Sophia's lack of medical knowledge
(C) the seriousness of Sophia's malady
(D) physicians' incompetence
(E) the arrogance of some physicians

3. In lines 14–15, "her mistress would not suffer her to be waked" is meant to suggest that

(A) Mrs. Honour has a short temper
(B) Mrs. Honour is devoted to her mistress
(C) Sophia has a kindly disposition
(D) Sophia lacks respect for her maid
(E) Sophia is unusually self-sufficient

4. In line 15, "equipped" might best be interpreted to mean

(A) prepared
(B) supported
(C) served
(D) provided for
(E) dressed

5. By stating that Sophia's malady was distinguished by "restless symptoms of a fever" and a mind that was "a little affected" (lines 6–7), the narrator lays the groundwork for Sophia's subsequent

(A) desire to get dressed without a maid's help
(B) request for a fire in her room
(C) urge to set out for London immediately
(D) willingness to yield to Mrs. Fitzpatrick
(E) effort to pass herself off as Jenny Cameron

6. The primary effect of the imagery and figures of speech in lines 11–23 is to

(A) affirm the luxury and glamor of Sophia's lifestyle
(B) emphasize the characters' spirituality
(C) suggest the social status of Sophia and Mrs. Fitzpatrick
(D) create an impression of Sophia's radiant beauty
(E) contrast exterior darkness with interior brightness

7. In lines 36–37, the reference to "greater" terrors and "less" terrors serves chiefly to show that Mrs. Fitzpatrick

   (A) would rather travel in the dark than displease Sophia
   (B) was paralyzed by a variety of fears
   (C) feared her husband more than she feared traveling in the dark
   (D) was torn between going with Sophia and remaining safe at the inn
   (E) would rather ignore her husband than defy Sophia

8. The structure of the sentence (lines 36–42) does all of the following EXCEPT

   (A) emphasize Mrs. Fitzpatrick's apprehensiveness
   (B) imply that some of Mrs. Fitzpatrick's behavior is difficult for an observer to understand
   (C) suggest that one mustn't believe all that Mrs. Fitzpatrick says
   (D) support the narrator's view that Mrs. Fitzpatrick lacks Sophia's self-assurance
   (E) provide evidence of Mrs. Fitzpatrick's indecisiveness

9. The description of Sophia in lines 43–45 has the primary effect of

   (A) revealing Mrs. Fitzpatrick's opinion of Sophia
   (B) suggesting that Sophia lacked determination
   (C) emphasizing that Sophia did not take Mrs. Fitzpatrick's fears seriously
   (D) providing evidence that Sophia was no less eccentric than Mrs. Fitzpatrick
   (E) showing that Sophia was extremely flexible and softhearted

10. Lines 43–52 of the passage indicate that the speaker believes which of the following to be true of Sophia?

   (A) She has deliberately developed charm and affability in order to attract men.
   (B) She has a secret affection for Mrs. Fitzpatrick's husband.
   (C) She has grown weary of her cousin's company.
   (D) She has a mean streak hidden beneath her charm.
   (E) She does not know her own mind when it comes to Jones.

11. During their visit to the inn, Sophia and Mrs. Fitzpatrick's state of mind can best be characterized by their

(A) dissatisfaction with their surroundings
(B) uncertainty about what to do next
(C) impatience with each other
(D) preoccupation with feeling safe and secure
(E) anxiety over offending other travelers

12. In line 57, "ravished" is best interpreted to mean

(A) transformed
(B) enthralled
(C) hypnotized
(D) impressed
(E) devastated

13. The narrator's allusions to Jenny Cameron and the Young Pretender (lines 58–59) serve primarily to

(A) imply the landlady's propensity for self-delusion
(B) illustrate Sophia's tendency to flaunt her charms
(C) exaggerate the effects of Sophia's personality
(D) capture the intensity of Sophia's ambition to raise her social status
(E) demonstrate that Sophia had recovered from her earlier "distemper" (line 8)

14. The function of the narrator of the passage can best be described as

(A) an omniscient observer
(B) a participant observer
(C) an involved spectator
(D) a disinterested bystander
(E) a concerned participant

15. The main concern of the passage is

(A) Sophia's trials and tribulations
(B) the impression Sophia creates on others
(C) Sophia's relationship with Mrs. Fitzpatrick
(D) Sophia's manner and appearance
(E) the differences between Sophia and Mrs. Fitzpatrick

Questions 16–26. Read the following poem carefully before you decide on your answers to the questions.

Dover Beach

The sea is calm tonight,
The tide is full, the moon lies fair
Upon the straits;—on the French coast the light
Line   Gleams and is gone; the cliffs of England stand,
(5)   Glimmering and vast, out in the tranquil bay.
Come to the window, sweet is the night-air!
Only, from the long line of spray
Where the sea meets the moon-blanched land,
Listen! you hear the grating roar
(10)   Of pebbles which the waves draw back, and fling,
At their return, up the high strand,
Begin, and cease, and then again begin,
With tremulous cadence slow, and bring
The eternal note of sadness in.

(15)   Sophocles long ago
Heard it on the Aegean, and it brought
Into his mind the turbid ebb and flow
Of human misery;[1] we
Find also in the sound a thought,
(20)   Hearing it by this distant northern sea.

The Sea of Faith
Was once, too, at the full, and round earth's shore
Lay like the folds of a bright girdle furled.
But now I only hear
(25)   Its melancholy, long, withdrawing roar,
Retreating, to the breath
Of the night-wind, down the vast edges drear
And naked shingles of the world.

Ah, love, let us be true
(30)   To one another! for the world, which seems
To lie before us like a land of dreams,
So various, so beautiful, so new,
Hath really neither joy, nor love, nor light,
Nor certitude, nor peace, nor help for pain;
(35)   And we are here as on a darkling[2] plain
Swept with confused alarms of struggle and flight,
Where ignorant armies clash by night.

— Matthew Arnold, c. 1850

---

[1] An allusion to Sophocles' *Antigone*
[2] dark, deeply shadowed

16. The poem's mood can best be described as

    (A) angry
    (B) mournful
    (C) mysterious
    (D) elegiac
    (E) caustic

17. In lines 1–14, all of the following stylistic techniques contribute to the poet's depiction of the sea EXCEPT

    (A) assonance
    (B) rhythm
    (C) diction
    (D) imagery
    (E) end rhyme

18. In the poem, the sea is depicted primarily through its

    (A) colors
    (B) movement
    (C) sounds
    (D) smells
    (E) tides

19. The allusion to Sophocles (lines 15–20) serves

     I.   to universalize the speaker's experience
     II. to indicate the timelessness of human suffering
     III. to compare the ancient world with contemporary England

    (A) I only
    (B) II only
    (C) I and II only
    (D) II and III only
    (E) I, II, and III

20. In the third stanza, the speaker's analogy compares

    (A) the effects of high tide to the effects of low tide
    (B) diminishing religious faith to the ebbing tide
    (C) the sound of the waves to the sound of breathing
    (D) the wind at night to the rise and fall of the sea
    (E) the shoreline to a piece of clothing

21. In line 22, "at the full" is best interpreted as

    (A) completely saturated
    (B) loud and forceful
    (C) overflowing
    (D) at its maximum height
    (E) abundant

22. Between lines 28 and 29, there is a shift from

    (A) loathing to acceptance of the status quo
    (B) apathy to immediate action
    (C) discontent to resignation
    (D) annoyance to pleasure
    (E) dejection to a plea for solace

23. The phrase "land of dreams" (line 31) serves primarily to support the notion that

    (A) idealists will inevitably be disappointed
    (B) hopefulness comes from having strong faith
    (C) goodness in the world is an illusion
    (D) optimism serves as a defense against a hostile world
    (E) love blinds one to reality

24. What is the subject of the verb "Hath" (line 33)?

    (A) "love" (line 29)
    (B) "world" (line 30)
    (C) "land" (line 31)
    (D) "dreams" (line 31)
    (E) "joy" (line 33)

25. The poem can best be described as

    (A) a villanelle
    (B) a narrative
    (C) an ode
    (D) a prose poem
    (E) a dramatic monologue

26. The primary theme of the poem is derived chiefly from

    (A) a comparison between the past and the present
    (B) the contrast between the peacefulness of nature and the tumult of battle
    (C) a description of the sea
    (D) the symbolism of The Sea of Faith
    (E) the speaker's disenchantment with the world

Questions 27–41. Read the following passage carefully before you decide on your answers to the questions.

Animals talk to each other, of course. There can be no question about that; but I suppose there are very few people who can understand them. I never knew but one man who could. I knew he could, however, because he told me so himself. He was a middle-aged,

Line
(5)   simple-hearted miner who had lived in a lonely corner of California, among the woods and mountains, a good many years, and had studied the ways of his only neighbors, the beasts and the birds, until he believed he could accurately translate any remark which they made. This was Jim Baker. According to Jim Baker, some animals

(10) have only a limited education, and use only very simple words, and scarcely ever a comparison or a flowery figure; whereas, certain other animals have a large vocabulary, a fine command of language and a ready and fluent delivery; consequently these latter talk a great deal; they like it; they are conscious of their talent, and they enjoy

(15) "showing off." Baker said, that after long and careful observation, he had come to the conclusion that the bluejays were the best talkers he had found among the birds and beasts. Said he:

"There's more *to* a bluejay than any other creature. He has got more moods, and more different kinds of feelings than other crea-

(20) tures; and, mind you, whatever a bluejay feels, he can put into language. And no mere commonplace language, either, but rattling, out-and-out book-talk—and bristling with metaphor, too—just bristling! And as for command of language—why *you* never see a bluejay get stuck for a word. No man ever did. They just boil out of

(25) him! And another thing: I've noticed a good deal, and there's no bird, or cow, or anything that uses as good grammar as a blue-jay. You may say a cat uses good grammar. Well, a cat does—but you let a cat get excited once; you let a cat get to pulling fur with another cat on a shed, nights, and you'll hear grammar that will give you

(30) lockjaw. Ignorant people think it's the *noise* which fighting cats make that is so aggravating, but it ain't so; it's the sickening grammar they use. Now I've never heard a jay use bad grammar but very seldom; and when they do, they are as ashamed as a human; they shut right down and leave.

(35) "You may call a jay a bird. Well, so he is, in a measure—because he's got feathers on him, and don't belong to no church, perhaps; but otherwise he is just as much a human as you be. And I'll tell you for why. A jay's gifts, and instincts, and feelings, and interests, cover the whole ground. A jay hasn't got any more principle than a Congress-

(40) man. A jay will lie, a jay will steal, a jay will deceive, a jay will betray; and four times out of five, a jay will go back on his solemnest promise. The sacredness of an obligation is a thing which you can't cram into no bluejay's head. Now, on top of all this, there's another

(45) thing a jay can outswear any gentleman in the mines. You think a cat can swear. Well, a cat can; but you give a bluejay a subject that calls for his reserve-powers, and where is your cat? Don't talk to *me*—I know too much about this thing. And there's yet another thing; in the one little particular of scolding—just good, clean, out-and-out scolding—a bluejay can lay over anything, human or divine. Yes, sir,

(50) a jay is everything a man is. A jay can cry, a jay can laugh, a jay can feel shame, a jay can reason and plan and discuss, a jay likes gossip and scandal, a jay has got a sense of humor, a jay knows when he is an ass just as well as you do—maybe better. If a jay ain't human, he better take in his sign, that's all. Now I'm going to tell you a perfectly

(55) true fact about some bluejays.

"When I first begun to understand jay language correctly, there was a little incident happened here. Seven years ago, the last man in this region but me moved away. There stands his house—been empty ever since; a log house, with a plank roof—just one big room, and

(60) no more; no ceiling—nothing between the rafters and the floor. Well, one Sunday morning I was sitting out here in front of my cabin, with my cat, taking the sun, and looking at the blue hills, and listening to the leaves rustling so lonely in the trees, and thinking of the home away yonder in the states, that I hadn't heard from in thir-

(65) teen years, when a bluejay lit on that house, with an acorn in his mouth, and says, 'Hello, I reckon I've struck something.' When he spoke, the acorn dropped out of his mouth and rolled down the roof, of course, but he didn't care; his mind was all on the thing he struck. It was a knot-hole in the roof. He cocked his head to one side, shut

(70) one eye and put the other one to the hole, like a possum looking down a jug; then he glanced up with his bright eyes, gave a wink or two with his wings—which signifies gratification, you understand— and says, 'It looks like a hole, it's located like a hole—blamed if I don't believe it *is* a hole!'"

(1880)

27. In the first paragraph, the author establishes the predominant tone for the rest of the passage primarily by

(A) comparing illiterate animals to animals with a good education
(B) overstating Jim Baker's qualifications to speak on the subject
(C) feigning a serious attitude toward a nonsensical subject
(D) making a generalization based on one piece of evidence
(E) exaggerating the naïveté of the speaker

28. The structure of the sentence beginning in line 4 ("He was . . .") does which of the following?

    I. It calls into question the straightforward assertions made in line 1.
    II. It implies the gullibility of the speaker.
    III. It raises doubts about the soundness of the speaker's judgment.

    (A) I only
    (B) II only
    (C) I and II only
    (D) II and III only
    (E) I, II, and III

29. The allusion to "certain other animals" (lines 11–12) is an indirect reference to

    (A) trained animals
    (B) mythical animals
    (C) domestic animals
    (D) human beings
    (E) purebred animals with pedigrees

30. Jim Baker's attitude toward cats (lines 27–34) might best be described as

    (A) grim indifference
    (B) bogus pity
    (C) avid hostility
    (D) counterfeit disdain
    (E) bitter resentment

31. The second, third, and fourth paragraphs of the passage differ stylistically from the first paragraph in all of the following ways EXCEPT

    (A) they contain passive sentences
    (B) they include colloquialisms
    (C) they address the reader directly
    (D) they make use of repetition
    (E) they contain instances of nonstandard usage

32. The discussion of poor grammar (lines 27–34) includes which of the following grammatical mistakes?

    (A) Faulty parallelism
    (B) Dangling modifier
    (C) Lack of agreement between subject and verb
    (D) Lack of agreement between pronoun and antecedent
    (E) Ambiguous pronoun reference

33. In the context of the passage, the phrase "cover the whole ground" (lines 38–39) is used as a metaphor for

    (A) come in a great many varieties
    (B) range from the best to the worst
    (C) match those of any human being
    (D) tend to remain hidden from human observers
    (E) are hard to define clearly

34. Jim Baker's allusion to "a Congressman" (lines 39–40) is meant primarily to

    (A) imply the speaker's underlying dissatisfaction with all politicians
    (B) express disapproval of the bluejay's personality and character
    (C) introduce material intended to disparage members of Congress
    (D) compare the loquacity of both bluejays and Congressmen
    (E) emphasize the deceptiveness of bluejays

35. In context, "and where is your cat?" (line 46) can best be paraphrased to read

    (A) and you'll be dumbfounded
    (B) and where do you think the cat will go?
    (C) and the cat will hide from shame
    (D) and a cat will run away
    (E) and a cat doesn't stand a chance

36. The use of the phrase "maybe better" (line 53) indicates that Jim Baker

    (A) holds humans in low regard
    (B) wishes to tease his listener
    (C) believes that bluejays are almost as smart as people
    (D) fears that the listener may doubt his word
    (E) knows that some bluejays tend to be stupid

37. The reader can infer that the "perfectly true fact" (lines 54–55) that follows will most likely be about

    (A) the humanlike qualities of bluejays
    (B) the bluejay's sense of humor
    (C) a foolish bluejay
    (D) a bluejay that behaved scandalously
    (E) a gossipy bluejay

38. The sentence that begins in line 56 signals a change in Jim Baker's

    (A) tone from critical to sentimental
    (B) use of rhetoric from generalizations to specific examples
    (C) use of language from informal to sedate
    (D) point of view from dispassionate to personal
    (E) purpose from persuasive to argumentative

39. Jim Baker relates the anecdote in lines 56–74 in order to

   (A) further inform his listener about the habits of bluejays
   (B) impress the listener by demonstrating his comprehension of bluejay language
   (C) reiterate his assertion that bluejays are virtually human
   (D) illustrate the bluejay's intelligence
   (E) provide evidence to support his previous claims regarding bluejays

40. Jim Baker's description of his life (lines 57–66) has the primary effect of

   (A) suggesting his discontent
   (B) indicating his perverse way of thinking
   (C) emphasizing his reclusiveness
   (D) criticizing his antisocial attitudes
   (E) reflecting his bizarre behavior

41. Jim Baker's overall tone in the passage can best be described as

   (A) whimsical
   (B) unrefined
   (C) smug
   (D) mock heroic
   (E) discreet

Questions 42–55. Read the following poem carefully before you decide on your answers to the questions

Snake

A snake came to my water-trough
On a hot, hot day, and I in pyjamas for the heat,
To drink there.

Line   In the deep, strange-scented shade of the great dark carob-tree
(5)   I came down the steps with my pitcher
And must wait, must stand and wait, for there he was at the trough before me.

He reached down from a fissure in the earth-wall in the gloom
And trailed his yellow-brown slackness soft-bellied down, over the
(10)   edge of the stone trough
And rested his throat upon the stone bottom,
And where the water had dripped from the tap, in a small clearness,
He sipped with his straight mouth,
Softly drank through his straight gums, into his slack long body,
(15)   Silently.

Someone was before me at my water-trough,
And I, like a second comer, waiting.

He lifted his head from his drinking, as cattle do,
And looked at me vaguely, as drinking cattle do,
(20)   And flickered his two-forked tongue from his lips, and mused a
            moment,
And stooped and drank a little more,
Being earth-brown, earth-golden from the burning bowels of the earth
On the day of Sicilian July, with Etna[1] smoking.

(25)   The voice of my education said to me
He must be killed,
For in Sicily the black, black snakes are innocent, the gold are
            venomous.

And voices in me said, If you were a man
(30)   You would take a stick and break him now, and finish him off.

But must I confess how I liked him,
How glad I was he had come like a guest in quiet, to drink at my
            water-trough

And depart peaceful, pacified, and thankless,
(35)   Into the burning bowels of this earth?

Was it cowardice, that I dared not kill him?
Was it perversity, that I longed to talk to him?
Was it humility, to feel so honoured?
I felt so honoured.

(40)   And yet those voices:
If you were not afraid, you would kill him!

And truly I was afraid, I was most afraid, But even so, honoured still
            more
That he should seek my hospitality
(45)   From out the dark door of the secret earth.

He drank enough
And lifted his head, dreamily, as one who has drunken,
And flickered his tongue like a forked night on the air, so black,
Seeming to lick his lips,
(50)   And looked around like a god, unseeing, into the air,

———————
[1] a volcano in Sicily

And slowly turned his head,
And slowly, very slowly, as if thrice adream,
Proceeded to draw his slow length curving round
And climb again the broken bank of my wall-face.

(55)   And as he put his head into that dreadful hole,
And as he slowly drew up, snake-easing his shoulders, and entered
   farther,
A sort of horror, a sort of protest against his withdrawing into that
   horrid black hole,
(60)   Deliberately going into the blackness, and slowly drawing himself
   after,
Overcame me now his back was turned.

I looked round, I put down my pitcher,
I picked up a clumsy log
(65)   And threw it at the water-trough with a clatter.

I think it did not hit him,
But suddenly that part of him that was left behind convulsed in
   undignified haste.
Writhed like lightning, and was gone
(70)   Into the black hole, the earth-lipped fissure in the wall-front,
At which, in the intense still noon, I stared with fascination.

And immediately I regretted it.
I thought how paltry, how vulgar, what a mean act!
I despised myself and the voices of my accursed human education.

(75)   And I thought of the albatross[2]
And I wished he would come back, my snake.

For he seemed to me again like a king,
Like a king in exile, uncrowned in the underworld,
Now due to be crowned again.

(80)   And so, I missed my chance with one of the lords
Of life.
And I have something to expiate:
A pettiness.

—D. H. Lawrence (1923)

---

[2]The Ancient Mariner in Coleridge's poem is forever
plagued by the albatross he thoughtlessly killed.

42. The speaker's experience in the poem is best described as

    (A) an unresolved conflict with Mother Nature
    (B) an escape from routine that causes remorse
    (C) an adventure in stalking a wild creature
    (D) an event leading to self-revelation
    (E) a spiritual awakening

43. After finding the snake, the speaker behaves as though he

    (A) has no prior claim on the water-trough
    (B) lacks the means with which to chase the snake away
    (C) has changed his mind about getting drunk
    (D) takes pride in his composure
    (E) feels threatened

44. The speaker provides the detail "and I in pyjamas" (line 2) most probably as

    (A) an indication of the time of day
    (B) a subtle manifestation of his state of mind
    (C) a sign of his vulnerability
    (D) a hint about his less-than-perfect health
    (E) an omen for something unusual

45. Which of the following best describes the prevailing poetic technique used in lines 8–15?

    (A) Hyperbole that stresses the snake's malevolence
    (B) Personification that endows the snake with a human personality
    (C) Imagery that captures the snake's intimidating appearance
    (D) Onomatopoetic words that replicate snake sounds
    (E) Diction that suggests the snake's slithering movement

46. Lines 18–22 imply that the foremost characteristic of the snake is its

    (A) awareness of potential dangers
    (B) indifference to the observer
    (C) similarity to other creatures
    (D) unquenchable thirst
    (E) unpredictable movement

47. The snake's origins, as described by the speaker, suggest that the snake

    (A) represents Satan or some other evil force
    (B) symbolizes the dark side of man
    (C) foreshadows the coming of the apocalypse
    (D) stands for temptation
    (E) indicates the innocence of the speaker

48. In line 25 and line 74, "education" is best interpreted to mean

    (A) the speaker's natural impulses
    (B) a code of ethical behavior
    (C) the things taught in school
    (D) society's beliefs and expectations
    (E) acquired inhibitions

49. Lines 29–35 emphasize that the speaker

    (A) resents competing with the snake for access to the water-trough
    (B) feels torn between his instinct and his education
    (C) both admires and fears the snake
    (D) has doubts about his own masculinity
    (E) regards the snake as welcome distraction from his usual routine

50. For the speaker, the snake is most like

    (A) a stroke of luck
    (B) an unexpected gift
    (C) a bothersome intruder
    (D) an univited guest
    (E) a welcome visitor

51. The questions that the speaker asks in lines 36–38 serve mainly to

    (A) illustrate conflicting feelings clashing inside him
    (B) hint that he intends to harm the snake
    (C) disclose that he identifies with the snake
    (D) suggest his awareness that snakes often have symbolic meaning
    (E) help him rationalize his reaction to the snake

52. Which of the following adjectives best describes the speaker's action in lines 55–65?

    (A) Instinctive
    (B) Premeditated
    (C) Reckless
    (D) Devious
    (E) Impulsive

53. The allusion to "the albatross" (line 75) most strongly conveys the speaker's

    (A) alienation from nature
    (B) disenchantment with his education
    (C) repentance for his action
    (D) affection for the snake
    (E) feelings of confusion

54. The word, "again" in "he seemed to me again like a king" (line 77) refers back to all of the following EXCEPT

    (A) "flickered his two-forked tongue from his lips, and mused a moment" (line 20)
    (B) "Being earth-brown, earth golden" (line 23)
    (C) "Was it humility, to feel so honoured?" (line 38)
    (D) "honoured still more/That he should seek my hospitality" (lines 42–43)
    (E) "And looked around . . . unseeing, into the air" (line 48)

55. At the end of the poem the speaker regards his encounter with the snake as

    (A) a cherished moment
    (B) a memorable experience
    (C) an unfulfilled opportunity
    (D) an unwanted diversion
    (E) an inspirational event

SECTION II
Essay Questions

TIME—2 HOURS

Suggested time for each essay—40 minutes
Each essay counts as one-third of the total essay section score

Instructions: This section of the exam consists of three questions that require responses in essay form. You may write the essays in any order you wish and return to work on a completed essay if time permits. Although it is suggested that you spend roughly 40 minutes on each essay, you may apportion your time as you see fit.

Each essay will be evaluated according to its clarity, effectiveness in dealing with the topics, and the overall quality of your writing. If you have the time, go over each essay, checking its punctuation, spelling, and diction. Unless plenty of time remains, try to avoid major revisions. In the end, the quality of each essay counts more than its quantity.

For Question 3, please choose a novel or play of at least the same literary merit as the works you have been assigned in your AP English course.

Essays should be written in pen, preferably with black or dark blue ink. Use lined paper and write as legibly as you can. Do not skip lines. Cross out any errors you make. Feel free to make notes and plan your essay on a piece of scrap paper. Please number your essays and begin each one on a new sheet of paper. Good luck.

ESSAY QUESTION 1

In each of the following poems, written about seventy years apart, the speaker comments on the phenomenon of forgetfulness. Read the poems carefully and then, in a well-organized essay, summarize each speaker's thoughts and analyze how the tone, imagery, sentence structure, or other poetic elements help to convey each speaker's state of mind.

Forgetfulness

Forgetfulness is like a song
That, freed from beat and measure, wanders.
Forgetfulness is like a bird whose wings are reconciled,
Line   Outspread and motionless, —
(5)   A bird that coasts the wind unwearyingly.

Forgetfulness is rain at night,
Or an old house in a forest,— or a child.
Forgetfulness is white, — white as a blasted tree,
And it may stun the sybil[1] into prophesy,
(10)   Or bury the Gods.

I can remember much forgetfulness.

                                    —Hart Crane, 1918

Forgetfulness

The name of the author is the first to go
followed obediently by the title, the plot,
the heartbreaking conclusion, the entire novel
Line   which suddenly becomes one you have never read, never even heard of.

(5)   It is as if, one by one, the memories you used to harbor
decided to retire to the southern hemisphere of the brain,
to a little fishing village where there are no phones.

Long ago you kissed the names of the nine Muses goodbye
and watched the quadratic equation pack its bag,
(10) and even now as you memorize the order of the planets,
something else is slipping away, a state flower perhaps,
the address of an uncle, the capital of Paraguay.

Whatever it is you are struggling to remember
it is not poised on the tip of your tongue,
(15) not even lurking in some obscure corner of your spleen.

It has floated away down a dark mythological river
whose name begins with an *L* as far as you can recall,
well on your own way to oblivion where you will join those
who have even forgotten how to swim and how to ride a bicycle.

(20) No wonder you rise in the middle of the night
to look up the date of a famous battle in a book on war.
No wonder the moon in the window seems to have drifted
out of a love poem that you used to know by heart.

                                  —Billy Collins, 1991

---

[1]In ancient myth, a female prophet or fortune teller

ESSAY QUESTION 2

(Suggested time—40 minutes. This question counts as one-third of your score for Section II of the exam.)

The following passage comes from the opening of "New Year's Day" (1924), a short story by Edith Wharton set in upper-class social circles of New York City early in the twentieth century. Read the passage carefully. Then, in a well-organized essay, analyze the literary devices Wharton uses to show that social values and customs of the day had changed since days gone by. You may wish to consider the structure of the excerpt as well as its diction, tone, or any other relevant literary element.

"She was *bad* . . . always. They used to meet at the Fifth Avenue Hotel," said my mother, as if the scene of the offence added to the guilt of the couple whose past she was revealing. Her spectacles
Line slanted on her knitting, she dropped the words in a hiss that might
(5) have singed the snowy baby-blanket which engaged her indefatigable fingers. (It was typical of my mother to be always employed in benevolent actions while she uttered uncharitable words.)

"They used to meet at the Fifth Avenue Hotel"; how the precision of the phrase characterized my old New York! A generation later,
(10) people would have said, in reporting an affair such as Lizzie Hazeldean's with Henry Prest: "They met in hotels"—and today who but a few superannuated spinsters, still feeding on the venom secreted in their youth, would take any interest in the tracing of such topographies?

(15) Life has become too telegraphic for curiosity to linger on any given point in a sentimental relation; as old Sillerton Jackson, in response to my mother, grumbled through his perfect "china set": "Fifth Avenue Hotel? They might meet in the middle of Fifth Avenue nowadays, for all that anybody cares."

(20) But what a flood of light my mother's tart phrase had suddenly focussed on an unremarked incident of my boyhood!

The Fifth Avenue Hotel . . . Mrs. Hazeldean and Henry Prest . . . the conjunction of these names had arrested her darting talk on a single point of my memory, as a search-light, suddenly checked in its
(25) gyrations, is held motionless while one notes each of the unnaturally sharp and lustrous images it picks out. At the time I was a boy of twelve, at home from school for the holidays. My mother's mother, Grandmamma Parrett, still lived in the house in West Twenty-third Street which Grandpapa had built in his pioneering youth, in days
(30) when people shuddered at the perils of living north of Union Square—days that Grandmamma and my parents looked back to

with a joking incredulity as the years passed and the new houses advanced steadily Park-ward, outstripping the Thirtieth Streets, taking the Reservoir at a bound, and leaving us in what, in my

(35) school-days, was already a dullish back-water between Aristocracy to the south and Money to the north.

    Even then fashion moved quickly in New York, and my infantile memory barely reached back to the time when Grandmamma, in lace lappers and creaking *"moire,"*[1] used to receive on New Year's day,

(40) supported by her handsome married daughters. As for old Sillerton Jackson, who, once a social custom had dropped into disuse, always affected never to have observed it, he stoutly maintained that the New Year's day ceremonial had never been taken seriously except among families of Dutch descent, and that was why Mrs. Henry

(45) van der Luyden had clung to it, in a reluctant half-apologetic way, long after her friends had closed their doors on the first of January, and the date had been chosen for those out-of-town parties which are so often used as a pretext for absence when the unfashionable are celebrating their rites.

(50)   Grandmamma, of course, no longer received. But it would have seemed to her an exceedingly odd thing to go out of town in winter, especially now that the New York houses were luxuriously warmed by the new hot-air furnaces, and searchingly illuminated by gas chandeliers. No, thank you—no country winters for the chilblained genera-

(55) tion of prunella[2] sandals and low-necked sarcenet,[3] the generation brought up in unwarmed and unlit houses, and shipped off to die in Italy when they proved unequal to the struggle of living in New York! Therefore Grandmamma, like most of her contemporaries, remained in town on the first of January, and marked the day by a

(60) family reunion, a kind of supplementary Christmas—though to us juniors the absence of presents and plum-pudding made it but a pale and moonlike reflection of the Feast.

---

[1] garments made of stylish, elegant fabric
[2] a silk fabric
[3] a dress made of soft, thin silky fabric

ESSAY QUESTION 3

(Suggested time—40 minutes. This question counts as one-third of your score for Section II of the exam.)

Many novels and plays focus on individuals involved in a struggle to find themselves or to seek a purpose in life. Sometimes the effort pays off; sometimes it doesn't.

Choose a novel or play of literary merit in which a character (not necessarily the protagonist) engages in a search for meaning or personal identity. In a well-organized essay, explain the search or struggle, assess to what extent it succeeds, and analyze how it contributes to the meaning of the work as a whole. You may use any of the works listed below, or choose one of comparable literary merit. Do not merely summarize the plot.

The Adventures of Augie March	*The House of Mirth*
The Adventures of Huckleberry Finn	*Joseph Andrews*
The Awakening	*The Jungle*
Death of a Salesman	*Madame Bovary*
Dr. Faustus	*Main Street*
A Farewell to Arms	*Moby Dick*
Great Expectations	*Oedipus Rex*
The Great Gatsby	*A Portrait of the Artist as a Young Man*
The Glass Menagerie	*The Red and the Black*
Hamlet	*Sister Carrie*
Heart of Darkness	*Tess of the d'Urbervilles*

STOP

END OF PRACTICE TEST 1

Answer Key
PRACTICE TEST 1

Section I

1. C	16. B	31. A	46. B
2. A	17. A	32. D	47. A
3. C	18. C	33. C	48. D
4. E	19. C	34. C	49. B
5. C	20. B	35. E	50. E
6. D	21. D	36. A	51. A
7. C	22. E	37. A	52. E
8. C	23. C	38. B	53. C
9. E	24. B	39. E	54. A
10. E	25. E	40. C	55. C
11. B	26. E	41. A	
12. B	27. C	42. D	
13. C	28. E	43. A	
14. C	29. D	44. B	
15. D	30. D	45. E	

SUMMARY OF ANSWERS IN SECTION I MULTIPLE-CHOICE

Number of correct answers _____

Use this information when you calculate your score on this examination. See page 250.

ANSWER EXPLANATIONS

Section I

1. **(C)** Sophia's fatigue and especially her "fever of the spirits" (line 9) seem to have been brought about by an unpleasant (but unspecified) occurrence in Upton. Choice (A) seems like a reasonable explanation for Sophia's "extreme fatigue." Her buoyant mood when she left Upton, however, suggests that a sleepless night was not a sufficient cause of her distemper, i.e., ill humor. Choice (B) may also seem like a possible answer because disputes of any kind can cause physical upset, but the passage fails to elaborate Jones's role, if any, in upsetting Sophia.

2. **(A)** The narrator evidently has no confidence in physicians, who cover their ignorance with high-sounding words and phrases that mean virtually nothing. Choices (D) and (E) may be implied by the narrator's comment, but neither specifically refers to physicians' use of meaningless medical jargon.

3. **(C)** Choice (E) may be implied by Sophia's decision not to awaken Mrs. Honour. (C) is a better choice, however, because it affords the narrator the opportunity to add a more laudable attribute to the list of Sophia's virtues, in this case Sophia's kindness and consideration, even for those on a lower rung of the social ladder.

4. **(E)** Choices (A)–(D) come close to the meaning of "equipped" but are too general. The more specific word "dressed" explains precisely what Mrs. Honour helped Sophia to do.

5. **(C)** Suffering from fatigue, from a "fever of the spirits," and from feelings that border on despair (line 33), Sophia cannot think clearly. She proposes to leave immediately for London in spite of the cold, the darkness, and the dangers of a nighttime journey. Because (A), (B), and (D) are not at all unusual, they don't merit being thought of as products of an aberrant mind. Disregard (E) because later in the passage it's the landlady—not Sophia—who fantasizes that her guest is Jenny Cameron in disguise.

6. **(D)** Radiant beauty is conveyed not only by the reference to Sophia's "greater glories" (line 17) but also by the maid's description of Sophia as an "angel upon the earth" (lines 22–23). Choice (A) may seem like a reasonable answer because such elegant beauty is not typical of women leading conventional, humdrum lives, but the passage contains more evidence to support (D).

7. **(C)** By fleeing from Upton at an "unseasonable" (line 38) hour, Mrs. Fitzpatrick shows that she feared her husband more than she feared traveling by night. Now that she is far from Mr. Fitzpatrick, her lesser fear—nighttime travel—has assumed greater importance. Choice (B) is true in part because Mrs. Fitzpatrick suffers from a variety of fears, but her escape from Upton indicates that she's not paralyzed by her angst.

8. **(C)** As described in lines 36–42, Mrs. Fitzpatrick is plagued with various fears that make her seem irresolute and uncertain, particularly in comparison to Sophia. The narrator admits in lines 40–41 that he doesn't grasp the nature of Mrs. F's "lesser terrors." There is no hint in lines 36–42 that she lacks credibility.

9. **(E)** By agreeing to stay the night at the inn, Sophia shows her essential goodness and affability. Choice (B) may seem like a good answer, but it contradicts one of the passage's main purposes—to portray Sophia in the best possible light.

10. **(E)** Although she claims to recoil at the thought of being overtaken by Jones (lines 47–48), the narrator thinks that "she rather wished than feared it" (line 49). The narrator attributes the discrepancy between what she says and what she feels to "those secret, spontaneous emotions of the soul to which the reason is often a stranger" (lines 51–52).

11. **(B)** Mrs. Fitzpatrick won't go to Bath after hearing that her husband had arrived in Upton. Sophia hopes to avoid her father, also newly arrived in Upton. She also wishes to stay away from "Jones" (line 47), although the narrator is not so sure (lines 48–49). In brief, the two women alter the itinerary according to their likes and dislikes, their whims and fears. Choice (D) has some validity, but the women's need to feel secure is only one of their concerns.

12. **(B)** The landlady is so enchanted by Sophia's sweetness and affability that she decides to become a Jacobite.

13. **(C)** The landlady's outlandish fantasy is reported to have been spawned by Sophia's "great sweetness and affability" (line 60). (A) is strongly suggested, but consider the narrator's focus throughout the passage—to acquaint the reader with Sophia. The traits of other characters are less important.

14. **(C)** Evidence of the narrator's viewpoint appears in short asides and comments, such as "I know not what" (line 40) and "I am afraid" (line 47), among others. The narrator's use of "our heroine" (line 15) and "We ought not . . ." (lines 20–22) reveals his concern for the characters. Thus, the narrator is a spectator but is far from an indifferent one.

15. **(D)** The narrator pays most attention to Sophia's charm and good looks.

16. **(B)** Such phrases as "eternal note of sadness" (line 14), "human misery" (line 18) and "Its melancholy, long, withdrawing roar" (line 25) turn the poem into a lament about the condition of the world. The speaker is disturbed about changes in the world, but his views are expressed more in sorrow than in anger.

17. **(A)** Words and images such as "straits," "coast," "grating roar of pebbles," "calm sea," and "ebb and flow" help to create a vivid picture of the poem's setting. Virtually every line rhymes with another, although the rhyming lines, except for 36–37, are sometimes two or more lines apart. The rhymes create a repetition of sound that may be likened to the waves breaking on the beach, but like the waves themselves, they are not evenly spaced nor of the same intensity. Likewise, the rhythm is irregular. In some parts of the poem (lines 10–11 and 32–33, for example) short phrases—usually iambic feet—suggest small, quick, repetitive waves. But intermittently, the rhythm slows, as in "Sophocles long ago/Heard it on the Aegean" (lines 15–16), mimicking long, slow rolling waves.

18. **(C)** In line 9, the speaker says, "Listen!" and then cites such sounds as the "roar of pebbles," and the "tremulous cadence" of the sea. Further on, the

speaker finds "in the sound a thought" (line 19) and says that "now I only hear/Its melancholy, long, withdrawing roar" (lines 24–25).

19. **(C)** Recalling that the Aegean Sea once evoked in Sophocles what the straits between England and France now evoke in him, the speaker both universalizes the experience and suggests that human misery has existed for a long, long time. The speaker never tries to compare ancient Greece with contemporary England.

20. **(B)** Reflecting on the ebbing of the sea, the speaker is reminded of the decline in religious faith.

21. **(D)** The speaker compares the Sea of Faith with the sea observed in lines 1–2. In both the tide is "full," or high. All the other choices imply amplitude and fullness in one form or other, but (D) is most applicable to the sea.

22. **(E)** In the third stanza the speaker is troubled by the diminution of faith in the world. As the next stanza begins, he aspires to use love as a possible antidote for the sadness and indifference that pervade the world.

23. **(C)** The phrase describes the appearance of the world as seen from a distance. What follows is a depiction of the world as it really is. The notion that goodness is a mere illusion is consistent with the speaker's pessimism about the world's condition.

24. **(B)** The grammatical subject is "world." Because the other nouns are either in the predicate or in a subordinate clause, they may not serve as the subject.

25. **(E)** A villanelle is a tightly structured nineteen-line poem with a prescribed pattern of rhymes. A narrative poem tells a story. An ode comes in various forms but usually glorifies a dignified or lofty subject. A prose poem is a piece of prose written in poetic language. A dramatic monologue consists of the words of a single person speaking to a listener who does not respond in words but may nevertheless influence the speaker.

26. **(E)** The poem is dominated by the speaker's melancholy over the state of the world, especially the loss of religious faith. In the final stanza, love may provide solace, but overall, the poem is suffused with references to human misery and sadness. (A) is a promising answer but is too general a description of the poem's primary theme. (B) refers to the contrast of war and peace found in lines 34–37. The absence of peace in the world, however, is just one cause of the speaker's grief.

27. **(C)** The author creates humor by taking an absurd premise and dealing with it in a serious, respectful manner. In effect, the author, like many good comedians, keeps a straight face while being funny. None of the other choices is broad enough to identify the overall tone of the passage.

28. **(E)** The speaker's informant is a "simple-hearted miner" living alone in the woods who "believed" that he could understand animal talk. To rely on such questionable authority raises doubts about the speaker's judgment. While the sentence beginning in line 3 doesn't disprove the assertion that animals talk, it tends to call it into question.

29. **(D)** The narrator of the passage reports what Jim Baker told him. The author, however, who speaks to the reader through the narrator, has human beings in mind, in particular big, puffed-up talkers who try to impress others with their command of language.

30. **(D)** Jim adopts a scornful tone while discussing cats but not because he despises them. Rather, he pretends to disapprove of cats because, compared with bluejays, they are grammatical disasters.

31. **(A)** The first paragraph contains no colloquial expressions such as "grammar that will give you lockjaw" (lines 29–30). Nor does it speak directly to the reader using second-person pronouns like "you." It contains no repetition like "bristling with metaphor, too—just bristling" (line 22). It also lacks usages that violate conventional English grammar, such as "ain't" (line 31) and "use bad grammar but very seldom" (line 32). Choice (A) is correct because nowhere in the passage does the author use passive sentence structure.

32. **(D)** In line 33, the plural pronoun "they" refers to the singular antecedent "jay." While you may find additional grammatical flaws in lines 24–32, none of them appears in the list of choices.

33. **(C)** Jim Baker uses the phrase while trying to prove that a jay is endowed with human qualities. That is, a bluejay "is just as much a human" as anyone reading or hearing the passage. In the next sentences, however, Jim Baker singles out members of Congress.

34. **(C)** Just prior to making the allusion, Jim Baker likens bluejays to humans. Once "a Congressman" is mentioned, however, he begins indirectly to charge members of Congress with lying, stealing, deceiving, and so forth. (A) probably has some validity, but the passage targets congressmen in particular. The other incorrect choices pertain mostly to bluejays instead of people.

35. **(E)** Jim Baker uses a colloquial expression to say that when it comes to swearing, a cat can't hold a candle to a bluejay.

36. **(A)** The phrase is supposed to get a laugh, but behind the humor lurks a misanthropic notion.

37. **(A)** Trying to make the case that a jay is everything a man is, Jim is about to cite a "perfectly true fact" to prove his point. All the other choices—(B) to (E)—are too specific to be inferred.

38. **(B)** Prior to line 56, Jim Baker's description of the bluejay's talents is full of generalities. After line 56, Jim tells about a specific bluejay in a specific place and time.

39. **(E)** While the anecdote doesn't actually prove that Jim comprehends bluejay talk, it tells of a specific time when he claims to have translated what a bluejay said.

40. **(C)** The details included in the description—from the empty house to the "leaves rustling so lonely in the trees" (line 63)—stress Jim's hermit-like existence.

41. **(A)** The speaker seems to revel in Jim Baker's fanciful notion of animals speaking articulately and following the rules of grammar.

42. **(D)** During his encounter with the snake the speaker allows his "education" to prevail over his instincts. Suddenly, he realizes that he has erred and must atone for his "pettiness." Choices (A), (B), and (C) describe something that occurs during the poem but (D) is the most all-inclusive answer and comes closest to the poem's meaning.

43. **(A)** The speaker, surprised to find the snake at the trough, waits patiently while the snake drinks its fill. He acts as though the snake has no less a right to drink there than he does.

44. **(B)** Ostensibly, the speaker wears pyjamas "for the heat," but also to imply that he meets the snake with an open mind, "undressed" as it were, or unencumbered by the ordinary contraints of society.

45. **(E)** Smooth-sounding phrases such as "yellow-brown slackness soft-bellied down" (line 9) and "slack long body,/Silently" (lines 14–15) recreate the sinuous flow of the snake over the ground.

46. **(B)** The snake seems to ignore the observer. It is intent on getting its fill of water.

47. **(A)** According to the speaker, the snake comes from and returns to "the burning bowels of the earth" (line 23). It also writhes into the "black hole" (line 70), and seems like the king "of the underworld" (line 78). In that respect, the snake is, or at least stands for, Satan.

48. **(D)** The speaker's mind resounds with the voices of a society that fears snakes and destroys them without compunction.

49. **(B)** The lines portray a man in conflict. One side of him says kill the snake; the other side appreciates the snake's visit. The lines also refer to ideas expressed by (C) and (D), but neither idea is as emphatic as that in (B).

50. **(E)** In line 32, the speaker says, "How glad I was he had come like a guest."

51. **(A)** Each of the questions sets up an either/or dichotomy, providing evidence of the ambivalence raging inside the speaker. Although he hurls a log at the snake later in the poem and also shows signs of empathy toward the creature, (B)–(E) fail to explain fully how the questions function in the poem.

52. **(E)** The speaker's action is precipitated by an ill-defined "sort of horror, a sort of protest" (line 58). Without knowing exactly why, he impulsively throws the log at the water-trough. (A) seems like a reasonable answer, but remember that the speaker's attitude toward snakes is not instinctive but rather learned behavior. (C) contains a kernel of truth, but recklessness implies that the individual is aware of the consequences of his action and chooses to ignore them. In contrast, an impulsive action (E) occurs without thinking.

53. **(C)** In *Rime of the Ancient Mariner*, the title character, after killing an albatross, is burdened by remorse and guilt. Even if you are not familiar with

Coleridge's poem, the speaker's regret for attacking the snake is evident in lines 72–73 and also in lines 80–84.

54. (**A**) All the quotations except that in Choice A suggest regal bearing, regal appearance, or an ordinary man's response to a regal presence.

55. (**C**) In lines 80–81, the speaker laments, "I missed my chance with one of the lords/Of life."

Section II

Although answers to essay questions will vary greatly, the following descriptions suggest an approach to each question and contain ideas that could be used in a response. Perhaps your essay contains many of the same ideas. If not, don't be alarmed. Your ideas may be at least as valid as those presented below.

Note: Don't mistake these descriptions for complete essays; essays written for the exam should be full-length, well organized, and fully developed. For an overview of how essays are graded, turn to "How Essays Are Scored," on page 45.

ESSAY QUESTION 1

Both poets define forgetfulness indirectly. Crane relies mostly on figures of speech: Similes such as "Forgetfulness is like a song" (line 1) and metaphors like "Forgetfulness is rain at night" (line 6). Collins describes forgetfulness with examples, naming specific types of facts that tend to escape from the memory—the names of authors, for instance, and the order of the planets.

Of the two poems, Crane's is the more abstract and elusive. Some of its images suggest the enigmatic nature of forgetfulness. It is "like a bird," says the speaker, "whose wings are reconciled,/outspread and motionless" (lines 3–4). In other words, the speaker in the poem finds forgetfulness hard to pin down and understand. It's an inexplicable, airy thing that follows no predictable pattern, like a "bird that coasts the wind unwearyingly" (line 5).

Some of Crane's images—"rain at night" (line 6), "an old house in the forest" (line 7)—refer to familiar, more tangible things. In context, rain has symbolic connotations, perhaps something in the dark that is heard but not seen or something that happens without our awareness, like forgetfulness itself, which takes us by surprise. Likewise, an old house in the forest evokes a sense of isolation, of loss, and disintegration, each an emotional by-product of forgetfulness.

Whether Crane set out to write an obscure poem is difficult to say, but its effect is puzzling and uncertain, just like the phenomenon of forgetfulness. In the last line, the speaker shifts the poem's focus to himself and offers a paradoxical thought about his own experience. Like all of us, he has been subject to forgetfulness, but he remembers that he has forgotten, a comment that adds still another dimension to the mystery of forgetfulness.

The speaker in the second poem takes a different tack. He describes forgetfulness as one of the common symptoms of growing old. He writes about himself, but he uses the second person, *you*, to suggest the universality of his experience. Although losing one's memory can be annoying, frustrating, even ominous in some cases, the speaker approaches it in a witty and breezy style, as if to say that since you can't do anything about it, you might as well live with it and carry on. The speaker's semi-serious tone is created in part by using everyday, conversational language. Through much of the poem, he scatters phrases suggesting that facts take their leave from the mind as though heading off on a trip: They decide to retire, pack their bags, kiss you goodbye, and slip away. The speaker's list of inconsequential details that are easily forgotten is also meant to amuse readers with a mild jolt of self-recognition. After all, which of us hasn't forgotten useless facts once filed away in our minds—names of the Muses, for example, and the capital of Paraguay?

Only in the fourth stanza does a note of foreboding enter the poem. It is brought in by a reference to "a dark mythological river," the "*L*," better known as the Lethe, one of the rivers of Hades. It is the river of oblivion and forgetfulness. A drink from the river erases all memory from the newly dead.

To avoid ending the poem in total gloom and doom, the speaker offers a modicum of encouragement in lines 20–21: To be sure, it's not easy to get up in the middle of the night to look up a date, but we do it because we refuse to let forgetfulness victimize us without a fight. The last two lines of the poem reassure us in still another way: Trivialities such as the words of a memorized love poem may vanish, but the poem nevertheless leaves residue behind that permits us still to be moved by the sight of the moon drifting by the window.

ESSAY QUESTION 2

To construct the passage, Wharton uses the words of a gentleman recalling his youth, a technique that allows the speaker to compare the past and the present. The narrator's remembrances of things past are triggered by a disapproving comment made by his aging mother about a promiscuous couple who once held trysts at the "Fifth Avenue Hotel," a location that suggests the epitome of high-class extravagance.

Scornfully, the narrator likens his mother's indictment of the couple to that of a snake's "hiss" (line 4), a notion developed later with a simile comparing his "superannuated" mother's remark to secretions of "venom" (line 12). All told, the narrator, who reflects contemporary values, has little stomach for the old-fashioned judgments issuing from his mother. He supports the view of Sillerton Jackson, an old gentleman grumbling through his false teeth—a "perfect 'china set'" (line 17)—that these days nobody cares about such so-called scandalous behavior (lines 18–19).

While rejecting his mother's outdated values, however, the narrator can't arrest the flood of his boyhood memories. Thinking back, he adopts a slightly mocking tone that says, in effect, how straight-laced and rigid his family's life had been. Among other things, he cites the perceived "perils of living north of Union Square" (lines 30–31), implying that the perils were more a threat to one's social standing than to one's physical well-being. He also cites the example of his grandmother, who, attired in clothing that bespoke of her social status, religiously followed the now-obsolete custom of receiving visitors on New Year's day. These days, the narrator maintains, fashionable people leave town in the winter.

ESSAY QUESTION 3

Any of the titles listed after the prompt would be an appropriate work on which to base an essay about a character's search for meaning and fulfillment.

An essay on *The Awakening* by Kate Chopin would most likely focus on Edna Pontellier, a wife and mother who has reached a point in life when she can no longer tolerate her respectable, upper-middle-class existence. Nothing pleases her more than doing what she chooses to do when she chooses to do it. Her gradual "awakening" includes letting go of some lifelong inhibitions, briefly taking a lover, falling in love, starting to paint, and leaving her husband. At one point she almost drowns while learning to swim, symbolizing inevitable difficulties encountered during journeys to self-fulfillment. Along the way, Edna realizes that virtually every decision she makes affects others, including her two children. Willing to risk social ostracism for herself, she can't let go of her maternal obligations. Because she refuses to live in misery, she sees death by drowning as her only path of escape. Before diving into the sea, she stands naked on the beach feeling reborn. Although she is about to destroy herself, for once she feels completely free to determine her own fate.

Fate is also the issue in Sophocles' play *Oedipus Rex.* In order to free Thebes of a deadly pestilence, the title character struggles to identify the murderer of Laius, his late father. After the blind seer, Tiresias, names Oedipus himself as the guilty party, Oedipus's efforts turn into a pursuit of self-knowledge As events unfold, Oedipus discovers that he had inadvertently fullfilled an ancient prophesy, not only by killing his own father but marrying his mother. Horrified, Jocasta hangs herself and Oedipus gouges out his eyes and goes into exile. Oedipus's effort to know himself and his origins obviously has tragic consequences. Finding the truth, instead of setting him free, destroys him. Events in the play suggest the inexorable power of fate and the tragic destiny that awaits those who fail to exercise moral self-restraint. Oedipus's downfall results not so much from preordained action, however, as from his uncontrollable pride (hubris), which figuratively and then literally blinds him.

Another work in which a character searches for meaning and fails tragically is *Death of a Salesman* by Arthur Miller. The hero, Willy Loman, devotes his life to building what may be called a typical American Dream: security, a successful career, a loving and happy family. But as hard as he tries, Willy can't make it. Too many social and economic barriers stand in his way. Even more, his own personality and temperament work against him. Unable to face his own shortcomings, he contrives fantasies to stave off the reality of his failures. He tries in vain to create an image of himself as a successful salesman but everyone, his sons included, sees through his posturing. Shattered after being fired from his job, Willy realizes that his life insurance makes him worth more dead than alive. Accordingly, he commits suicide. Willy represents a malaise that infects vast numbers in our society, and *Death of a Salesman* can be viewed as an implicit indictment of capitalism as a way of life.

SELF-SCORING GUIDE FOR PRACTICE TEST 1
Scoring Section 2   ESSAYS

After referring to "How Essays Are Scored," on page 45 of this book, use this guide to help you evaluate each essay. Do your best to evaluate your performance in each category by using the criteria spelled out below. Because it is hard to achieve objectivity when assessing your own writing, you may improve the validity of your score by having a trusted and well-informed friend or experienced teacher read and rate your essay.

On the following Rating Chart, enter a number (from 1 to 6) that you think represents your level of performance in each category (A–F).

Category A: OVERALL PURPOSE/MAIN IDEA
- 6 clearly establishes and cogently defines an insightful purpose
- 5 clearly establishes and generally defines an appropriate purpose
- 4 identifies and defines an appropriate purpose
- 3 identifies and develops a mostly appropriate purpose
- 2 attempts to identify but falls short of defining a clear purpose
- 1 fails to identify the purpose of the essay

Category B: HANDLING OF THE PROMPT
- 6 clearly and completely addresses and directly answers each part of the prompt
- 5 directly addresses and answers each part of the prompt
- 4 answers each part of the prompt directly or indirectly
- 3 answers most parts of the prompt directly or indirectly
- 2 fails to address important parts of the prompt directly or indirectly
- 1 does not address the prompt or misinterprets requirements of the prompt

Category C: ORGANIZATION AND DEVELOPMENT
- 6 insightfully organizes sequence of ideas according to the purpose of the essay; presents a cogent analysis using fully-developed, coherent paragraphs
- 5 organizes material clearly and develops ideas with generally insightful evidence in unified paragraphs
- 4 organizes conventional evidence or commentary in appropriate but perfunctorily arranged, formulaic paragraphs
- 3 organizes material with little relation to the point or purpose of the essay; develops ideas adequately but with occasional irrelevancies
- 2 organizes weak material in a confusing manner; generally ignores appropriate paragraph development
- 1 lacks discernible organization; ignores relevant development of ideas

Category D: SENTENCE STRUCTURE

    6 uses clear, precise, and appropriately varied sentences to convey meaning and create effects

    5 uses clear sentences with appropriately varied structures to create interest

    4 consists of mostly clear sentences with some structural variety

    3 contains minor sentence errors and little sentence variety

    2 includes sentence errors that sometimes interfere with meaning

    1 contains serious sentence errors that obscure meaning

Category E: USE OF LANGUAGE

    6 uses precise and effective vocabulary extremely well-suited to the subject and the audience

    5 contains vocabulary that clearly and accurately convey meaning

    4 uses conventional but generally correct and appropriate vocabulary

    3 uses ordinary vocabulary with some errors in diction or idiom

    2 contains awkward word choices and frequent errors in diction or idiom

    1 uses words that often obscure meaning

Category F: GRAMMAR AND USAGE

    6 avoids all or virtually all grammar and usage errors

    5 includes occasional minor errors in standard English grammar and usage

    4 uses standard English grammar and usage but with several minor errors in standard English

    3 contains errors in standard English grammar and usage that occasionally obscure meaning

    2 contains errors in standard English grammar and usage that frequently obscure meaning

    1 contains several major errors in standard English grammar and usage that block meaning

RATING CHART

<table>
<tr><th colspan="4">RATING CHART</th></tr>
<tr><td>Rate your essay:</td><td>Essay 1</td><td>Essay 2</td><td>Essay 3</td></tr>
<tr><td>Overall Purpose/Main Idea</td><td>_____</td><td>_____</td><td>_____</td></tr>
<tr><td>Handling of the Prompt</td><td>_____</td><td>_____</td><td>_____</td></tr>
<tr><td>Organization and Development</td><td>_____</td><td>_____</td><td>_____</td></tr>
<tr><td>Sentence Structure</td><td>_____</td><td>_____</td><td>_____</td></tr>
<tr><td>Use of Language</td><td>_____</td><td>_____</td><td>_____</td></tr>
<tr><td>Grammar and Usage</td><td>_____</td><td>_____</td><td>_____</td></tr>
<tr><td>Composite Scores (Sum of each column)</td><td>_____</td><td>_____</td><td>_____</td></tr>
</table>

By using the following chart, in which composite scores are converted to the 9-point AP rating scale, you may determine the final score for each essay:

Composite Score	AP Essay Score
33–36	9
29–32	8
25–28	7
21–24	6
18–20	5
15–17	4
10–14	3
7–9	2
6 or below	1

AP Essay Scores   Essay 1 _____   Essay 2 _____   Essay 3 _____

TEST SCORE WORKSHEET

Calculating Your AP Score on Practice Test 1

The scores you have earned on the multiple-choice and essay sections of the exam may now be converted to the AP 5-point scale by doing the following calculations:

I. Determine your score for Section I (Multiple-Choice)

    Step A: Number of correct answers _____

    Step B: Multiply the figure in Step A by 1.2272 to find your Multiple-Choice Score _____. (Do not round)

II. Determine your score for Section II (Essays)[1]

    Step A: Enter your score for Essay 1 (out of 9) _____

    Step B: Enter your score for Essay 2 (out of 9) _____

    Step C: Enter your score for Essay 3 (out of 9) _____

    Step D: Add the figures in Steps A, B, and C _____

    Step E: Multiply the figure in Step D by 3.0556 _____ (Do not round). This is your Essay Score.

III. Determine Your Total Score

    Add the scores for I and II to find your composite score _____ .

                               (Round to the nearest whole number)

To convert your composite score to the AP 5-point scale, use the chart below. The range of scores only approximates what you would earn on the actual test because the exact figures may vary from test to test. Be aware, therefore, that your score on this test, as well as on other tests in this book, may differ slightly from your score on an actual AP exam.

Composite Score	AP Grade
114–150	5
98–113	4
81–97	3
53–80	2
0–52	1

---

[1]After the AP exam, essays are judged in relation to other essays written on the same topic at the same time. Therefore, the score you assign yourself for an essay may not be the same as the score you would earn on an actual exam.

Answer Sheet
PRACTICE TEST 2

Section I

1 Ⓐ Ⓑ Ⓒ Ⓓ Ⓔ   16 Ⓐ Ⓑ Ⓒ Ⓓ Ⓔ   31 Ⓐ Ⓑ Ⓒ Ⓓ Ⓔ   46 Ⓐ Ⓑ Ⓒ Ⓓ Ⓔ
2 Ⓐ Ⓑ Ⓒ Ⓓ Ⓔ   17 Ⓐ Ⓑ Ⓒ Ⓓ Ⓔ   32 Ⓐ Ⓑ Ⓒ Ⓓ Ⓔ   47 Ⓐ Ⓑ Ⓒ Ⓓ Ⓔ
3 Ⓐ Ⓑ Ⓒ Ⓓ Ⓔ   18 Ⓐ Ⓑ Ⓒ Ⓓ Ⓔ   33 Ⓐ Ⓑ Ⓒ Ⓓ Ⓔ   48 Ⓐ Ⓑ Ⓒ Ⓓ Ⓔ
4 Ⓐ Ⓑ Ⓒ Ⓓ Ⓔ   19 Ⓐ Ⓑ Ⓒ Ⓓ Ⓔ   34 Ⓐ Ⓑ Ⓒ Ⓓ Ⓔ   49 Ⓐ Ⓑ Ⓒ Ⓓ Ⓔ
5 Ⓐ Ⓑ Ⓒ Ⓓ Ⓔ   20 Ⓐ Ⓑ Ⓒ Ⓓ Ⓔ   35 Ⓐ Ⓑ Ⓒ Ⓓ Ⓔ   50 Ⓐ Ⓑ Ⓒ Ⓓ Ⓔ
6 Ⓐ Ⓑ Ⓒ Ⓓ Ⓔ   21 Ⓐ Ⓑ Ⓒ Ⓓ Ⓔ   36 Ⓐ Ⓑ Ⓒ Ⓓ Ⓔ   51 Ⓐ Ⓑ Ⓒ Ⓓ Ⓔ
7 Ⓐ Ⓑ Ⓒ Ⓓ Ⓔ   22 Ⓐ Ⓑ Ⓒ Ⓓ Ⓔ   37 Ⓐ Ⓑ Ⓒ Ⓓ Ⓔ   52 Ⓐ Ⓑ Ⓒ Ⓓ Ⓔ
8 Ⓐ Ⓑ Ⓒ Ⓓ Ⓔ   23 Ⓐ Ⓑ Ⓒ Ⓓ Ⓔ   38 Ⓐ Ⓑ Ⓒ Ⓓ Ⓔ   53 Ⓐ Ⓑ Ⓒ Ⓓ Ⓔ
9 Ⓐ Ⓑ Ⓒ Ⓓ Ⓔ   24 Ⓐ Ⓑ Ⓒ Ⓓ Ⓔ   39 Ⓐ Ⓑ Ⓒ Ⓓ Ⓔ   54 Ⓐ Ⓑ Ⓒ Ⓓ Ⓔ
10 Ⓐ Ⓑ Ⓒ Ⓓ Ⓔ   25 Ⓐ Ⓑ Ⓒ Ⓓ Ⓔ   40 Ⓐ Ⓑ Ⓒ Ⓓ Ⓔ   55 Ⓐ Ⓑ Ⓒ Ⓓ Ⓔ
11 Ⓐ Ⓑ Ⓒ Ⓓ Ⓔ   26 Ⓐ Ⓑ Ⓒ Ⓓ Ⓔ   41 Ⓐ Ⓑ Ⓒ Ⓓ Ⓔ
12 Ⓐ Ⓑ Ⓒ Ⓓ Ⓔ   27 Ⓐ Ⓑ Ⓒ Ⓓ Ⓔ   42 Ⓐ Ⓑ Ⓒ Ⓓ Ⓔ
13 Ⓐ Ⓑ Ⓒ Ⓓ Ⓔ   28 Ⓐ Ⓑ Ⓒ Ⓓ Ⓔ   43 Ⓐ Ⓑ Ⓒ Ⓓ Ⓔ
14 Ⓐ Ⓑ Ⓒ Ⓓ Ⓔ   29 Ⓐ Ⓑ Ⓒ Ⓓ Ⓔ   44 Ⓐ Ⓑ Ⓒ Ⓓ Ⓔ
15 Ⓐ Ⓑ Ⓒ Ⓓ Ⓔ   30 Ⓐ Ⓑ Ⓒ Ⓓ Ⓔ   45 Ⓐ Ⓑ Ⓒ Ⓓ Ⓔ

SECTION I

Multiple-choice Questions

TIME—1 HOUR

Percent of total grade on the exam: 45 percent

Instructions: This section of the exam consists of selections from literary works and questions on their content, form, and style. After reading each passage and poem, choose the best answer to each question and then fill in the corresponding oval on the answer sheet.

Questions 1–11. Read the following poem carefully before you decide on your answers to the questions.

La Belle Dame Sans Merci[1]

O what can ail thee, Knight-at-arms,
    Alone and palely loitering?
The sedge[2] is withered from the Lake,
    And no birds sing!

Line
(5)   O what can ail thee, Knight-at-arms,
    So haggard and so woebegone?
The Squirrel's granary is full,
    And the harvest's done.

I see a lily on thy brow,
(10)   With anguish moist and fever dew;
And on thy cheek a fading rose
    Fast withereth too.

"I met a Lady in the Meads,[3]
    Full beautiful, a faery's child;
(15) Her hair was long, her foot was light,
    And her eyes were wild.

"I made a Garland for her head,
    And bracelets too, and fragrant Zone;[4]
She looked at me as she did love,
(20)   And made sweet moan

---

[1]The Beautiful Woman Without Mercy
[2]grassy marsh plant
[3]meadows
[4]a belt of flowers

"I set her on my pacing steed,
   And nothing else saw all day long,
For sidelong would she bend and sing
   A faery's song.

(25)   "She found me roots of relish sweet,
   And honey wild, and manna dew;
And sure in language strange she said—
   'I love thee true.'

"She took me to her elfin grot,[5]
(30)   And there she wept and sighed full sore,
And there I shut her wild wild eyes
   With kisses four.

"And there she lullèd me asleep
   And there I dreamed—Ah woe betide!
(35) The latest dream I ever dreamt
   On the cold hill side.

"I saw pale Kings, and Princes too,
   Pale warriors, death-pale were they all;
They cried—'La Belle Dame sans Merci
(40)   Hath thee in thrall!'

"I saw their starved lips in the gloam,
   With horrid warning gapèd wide,
And I awoke, and found me here
   On the cold hill's side.

(45)   "And this is why I sojourn here,
   Alone and palely loitering;
Though the sedge is wither'd from the Lake,
   And no birds sing."

                      —John Keats, 1819

----

[5]grotto

1. The narrator in the poem observes the autumn season primarily through

   (A) tastes and feelings
   (B) light and dark
   (C) odors and colors
   (D) sights and sounds
   (E) land and sky

2. The significant shift in the poem's structure occurs between lines

    (A) 4 and 5
    (B) 12 and 13
    (C) 24 and 25
    (D) 32 and 33
    (E) 46 and 47

3. By setting the poem in autumn, the poet is

    (A) implying that the fate of humanity depends in part on nature
    (B) suggesting that the knight's life, like the year, is approaching its end
    (C) endowing the season with human attributes
    (D) using a metaphor that helps readers grasp the poem's underlying meaning
    (E) casting the narrative in a mournful mood

4. The tone of the poem can be described by all of the following EXCEPT

    (A) melancholic
    (B) despairing
    (C) horrifying
    (D) mysterious
    (E) magical

5. Which of the following literary techniques most significantly contributes to the overall effect of the poem?

    (A) Its pattern of rhymes
    (B) The capitalization of certain words
    (C) The use of figurative language
    (D) Its interplay of the setting and mood
    (E) Its repetition of sounds

6. The metaphors in lines 9–12 are meant to

    (A) contrast the hues in the flowers with the absence of color in the countryside
    (B) suggest the religious affiliation of the knight
    (C) show that the knight is behaving strangely
    (D) imply that the knight has been on a romantic quest
    (E) depict the pallor of the knight's face

7. In line 19, "as she did love" means

   (A) trying to love
   (B) as though she loved
   (C) when she was loved
   (D) like someone craving love
   (E) experienced in the art of love

8. Which of the following best paraphrases the meaning of line 22?

   (A) And rode on with my eyes closed
   (B) And she blocked my vision
   (C) And was preoccupied by my horse
   (D) And could think of nothing else for the rest of the day
   (E) And was blinded by love

9. The phrase "Ah woe betide!" (line 34) serves primarily to

   (A) overstate the knight's compassion
   (B) indicate the knight's awareness that he has made a mistake
   (C) heighten the emotional intensity of the knight's story
   (D) change the spirit established by "lullèd me asleep" in line 33
   (E) suggest the conflict going on in the knight's mind

10. The pronoun "this" in line 45 refers to

    (A) awakening alone on the cold hillside instead of in the lady's grotto
    (B) the deathly pale warriors, kings, and princes
    (C) words that he heard uttered in his dream
    (D) the lady's declaration of love for the knight
    (E) the loss of the knight's horse

11. Which of the following describes the main theme of the poem?

    (A) Untrustworthy women
    (B) The power of dreams to foretell the future
    (C) Unrequited love
    (D) How time heals wounds
    (E) The consequences of hypocrisy

Questions 12–20. Read the following dialogue carefully before you decide on your answers to the questions.

RAMSDEN [*very deliberately*] Mr. Tanner: you are the most impudent person I have ever met.

Line
(5)

TANNER [*seriously*] I know it, Ramsden. Yet even I cannot wholly conquer shame. We live in an atmosphere of shame. We are ashamed of everything that is real about us; ashamed of ourselves, of our relatives, of our incomes, of our accents, of our opinions, of our experience, just as we are ashamed of our naked skins. Good Lord, my dear Ramsden, we are ashamed to walk, ashamed to ride in an omnibus, ashamed to hire a hansom instead of keeping a carriage, ashamed of keeping one horse instead of two and a groom-gardener instead of a coachman and footman. The more things a man is ashamed of, the more respectable he is. Why, you're ashamed to buy my book, ashamed to read it: the only thing you're not ashamed of is to judge me for it without having read it; and even that only means that you're ashamed to have heterodox opinions. Look at the effect I produce because my fairy godmother withheld from me this gift of shame. I have every possible virtue that a man can have except—

(10)

(15)

RAMSDEN. I am glad you think so well of yourself.

TANNER. All you mean by that is that you think I ought to be ashamed of talking about my virtues. You don't mean that I haven't got them: you know perfectly well that I am as sober and honest a citizen as yourself, as truthful personally, and much more truthful politically and morally.

(20)

RAMSDEN [*touched on his most sensitive point*] I deny that. I will not allow you or any man to treat me as if I were a mere member of the British public. I detest its prejudices; I scorn its narrowness; I demand the right to think for myself. You pose as an advanced man. Let me tell you that I was an advanced man before you were born.

(25)

TANNER. I knew it was a long time ago.

RAMSDEN. I am as advanced as ever I was. I defy you to prove that I have ever hauled down the flag. I am *more* advanced than ever I was. I grow more advanced every day.

(30)

TANNER. More advanced in years, Polonius.[1]

RAMSDEN. Polonius! So you are Hamlet, I suppose.

---

[1]A character in *Hamlet* known for verbosity and deviousness

(35)   TANNER. No: I am only the most impudent person you've ever met. That's your notion of a thoroughly bad character. When you want to give me a piece of your mind, you ask yourself, as a just and upright man, what is the worst you can fairly say to me. Thief, liar, forger, adulterer, perjurer, glutton, drunkard? Not one of these names

(40)   fits me. You have to fall back on my deficiency in shame. Well, I admit it. I even congratulate myself; for if I were ashamed of my real self, I should cut as stupid a figure as any of the rest of you. Cultivate a little impudence, Ramsden; and you will become quite a remarkable man.

(45)   RAMSDEN. I have no—

         TANNER. You have no desire for that sort of notoriety. Bless you, I knew that answer would come as well as I know that a box of matches will come out of an automatic machine when I put a penny in the slot: you would be ashamed to say anything else.

                                                                          (1903)

12. Which of the following adjectives best describes the tone of the conversation?

    (A) Flippant
    (B) Pretentious
    (C) Argumentative
    (D) Humorous
    (E) Pragmatic

13. Ramsden's characterization of Tanner in lines 1–2 is borne out in the remainder of the dialogue by all of the following EXCEPT

    (A) Tanner's assessment of himself
    (B) Tanner's advice to Ramsden
    (C) Tanner's overall arrogance
    (D) Tanner's remark, "More advanced in years, Polonius" (line 33)
    (E) Tanner's physical appearance

14. The sentiment expressed in lines 11–12, "The more things . . . is," is an example of which of the following?

    (A) An analogy
    (B) An understatement
    (C) A mixed metaphor
    (D) A metonymy
    (E) A paradox

15. The repeated use of "ashamed" in lines 4–17 indicates that Tanner

    (A) wishes to emphasize the pervasiveness of shame
    (B) hopes to provoke Ramsden into an argument
    (C) expects Ramsden to take back his nasty remark about Tanner's impudence
    (D) doubts that Ramsden can readily absorb the message
    (E) wants to impress his listener with the breadth and depth of his thinking about the issue

16. Tanner's allusion to "my fairy godmother" (line 16) serves to

    (A) add a spiritual dimension to his thinking
    (B) lighten the tone of his remarks
    (C) turn the style of the passage from personal to analytical
    (D) assert the sincerity of his beliefs
    (E) provide evidence that his theory of human behavior is correct

17. Ramsden's reference to "a mere member of the British public" (lines 25–26) does which of the following?

    (A) Reveals a major difference between himself and Tanner
    (B) Proves that he is well-informed about current British society
    (C) Asserts that he considers himself an entrenched member of the upper class
    (D) Demonstrates a lack of concern about what Tanner thinks of him
    (E) Shows that he wishes to be regarded as a radical political thinker

18. In lines 30–33 "advanced" is used in the sense of

    (A) tolerant of others
    (B) experienced
    (C) unorthodox
    (D) conservative
    (E) aged

19. The metaphor in line 31, "hauled down the flag," is best interpreted to mean

    (A) retreated into the past
    (B) accepted less than the best
    (C) insulted my colleagues
    (D) violated my principles
    (E) surrendered

20. By comparing Ramsden to an "automatic machine" (line 48), Tanner suggests Ramsden's

    (A) composure
    (B) conservatism
    (C) callousness
    (D) conventionality
    (E) lack of judgment

Questions 21–35. Read the following passage carefully before you decide on your answers.

I am a rather elderly man. The nature of my avocations, for the last thirty years, has brought me into more than ordinary contact with what would seem an interesting and somewhat singular set of
Line men, of whom, as yet, nothing, that I know of, has ever been
(5) written—I mean, the law-copyists, or scriveners.[1] I have known very many of them, professionally and privately, and, if I pleased, could relate diverse histories, at which good-natured gentlemen might smile, and sentimental souls might weep. But I waive the biographies of all other scriveners, for a few passages in the life of Bartleby, who
(10) was a scrivener, the strangest I ever saw, or heard of. While, of other law-copyists, I might write the complete life, of Bartleby nothing of that sort can be done. I believe that no materials exist for a full and satisfactory biography of this man. It is an irreparable loss to literature. Bartleby was one of those beings of whom nothing is ascertain-
(15) able, except from the original sources, and, in his case, those are very small. What my own astonished eyes saw of Bartleby, *that* is all I know of him, except, indeed, one vague report, which will appear in the sequel.

Ere introducing the scrivener, as he first appeared to me, it is fit I
(20) make some mention of myself, my employees, my business, my chambers, and general surroundings; because some such description is indispensable to an adequate understanding of the chief character about to be presented. Imprimis:[2] I am a man who, from his youth upwards, has been filled with a profound conviction that the easiest
(25) way of life is the best. Hence, though I belong to a profession proverbially energetic and nervous, even to turbulence, at times, yet nothing of that sort have I ever suffered to invade my peace. I am one of those unambitious lawyers who never addresses a jury, or in any way draws down public applause; but, in the cool tranquillity of
(30) a snug retreat, do a snug business among rich men's bonds, and mortgages, and title-deeds. All who know me, consider me an

---

[1]Clerks whose job was to copy documents by hand
[2]A legal term meaning "in the first place"

eminently *safe* man. The late John Jacob Astor,[3] a personage little
given to poetic enthusiasm, had no hesitation in pronouncing my
first grand point to be prudence; my next, method. I do not speak it
(35) in vanity, but simply record the fact, that I was not unemployed in
my profession by the late John Jacob Astor; a name which, I admit, I
love to repeat; for it hath a rounded and orbicular sound to it, and
rings like unto bullion. I will freely add, that I was not insensible to
the late John Jacob Astor's good opinion.

(40)   Some time prior to the period at which this little history begins,
my avocations had been largely increased. The good old office, now
extinct in the State of New York, of a Master in Chancery,[4] had been
conferred upon me. It was not a very arduous office, but very pleas-
antly remunerative. I seldom lose my temper; much more seldom
(45) indulge in dangerous indignation at wrongs and outrages; but, I
must be permitted to be rash here, and declare that I consider the
sudden and violent abrogation of the office of Master in Chancery,
by the new Constitution, as a—premature act; inasmuch as I had
counted upon a life-lease of the profits, whereas I only received those
(50) of a few short years. But this is by the way.

My chambers were up stairs, at No.——Wall Street. At one end,
they looked upon the white wall of the interior of a spacious skylight
shaft, penetrating the building from top to bottom.

This view might have been considered rather tame than otherwise,
(55) deficient in what landscape painters call "life." But, if so, the view
from the other end of my chambers offered, at least, a contrast, if
nothing more. In that direction, my windows commanded an unob-
structed view of a lofty brick wall, black by age and everlasting shade;
which wall required no spyglass to bring out its lurking beauties, but,
(60) for the benefit of all near-sighted spectators, was pushed up to within
ten feet of my window panes. Owing to the great height of the surrounding buildings, and my chambers being on the second floor, the
interval between this wall and mine not a little resembled a huge
square cistern.

(1853)

---

[3]In the mid-nineteenth century Astor was one of America's wealthiest men
[4]A type of court that handled issues of fairness; abolished in New York in 1846

21. On the whole, the passage is about

(A) the narrator's qualifications to write Bartleby's story
(B) the narrator's background
(C) the setting in which the story takes place
(D) practicing law in New York
(E) Bartleby's eccentricities

Practice Test 2

22. The relationship between the narrator and Bartleby can best be described as

    (A) distant
    (B) alienated
    (C) bitter
    (D) sentimental
    (E) easygoing

23. Grammatically, the phrase "law-copyists, or scriveners" (line 5) functions as

    (A) an objective complement
    (B) a comparison
    (C) a direct object
    (D) a predicate nominative
    (E) an appositive modifier

24. In lines 8–18 of the passage, the narrator is most concerned with

    (A) spurring readers' curiosity about Bartleby
    (B) explaining why it's difficult to find material on Bartleby
    (C) creating the impression that he is an established author
    (D) lamenting the absence of sources for a biography of Bartleby
    (E) apologizing for his failure to locate information about Bartleby

25. The sentence starting in line 12 does which of the following?

    (A) It contradicts an opinion expressed by the narrator in the previous sentence.
    (B) It introduces the thought that literature has suffered an "irreparable loss."
    (C) It explains the assertion made in the previous sentence.
    (D) It develops the statement that Bartleby was the strangest of all scriveners.
    (E) It functions as a transition between the preceding and following sentences.

26. The phrase "original sources" (line 15) can best be understood to mean

    (A) material written in Bartleby's hand
    (B) documents pertaining to Bartleby's life
    (C) stories told by Bartleby's friends and colleagues
    (D) information provided by Bartleby himself
    (E) sketches and drawings

27. Lines 23–29 serve mainly to show that the narrator

    (A) came into his profession late in life
    (B) reveres people with money
    (C) takes a dim view of attorneys
    (D) prefers not to work very hard
    (E) adheres to a set of strong beliefs and principles

28. In lines 24–39, the narrator uses all of the following stylistic devices EXCEPT

    (A) apostrophe
    (B) alliteration
    (C) litotes
    (D) simile
    (E) repetition

29. In its context, "suffered" (line 27) can best be interpreted to mean

    (A) endured
    (B) agonized
    (C) permitted
    (D) damaged
    (E) forced

30. Which of the following best characterizes the narrator's style?

    (A) Flippant and condescending
    (B) Didactic and detached
    (C) Patronizing and pompous
    (D) Personal and low-key
    (E) Opinionated and contentious

31. The narrator chooses the phrase "a—premature act" (line 48) most probably

    (A) as a euphemism for something that galls him
    (B) to express disapproval of the new Constitution
    (C) to use a familiar term of legal jargon
    (D) to characterize an injustice once done to him
    (E) as an understatement meant to ridicule New York attorneys

32. As used in line 32, the word "*safe*" means which of the following?

    (A) Secure and conscientious
    (B) Honest and reputable
    (C) Unbiased and discreet
    (D) Well-informed and dependable
    (E) Level-headed and competent

Practice Test 2

33. The allusion to the late John Jacob Astor (line 32) serves mainly to

   (A) illustrate the narrator's affection for money
   (B) indicate the prestige of the narrator's law practice
   (C) show that the narrator pursued clients from the upper reaches of society
   (D) suggest why the narrator located his office on Wall Street
   (E) exemplify the social status of clients that the narrator typically served

34. The shift in the narrator's rhetorical stance between lines 51–53 and lines 54–64 can best be described as one from

   (A) subjective to objective
   (B) factual to impressionistic
   (C) critical to nurturing
   (D) effusive to reserved
   (E) confident to uncertain

35. The narrator establishes the tone of the last paragraph (lines 54–64), primarily by

   (A) using the language of aesthetics to describe the views from his office windows
   (B) emphasizing black and white visual images
   (C) comparing the narrow shaft outside his window with a "huge square cistern" (lines 63–64)
   (D) exaggerating the size of the surrounding structures
   (E) contrasting the view from windows at opposite ends of his office

Questions 36–45. Read the following poem carefully before you decide on your answers to the questions.

The Broken Heart

He is stark mad, whoever says,
    That he hath been in love an hour,
Yet not that love so soon decays,
Line   But that it can ten in less space devour;
(5) Who will believe me, if I swear
That I have had the plague a year?
    Who would not laugh at me, if I should say
    I saw a flash of powder burn a day?

Ah, what a trifle is a heart,
(10)   If once into love's hands it come!
All other griefs allow a part
    To other griefs, and ask themselves but some;
They come to us, but us love draws;
He swallows us and never chaws;
(15)   By him, as by chain'd shot, whole ranks do die;
    He is the tyrant pike,[1] our hearts the fry.[2]

If 'twere not so, what did become
    Of my heart when I first saw thee?
I brought a heart into the room,
(20)   But from the room I carried none with me;
If it had gone to thee, I know
Mine would have taught thine heart to show
    More pity unto me ; but Love, alas!
    At one first blow did shiver[3] it as glass.

(25) Yet nothing can to nothing fall,
    Nor any place be empty quite;
Therefore I think my breast hath all
    Those pieces still, though they be not unite;
And now, as broken glasses show
(30) A hundred lesser faces, so
    My rags of heart can like, wish, and adore,
    But after one such love, can love no more.

—John Donne, 1633

---

[1]predatory fish
[2]small fish, easily devoured
[3]shatter

36. The speaker in the poem would most likely characterize his experience in love as

    (A) annoying
    (B) tedious
    (C) lamentable
    (D) pointless
    (E) odious

37. The purpose of the first stanza (lines 1–8) is primarily to

    (A) reveal the speed and potency of love
    (B) compare being in love with being "stark mad"
    (C) caution readers about the hazards of love
    (D) suggest that love is infectious as the plague
    (E) pity anyone who falls in love

38. Line 10 includes an example of

    (A) a conceit
    (B) a paradox
    (C) irony
    (D) personification
    (E) an oxymoron

39. The imagery in the poem is dominated by

    (A) references to rationality and madness
    (B) allusions to violence and destruction
    (C) the use of anatomical language
    (D) references to grief and mourning
    (E) an emphasis on stealth and secrecy

40. Which sentence best paraphrases line 13?

    (A) Distress comes in many forms, but none lasts as long as heartache.
    (B) Emotions can damage us, but none as severely as love.
    (C) Love tends to grab us and never let go.
    (D) We fall in love easily, but no one knows why.
    (E) Unbidden pains afflict us, but lovesickness pulls us to them.

41. The metaphors in lines 14–16 are meant to suggest all of the following about love EXCEPT that

    (A) love is beyond man's control
    (B) love is ruthless
    (C) love is like a force of nature
    (D) love is a predatory beast
    (E) love is hateful

42. Which of the following best describes the function(s) of lines 21–26?

    (A) They show the speaker applying logic to explain a highly emotional event.
    (B) They contrast the effects of love on men and on women.
    (C) They argue against pitying a lover with a broken heart.
    (D) They condemn love's damaging effects on the speaker's heart.
    (E) They caution readers not to fall uncontrollably in love.

43. The literary device that most significantly contributes to the unity of the poem is its

    (A) structured pattern of rhymes
    (B) use of alliteration
    (C) repetition of words and sounds
    (D) archaic diction
    (E) use of the first person

44. Lines 31–32 most strongly express the speaker's

    (A) acknowledgment of a weakness in his personality
    (B) urge to "like, wish, and adore," but not fall in love
    (C) desire to fall in love again
    (D) awareness of his lost capacity to love
    (E) hopes to keep himself from falling recklessly in love again

45. Which of the following best describes the development of the poem?

    (A) Past to present
    (B) Abstract to specific
    (C) Idealistic to realistic
    (D) Subjective to objective
    (E) Conjectural to assertive

Questions 46–55. Read the following passage carefully before you decide on your answers to the questions.

After their marriage they busied themselves, with marked success, in enlarging the circle of their acquaintance. Thirty people knew them by sight; twenty more with smiling demonstrations tolerated
Line their occasional presence within hospitable thresholds; at least fifty
(5) others became aware of their existence. They moved in their enlarged world amongst perfectly delightful men and women who feared emotion, enthusiasm, or failure, more than fire, war, or moral disease; who tolerated only the commonest formulas of commonest thoughts, and recognized only profitable facts. It was an extremely
(10) charming sphere, the abode of all the virtues, where nothing is realized and where all joys and sorrows are cautiously toned down into pleasures and annoyances. In that serene region, then, where noble sentiments are cultivated in sufficient profusion to conceal the pitiless materialism of thoughts and aspirations Alvan Hervey and his
(15) wife spent five years of prudent bliss unclouded by any doubt as to the moral propriety of their existence. She, to give her individuality fair play, took up all manner of philanthropic work and became a member of various rescuing and reforming societies patronized or presided over by ladies of title. He took an active interest in politics;
(20) and having met quite by chance a literary man—who nevertheless was related to an earl—he was induced to finance a moribund society paper. It was a semi-political, and wholly scandalous publication, redeemed by excessive dulness [sic]; and as it was utterly faithless, as it contained no new thought, as it never by any chance had a
(25) flash of wit, satire, or indignation in its pages, he judged it respectable enough, at first sight. Afterwards, when it paid, he promptly perceived that upon the whole it was a virtuous undertaking. It paved the way of his ambition; and he enjoyed also the special kind of importance he derived from this connection with what he
(30) imagined to be literature.

This connection still further enlarged their world. Men who wrote or drew prettily for the public came at times to their house, and his editor came very often. He thought him rather an ass because he had such big front teeth (the proper thing is to have small, even teeth)
(35) and wore his hair a trifle longer than most men do. However, some dukes wear their hair long, and the fellow indubitably knew his business. The worst was that his gravity, though perfectly portentous, could not be trusted. He sat, elegant and bulky, in the drawing-room, the head of his stick hovering in front of his big teeth, and
(40) talked for hours with a thick-lipped smile (he said nothing that could be considered objectionable and not quite the thing), talked in an

(45)

(50)

(55)

(60)

unusual manner—not obviously—irritatingly. His forehead was too lofty—unusually so—and under it there was a straight nose, lost between the hairless cheeks, that in a smooth curve ran into a chin shaped like the end of a snow-shoe. And in this face that resembled the face of a fat and fiendishly knowing baby there glinted a pair of clever, peering, unbelieving black eyes. He wrote verses too. Rather an ass. But the band of men who trailed at the skirts of his monumental frock-coat seemed to perceive wonderful things in what he said. Alvan Hervey put it down to affectation. Those artist chaps, upon the whole, were so affected. Still, all this was highly proper— very useful to him—and his wife seemed to like it—as if she also had derived some distinct and secret advantage from this intellectual connection. She received her mixed and decorous guests with a kind of tall, ponderous grace, peculiarly her own and which awakened in the mind of intimidated strangers incongruous and improper reminiscences of an elephant, a giraffe, a gazelle; of a gothic tower—of an overgrown angel. Her Thursdays were becoming famous in their world; and their world grew steadily, annexing street after street. It included also Somebody's Gardens, a Crescent—a couple of Squares.

(1913)

46. The primary rhetorical function of the sentence beginning on line 2 is to

(A) define a term used in the preceding sentence
(B) reinforce the idea that the couple were newlyweds
(C) prepare the reader for an anecdote later in the passage
(D) provide supporting details for the main idea of the previous sentence
(E) digress from the main topic of the paragraph

47. In lines 5–9 ("They moved . . . facts"), the narrator makes use of all the following EXCEPT

(A) pathos
(B) repetition
(C) insult
(D) comparison
(E) irony

48. From the comment that Alvan Hervey met a literary man "who nevertheless was related to an earl" (lines 20–21), the reader can infer that

    (A) the man pursued his literary endeavors rather casually
    (B) it surprised Alvan to find a literary person who was also a nobleman
    (C) the man was a second-rate writer
    (D) the man was wealthy but went slumming in a low-paying profession
    (E) the man's social status was more impressive than his literary ability

49. The humor in the passage derives mainly from

    (A) the Herveys' belief in their moral superiority
    (B) the Herveys' efforts to expand their circle of friends and acquaintances
    (C) the irony of Alvan's disdain for literary and artistic people
    (D) the narrator's sarcasm as it relates to the characters' pretentiousness
    (E) the uniqueness of the Herveys' behavior

50. Which trait of the Herveys is given the most emphasis in the passage?

    (A) Their obsession to build a good reputation
    (B) Their need to be superior to everyone around them
    (C) Their desire to keep up with their friends and acquaintances
    (D) Their inclination to do charitable works
    (E) Their interest in supporting the arts

51. The reason that Mrs. Hervey joined "various rescuing and reforming societies" (line 18) was to

    (A) form bonds with members of the upper class
    (B) develop her reputation for helping others
    (C) enlarge her circle of acquaintance in the community
    (D) do what Alvan expected of her
    (E) create an identity for herself apart from her husband

52. Lines 19–30 serve to show all of the following about Alvan Hervey EXCEPT that he

    (A) was ambitious
    (B) determined the value of things by their profitability
    (C) lacked wit and a sense of humor
    (D) enjoyed being associated with literary people
    (E) craved the approval of others

53. The narrator describes Alvan Hervey's editor primarily in terms of his

    (A) intellectual gifts
    (B) many talents
    (C) professional skill
    (D) manner of speaking
    (E) physical appearance

54. In lines 55–56, the strangers are "intimidated" in the sense that they

    (A) didn't fit into the crowd
    (B) felt themselves being bullied by Mrs. Hervey
    (C) were overwhelmed by Mrs. Hervey's manner and appearance
    (D) could not control their vivid imaginations
    (E) were frightened in Mrs. Hervey's presence

55. In lines 60–61, the narrator's use of "Somebody's Gardens, a Crescent—a couple of Squares" rather than the names of specific places suggests that

    (A) the Herveys continue to expand their world for no other reason than to expand their world
    (B) the community has grown beyond recognition since the Herveys settled there
    (C) the Herveys have made themselves known in more places than they can remember
    (D) the Herveys have become less discriminating in their choice of friends and acquaintances
    (E) the reputation of Mr. and Mrs. Hervey has spread further than they are aware

SECTION II
Essay Questions

TIME—2 HOURS

Suggested time for each essay—40 minutes
Each essay counts as one-third of the total essay section score

Instructions: This section of the exam consists of three questions that require responses in essay form. You may write the essays in any order you wish and return to work on a completed essay if time permits. Although it is suggested that you spend roughly 40 minutes on each essay, you may apportion your time as you see fit.

Each essay will be evaluated according to its clarity, effectiveness in dealing with the topics, and the overall quality of your writing. If you have the time, go over each essay, checking its punctuation, spelling, and diction. Unless plenty of time remains, try to avoid major revisions. In the end, the quality of each essay counts more than its quantity.

For Question 3, please choose a novel or play of at least the same literary merit as the works you have been assigned in your AP English course.

Essays should be written in pen, preferably with black or dark blue ink. Use lined paper and write as legibly as you can. Do not skip lines. Cross out any errors you make. Feel free to make notes and plan your essay on a piece of scrap paper. Please number your essays and begin each one on a new sheet of paper. Good luck.

ESSAY QUESTION 1

(Suggested time—40 minutes. This question counts as one-third of your score for Section II of the exam.)

Read the following poem carefully, paying particular attention to the personalities of the two neighbors. Then write a well-organized essay in which you explain how the speaker conveys not only the differences between himself and his neighbor but the implications of those differences. You may wish to include analysis of such poetic elements as diction, tone, figurative language, and imagery, among others.

Mending Wall

Something there is that doesn't love a wall,
That sends the frozen-ground-swell under it,
And spills the upper boulders in the sun,
Line   And makes gaps even two can pass abreast.
(5)   The work of hunters is another thing:
I have come after them and made repair
Where they have left not one stone on a stone,
But they would have the rabbit out of hiding,
To please the yelping dogs. The gaps I mean,
(10)   No one has seen them made or heard them made,
But at spring mending-time we find them there.
I let my neighbor know beyond the hill;
And on a day we meet to walk the line
And set the wall between us once again.
(15)   We keep the wall between us as we go.
To each the boulders that have fallen to each.
And some are loaves and some so nearly balls
We have to use a spell to make them balance:
'Stay where you are until our backs are turned!'
(20)   We wear our fingers rough with handling them.
Oh, just another kind of out-door game,
One on a side. It comes to little more:
There where it is we do not need the wall:
He is all pine and I am apple orchard.
(25)   My apple trees will never get across
And eat the cones under his pines, I tell him.
He only says, 'Good fences make good neighbors'.
Spring is the mischief in me, and I wonder
If I could put a notion in his head:
(30)   'Why do they make good neighbors? Isn't it
Where there are cows?
But here there are no cows.
Before I built a wall I'd ask to know
What I was walling in or walling out,
(35)   And to whom I was like to give offense.
Something there is that doesn't love a wall,
That wants it down.' I could say 'Elves' to him,
But it's not elves exactly, and I'd rather
He said it for himself. I see him there
(40)   Bringing a stone grasped firmly by the top
In each hand, like an old-stone savage armed.
He moves in darkness as it seems to me
Not of woods only and the shade of trees.
He will not go behind his father's saying,
(45)   And he likes having thought of it so well
He says again, "Good fences make good neighbors."

—Robert Frost, 1915

ESSAY QUESTION 2

(Suggested time—40 minutes. This question counts as one-third of your score for Section II of the exam.)

The passage below is an excerpt from a short story, "Egotism; or The Bosom Serpent" (1843) by Nathaniel Hawthorne. Roderick Elliston, the story's main character, suffers from a rare and puzzling condition, the nature of which is described in the passage. Read the excerpt carefully. Then, in a well-organized essay, analyze the techniques the author uses to explain Elliston's ailment and the reaction it evokes. Consider diction, choice of details, structure, and any other relevant literary element.

        Shortly after Elliston's separation from his wife—now nearly four years ago—his associates had observed a singular gloom spreading over his daily life, like those chill, gray mists that sometimes steal
Line away the sunshine from a summer's morning. The symptoms caused
(5) them endless perplexity. They knew not whether ill health were robbing his spirits of elasticity, or whether a canker of the mind was gradually eating, as such cankers do, from his moral system into the physical frame, which is but the shadow of the former. They looked for the root of this trouble in his shattered schemes of domestic
(10) bliss,—willfully shattered by himself,—but could not be satisfied of its existence there. Some thought that their once brilliant friend was in an incipient stage of insanity, of which his passionate impulses had perhaps been the forerunners; others prognosticated a general blight and gradual decline. From Roderick's own lips they could learn
(15) nothing. More than once, it is true, he had been heard to say, clutching his hands convulsively upon his breast,—"It gnaws me! It gnaws me!"—but, by different auditors, a great diversity of explanation was assigned to this ominous expression. What could it be that gnawed the breast of Roderick Elliston? Was it sorrow? Was it merely the
(20) tooth of physical disease? Or, in his reckless course, often verging upon profligacy, if not plunging into its depths, had he been guilty of some deed which made his bosom a prey to the deadlier fangs of remorse? There was plausible ground for each of these conjectures; but it must not be concealed that more than one elderly gentleman,
(25) the victim of good cheer and slothful habits, magisterially pronounced the secret of the whole matter to be Dyspepsia![1]
        Meanwhile, Roderick seemed aware how generally he had become the subject of curiosity and conjecture, and, with a morbid repugnance to such notice, or to any notice whatsoever, estranged himself
(30) from all companionship. Not merely the eye of man was a horror to him; not merely the light of a friend's countenance; but even the blessed sunshine, likewise, which in its universal beneficence typifies

---

[1]indigestion

the radiance of the Creator's face, expressing his love for all the creatures of his hand. The dusky twilight was now too transparent for
(35) Roderick Elliston; the blackest midnight was his chosen hour to steal
abroad; and if ever he were seen, it was when the watchman's lantern
gleamed upon his figure, gliding along the street, with his hands
clutched upon his bosom, still muttering, "It gnaws me! It gnaws
me!" What could it be that gnaws him?

ESSAY QUESTION 3

(Suggested time—40 minutes. This question counts as one-third of your score for
Section II of the exam.)

The literary scholar and critic Louise Rosenblatt offers these thoughts about
authors and readers:

> The writer of a literary work "leads us to perceive selected images, personalities, and
> events in special relation to one another. Thus, out of the matrix of elements with
> common meaning for him and his readers, he builds up a new sequence, a new
> structure, that enables him to evoke in the reader's mind a special emotion, a new or
> deeper understanding—that enables him, in short, to communicate with his reader."

Choose a work from the list below or pick a novel or play of comparable literary
merit that evokes in the reader "a special emotion" or a "new or deeper understanding." In a well-written essay identify the emotion or understanding that the work
brings about and explain the relationship between how the writer achieves his purpose
and the meaning of the work as a whole.

Alias Grace	*Heart of Darkness*
All My Sons	*Invisible Man*
All the King's Men	*Joe Turner's Come and Gone*
All the Pretty Horses	*King Lear*
Antigone	*Light in August*
Beloved	*Macbeth*
Billy Budd	*Middlemarch*
The Bridge of San Luis Rey	*Oedipus Rex*
Cold Mountain	*Orlando*
Crime and Punishment	*Tess of the d'Urbervilles*
Fathers and Sons	*The Scarlet Letter*
Ghosts	*The Sound and the Fury*
The Grapes of Wrath	*Their Eyes Were Watching God*
Great Expectations	*The Things They Carried*
Gulliver's Travels	*Waiting for Godot*

END OF PRACTICE TEST 2

Answer Key
PRACTICE TEST 2

Section I

1. D	16. B	31. A	46. D
2. B	17. C	32. E	47. A
3. E	18. C	33. A	48. B
4. C	19. A	34. B	49. D
5. D	20. D	35. A	50. A
6. E	21. B	36. C	51. E
7. B	22. A	37. A	52. C
8. E	23. E	38. D	53. E
9. C	24. A	39. B	54. C
10. A	25. C	40. E	55. A
11. C	26. D	41. E	
12. C	27. D	42. D	
13. E	28. A	43. A	
14. E	29. C	44. D	
15. A	30. D	45. B	

SUMMARY OF ANSWERS IN SECTION I MULTIPLE-CHOICE

Number of correct answers _____

Use this information when you calculate your score on this examination. See page 288.

ANSWER EXPLANATIONS

Section I

1. **(D)** Autumn is described with such images as the withered sedge, the absence of birdsong, the completion of the harvest—in other words, through its sights and sounds.

2. **(B)** The poem consists of two sections. In the first part the narrator sets the scene and asks the knight what ails him. The second, and major, part of the poem contains the knight's response, which begins on line 13.

3. **(E)** In autumn, the season of change, summer dries up and fades away just as the knight's happiness dissolves upon waking from his dream and discovering that he's been jilted. Devastated by loss, he mourns for his lost love while loitering sick at heart around the countryside. (B) has some validity because the fading of the knight's cheeks and the pallor on his forehead might be interpreted as foreshadowing his death, but these qualities are more akin to a debilitating sorrow than to dying. (D) also has possibilities as an answer, but autumn has less to do with the poem's meaning than with its emotional impact.

4. **(C)** Melancholy images prevail in the knight's description of his encounter with the lady. That the knight despairs is obvious in the first two lines of the poem. The woman mysteriously entrances the knight, just as she had enthralled other men (kings, princes, and warriors). While the woman's behavior may be appalling, to call it horrifying is an overstatement.

5. **(D)** The dreary setting of the poem goes hand in hand with the knight's "haggard and so woebegone" condition and with the melancholy mood of the poem. The other choices name poetic features of the poem but have less importance than (D).

6. **(E)** The lily suggests the whiteness of the knight's forehead, while the "fading rose" implies his increasingly pale cheeks. Both metaphors reinforce the image of the knight "palely loitering," introduced in line 2 and reiterated in line 46. (A) would be a reasonable answer only if the poet had depicted the colors of the landscape. Only the word "sedge" (lines 3 and 47) provides a hint of color—the pale brown hues of dying marsh grass.

7. **(B)** At this point in the story, the knight is explaining why he was attracted to the lady. One reason is that her irresistible gaze said, "I love you," a sentiment she puts into words in line 28.

8. **(E)** Lines 23–24 explain why the knight "nothing else saw all day long." Ordinarily a "faery's song" would not obstruct one's vision, but in this case it blinded the knight with love. (A) and (B) also refer to the knight's ability to see, but neither paraphrases line 22 as accurately as (E).

9. **(C)** Line 34 marks a turning point in the knight's story. Before exclaiming "Ah woe betide!" he simply tells what happened during his brief affair with the lady. With the dream come disappointment and anguish heightened by this uncontrollable outburst of emotion.

10. **(A)** Although all the choices allude to events in the knight's story, "this" refers directly to the shock of finding himself "here/ /On the cold hill's side" (lines 43–44) after having been lulled to sleep in the lady's "elfin grot" (line 29).

11. **(C)** The poem is basically a story of a lovestruck man saddened by a woman who pretends to love him but then leaves him in the lurch. (A) is a poor choice because it is an overgeneralized conclusion based on a story of only one deceptive female.

12. **(C)** The conversation is essentially a contentious discussion in which Tanner and Marsden bluntly exchange opinions of themselves and each other. If you chose (B), you've missed the mark, but only slightly, because both speakers—Tanner, especially—characterize themselves as naturally superior to other people.

13. **(E)** Twice during the conversation Tanner agrees that he is impudent. In lines 43–44, he advises Ramsden to cultivate a little impudence himself in order to "become quite a remarkable man." Tanner's cockiness and insolence are revealed by almost everything he says. His vicious comment in line 33 is particularly hurtful. Only Choice (E), Tanner's appearance, is not related to his impudence.

14. **(E)** The statement seems self-contradictory but Tanner nevertheless believes it to be true. The validity of Tanner's paradox is supported by much of the dialogue that both precedes and follows it.

15. **(A)** Tanner harps on the word "ashamed" in arguing that people are conformists and that their fear of shame lies behind almost everything they do.

16. **(B)** Tanner uses his speech to indict people for their conventionality. By alluding to his fairy godmother, he manages to soften the polemical tone of his remarks.

17. **(C)** Ramsden refuses to let Tanner treat him as a member of Britain's middle and working classes presumably because he regards himself superior to them. His disdainful comment is one that Tanner, as a compatriot in the upper reaches of British society, would fully appreciate.

18. **(C)** Ramsden contradicts Tanner's implication that he is a conformist. In fact, Ramsden regards himself as an unconventional, progressive thinker.

19. **(A)** By calling himself "advanced," Ramsden claims to keeps abreast of advanced ideas and thinking. "Hauling down the flag," therefore, refers to taking a step backward, or returning to the past—something he denies ever having done.

20. **(D)** To Tanner, Ramsden seems utterly conventional, so ordinary, in fact, that he can predict what Ramsden will say.

21. **(B)** Three-fourths of the passage, beginning with line 19, is devoted to a description of the narrator's avocation, his likes and dislikes, and the office over which he presides.

22. **(A)** The narrator says in lines 11–15 that he knows virtually nothing about Bartleby except what he has observed. Evidently, Bartleby kept to himself

while in the narrator's employ. Nothing in the passage suggests the existence of affection or friction between the two men.

23. **(E)** Appositive modifiers repeat or specify in different words the expression they modify, in this case "set of men" (lines 3–4).

24. **(A)** The narrator provokes curiosity about Bartleby by describing him as "the strangest [scrivener] I ever saw" (line 10). The reference in line 17 to a "vague report" is also meant to hook the reader's interest. The other choices, (B)–(E), touch on facts that to some degree relate to the passage, but they are incidental to the narrator's major concern.

25. **(C)** In the given sentence the narrator amplifes the idea in the previous sentence that the complete life story of Bartleby cannot be written.

26. **(D)** The phrase means the same as "primary" sources, that is, the words and revelations of Bartleby himself. The narrator says in line 9 that he plans to write "a few passages" about Bartleby because no information exists for a full-length biography. (A) could also be construed as an "original source" for a biography but only if the material pertained to Bartleby himself. A sample of his handwriting on a legal document would be of limited value as a source, especially in comparison to personal information that Bartleby left behind.

27. **(D)** Several phrases indicate that the narrator favors the "easiest way of life" (lines 23–26). He admits to being "unambitious," and he prefers "cool tranquillity of a snug retreat" (lines 29–30) rather than laboring in public.

28. **(A)** Examples of alliteration include "profession proverbially energetic" (lines 25–26) and "pronouncing my first grand point to be prudence" (lines 33–34). Litotes appear in line 35 ("I was not unemployed") and in line 38 ("I was not insensible"). The comment that John Jacob Astor's name "rings like unto bullion" contains a simile, and the word "snug" is repeated in line 30. Only Choice (A), apostrophe—addressing a person or thing not present—is missing.

29. **(C)** The word "suffered" has multiple meanings. Here it is used as a synonym for "tolerated" or "allowed." As one who values tranquillity and peace, the narrator has never allowed frenetic lawyers to influence him.

30. **(D)** The choices containing negative connotations should be eliminated because the passage for the most part is written in a friendly, matter-of-fact tone. Although the narrator casts aspersions on hyperactive lawyers and laments the abolition of the office of Master in Chancery, those are incidental to his main purpose—to tell the story of an unusual scrivener.

31. **(A)** The dash between "a" and "premature" implies that the narrator paused to think of a suitable word. He claims to have been indignant about the abrogation of the Master in Chancery and is about to say something rash about it (lines 45–46) when he apparently changes his mind and utters "premature," instead of a more expressive word. (B) and (D) are tempting answers, but neither accurately describes what occurred. The narrator doesn't denounce the Constitution, only the elimination of the Master in Chancery, a position he hoped to hold for a long time. Likewise, the provision of the

Constitution that abolished his job was not meant to violate the narrator's rights; the narrator merely chooses to see it that way.

32. **(E)** To illustrate the meaning of "safe," the narrator cites the opinions of John Jacob Astor, who, in spite of a shortage of "poetic enthusiasm," praised the narrator's "prudence" and "method." In other words, Astor singled out what he believed were the narrator's best qualities: caution and skill in the practice of law.

33. **(A)** Claiming that he does not cite Astor out of vanity (lines 33–35), the narrator instead loves to say Astor's name because to him it "rings like unto bullion" (line 38). That is, it sounds like money. (B)–(E) are certainly implied, but the narrator's attraction to Astor's riches is what he emphasizes.

34. **(B)** In lines 51–53, the narrator briefly describes a few facts about his office. In the following lines, he interprets the facts, engaging in whimsy, particularly with respect to the views from his windows.

35. **(A)** Both windows face unsightly blank walls. With his tongue lodged firmly in his cheek, and using such phrases as "deficient in what landscape painters call 'life'," and "lurking beauties," the narrator describes the views as though they were works of art.

36. **(C)** Throughout the poem, the speaker laments bitterly about falling in love and being rejected. The poem's title also suggests the emotional state of the speaker.

37. **(A)** The speaker says in line 4 that love can devour ten people in less than an hour. To think otherwise is as crazy as believing that a person can survive the plague for a year or that a quantity of gunpowder can burn for a year instead of exploding instantly.

38. **(D)** The phrase "love's hands" gives love a human characterisitic.

39. **(B)** Although the poem contains some imagery related to Choices (A), (C), and (D), most images relate to war and devastation: for example, "flash of powder," "chain'd shot," "ranks do die," and "broken glass"—all suggesting the brutality of love.

40. **(E)** The speaker asserts that love draws us to it, while other "griefs," come to us, perhaps even seek us out.

41. **(E)** The lines in question characterize love as an uncontrollable force that can swallow us whole, as a ruthless destroyer of men, and as a large fish (a "pike") that feeds on our hearts. No suggestion is made that love is hateful.

42. **(D)** In lines 19 and 20, the speaker asserts, "I brought a heart into the room,/But from the room I carried none with me." In line 21, he begins to reconsider that account of what had happened, figuring that, had he left his heart behind, his beloved would have taken pity on him. In addition, the speaker concludes that an absent heart could not have shattered like glass within his breast. (E) is implied by the entire poem but not particularly by these lines.

43. **(A)** The pattern of rhymes, in particular the concluding couplet in each stanza, endows the poem with a cohesiveness it might not otherwise have.

44. **(D)** The speaker realizes to his chagrin that with a shattered heart he'll never love again.

45. **(B)** The poem begins with some general remarks about the nature of love. Subsequently, the speaker relates his own experience as a lover. Therefore, what starts as theoretical and abstract gradually becomes highly personal and specific.

46. **(D)** Because the sentence in question enumerates the people entering the Herveys' circle of acquaintance, it supports the first sentence in the passage.

47. **(A)** An example of repetition is "commonest formulas of commonest thought" (lines 8–9). The overall tone is ironic and meant to degrade the "perfectly delightful"—but also commonplace and money-grubbing—"men and women" in the couple's social circle. The narrator also makes a comparison between what these people feared and what they feared even more (lines 6–8). Only pathos, that element in literature that provokes the reader's pity or sorrow, is absent.

48. **(B)** The word "nevertheless" suggests that the man was somehow out of the ordinary. Indeed, being a writer, a poet, or a critic would be unusual for an earl or even an earl's relative.

49. **(D)** Using sarcasm, the narrator portrays the Herveys searching for happiness "where noble sentiments are cultivated in sufficient profusion to conceal . . . pitiless materialism of thoughts and aspirations" (lines 12–13). That is, they put on airs, mouthed the proper words, and partook of culture not because they wanted to but because it made a good impression on others. In other words, they were phonies, just like everyone else in their circle of acquaintances. (B) may seem like a promising answer because the passage often mentions people the Herveys came to know. The humor, however, derives mainly from the narrator's tone—that is, his implied criticism of the Herveys and others who value appearance above all else and aim to improve their standing in society by doing what they think is expected of them.

50. **(A)** All the choices more or less describe the Herveys, but almost everything they do is intended to enhance and spread their good name.

51. **(E)** According to lines 16–17, she volunteered her services in order "to give her individuality fair play."

52. **(C)** Nothing in the passage provides evidence that Alvan Hervey, although he may well have been duller than dishwater, lacked wit and sense of humor. The society paper he backed with his money was devoid of wit, but he had nothing to do with its contents.

53. **(E)** The description (lines 33–47) focuses mainly on the man's appearance, particularly on his facial features.

54. **(C)** Mrs. Hervey's "tall, ponderous grace" (line 55) so impressed some guests that they could not help being reminded of other tall creatures and objects such as a giraffe and a gothic tower (line 57).

55. **(A)** The main point of the passage relates to the expansion of the Herveys' social circle. Over time, they have become so caught up in the process—even

to the extent of befriending a man they consider "rather an ass"—that they continue to do it just for the sake of doing it. (C), (D), and (E) are likely consequences of the Herveys' behavior, but none of these choices is discussed or implied in the passage.

Section II

Although answers to essay questions will vary greatly, the following descriptions suggest an approach to each question and contain ideas that could be used in a response. Perhaps your essay contains many of the same ideas. If not, don't be alarmed. Your ideas may be at least as valid than those presented below.

Note: Don't mistake these descriptions for complete essays; essays written for the exam should be full-length, well organized, and fully developed. For an overview of how essays are graded, turn to "How Essays Are Scored," on page 45.

ESSAY QUESTION 1

In lines 1–10 the speaker explains the impetus for the poem: Each winter "something" unseen and unheard knocks down sections of the stone wall that marks the boundary between his and his neighbor's property. Cycles of freezing and thawing, as well as hunters are probably responsible, but the truth remains uncertain, implying that the speaker may probe into deeper questions, perhaps age-old philosophical questions that can never be fully answered. Based on the narrative section of the poem, the speaker has in mind such matters as the barriers between people, the lack of trust that separates one man from another, and the eternal conflict that pits the forces of change against desires to preserve the status quo.

Although the speaker is the one who summons his neighbor to "walk the line/And set the wall between" them once again, he questions the necessity for this annual ritual. He considers it a "game" instead of a serious undertaking and thinks of several sensible and humorous (to him) reasons to abandon it, such as "He is all pine and I am apple orchard./My apple trees will never get across/And eat the cones under his pines" (lines 24–26). The neighbor, however, thinks otherwise, and twice quotes an epigram, "Good fences make good neighbors," passed down to him from his father. To the speaker, this recitation evokes an image of a superstitious savage (lines 41–44), an ignorant man who "moves in darkness" (read *ignorance*), and refuses to "go behind," or relinquish, his father's saying.

The plain language of the poem and frequent references to nature and the land (stones, hills, boulders, pine trees, apple orchard, cows) befit the poem's setting. The lack of rhyme and the colloquial speech of the two neighbors underscore the poem's folksy informality. Yet, the reflections of the speaker, who admits he's full of "mischief" (line 28) raise profound issues. For example, why is the wall rebuilt each year despite the speaker's objections? Are the two farmers in a rut? Is it because they can't communicate? Are barriers between people essential to society? Does the permanence of the barrier symbolize the state of the world? Would it be fair to say, perhaps, that "Mending Wall" is a metaphor for life?

ESSAY QUESTION 2

The excerpt consists of two paragraphs, each written from a different point of view. The first describes Elliston's symptoms as observed by his "associates." The second deals with Elliston's reaction to his own ailment. Although the focus of the two paragraphs differs, the horrific tone of each unites them. In addition, both show Elliston the victim of a woeful ailment, exacerbated by the mystery of its cause and ignorance of its antidote.

A sense of darkness and ominous decay pervades the entire passage, reflecting Elliston's physical and emotional condition. Images such as "chill, gray mists that sometimes steal away the sunshine" (lines 3–4) and "their once brilliant friend" express changes that have forced Elliston into seclusion. He is so blighted that he can no longer face "the blessed sunshine" (line 32), nor even the "dusky twilight" (line 34). Only "blackest midnight" (line 35) draws him out, but even then he clutches himself and continues to mutter chillingly, "It gnaws me! It gnaws me!"

To add still darker dimensions to the portrait of this unfortunate man, the author alludes to the possibility that he has "canker" (cancer) or that he appears to be going insane. What's worse, however, are hints in each paragraph that Elliston's physical decline may reflect a moral and spiritual decline as well. In lines 32–33, for example, the speaker suggests that by rejecting "blessed sunshine" Elliston is also turning his back on "the radiance of the Creator's face," which is likened to an expression of "love for all creatures of his hand," a first-rate irony considering Elliston's condition. Is the author implying that Elliston is not a creature of God's hand? Or is the poor fellow possessed by some sort of demon?

Because the origins of Elliston's malady remain an "endless perplexity" (line 5), the author crowds the passage with questions asked by people who have seen or heard Elliston in agony and can't figure out what's wrong. Only a group of elderly gentlemen, called by the author victims of "good cheer and slothful habits" (line 25) a label suggesting that they may be slightly out to lunch, dismiss Elliston's problem as indigestion. Their diagnosis adds a surprisingly perverse touch to an account of human suffering at its worst.

ESSAY QUESTION 3

An essay on any one of the three titles discussed below would be appropriate:

In *Antigone* by Jean Anouilh (based on the play by Sophocles), the author raises insightful and thought-provoking questions about loyalty, duty, and responsibility.

As the play opens, the title character's life has been turned upside down by the death of her brothers. What grieves her most is not her loss, however, but her uncle's (King Creon) decree that one brother, Polynices, is a traitor to the kingdom of Thebes and, therefore, may not be honored with a proper burial. Antigone, whose allegiance to her brother is stronger than her obligation to follow the rule of law, defies Creon's word and throws dirt onto the corpse. Her actions, which contribute to social mayhem in Thebes, lead ultimately to her own death and the death of others. They also introduce painful questions regarding family obligations and the social good, such as: Which should take precedence—personal freedom or the need for order in society? Antigone may seem like a martyr to her cause, but her behavior raises the issue of whether it is always right to stand up for one's principles and do what one desires regardless of the consequences to oneself and others.

Anouilh provides no answers to these questions. Rather, he presents a situation that obliges the audience to think about Antigone's rebelliousness and decide whether it can or cannot be justified. Emotionally, many readers (or audiences) are apt to side with Antigone in spite of the havoc and grief she causes. She's the underdog, after all, and is bullied by her ruthless, powerful uncle. One could argue, however, that Creon is not a tyrant. Rather, he's just doing the best he can at his job, which includes, among other things, maintaining order and the rule of law in his kingdom.

The Bridge of San Luis Rey raises issues about basic causes of human events. More specifically, are human events accidental and, therefore, meaningless? Or are they part of a predetermined plan? Thornton Wilder's novel interweaves the stories of five victims of a bridge collapse in 1714. Brother Juniper, a Franciscan monk who has witnessed the catastrophe, tries to piece together evidence that explains why God chose these five people for premature death. Juniper's investigation uncovers some common traits among the victims and highlights some extraordinary coincidences that brought them to the bridge at the same time.

His quest, however, leads the authorities of the Inquisition to condemn him as a heretic. They burn him at the stake for attempting to assign meaning to what they view clearly as an act of God. In a sense, then, the novel is about meaning—how we seek and perceive meaning, and particularly how some of us assume that we are wise enough to assign meaning to providential occurrences in our daily lives. Was the collapse of the bridge a random event? Or was it destined to happen at that moment in time? The author won't tell us, but he provides enough food for thought to give readers a chance to figure out answers for themselves.

What is more important in the development of a person—nature? or nurture? That is, do natural-born qualities play a more significant role in determining the fate of a human being than the environment in which a person lives?

In *Native Son* by Richard Wright, Bigger Thomas, a young black man in Depression-era Chicago, finds himself stuck in a hopeless life of misery and poverty. A social welfare agency, however, offers him a chance with a chauffeur's job at the Daltons, a wealthy white family. One night he accidentally suffocates the daughter, May Dalton. After burning her body to destroy the evidence, he fabricates a kidnap plot intended to extort money from the family. A manhunt follows. Bigger is caught, tried, and sentenced to die.

Implicit in the story is the question of how Bigger arrived at death's door. Was it nature or was it nurture? Did Bigger's innate qualities of mind and heart doom him to a life of violence and degradation? Or did social forces destroy him? While Bigger makes a number of self-destructive decisions, the author, in Louise Rosenblatt's words, "chooses those particular elements that have significant relevance to his insight." Although he gives the character a hot-tempered, incorrigible personality, Wright primarily blames society's callousness for Bigger's fate. Just as Bigger is blind to his own potential, white America is blindly unaware of his and other black people's suffering.

SELF-SCORING GUIDE FOR PRACTICE TEST 2
Scoring Section 2 ESSAYS

After referring to "How Essays Are Scored," on page 45 of this book, use this guide to help you evaluate each essay. Do your best to evaluate your performance in each category by using the criteria spelled out below. Because it is hard to achieve objectivity when assessing your own writing, you may improve the validity of your score by having a trusted and well-informed friend or experienced teacher read and rate your essay.

    On the following Rating Chart, enter a number (from 1 to 6) that you think represents your level of performance in each category (A–F).

Category A: OVERALL PURPOSE/MAIN IDEA
6 clearly establishes and cogently defines an insightful purpose
5 clearly establishes and generally defines an appropriate purpose
4 identifies and defines an appropriate purpose
3 identifies and develops a mostly appropriate purpose
2 attempts to identify but falls short of defining a clear purpose
1 fails to identify the purpose of the essay

Category B: HANDLING OF THE PROMPT
6 clearly and completely addresses and directly answers each part of the prompt
5 directly addresses and answers each part of the prompt
4 answers each part of the prompt directly or indirectly
3 answers most parts of the prompt directly or indirectly
2 fails to address important parts of the prompt directly or indirectly
1 does not address the prompt or misinterprets requirements of the prompt

Category C: ORGANIZATION AND DEVELOPMENT
6 insightfully organizes sequence of ideas according to the purpose of the essay; presents a cogent analysis using fully-developed, coherent paragraphs
5 organizes material clearly and develops ideas with generally insightful evidence in unified paragraphs
4 organizes conventional evidence or commentary in appropriate but perfunctorily arranged, formulaic paragraphs
3 organizes material with little relation to the point or purpose of the essay; develops ideas adequately but with occasional irrelevancies
2 organizes weak material in a confusing manner; generally ignores appropriate paragraph development
1 lacks discernible organization; ignores relevant development of ideas

Category D: SENTENCE STRUCTURE

    6 uses clear, precise, and appropriately varied sentences to convey meaning and create effects

    5 uses clear sentences with appropriately varied structures to create interest

    4 consists of mostly clear sentences with some structural variety

    3 contains minor sentence errors and little sentence variety

    2 includes sentence errors that sometimes interfere with meaning

    1 contains serious sentence errors that obscure meaning

Category E: USE OF LANGUAGE

    6 uses precise and effective vocabulary extremely well-suited to the subject and the audience

    5 contains vocabulary that clearly and accurately convey meaning

    4 uses conventional but generally correct and appropriate vocabulary

    3 uses ordinary vocabulary with some errors in diction or idiom

    2 contains awkward word choices and frequent errors in diction or idiom

    1 uses words that often obscure meaning

Category F: GRAMMAR AND USAGE

    6 avoids all or virtually all grammar and usage errors

    5 includes occasional minor errors in standard English grammar and usage

    4 uses standard English grammar and usage but with several minor errors in standard English

    3 contains errors in standard English grammar and usage that occasionally obscure meaning

    2 contains errors in standard English grammar and usage that frequently obscure meaning

    1 contains several major errors in standard English grammar and usage that block meaning

RATING CHART

RATING CHART			
Rate your essay:	Essay 1	Essay 2	Essay 3
Overall Purpose/Main Idea	_____	_____	_____
Handling of the Prompt	_____	_____	_____
Organization and Development	_____	_____	_____
Sentence Structure	_____	_____	_____
Use of Language	_____	_____	_____
Grammar and Usage	_____	_____	_____
Composite Scores (Sum of each column)	_____	_____	_____

By using the following chart, in which composite scores are converted to the 9-point AP rating scale, you may determine the final score for each essay:

Composite Score	AP Essay Score
33–36	9
29–32	8
25–28	7
21–24	6
18–20	5
15–17	4
10–14	3
7–9	2
6 or below	1

AP Essay Scores   Essay 1 _____   Essay 2 _____   Essay 3 _____

TEST SCORE WORKSHEET

Calculating Your AP Score on Practice Test 2

The scores you have earned on the multiple-choice and essay sections of the exam may now be converted to the AP 5-point scale by doing the following calculations:

I. Determine your score for Section I (Multiple-Choice)

   Step A: Number of correct answers _____

   Step B: Multiply the figure in Step A by 1.2272 to find your Multiple-Choice Score _____. (Do not round)

II. Determine your score for Section II (Essays)[1]

   Step A: Enter your score for Essay 1 (out of 9) _____

   Step B: Enter your score for Essay 2 (out of 9) _____

   Step C: Enter your score for Essay 3 (out of 9) _____

   Step D: Add the figures in Steps A, B, and C _____

   Step E: Multiply the figure in Step D by 3.0556 _____ (Do not round). This is your Essay Score.

III. Determine Your Total Score

   Add the scores for I and II to find your composite score _____ .

   (Round to the nearest whole number)

To convert your composite score to the AP 5-point scale, use the chart below. The range of scores only approximates what you would earn on the actual test because the exact figures may vary from test to test. Be aware, therefore, that your score on this test, as well as on other tests in this book, may differ slightly from your score on an actual AP exam.

Composite Score	AP Grade
114–150	5
98–113	4
81–97	3
53–80	2
0–52	1

---

[1]After the AP exam, essays are judged in relation to other essays written on the same topic at the same time. Therefore, the score you assign yourself for an essay may not be the same as the score you would earn on an actual exam.

Answer Sheet
PRACTICE TEST 3

Section I

1 (A) (B) (C) (D) (E)
2 (A) (B) (C) (D) (E)
3 (A) (B) (C) (D) (E)
4 (A) (B) (C) (D) (E)
5 (A) (B) (C) (D) (E)
6 (A) (B) (C) (D) (E)
7 (A) (B) (C) (D) (E)
8 (A) (B) (C) (D) (E)
9 (A) (B) (C) (D) (E)
10 (A) (B) (C) (D) (E)
11 (A) (B) (C) (D) (E)
12 (A) (B) (C) (D) (E)
13 (A) (B) (C) (D) (E)
14 (A) (B) (C) (D) (E)
15 (A) (B) (C) (D) (E)

16 (A) (B) (C) (D) (E)
17 (A) (B) (C) (D) (E)
18 (A) (B) (C) (D) (E)
19 (A) (B) (C) (D) (E)
20 (A) (B) (C) (D) (E)
21 (A) (B) (C) (D) (E)
22 (A) (B) (C) (D) (E)
23 (A) (B) (C) (D) (E)
24 (A) (B) (C) (D) (E)
25 (A) (B) (C) (D) (E)
26 (A) (B) (C) (D) (E)
27 (A) (B) (C) (D) (E)
28 (A) (B) (C) (D) (E)
29 (A) (B) (C) (D) (E)
30 (A) (B) (C) (D) (E)

31 (A) (B) (C) (D) (E)
32 (A) (B) (C) (D) (E)
33 (A) (B) (C) (D) (E)
34 (A) (B) (C) (D) (E)
35 (A) (B) (C) (D) (E)
36 (A) (B) (C) (D) (E)
37 (A) (B) (C) (D) (E)
38 (A) (B) (C) (D) (E)
39 (A) (B) (C) (D) (E)
40 (A) (B) (C) (D) (E)
41 (A) (B) (C) (D) (E)
42 (A) (B) (C) (D) (E)
43 (A) (B) (C) (D) (E)
44 (A) (B) (C) (D) (E)
45 (A) (B) (C) (D) (E)

46 (A) (B) (C) (D) (E)
47 (A) (B) (C) (D) (E)
48 (A) (B) (C) (D) (E)
49 (A) (B) (C) (D) (E)
50 (A) (B) (C) (D) (E)
51 (A) (B) (C) (D) (E)
52 (A) (B) (C) (D) (E)
53 (A) (B) (C) (D) (E)
54 (A) (B) (C) (D) (E)
55 (A) (B) (C) (D) (E)

Practice Test 3

SECTION I

Multiple-choice Questions

TIME—1 HOUR

Percent of total grade on the exam: 45 percent

Instructions: This section of the exam consists of selections from literary works and questions on their content, form, and style. After reading each passage and poem, choose the best answer to each question and then fill in the corresponding oval on the answer sheet.

Questions 1–10. Read the following poem carefully before you decide on your answers to the questions.

Berry Picking

Silently my wife walks on the still wet furze[1]
Now darkgreen the leaves are full of metaphors
Now lit up is each tiny lamp of blueberry.
The white nails of rain have dropped and the sun is free.

Line
(5)   And whether she bends or straightens to each bush
To find the children's laughter among the leaves
Her quiet hands seem to make the quiet summer hush—
Berries or children, patient she is with these.

I only vex and perplex her; madness, rage
(10) Are endearing perhaps put down upon the page;
Even silence daylong and sullen can then
Enamor as restraint or classic discipline.

So I envy the berries she puts in her mouth,
The red and succulent juice that stains her lips;
(15) I shall never taste that good to her, nor will they
Displease her with a thousand barbarous jests.

How they lie easily for her hand to take,
Part of the unoffending world that is hers;
Here beyond complexity she stands and stares
(20) And leans her marvelous head as if for answers.

No more the easy soul my childish craft deceives
Nor the simpler one for whom yes is always yes;
No, now her voice comes to me from a far way off
Though her lips are redder than the raspberries.

                  —Irving Layton, 1958

---

[1] a low-lying evergreen shrub

1. Which of the following best describes the attitude of the speaker toward his wife?

    (A) Sadness
    (B) Envy
    (C) Infatuation
    (D) Frustration
    (E) Confusion

2. In line 1, the image "the still wet furze" exemplifies which of the following poetic techniques?

    (A) Caesura
    (B) Consonance
    (C) Onomatopoeia
    (D) Ambiguity of meaning
    (E) Allusion

3. The woman in the poem is characterized primarily by her

    (A) antisocial behavior
    (B) patience
    (C) serenity
    (D) indifference to her husband
    (E) hearty appetite

4. Between line 8 and line 9, the speaker shifts from

    (A) present events to recalled events
    (B) concrete language to abstract language
    (C) specificity to generalization
    (D) cause to effect
    (E) respect to disapproval

5. In line 12, the verb "Enamor" is best interpreted as

    (A) charm
    (B) inflame with love
    (C) captivate
    (D) be construed
    (E) trick

6. The notion that the "leaves are full of metaphors" (line 2) is supported by all of the following EXCEPT

   (A) "tiny lamp of blueberry" (line 3)
   (B) "white nails of rain" (line 4)
   (C) "sun is free" (line 4)
   (D) "she bends or straightens" (line 5)
   (E) "children's laughter among the leaves" (line 6)

7. Throughout the poem, the choice of details and images suggests that

   (A) the events taking place are imaginary
   (B) the husband and wife have recently had an argument
   (C) the woman is totally absorbed in what she is doing
   (D) the man considers himself a second-rate poet
   (E) the man longs to have as much patience as his wife

8. The woman in the poem is portrayed primarily through her

   (A) actions
   (B) facial expressions
   (C) words
   (D) physical traits
   (E) body language

9. In the course of the poem the speaker discloses that he

   (A) no longer loves his wife
   (B) has often spoken cruelly to his wife
   (C) rarely consults his wife while making decision
   (D) fears growing estranged from his wife
   (E) feels guilty about having deceived his wife

10. Which of the following most significantly contributes to the unity of the poem?

   (A) The poem's last two lines
   (B) The arrangement of rhymes
   (C) Figures of speech
   (D) Repetition of certain sounds
   (E) The warmth and delicacy of the speaker's feelings

Questions 11–25. Read the following passage carefully before you decide on your answers to the questions.

The wound in my uncle *Toby's* groin, which he received at the siege of *Namur,* rendering him unfit for the service, it was thought expedient he should return to *England,* in order, if possible, to be set to rights.

Line
(5)   He was four years totally confined,—part of it to his bed, and all of it to his room; and in the course of his cure, which was all that time in hand, suffer'd unspeakable miseries,—owing to a succession of exfoliations from the *os pubis,*[1] and the outward edge of that part of the *coxendix* called the *os ilium,*[2]—both which bones were dismally
(10)   crush'd, as much by the irregularity of the stone, which I told you was broke off the parapet,—as by its size,—(though it was pretty large) which inclined the surgeon all along to think, that the great injury which it had done my uncle *Toby's* groin, was more owing to the gravity of the stone itself, than to the projectile force of it,—
(15)   which he would often tell him was a great happiness.

My father at that time was just beginning business in *London* and had taken a house;—and as the truest friendship and cordiality subsisted between the two brothers,—and that my father thought my uncle *Toby* could no where be so well nursed and taken care of as in
(20)   own house,—he assign'd him the very best apartment in it.—And what was a much more sincere mark of his affection still, he would never suffer a friend or an acquaintance to step into the house on any occasion, but he would take him by the hand, and lead him up stairs to see his brother *Toby,* and chat an hour by his bed side.

(25)   The history of a soldier's wound beguiles the pain of it;—my uncle's visitors, at least, thought so, and in their daily calls upon him, from the courtesy arising out of that belief, they would frequently turn the discourse to that subject,—and from that subject the discourse would generally roll on to the siege itself.

(30)   These conversations were infinitely kind; and my uncle *Toby* received great relief from them, and would have received much more, but that they brought him into some unforeseen perplexities, which, for three months together, retarded his cure greatly; and if he had not hit upon an expedient to extricate himself out of them, I verily
(35)   believe they would have laid him in his grave.

What these perplexities of my uncle *Toby* were,—'tis impossible for you to guess;—if you could,—I should blush; not as a relation,—not as a man,—nor even as a woman,—but I should blush as an author; inasmuch as I set no small store by myself upon this very
(40)   account, that my reader has never yet been able to guess at any thing.

---

[1]the hipbone
[2]bone in the upper part of the pelvis

> And in this, Sir, I am of so nice a singular humour, that if I thought you was able to form the least judgment or probable conjecture to yourself, of what was to come in the next page,—I would tear it out of my book.

(1760)

11. The phrase "rendering him unfit for service" (line 2) is reinforced by all of the following EXCEPT

    (A) "should return to *England*" (line 3)
    (B) "four years totally confined" (line 5)
    (C) "suffer'd unspeakable miseries" (line 7)
    (D) "succession of exfoliations" (lines 7–8)
    (E) "bones were dismally crush'd" (lines 9–10)

12. In context, the word "expedient" (line 3) is best interpreted to mean

    (A) opportune
    (B) in haste
    (C) practical
    (D) advisible
    (E) efficient

13. The phrase "if possible" in line 3 casts into doubt that Toby

    (A) can be transported back to England
    (B) has the wherewithal to make it back to England on his own
    (C) will recover from his wound
    (D) will ever be well enough to return to the service
    (E) has the strength to endure a lengthy convalescence

14. The narrator uses the Latin names of Toby's bones (lines 8–9) primarily to

    (A) suggest that physicians treated Toby as a specimen not a patient
    (B) show respect for the reader's erudition
    (C) endow the passage with the ring of truth
    (D) reveal the level of anatomical information available at the time
    (E) impress readers with his knowledge of Latin

15. Prior to this passage, the author evidently wrote

    (A) a biography of his father
    (B) a history of England's military operations in foreign lands
    (C) an exposé of medical practices in London
    (D) a portrait of his family
    (E) an account of Toby's experience at the siege of *Namur*

16. By using the phrase "a great happiness" (line 15), the speaker is suggesting that Uncle Toby's surgeon has which of the following characteristics?

    (A) He is familiar with wounds suffered in war.
    (B) He is witty.
    (C) He tends to be sarcastic.
    (D) He has compassion for his patient.
    (E) He has considerable medical expertise.

17. The best interpretation of the word "subsisted" in lines 17–18 is

    (A) supported
    (B) receded
    (C) held
    (D) fed
    (E) obtained

18. The narrator's attitude toward his father may best be described as

    (A) awestruck
    (B) bewildered
    (C) dutiful
    (D) reverential
    (E) respectful

19. Which of the following statements about Toby's condition does the narrator imply?

    (A) Toby's wounds healed more rapidly than expected.
    (B) Frequent conversations about the siege of *Namur* slowed Toby's recovery.
    (C) Toby would have recovered sooner had his surgeon administered the proper treatment.
    (D) The dimensions of the rock that hit Toby had little to do with the seriousness of the wound.
    (E) Toby's brother aided considerably in Toby's recovery.

20. The sentence beginning in line 20 ("And what was . . .") does which of the following?

    (A) It lends support to the sentence that preceded it.
    (B) It implies the narrator's real feelings about Toby.
    (C) It addresses details that had been lacking in earlier paragraphs.
    (D) It casts doubt on the accuracy of the previous sentence.
    (E) It adds important details to the portrait of Toby.

21. The sentence "The history of a soldier's wound beguiles the pain of it" (line 25) does which of the following?

    (A) It shifts the focus of the passage from a specific case to generalities.
    (B) It explains why Toby's visitors brought up a particular topic of conversation.
    (C) It introduces a problem that interferes with Toby's recovery.
    (D) It articulates a widely accepted theory of medical professionals.
    (E) It violates a military tradition that keeps wounded soldiers from discussing their wounds with civilians.

22. The phrase "if you could" (line 37) suggests that the narrator places great value on

    (A) keeping readers well informed
    (B) keeping his readers in suspense
    (C) shocking readers with gruesome details
    (D) taking readers into his confidence
    (E) flattering his readers

23. The last paragraphs (lines 36–44) suggest that this passage is likely to precede an account of

    (A) how Toby overcame unexpected barriers to his recuperation
    (B) Toby's return to military service
    (C) Toby's near-death experiences
    (D) conversations that took place at Toby's bedside
    (E) the outcome of the siege of *Namur*

24. The last paragraph of the passage differs from those that preceded it in all of the following ways EXCEPT

    (A) it addresses the reader directly
    (B) it turns away from the past in order to discuss Toby's future
    (C) it focuses on the narrator instead of on Toby
    (D) it shifts from third person to first person
    (E) it reveals a new aspect of the narrator's personality

25. Which of the following pairs of adjectives best describe the tone of the passage?

    (A) Disdainful/scornful
    (B) Haughty/pompous
    (C) Courteous/deferential
    (D) Solemn/measured
    (E) Satirical/critical

Questions 26–40. Read the following poem carefully before you decide on your answers to the questions.

Gascoigne's Goodnight

When thou has spent the lingering day in pleasure and delight,
Or after toil and weary way, dost seek to rest at night,
Unto thy pains or pleasures past, add this one labor yet:
Ere sleep close up thine eye too fast, do not thy God forget, *Line*
But search within thy secret thoughts, what deeds did thee befall; (5)
And if thou find amiss in aught,[1] to God for mercy call.
Yea, though thou find nothing amiss which thou canst call to mind,
Yet evermore remember this: there is the more behind;
And think how well so ever it be that thou hast spent the day,
It came of God, and not of thee, so to direct thy way. (10)
Thus, if thou try thy daily deeds and pleasure in this pain,
Thy life shall cleanse thy corn from weeds, and thine shall be the gain;
But if thy sinful, sluggish eye will venture for to wink,
Before thy wading will may try how far thy soul may sink,
Beware and wake; for else, thy bed, which soft and smooth is made, (15)
May heap more harm upon thy head than blows of en'my's blade.
Thus if this pain procure thine ease, in bed as thou dost lie,
Perhaps it shall not God displease to sing thus, soberly:
"I see that sleep is lent me here to ease my weary bones,
As death at last shall eke[2] appear, to ease my grievous groans. (20)
My daily sports, my paunch full fed, have caused my drowsy eye,
As careless life, in quiet led, might cause my soul to die.
The stretching arms, the yawning breath, which I to bedward use,
Are patterns of the pangs of death, when life will me refuse.
And of my bed each sundry part in shadows doth resemble (25)
The sundry shapes of death, whose dart shall make my flesh to tremble.
My bed itself is like the grave, my sheets the winding sheet,
My clothes the mold which I must have to cover me most meet;[3]
The hungry fleas, which frisk so fresh, to worms I can compare,
Which greedily shall gnaw my flesh and leave the bones full bare. (30)
The waking cock, that early crows to wear the night away
Puts in my mind the trump that blows before the Latter Day.
And as I rise up lustily when sluggish sleep is past,
So hope I to rise joyfully to Judgment at the last.
Thus will I wake, thus will I sleep, thus will I hope to rise, (35)
Thus will I neither wail nor weep, but sing in godly wise;
My bones shall in this bed remain, my soul in God shall trust,
By whom I hope to rise again from death and earthly dust."

—George Gascoigne (1539–1578)

---

[1] anything, to any degree
[2] also
[3] properly, exactly

26. In context, "there is the more behind" (line 8) is best interpreted to mean

    (A) it's impossible for one to remember everything that happens in a day
    (B) a day has more meaning to it than you think
    (C) another day will be coming tomorrow
    (D) don't end a day without reflecting on it
    (E) no day passes during which one can do everything properly

27. The mood of the poem can best be described as

    (A) inspirational
    (B) suspenseful
    (C) pious
    (D) skeptical
    (E) haunting

28. In the metaphor in line 12, "weeds" is used to stand for

    (A) wasted lives
    (B) wickedness
    (C) undesirable labor
    (D) God's wrath
    (E) weariness

29. Which of the following stylistic devices is most evident in lines lines 1–19?

    (A) The use of epigrams
    (B) An extended metaphor
    (C) The use of archaic pronouns such as "thou" and "thee"
    (D) A series of sentences in the subjunctive mood
    (E) One declarative statement after another

30. The pronoun "it" in line 18 refers to

    (A) "ease" in line 17
    (B) the recitation of lines 19–39
    (C) the "song" quoted from line 19 to line 39
    (D) the bed alluded to in lines 15 and 17
    (E) the pain mentioned in line 17

31. Lines 19–24 contain all of the following poetic devices EXCEPT

    (A) personification
    (B) analogy
    (C) alliteration
    (D) internal rhyme
    (E) synecdoche

32. The main purpose of the comment "My daily sports, my paunch full fed, have caused my drowsy eye,/As careless life, in quiet led, might cause my soul to die" (lines 21–22) is to

    (A) caution the reader against a life devoid of spiritual things
    (B) mock anyone who lives only for the present
    (C) cite reasons why some men ignore God
    (D) suggest that bodily functions cause fatigue
    (E) assert that lack of self-control may lead to dire consequences

33. Which of the following best characterizes the poem's language?

    (A) It uses numerous images of farm life.
    (B) It argues logically in behalf of leading a spiritual life.
    (C) It expresses poetically the need for organized worship to give meaning to life.
    (D) Its religious nature is partly derived from images of death.
    (E) Its tone implies a warning to nonbelievers that they will suffer in the afterlife.

34. Lines 23–29 most resemble which of the following rhetorical devices?

    (A) An elegy
    (B) A metonymy
    (C) A paradoxical understatement
    (D) A mixed metaphor
    (E) An analogy

35. Which of the following is a major concern of the speaker in the poem?

    (A) Fear of dying
    (B) Preparing for sleep
    (C) An unexamined life
    (D) Leading a life without joy
    (E) Excessive hedonism

36. In line 33, "lustily" is best interpreted to mean

    (A) full of desire
    (B) eagerly
    (C) loudly
    (D) without modesty
    (E) with good intentions

37. The poem is best described as a

    (A) case study of a sinner
    (B) lesson in moral behavior
    (C) type of sermon
    (D) didactic fable
    (E) prayer to God

38. Based on the content of the poem, with which of the following statements is the speaker most likely to agree?

    I. People are so caught up in the daily affairs of life that they neglect God.
    II. Through nature God has provided humanity with a source of freshness and inspiration.
    III. To assure that their souls will ultimately rise to heaven, people must acknowledge and respect God.

    (A) II only
    (B) I and II only
    (C) I and III only
    (D) II and III only
    (E) I, II, and III

39. The "sundry shapes of death" (line 26) include all of the following EXCEPT

    (A) "shadows" (line 25)
    (B) "the winding sheet" (line 27)
    (C) "the mold" (line 28)
    (D) "worms" (line 29)
    (E) "the trump" (line 32)

40. Throughout the poem, the speaker's attitude toward death is best characterized as

    (A) an escape from the burdens of life
    (B) something for which one should prepare
    (C) something to look forward to
    (D) acceptance of the inevitable
    (E) detached indifference

Questions 41–55. Read the following passage carefully before you decide on your answers to the questions.

He never asked her whether she had seen Morris again, because he was sure that if this had been the case she would tell him. She had, in fact, not seen him; she had only written him a long letter. The
Line letter, at least, was long for her; and, it may be added, that it was
(5) long for Morris; it consisted of five pages, in a remarkably neat and handsome hand. Catherine's handwriting was beautiful, and she was even a little proud of it; she was extremely fond of copying, and possessed volumes of extracts which testified to this accomplishment; volumes which she had exhibited one day to her lover, when the bliss
(10) of feeling that she was important in his eyes was exceptionally keen. She told Morris, in writing, that her father had expressed the wish that she should not see him again, and that she begged he would not come to the house until she should have 'made up her mind.' Morris replied with a passionate epistle, in which he asked to what, in
(15) Heaven's name, she wished to make up her mind. Had not her mind been made up two weeks before, and could it be possible that she entertained the idea of throwing him off? Did she mean to break down at the very beginning of their ordeal, after all the promises of fidelity she had both given and extracted? And he gave an account of
(20) his own interview with her father—an account not identical at all points with that offered in these pages. 'He was terribly violent,' Morris wrote, 'but you know my self-control. I have need of it all when I remember that I have it in my power to break in upon your cruel captivity.' Catherine sent him, in answer to his, a note of three
(25) lines. 'I am in great trouble; do not doubt my affection, but let me wait a little and think.' The idea of a struggle with her father, of setting up her will against his own, was heavy on her soul, and it kept her quiet, as a great physical weight keeps us motionless. It never entered into her mind to throw her lover off; but from the first
(30) she tried to assure herself that there would be a peaceful way out of their difficulty. The assurance was vague, for it contained no element of positive conviction that her father would change his mind. She only had an idea that if she should be very good, the situation would in some mysterious manner improve. To be good she must be
(35) patient, outwardly submissive, abstain from judging her father too harshly, and from committing any act of open defiance. He was perhaps right, after all, to think as he did; by which Catherine meant not in the least that his judgement of Morris's motives in seeking to marry her was perhaps a just one, but that it was probably natural
(40) and proper that conscientious parents should be suspicious and even unjust. There were probably people in the world as bad as her father supposed Morris to be, and if there were the slightest chance of Morris being one of these sinister persons, the Doctor was right in

taking it into account. Of course he could not know what she

(45) knew—how the purest love and truth were seated in the young man's eyes; but Heaven, in its time, might appoint a way of bringing him to such knowledge. Catherine expected a good deal of Heaven, and referred to the skies the initiative, as the French say, in dealing with her dilemma. She could not imagine herself imparting any kind of

(50) knowledge to her father; there was something superior even in his injustice, and absolute in his mistakes. But she could at least be good, and if she were only good enough, Heaven would invent some way of reconciling all things—the dignity of her father's errors and the sweetness of her own confidence, the strict performance of her

(55) filial duties, and the enjoyment of Morris Townsend's affection.

(1880)

41. The comment that Catherine's letter to Morris "was long for her" (line 4) is most likely intended to

   (A) illustrate one aspect of Catherine's character
   (B) suggest that Catherine is semiliterate
   (C) turn the reader against Catherine
   (D) imply that Catherine usually has more important things to do
   (E) show that Catherine's love for Morris had cooled

42. The "accomplishment" mentioned in line 8 refers to

   (A) Catherine's beautiful handwriting
   (B) an extraordinary letter from Morris to Catherine
   (C) the five-page letter Catherine wrote to Morris
   (D) Catherine's fondness for copying
   (E) Catherine's collection of books containing copied excerpts

43. In lines 9–10, "when the bliss of feeling that she was important in his eyes was exceptionally keen" implies that

   (A) Catherine fears that she has lost Morris's love
   (B) Morris is determined to end his affair with Catherine
   (C) Catherine's attitude toward Morris has undergone a change
   (D) Catherine and Morris have yet to declare their love for each other
   (E) Morris has betrayed Catherine

44. The phrase "in Heaven's name" (lines 14–15) is meant to show

    (A) that Morris is incredulous that Catherine has betrayed him
    (B) that Morris doubts Catherine's commitment to him
    (C) how desperately Morris loves Catherine
    (D) Morris's religious bent
    (E) Morris's perplexity over Catherine's words

45. The description of Morris's exchange of letters with Catherine (lines 11–26) suggests that this passage most probably comes after

    I. an account of the the couple's declaration of love for each other
    II. a narrative of a meeting that occurred between Morris and Catherine's father
    III. a scene in which Catherine's father instructs his daughter to break up with Morris

    (A) II only
    (B) III only
    (C) I and II only
    (D) II and III only
    (E) I, II, and III

46. Which of the following best describes the shift in the tone of Morris's words between lines 13–20 (beginning with "Morris replied…") and lines 21–24 (beginning with "He was terribly violent…")?

    (A) Bewildered to aggressive
    (B) Contrite to pretentious
    (C) Confident to apprehensive
    (D) Hostile to conciliatory
    (E) Forlorn to optimistic

47. Grammatically, the word "note" (line 24) serves as

    (A) the direct object of the verb "sent" (line 24)
    (B) the subject of the sentence in which the word appears (lines 24–25)
    (C) the indirect object of the verb "sent" (line 24)
    (D) the object of the preposition "in" (line 24)
    (E) an appositive for "answer" (line 24)

48. By comparing the "idea of a struggle with her father" (line 26) with "a great physical weight keeps us motionless" (line 28) the narrator invites the thought that

    (A) Catherine is really looking for an excuse to break off with Morris
    (B) Catherine is unaccustomed to talking back to her father
    (C) Catherine is not likely to solve her problem without assistance
    (D) Catherine and Morris are destined sooner or later to go their separate ways
    (E) Catherine's father is some sort of petty tyrant

49. The main reasons that prevent Catherine from solving the problem with her father include all of the following EXCEPT

    (A) his presumption of his own infallibility
    (B) proving to him that Morris is a truthful and loving person
    (C) his desire to be a conscientious parent
    (D) his propensity for violence
    (E) her unwillingness to defy or oppose him

50. Catherine's intuition tells her that her father will change his mind about Morris if she does all of the following EXCEPT

    (A) refrain from exhibiting her true feelings about what her father has done
    (B) adhere to her father's wishes
    (C) seek help from a reputable third party to intervene in her behalf
    (D) try to be a model daughter
    (E) give her father a chance to reconsider by letting an ample amount of time go by

51. The structure of the sentence beginning in line 36 and ending on line 41 achieves which of the following?

    (A) It implies that Catherine is accustomed to being treated unjustly by her father.
    (B) It indicates that Catherine, while differing from her father, is aware that he has the right to be unjust.
    (C) It contradicts Catherine's assertion in the previous sentence that she must not judge her father too harshly.
    (D) It suggests that her father's opinion of Morris may be more accurate than her own.
    (E) It emphasizes the callousness of Catherine's father.

52. In context, the phrase "referred to the skies" in line 48 is best interpreted to mean

    (A) left in the hands of God
    (B) relied on the movement of the stars
    (C) remained optimistic
    (D) believed that God controlled her father's behavior
    (E) waited for Fate to act

53. Catherine's primary dilemma consists mainly of a conflict between

    (A) satisfying herself and keeping Morris happy
    (B) protesting her father's decision and displaying her usual tranquillity
    (C) convincing her father to change his mind and letting fate take its course
    (D) being a dutiful daughter and basking in a loving relationship with Morris
    (E) adhering to her pledge to Morris and wrestling with her conscience

54. Catherine's feelings for her father might best be described as a combination of

    (A) disdain and cynicism
    (B) respect and fear
    (C) deference and resentment
    (D) faithfulness and naïveté
    (E) appreciation and admiration

55. The passage is chiefly concerned with a

    (A) misunderstanding and its clarification
    (B) romance and its dissolution
    (C) conflict and its aftereffects
    (D) plan and its undoing
    (E) rite of passage and suffering it induces

SECTION II
Essay Questions

TIME—2 HOURS

Suggested time for each essay—40 minutes
Each essay counts as one-third of the total essay section score

Instructions: This section of the exam consists of three questions that require responses in essay form. You may write the essays in any order you wish and return to work on a completed essay if time permits. Although it is suggested that you spend roughly 40 minutes on each essay, you may apportion your time as you see fit.

Each essay will be evaluated according to its clarity, effectiveness in dealing with the topics, and the overall quality of your writing. If you have the time, go over each essay, checking its punctuation, spelling, and diction. Unless plenty of time remains, try to avoid major revisions. In the end, the quality of each essay counts more than its quantity.

For Question 3, please choose a novel or play of at least the same literary merit as the works you have been assigned in your AP English course.

Essays should be written in pen, preferably with black or dark blue ink. Use lined paper and write as legibly as you can. Do not skip lines. Cross out any errors you make. Feel free to make notes and plan your essay on a piece of scrap paper. Please number your essays and begin each one on a new sheet of paper. Good luck.

ESSAY QUESTION 1

(Suggested time—40 minutes. This question counts as one-third of your score for Section II of the exam.)

The following poem was inspired by "The Man with the Hoe," a painting by Millet. Read the poem carefully and then write an essay in which you characterize the speaker's views of the figure in the painting. Then, analyze how the speaker conveys those views. Consider the poem's structure, figurative language, diction, imagery, or any other relevant poetic devices.

The Man with the Hoe

(Written after seeing Millet's world-famous painting of a brutalized toiler)

God made man in His own image, in the image of God made He him.

—Genesis

Bowed by the weight of centuries he leans
Upon his hoe and gazes on the ground,
The emptiness of ages in his face,
And on his back the burden of the world.
(5)   Who made him dead to rapture and despair,
A thing that grieves not and that never hopes,
Stolid and stunned, a brother to the ox?
Who loosened and let down this brutal jaw?
Whose was the hand that slanted back this brow?
(10)   Whose breath blew out the light within this brain?

Is this the Think the Lord God made and gave
To have dominion over sea and land;
To trace the stars and search the heavens for power;
To feel the passion of Eternity?
(15)   Is this the dream He dreamed who shaped the suns
And marked their ways upon the ancient deep?
Down all the caverns of Hell to their last gulf
There is no shape more terrible than this—
More tongued with censure of the world's blind greed—
(20)   More filled with signs and portents for the soul—
More packed with danger to the universe.

What gulfs between him and seraphim!
Slave of the wheel of labor, what to him
Are Plato and the swing of Pleiades?
(25)   What the long reaches of the peaks of song,
The rift of dawn, the reddening of the rose?
Thru this dread shape the suffering ages look;
Time's tragedy is in that aching stoop;
Thru this dread shape humanity betrayed,
(30)   Plundered, profaned and disinherited,
Cries protest to the Judges of the World,
A protest that is also prophesy.

O masters, lords and rulers in all lands,
Is this the handiwork you give to God,
(35)   This monstrous thing distorted and soul-quenched?
How will you ever straighten up this shape;

Line refers to line 4; (5), (10), (15), (20), (25), (30), (35) are line numbers.

Touch it again with immortality;
Give back the upward looking and the light;
Rebuild in it the music and the dream;
(40)   Make right the immemorial infamies,
Perfidious wrongs, immedicable woes?

O masters, lords and rulers in all lands,
How will the future reckon with this Man?
How answer his brute question in that hour
(45)   When whirlwinds of rebellion shake all shores?
How will it be with kingdoms and with kings—
With those who shaped him to the thing he is—
When this dumb Terror shall rise to judge the world,
After the silence of the centuries?

—Edwin Markham, 1899

ESSAY QUESTION 2

(Suggested time—40 minutes. This question counts as one-third of your score for Section II of the exam.)

After reading the following excerpt from the British novel, *Vanity Fair* (1848) by William Makepeace Thackery, please write an essay that analyzes how the character of the woman is revealed and how the characterization serves the author's purpose. You may focus on tone, point of view, imagery, diction, choice of detail, or any other literary elements you deem important.

       Sometimes—once or twice a week—that lady visited the upper
regions in which the child lived. She came like a vivified figure out of
the *Magazin des Modes*—blandly smiling in the most beautiful new
Line clothes and little gloves and boots. Wonderful scarves, laces, and
(5) jewels glittered about her. She had always a new bonnet on: and
flowers bloomed perpetually in it: or else magnificent curling ostrich
feathers, soft and snowy as camellias. She nodded twice or thrice
patronisingly to the little boy, who looked up from his dinner or
from the pictures of soldiers he was painting. When she left the
(10) room, an odour of rose, or some other magical fragrance, lingered
about the nursery. She was an unearthly being in his eyes, superior to
his father—to all the world: to be worshipped and admired at a distance. To drive with that lady in the carriage was an awful rite: he sat
up in the back seat, and did not dare to speak: he gazed with all his
(15) eyes at the beautifully dressed princess opposite him. Gentlemen on
splendid prancing horses came up, and smiled and talked with her.
How her eyes beamed upon them! Her hand used to quiver and
wave gracefully as they passed. When he went out with her he had
his new red dress on. His old brown holland[1] was good enough

---
[1] a linen or cotton shirt

(20)   when he stayed at home. Sometimes when she was away, and Dolly
his maid was making the bed, he came into his mother's room. It was
the abode of a fairy to him—a mystic chamber of splendor and
delights. There in the wardrobe hung those wonderful robes—pink
and blue, and many-tinted. There was the jewel-case, silver-clasped:
(25)   and the wondrous bronze hand on the dressing-table, glistening all
over a hundred rings. There was the cheval-glass, that miracle of art,
in which he could just see his own wondering head, and the reflection of Dolly (queerly distorted, and as if up in the ceiling), plump-
ing and patting the pillows of the bed. Oh, thou poor lonely little
(30)   benighted boy! Mother is the name of God in the lips and hearts of
little children; and here was one who was worshipping a stone!

ESSAY QUESTION 3

(Suggested time—40 minutes. This question counts as one-third of your score for
Section II of the exam.)

In many works of literature a character conquers great obstacles to achieve a worthy
goal. Sometimes the obstacle is a personal impediment, at other times it consists of
the attitudes and beliefs of others.

Pick a play or novel in which an important character must overcome a personal
or social obstacle in order to achieve a worthwhile goal. Then write a well-organized
essay that explains the goal and how the character reaches it. Also explain the ways
in which the character's struggle contributes to the meaning of the work as a whole.
Do not merely summarize the plot.

Choose a title from the following list or another play or novel of comparable literary merit.

Crime and Punishment	*King Lear*
The Crucible	*Madame Bovary*
Cyrano de Bergerac	*Native Son*
An Enemy of the People	*The Picture of Dorian Gray*
Ethan Frome	*A Portrait of the Artist as a Young Man*
The Glass Menagerie	*The Red and the Black*
The Grapes of Wrath	*The Scarlet Letter*
Great Expectations	*The Stranger*
The Great Gatsby	*Tess of the d'Urbervilles*
Gulliver's Travels	*Their Eyes Were Watching God*
Heart of Darkness	*Washington Square*

STOP

END OF PRACTICE TEST 3

Answer Key
PRACTICE TEST 3

Section I

1. A	16. D	31. E	46. A
2. D	17. C	32. A	47. A
3. C	18. E	33. D	48. B
4. A	19. E	34. E	49. D
5. D	20. A	35. B	50. C
6. D	21. B	36. B	51. B
7. C	22. B	37. C	52. A
8. A	23. A	38. C	53. D
9. B	24. B	39. A	54. B
10. A	25. D	40. B	55. C
11. A	26. B	41. A	
12. D	27. C	42. D	
13. C	28. B	43. C	
14. C	29. D	44. E	
15. E	30. B	45. E	

SUMMARY OF ANSWERS IN SECTION I MULTIPLE-CHOICE

Number of correct answers _____

Use this information when you calculate your score on this examination. See page 322.

ANSWER EXPLANATIONS

Section I

1. **(A)** As the speaker observes his wife, he admits that she seems more content picking berries than she is being with him. The observation saddens him. No doubt she frustrates (D) and confuses (E) him, but his downheartedness pervades the poem.

2. **(D)** The word "still" is somewhat ambiguous. It often means *quiet*, an adjective that certainly fits the tranquil setting of the poem. But the phrase "still wet" also describes foliage that has remained wet after the rain.

3. **(C)** Starting with the word "Silently" in line 1, the poet piles detail upon detail to portray his wife as a quiet, reserved person. Line 7 ("Her quiet hands seem to make the quiet summer hush") is perhaps the most telling description of her serenity. (D) characterizes the woman, too, but her aloofness is not stated outright. Rather, it is suggested between the lines.

4. **(A)** The first two stanzas are devoted to describing the site and the woman's behavior while picking berries. In the third stanza the poet begins to think about how his wife usually responds to him.

5. **(D)** Ordinarily *enamor* relates to love, but in this context it suggests misinterpretation. At the end of the day, the poet's long and sullen silence can be mistaken for "restraint or classic discipline."

6. **(D)** All of the choices except "she bends or straightens" are figures of speech: (A), (B), and (E) are metaphors; in (C), the sun is personified.

7. **(C)** Through much of the poem the speaker scrutinizes the woman, noting that berry picking not only gives her peace of mind but commands her undivided attention. For example, see lines 7–8.

8. **(A)** The speaker concentrates on what the woman does while berry picking. Among other things, he shows her walking, bending, straightening up, and eating the berries.

9. **(B)** The speaker admits in line 16 that he has displeased his wife "with a thousand barbarous jests." (A) may be true, but it remains unclear whether the speaker no longer loves his wife.

10. **(A)** The last line succinctly expresses the speaker's feelings, echoing sentiments expressed earlier in the poem. Briefly, he realizes that his wife derives more pleasure and satisfaction from the red and succulent berries than she does from him.

11. **(A)** All the choices except (A) cite a reason that Toby can no longer serve. Choice (A), on the other hand, names a consequence, not a cause, of his inability to serve.

12. **(D)** The dictionary lists several definitions for "expedient," including *proper, advantageous, opportune, suitable,* and *politic.* In the context of this passage, the best definition is *advisible* because Toby's wound needed expert attention as soon as possible.

13. **(C)** In context the phrase refers to "be set to rights." In other words, Toby's wound was so serious that his recovery was questionable. (D) is also implied, but a more pressing concern was Uncle Toby's recovery from his wound.

14. **(C)** Using Latin nomenclature creates the impression that the passage was well researched and is scientifically accurate. Using Latin terms could also be construed as a compliment to readers (Choice B), although in the eighteenth century, when the passage was written, educated readers were apt to be familiar with Latin. A modern reader might accuse the doctor of showing off his erudition (Choice E), but it's more likely that the author is simply recording the ordinary language of medical professionals.

15. **(E)** Support for this answer is found in lines 10–11, where the narrator mentions that he had previously said that the stone that wounded Toby "broke off the parapet."

16. **(D)** Using a compassionate bedside manner, the surgeon encourages Uncle Toby by saying it's a "great happiness" that the wound resulted from a falling stone instead of an object fired at him. (A) and (E) are possible answers, but they are assumptions that the passage doesn't clearly support.

17. **(C)** The word is used to indicate that the brothers were held together by a firm and friendly bond.

18. **(E)** The passage is full of details that imply the narrator's respect for his father. In particular, see lines 16–24. (A) and (E) approximate the narrator's attitude toward his father, but they are too extreme. (C) also has some validity, but "dutiful" suggests obligation, while "respectful" is voluntary.

19. **(E)** Toby's brother went out of his way to help. Toby received particular relief from the conversations with people his brother ushered to his bedside.

20. **(A)** The sentence supports the previous one in which the narrator describes how his father took pains to care for his wounded brother.

21. **(B)** The paragraph following the given sentence says that visitors thought they would be doing Toby a good turn by inviting him to talk about his wound.

22. **(B)** The phrase appears in a brief discussion of the author's desire to keep readers in the dark about what comes next. He would blush if readers could guess.

23. **(A)** In this section of the passage the speaker alludes to "unforeseen perplexities" that he intends to explain next.

24. **(B)** The speaker virtually ignores Toby's past and future in the final paragraph.

25. **(D)** Uncle Toby's story is told in a basically sober and straightforward manner.

26. **(B)** Lines 9–10 explain the meaning of the clause in line 8—namely, that a single day has more significance than you might think because God gave it to you as a gift for which you ought to be grateful.

27. **(C)** The speaker in the poem, as though delivering a sermon, promotes piety. Some readers may be inspired by the poem's message (Choice A).

Some may also be haunted (Choice E) by the comparison drawn between sleep and death, but the mood of the poem is consistently pious.

28. **(B)** The couplet in which the word appears makes the point that assessing each day's experiences will enable you to distinguish between the good things you did ("corn") and the wicked things ("weeds"), and will ultimately work to your advantage ("thine shall be the gain").

29. **(D)** At least four of the half-dozen sentences between lines 1–18 use "if" to express a hypothetical condition. In other words, "*if* such-and-such occurred, then the following would happen." The repeated use of "if" sentences corresponds with the speaker's purpose—to show readers the rewards that await them *if* they change their behavior.

30. **(B)** Because the entire quotation reads "Perhaps it shall not God displease to sing thus, soberly:" the pronoun "it" refers to the act of singing or reciting the words of the "song" that follows.

31. **(E)** In line 20 death is personified. Also in line 20 you'll find an example of alliteration ("grievous groans"). Lines 23–24 contain an analogy. The lines also contain internal rhymes, as in "fed" and "led" (lines 21–22). Only a synecdoche is missing, making (E) the correct answer.

32. **(A)** The lines describe the sort of life that causes a "soul to die," meaning a life fit more for a beast perhaps than for a person intent on saving his soul for the hereafter.

33. **(D)** The language is full of religious words and phrases, many alluding to death, especially in the second half of the poem. Aside from a reference to corn and to the crowing of a cock (Choice A), the poem has no images related to life on a farm. (B) is a poor choice because the speaker's argument is based on faith, not on logic. (C) and (E) may be vaguely implied, but the language in the poem never refers specifically to those issues.

34. **(E)** In the given lines, the speaker makes an analogy. Using a series of similes, he compares dying and going to sleep.

35. **(B)** The speaker in the poem is preoccupied with the rituals associated with going to sleep. He repeatedly makes the point that you shouldn't drop off at the end of a day without thanking God for the gifts He has bestowed upon you. Note that the poem's title suggests the speaker's main concern.

36. **(B)** The word is used to describe the manner in which a devout worshipper might rise from his bed after a good night's sleep. Expecting God to take his soul into Heaven, he awakens eagerly, as though he is answering God's call to Judgment.

37. **(C)** The prayer (lines 19–39) illustrates what one might say to please God. But the overall purpose of the poem is to persuade readers to let God into their lives. In that sense, the speaker is much like a preacher delivering an inspirational sermon to his flock.

38. **(C)** Statement I is discussed in the first half of the poem, especially in lines 1–10. The latter half of the poem—particularly lines 34–39—deals with the idea expressed in Statement III. Statement II has no relevancy to the poem.

39. **(A)** The "winding sheet" refers to the cloth in which corpses are wrapped. The "mold" and "worms" allude to the decay and gradual decomposition of an interred body. The "trump" is the trumpet blown to announce Judgment Day. Only the word "shadows" fails to count as one of the "sundry shapes" of death.

40. **(B)** According to the poem, because death may come at any time, you must prepare by always trusting God and striving to be in His good graces. With faith in God, you need not fear your demise. On the Day of Judgment your soul will be raised "from death and earthly dust."

41. **(A)** The comment reveals a dimension of Catherine's personality, namely, that she shuns writing lengthy letters, especially at a time like this, when her relationship with Morris appears to be in jeopardy. Her father's insistence that she and Morris never see each other again could also have kept her from writing a longer letter.

42. **(D)** The passage states that Catherine owned volumes of extracts "which testified to this accomplishment," referring to the previous clause, "she was extremely fond of copying" (line 7).

43. **(C)** Only when Catherine had been confident that Morris loved and treasured her unconditionally had she dared to show him volumes of extracts she had copied. The narrator mentions this fact to suggest that in her present state of mind Catherine could no longer do such a thing.

44. **(E)** To Morris it is inconceivable that Catherine would consider siding with her father against him. Therefore, he either feigns bewilderment or is truly puzzled by her assertion that she needs time to think about whether to see him again.

45. **(E)** Morris's letter refers to the time two weeks earlier when he and Catherine had promised fidelity to each other (lines 15–17). The narrator also mentions that an account of Morris's meeting with Catherine's father had been offered earlier "in these pages" (lines 20–21). Catherine's letter alludes to a conversation during which her father had exhorted her not to see Morris again (lines 11–13). Directly or indirectly, therefore, the letters suggest that events I, II, and III appeared earlier in the text.

46. **(A)** At first Morris puzzles over suddenly being excluded from Catherine's house and Catherine's apparent change of heart. Later, his words become threatening as he reminds her of the power he has "to break in upon" her "cruel captivity." In other words, he claims to know how to stir up some sort of trouble—but the passage fails to explain what the trouble might be.

47. **(A)** A direct object receives the action of a verb or shows the consequence of the action. In this case, Catherine "sent" (verb) a "note" (the object receiving the action).

48. **(B)** The reason that a potential struggle with her father weighs on Catherine's soul (lines 26–27) is that she is unused to disobeying or challenging his authority. Even her affection for Morris cannot break a longstanding pattern of giving in to her father.

49. **(D)** Although Morris reports that Catherine's father was "terribly violent," during their conversation, Catherine disregards the allegation. She is very aware, however, that her father was not one to acknowledge his own mistakes (line 51), that she would be unable to alter her father's opinion of Morris (lines 33–34), and that a conscientious parent should be expected to be suspicious of a daughter's beaus (lines 38–41). In addition, the thought of struggling with her father weighed Catherine down (lines 26–27).

50. **(C)** Lines 32–36 contain a list of things that Catherine thinks she ought to do. Each of the choices shows up on her list except (C), calling on a third party to intervene.

51. **(B)** The sentence consists of three clauses. The first one consists of Catherine's acknowledgment of her father's right to think as he does. The last, or third, clause explains why, and the clause between them describes Catherine's feelings about the matter.

52. **(A)** Several allusions to Heaven toward the end of the passage suggest Catherine's inability to change her father's way of thinking about Morris. Therefore, she has no choice but to rely on Heaven, or God, to help solve her dilemma.

53. **(D)** Catherine's dilemma, described in lines 49–55, alludes to the conflict between "the strict performance of her filial duties, and the enjoyment of Morris Townsend's affection."

54. **(B)** Although Catherine thinks that her father has misjudged Morris, she respects his role as one that is "natural and proper" for a conscientious parent. At the same time she is afraid of setting herself up against him and unwilling to engage him in a struggle that she will certainly lose.

55. **(C)** The passage is devoted first to providing background information about a dispute that has arisen between Catherine and her father. It then shows the effect of the conflict on Catherine and to some extent on Morris.

Section II

Although answers to essay questions will vary greatly, the following descriptions suggest an approach to each question and contain ideas that could be used in a response. Perhaps your essay contains many of the same ideas. If not, don't be alarmed. Your ideas may be at least as valid as those presented below.

Note: Don't mistake these descriptions for complete essays; essays written for the exam should be full-length, well organized, and fully developed. For an overview of how essays are graded, turn to "How Essays Are Scored," on page 45.

ESSAY QUESTION 1

The figure in the painting horrifies and distresses the speaker. As depicted, he is physically strong ("brother to the ox") but stooped from carrying the "burden of the world" on his back. His head, with its "slanted back" brow, resembles that of a Neanderthal. A victim of death in life ("dead to rapture and despair") the man is a less-than-human creature.

In the second stanza, the speaker rails against the existence of such a brute and asks whether God could have had such a being in mind when He made a man in His own image. The question alludes to the quotation from *Genesis* that precedes the first stanza of the poem.

Next, the speaker decries the huge chasm separating this subhuman beast and the angels (line 22). The man, in effect is "humanity betrayed,/Plundered, profaned and disinherited" (lines 29–30).

In the fourth stanza, the speaker addresses those responsible for such an atrocity, namely the "masters, lords, and rulers in all lands," and demands to know what they intend to do to set things right, to restore the man's humanity.

And in the last stanza, the speaker warns the masters, lords, and rulers that they'd better do something because, when "this Man" (now capitalized to suggest that he represents the downtrodden masses of the world) rises in rebellion, they will have to answer for their actions.

The speaker's response to the painting, then, begins viscerally but evolves into a social/political polemic delivered at a fever pitch with passionate, highly charged diction, including such evocative images as "The emptiness of ages on his face" (line 3), "Down all the caverns of Hell to their last gulf/There is no shape more terrible than this—" (lines 17–18), and "whirlwinds of rebellion shake the world" (line 45). In short, to express his wrath, the speaker relies on hyperbolic, often alliterative bombast: "on his back the burden of the world" (line 4), "Plato and the swing of Pleiades" (line 24), "The rift of dawn, the reddening of the rose" (line 26).

Further, the poem is written in blank verse, a form that fits the content, for a finely crafted rhyme scheme would ill befit the speaker's effusive torrent of fiery words. The poem's emotionalism is heightened still further by a rush of rhetorical questions meant to represent the speaker's moral outrage: "Who loosened and let down this brutal jaw? /. . .Whose breath blew out the light within this brain?" (lines 8 and 10). The speaker answers his own questions. He indicts the demons who remain anonymous but are vaguely categorized as the "masters, lords and rulers in all lands."

The author of "The Man with the Hoe," has tried to be profound and grandiose in thought, language, and idea. Whether he succeeds or whether the poem is little more than windy, melodramatic rant is arguable. Regardless, it's difficult to remain unimpressed by the speaker's empathy for the wretched masses of the world.

ESSAY QUESTION 2

The woman in the passage seems like a nineteenth century version of a glamor queen. Details about her appearance, her clothes, and the impact she leaves on her admirers dominate her portrait. The imagery is rich in sensuality—for example, her glittering jewels (line 5), her "magnificent curling ostrich feathers, soft and snowy as camellias" (lines 6–7), and the "odour of rose, or some other magical fragrance" (line 10) that she leaves behind after exiting a room.

The voice of the narrator, prevailing in the early part of the passage, gives way to the point of view of the little boy in lines 11–12. From then on, we observe the woman through the innocent eyes of her son, until line 39 when the narrator returns to pass judgment on his subject. To the boy, the woman is like a fairy goddess, an unearthly being deserving of worship and admiration. The narrator, whose opinion differs, however, declares that she patronizes the little boy (lines 7–8). Both the narrator and her son at one point refer to the woman as "that lady," a scornful turn of phrase that suggests her vanity and self-indulgence. Indeed, her aloofness is illustrated by calling her a "beautifully dressed princess" (line 15) who waves gracefully from her carriage. As much as the little boy admires his mother, the two remain distant from each other. For him riding in a carriage with her is "an awful rite" (line 13) for she ignores him and pays attention only to passing gentlemen on horseback.

The last several lines of the passage reinforce how distant the woman is from her son. The boy enters his mother's "mystic chamber of splendor and delights" (lines 22–23) and is virtually overcome with the wardrobe and the room's furnishings. But all this occurs only in her absence.

Concluding the passage, the narrator undercuts everything favorable about the woman by calling her a "stone"—a terrible indictment. At the same time he creates sympathy for her son, referring to him as a "little benighted boy!"

ESSAY QUESTION 3

All of the listed titles contain material with which to answer the question.

Tom Wingfield in *The Glass Menagerie* by Tennessee Williams, exemplifies a young man leading a life of frustrated dreams. He has the mind and heart of a poet and would like to go out and see the world instead of coping every day with an overbearing mother, a semi-invalid sister, and a job that bores him to tears. One tragic night his patience runs out. He abandons his family and leaves town for good. But he fails to escape completely. As he wanders the earth searching for some elusive paradise, the memory of his sister haunts him. The ending of the play leaves audiences with the thought that happiness, like so much else in Tom's life, is an illusion.

Another character, Pip, the hero of *Great Expectations* by Charles Dickens, would also serve as the subject of an essay on overcoming obstacles. Pip, who has an abiding dream to be a gentleman, is hindered in his pursuit of success by his low-class background and rustic manners. Throughout the novel Pip struggles to create his own identity. As he matures he realizes the corrupting power of wealth. He also learns to distrust other people and becomes convinced that life will disappoint him. Yet, he maintains a basic goodness. After years of frustration, he achieves the stature he has sought and wins the hand and heart of Estella, a woman he has long but unsuccessfully pursued.

Tom Joad, the protagonist of John Steinbeck's *The Grapes of Wrath*, also represents a man struggling to achieve a goal. Throughout the novel he seeks contentment and security in a world that scorns not only him but his family and countless other refugees from the Dust Bowl of Oklahoma who crisscross the valleys of California in search of work. Tom gets into trouble by killing a deputy sheriff. Suddenly a fugitive, he leaves his family and sets out on his own. What had once been a search for individual happiness broadens into a mini-crusade in behalf of the masses of poor, exploited workers. Tom, in fact, embodies what is perhaps the book's main message—that by working together, people will overcome adversity.

SELF-SCORING GUIDE FOR PRACTICE TEST 3
Scoring Section 2 ESSAYS

After referring to "How Essays Are Scored," on page 45 of this book, use this guide to help you evaluate each essay. Do your best to evaluate your performance in each category by using the criteria spelled out below. Because it is hard to achieve objectivity when assessing your own writing, you may improve the validity of your score by having a trusted and well-informed friend or experienced teacher read and rate your essay.

On the following Rating Chart, enter a number (from 1 to 6) that you think represents your level of performance in each category (A–F).

Category A: OVERALL PURPOSE/MAIN IDEA
  6 clearly establishes and cogently defines an insightful purpose
  5 clearly establishes and generally defines an appropriate purpose
  4 identifies and defines an appropriate purpose
  3 identifies and develops a mostly appropriate purpose
  2 attempts to identify but falls short of defining a clear purpose
  1 fails to identify the purpose of the essay

Category B: HANDLING OF THE PROMPT
  6 clearly and completely addresses and directly answers each part of
    the prompt
  5 directly addresses and answers each part of the prompt
  4 answers each part of the prompt directly or indirectly
  3 answers most parts of the prompt directly or indirectly
  2 fails to address important parts of the prompt directly or indirectly
  1 does not address the prompt or misinterprets requirements of
    the prompt

Category C: ORGANIZATION AND DEVELOPMENT
  6 insightfully organizes sequence of ideas according to the purpose of
    the essay; presents a cogent analysis using fully-developed, coherent
    paragraphs
  5 organizes material clearly and develops ideas with generally insightful
    evidence in unified paragraphs
  4 organizes conventional evidence or commentary in appropriate but
    perfunctorily arranged, formulaic paragraphs
  3 organizes material with little relation to the point or purpose of the
    essay; develops ideas adequately but with occasional irrelevancies
  2 organizes weak material in a confusing manner; generally ignores
    appropriate paragraph development
  1 lacks discernible organization; ignores relevant development of ideas

Category D: SENTENCE STRUCTURE

  6 uses clear, precise, and appropriately varied sentences to convey meaning and create effects

  5 uses clear sentences with appropriately varied structures to create interest

  4 consists of mostly clear sentences with some structural variety

  3 contains minor sentence errors and little sentence variety

  2 includes sentence errors that sometimes interfere with meaning

  1 contains serious sentence errors that obscure meaning

Category E: USE OF LANGUAGE

  6 uses precise and effective vocabulary extremely well-suited to the subject and the audience

  5 contains vocabulary that clearly and accurately convey meaning

  4 uses conventional but generally correct and appropriate vocabulary

  3 uses ordinary vocabulary with some errors in diction or idiom

  2 contains awkward word choices and frequent errors in diction or idiom

  1 uses words that often obscure meaning

Category F: GRAMMAR AND USAGE

  6 avoids all or virtually all grammar and usage errors

  5 includes occasional minor errors in standard English grammar and usage

  4 uses standard English grammar and usage but with several minor errors in standard English

  3 contains errors in standard English grammar and usage that occasionally obscure meaning

  2 contains errors in standard English grammar and usage that frequently obscure meaning

  1 contains several major errors in standard English grammar and usage that block meaning

RATING CHART

RATING CHART

Rate your essay:	Essay 1	Essay 2	Essay 3
Overall Purpose/Main Idea	_____	_____	_____
Handling of the Prompt	_____	_____	_____
Organization and Development	_____	_____	_____
Sentence Structure	_____	_____	_____
Use of Language	_____	_____	_____
Grammar and Usage	_____	_____	_____
Composite Scores (Sum of each column)	_____	_____	_____

By using the following chart, in which composite scores are converted to the 9-point AP rating scale, you may determine the final score for each essay:

Composite Score	AP Essay Score
33–36	9
29–32	8
25–28	7
21–24	6
18–20	5
15–17	4
10–14	3
7–9	2
6 or below	1

AP Essay Scores   Essay 1 _____   Essay 2 _____   Essay 3 _____

TEST SCORE WORKSHEET

Calculating Your AP Score on Practice Test 3

The scores you have earned on the multiple-choice and essay sections of the exam may now be converted to the AP 5-point scale by doing the following calculations:

I.   Determine your score for Section I (Multiple-Choice)

Step A: Number of correct answers _____

Step B: Multiply the figure in Step A by 1.2272 to find your Multiple-Choice Score _____. (Do not round)

II. Determine your score for Section II (Essays)[1]

Step A: Enter your score for Essay 1 (out of 9) _____

Step B: Enter your score for Essay 2 (out of 9) _____

Step C: Enter your score for Essay 3 (out of 9) _____

Step D: Add the figures in Steps A, B, and C _____

Step E: Multiply the figure in Step D by 3.0556 _____ (Do not round). This is your Essay Score.

III. Determine Your Total Score

Add the scores for I and II to find your composite score _____ .

(Round to the nearest whole number)

To convert your composite score to the AP 5-point scale, use the chart below. The range of scores only approximates what you would earn on the actual test because the exact figures may vary from test to test. Be aware, therefore, that your score on this test, as well as on other tests in this book, may differ slightly from your score on an actual AP exam.

Composite Score	AP Grade
114–150	5
98–113	4
81–97	3
53–80	2
0–52	1

---

[1]After the AP exam, essays are judged in relation to other essays written on the same topic at the same time. Therefore, the score you assign yourself for an essay may not be the same as the score you would earn on an actual exam.

Answer Sheet

PRACTICE TEST 4

Section I

1 Ⓐ Ⓑ Ⓒ Ⓓ Ⓔ	16 Ⓐ Ⓑ Ⓒ Ⓓ Ⓔ	31 Ⓐ Ⓑ Ⓒ Ⓓ Ⓔ	46 Ⓐ Ⓑ Ⓒ Ⓓ Ⓔ
2 Ⓐ Ⓑ Ⓒ Ⓓ Ⓔ	17 Ⓐ Ⓑ Ⓒ Ⓓ Ⓔ	32 Ⓐ Ⓑ Ⓒ Ⓓ Ⓔ	47 Ⓐ Ⓑ Ⓒ Ⓓ Ⓔ
3 Ⓐ Ⓑ Ⓒ Ⓓ Ⓔ	18 Ⓐ Ⓑ Ⓒ Ⓓ Ⓔ	33 Ⓐ Ⓑ Ⓒ Ⓓ Ⓔ	48 Ⓐ Ⓑ Ⓒ Ⓓ Ⓔ
4 Ⓐ Ⓑ Ⓒ Ⓓ Ⓔ	19 Ⓐ Ⓑ Ⓒ Ⓓ Ⓔ	34 Ⓐ Ⓑ Ⓒ Ⓓ Ⓔ	49 Ⓐ Ⓑ Ⓒ Ⓓ Ⓔ
5 Ⓐ Ⓑ Ⓒ Ⓓ Ⓔ	20 Ⓐ Ⓑ Ⓒ Ⓓ Ⓔ	35 Ⓐ Ⓑ Ⓒ Ⓓ Ⓔ	50 Ⓐ Ⓑ Ⓒ Ⓓ Ⓔ
6 Ⓐ Ⓑ Ⓒ Ⓓ Ⓔ	21 Ⓐ Ⓑ Ⓒ Ⓓ Ⓔ	36 Ⓐ Ⓑ Ⓒ Ⓓ Ⓔ	51 Ⓐ Ⓑ Ⓒ Ⓓ Ⓔ
7 Ⓐ Ⓑ Ⓒ Ⓓ Ⓔ	22 Ⓐ Ⓑ Ⓒ Ⓓ Ⓔ	37 Ⓐ Ⓑ Ⓒ Ⓓ Ⓔ	52 Ⓐ Ⓑ Ⓒ Ⓓ Ⓔ
8 Ⓐ Ⓑ Ⓒ Ⓓ Ⓔ	23 Ⓐ Ⓑ Ⓒ Ⓓ Ⓔ	38 Ⓐ Ⓑ Ⓒ Ⓓ Ⓔ	53 Ⓐ Ⓑ Ⓒ Ⓓ Ⓔ
9 Ⓐ Ⓑ Ⓒ Ⓓ Ⓔ	24 Ⓐ Ⓑ Ⓒ Ⓓ Ⓔ	39 Ⓐ Ⓑ Ⓒ Ⓓ Ⓔ	54 Ⓐ Ⓑ Ⓒ Ⓓ Ⓔ
10 Ⓐ Ⓑ Ⓒ Ⓓ Ⓔ	25 Ⓐ Ⓑ Ⓒ Ⓓ Ⓔ	40 Ⓐ Ⓑ Ⓒ Ⓓ Ⓔ	55 Ⓐ Ⓑ Ⓒ Ⓓ Ⓔ
11 Ⓐ Ⓑ Ⓒ Ⓓ Ⓔ	26 Ⓐ Ⓑ Ⓒ Ⓓ Ⓔ	41 Ⓐ Ⓑ Ⓒ Ⓓ Ⓔ	
12 Ⓐ Ⓑ Ⓒ Ⓓ Ⓔ	27 Ⓐ Ⓑ Ⓒ Ⓓ Ⓔ	42 Ⓐ Ⓑ Ⓒ Ⓓ Ⓔ	
13 Ⓐ Ⓑ Ⓒ Ⓓ Ⓔ	28 Ⓐ Ⓑ Ⓒ Ⓓ Ⓔ	43 Ⓐ Ⓑ Ⓒ Ⓓ Ⓔ	
14 Ⓐ Ⓑ Ⓒ Ⓓ Ⓔ	29 Ⓐ Ⓑ Ⓒ Ⓓ Ⓔ	44 Ⓐ Ⓑ Ⓒ Ⓓ Ⓔ	
15 Ⓐ Ⓑ Ⓒ Ⓓ Ⓔ	30 Ⓐ Ⓑ Ⓒ Ⓓ Ⓔ	45 Ⓐ Ⓑ Ⓒ Ⓓ Ⓔ	

SECTION I

Multiple-choice Questions

TIME—1 HOUR

Percent of total grade on the exam: 45 percent

Instructions: This section of the exam consists of selections from literary works and questions on their content, form, and style. After reading each passage and poem, choose the best answer to each question and then fill in the corresponding oval on the answer sheet.

Questions 1–15. Read the following passage carefully before you decide on your answers to the questions.

> When we went down-stairs, we were presented to Mr. Skimpole, who was standing before the fire, telling Richard how fond he used to be, in his school-time, of football. He was a little bright creature, with a rather large head; but a delicate face, and a sweet voice, and there was a perfect charm in him. All he said was so free from effort and spontaneous, and was said with such a captivating gaiety, that it was fascinating to hear him talk. Being of a more slender figure than Mr. Jarndyce, and having a richer complexion, with browner hair, he looked younger. Indeed, he had more the appearance, in all respects, of a damaged young man, than a well-preserved elderly one. There was an easy negligence in his manner, and even in his dress (his hair carelessly disposed, and his neckerchief loose and flowing, as I have seen artists paint their own portraits), which I could not separate from the idea of a romantic youth who had undergone some unique process of depreciation. It struck me as being not at all like the manner or appearance of a man who had advanced in life, by the usual road of years, cares, and experiences.
>
> I gathered from the conversation, that Mr. Skimpole had been educated for the medical profession, and had once lived in his professional capacity, in the household of a German prince. He told us, however, that as he had always been a mere child in points of weights and measures, and had never known anything about them (except that they disgusted him), he had never been able to prescribe with the requisite accuracy of detail. In fact, he said, he had no head for detail. And he told us, with great humour, that when he was wanted to bleed the prince, or physic any of his people, he was generally found lying on his back, in bed, reading the newspapers, or making fancy sketches in pencil, and couldn't come. The prince, at last objecting to this, 'in which,' said Mr. Skimpole, in the frankest manner, 'he was perfectly right,' the engagement terminated, and

Line
(5)

(10)

(15)

(20)

(25)

(30)

Mr. Skimpole having (as he added with delightful gaiety) 'nothing to live upon but love, fell in love, and married, and surrounded himself with rosy cheeks.' His good friend Jarndyce and some other of his good friends then helped him, in quicker or slower succession, to

(35) several openings in life; but to no purpose, for he must confess to two of the oldest infirmities in the world: one was, that he had no idea of time; the other, that he had no idea of money. In consequence of which he never kept an appointment, never could transact any business, and never knew the value of anything! Well! So he had

(40) got on in life, and here he was! He was very fond of reading the papers, very fond of making fancy sketches with a pencil, very fond of nature, very fond of art. All he asked of society was, to let him live. *That* wasn't much. His wants were few. Give him the papers, conversation, music, mutton, coffee, landscape, fruit in the season, a

(45) few sheets of Bristol-board, and a little claret, and he asked no more. He was a mere child in the world, but he didn't cry for the moon. He said to the world, 'Go your several ways in peace! Wear red coats, blue coats, lawn sleeves, put pens behind your ears, wear aprons; go after glory, holiness, commerce, trade, any object you prefer; only—

(50) let Harold Skimpole live!'

All this, and a great deal more, he told us, not only with the utmost brilliancy and enjoyment, but with a certain vivacious candour—speaking of himself as if he were not at all his own affair, as if Skimpole were a third person, as if he knew that Skimpole had

(55) his singularities, but still had his claims too, which were the general business of the community and must not be slighted. He was quite enchanting. If I felt at all confused at that early time, in endeavoring to reconcile anything he said with anything I had thought about the duties and accountabilities of life (which I am far from sure of), I

(60) was confused by not exactly understanding why he was free of them. That he *was* free of them, I scarcely doubted; he was so very clear about it himself.

(1852)

1. The narrator is quickly caught up in Skimpole's story mainly because of

(A) the respect he has for Skimpole
(B) Skimpole's youthful appearance
(C) their mutual interest in football
(D) their similar background and education
(E) Skimpole's manner of speaking

2. The narrator is puzzled by one aspect of Skimpole's story primarily because

   (A) the narrator considers Skimpole a kindred spirit
   (B) the narrator lacks experience in the world
   (C) the narrator, like Skimpole, has no head for detail
   (D) Skimpole jumps from subject to subject
   (E) the narrator is overwhelmed by Skimpole's personality

3. In line 10, "damaged" is best interpreted to mean

   (A) unconventional
   (B) secretly wounded
   (C) emotionally upset
   (D) worn out
   (E) troubled

4. The antecedent of the relative pronoun "which" in line 13 is

   (A) negligence (line 11)
   (B) manner (line 11)
   (C) dress (line 11)
   (D) hair (line 11)
   (E) neckerchief (line 12)

5. Which of the following pairs of adjectives best describe the narrator's tone?

   (A) Solemn and proud
   (B) Derisive and flippant
   (C) Affable and affectionate
   (D) Laudatory and worshipful
   (E) Envious and uncertain

6. Which of the following best describes the purpose(s) of the passage?

   I. To introduce Skimpole through the eyes of the narrator
   II. To reveal some of the narrator's values and biases
   III. To compare Skimpole and the narrator

   (A) I only
   (B) I and II only
   (C) I and III only
   (D) II and III only
   (E) I, II, and III

7. The chief effect of the diction and imagery in lines 3–17 is to

(A) affirm the congeniality of the gathering taking place downstairs
(B) suggest that Skimpole is a pretentious braggart
(C) establish a mood of foreboding about Skimpole's future
(D) create an impression of an unconventional man
(E) provoke the suspicion that Skimpole is concealing something about his past

8. The shift that occurs between the first and second paragraphs of the passage can best be described as one from

(A) stating generalities to focusing on details
(B) expressing opinions to doling out impressions
(C) presenting hypotheses to drawing conclusions
(D) observing the present to recalling the past
(E) reporting facts to explaining implications

9. The phrase "rosy cheeks" (line 33) is an example of

(A) synecdoche
(B) personification
(C) metaphor
(D) metonymy
(E) onomatopoeia

10. In line 34, "in quicker or slower succession" is best interpreted to mean that

(A) help was rendered according to a prearranged plan
(B) some of Skimpole's friends lacked the enthusiasm to lend a hand
(C) Skimpole asked for help from his friends as he needed it
(D) Jarndyce and others knew that helping Skimpole would be fruitless
(E) Skimpole received help as job opportunities became available

11. The narrator's interjection, "Well! So he had got on in life, and here he was" (lines 39–40), functions in all of the following ways EXCEPT

(A) it conveys the idea that Skimpole had no regrets about his weaknesses
(B) it editorializes about Skimpole's ineptitude
(C) it prepares readers for Skimpole's plea to society to "let him live" (lines 39–50)
(D) it suggests that Skimpole's infirmities had no long-lasting effect on him
(E) it serves as a transition between sections of Skimpole's story

12. The structure of the sentence beginning in line 47 ("Wear red . . .") does which of the following?

    (A) It demonstrates the intensity of Skimpole's frustrations.
    (B) It reflects the failure of society to accept a character like Skimpole.
    (C) It supports the earlier assertion that "he didn't cry for the moon" (line 46).
    (D) It suggests that Skimpole may be deranged.
    (E) It illustrates Skimpole's broadmindedness.

13. The last paragraph (lines 51–62) suggests that this passage most probably precedes an account of

    (A) the narrator's increased understanding of what Skimpole was all about
    (B) how Skimpole acquired his skill as a *bon vivant*
    (C) Skimpole's continued efforts to make something of himself
    (D) the narrator's efforts to befriend Skimpole
    (E) the narrator's decision to make Skimpole his role model and to follow in his footsteps

14. The dominant impression that Skimpole leaves on the narrator is that of

    (A) a failure
    (B) a playboy
    (C) a rogue
    (D) a nonconformist
    (E) a freeloader

15. The passage as a whole draws a contrast between

    (A) inclusion and exlusion
    (B) knowledge and ignorance
    (C) conformity and individuality
    (D) illusion and reality
    (E) youth and age

Questions 16–25. Read the following poem carefully before you decide on your answers.

Sadness

It was everywhere, in the streets and houses,
    on the farms and now in the air itself.
It had come from history and we were history
Line   so it had come from us.
(5) I told my artist friends who courted it
    not to suffer
on purpose, not to fall in love
    with sadness
because it would be naturally theirs
(10)   without assistance,
I had sad stories of my own,
    but they made me quiet
the way my parents' failures once did,
    nobody's business
(15) but our own, and, besides, what was left to say
    these days
when the unspeakable was out there being spoken,
    exhausting all sympathy?
Yet, feeling it, how difficult to keep
(20)   the face's curtains
closed—she left, he left, they died—
    the heart rising
into the mouth and eyes, everything so basic,
    so unhistorical
(25) at such times. And then, too, the woes
    of others would get in,
but mostly I was inured and out
    to make a decent buck
or in pursuit of some slippery pleasure
(30)   that was sadness disguised.
I found it, it found me, oh
    my artist friends
give it up, just mix your paints,
    stroke,
(35) the strokes unmistakably will be yours.

                  —Stephen Dunn (1989)

16. Which of the following best expresses the meaning of "courted" in line 5?

    (A) asked for
    (B) kept company with
    (C) caused
    (D) paid attention to
    (E) embraced

17. The basic mood of the poem can best be described as

    (A) angry
    (B) cranky
    (C) gloomy
    (D) resentful
    (E) melodramatic

18. Which of the following phrases best reiterates the idea expressed in lines 9–10 that "it would be naturally theirs/without assistance"?

    (A) "in the air itself" (line 2)
    (B) "nobody's business" (line 14)
    (C) "what was left to say/these days" (lines 15–16)
    (D) "sadness disguised" (line 30)
    (E) "strokes unmistakably will be yours" (line 35)

19. Between lines 10 and 11, there is a shift in the speaker's rhetorical stance from

    (A) subjectivity to objectivity
    (B) figurative to literal language
    (C) pretense to honesty
    (D) factual information to editorial opinion
    (E) external to internal concerns

20. In context, the phrase "the unspeakable" (line 17) refers to

    (A) gossip about the personal tragedies of others
    (B) the depth of sadness once experienced by the speaker
    (C) an inability to express emotions in words
    (D) "sad stories" (line 11)
    (E) "parents' failures" (line 13)

21. The metaphor "face's curtains" (line 20) can best be interpreted to mean

    (A) a mask that hides emotions
    (B) a look of sorrow
    (C) changing one's appearance
    (D) facial blemishes
    (E) the application of makeup

22. Which of the following inferences can be drawn from the speaker's statement that "the woes of others would get in" (lines 25–26)?

    I. The speaker has experienced sadness vicariously.
    II. Sadness breeds more sadness.
    III. The speaker had no control over the sadness he felt for others.

    (A) I only
    (B) III only
    (C) I and II only
    (D) II and III only
    (E) I, II, and III

23. Throughout the poem, the speaker implies which of the following about the nature of sadness?

    (A) Its effects can be eliminated with the right kind of help.
    (B) It represents personal weakness and should be avoided.
    (C) It helps to build an individual's character and strength.
    (D) It is an integral part of the human condition.
    (E) It is often used as a substitute for other emotions.

24. In lines 25–31, the speaker conveys a sense of

    (A) hopelessness
    (B) resentment
    (C) guilt
    (D) shamelessness
    (E) proportion

25. The pronoun "it" in line 33 refers to the artists'

    (A) customary pessimism
    (B) pursuit of sadness
    (C) sad stories
    (D) self-pity
    (E) rejection of pleasure

Questions 26–35. Read the following passage carefully before you decide on your answers to the questions.

STREPSIADES: O dear! O dear!
O Lord! O Zeus! these nights, how long they are.
Will they ne'er pass? will the day never come?
Line   Surely I heard the cock crow, hours ago.
(5)   Yet my servants still snore. These are new customs.
O 'ware of war for many various reasons;
One fears in war even to flog one's servants.
And here's this hopeful son of mine wrapped up
Snoring and sweating under five thick blankets.
(10)   Come, we'll wrap up and snore in opposition.
                                        (*Tries to sleep.*)
But I can't sleep a wink, devoured and bitten
By ticks, and bugbears,[1] duns,[2] and race-horses,
All through this son of mine. *He* curls his hair,
(15)   And sports his thoroughbreds, and drives his tandem;[3]
Even in dreams he rides: while I—I'm ruined,
Now that the Moon has reached her twentieths,[4]
And paying time comes on. Boy! light a lamp,
And fetch my ledger: now I'll reckon up
(20)   Who are my creditors, and what I owe them.
Come, let me see then. *Fifty pounds to Pasias!*
Why fifty pounds to Pasias? what were they for?
O, for the hack[5] from Corinth. O dear! O dear!
I wish my eye had been hacked out before—

(25)   PHEIDIPPIDES (*in his sleep*). You are cheating, Philon; keep
        to your own side.

STREPSIADES: Ah! there it is! that's what has ruined me!
Even in his very sleep he thinks of horses.
. . . Well then, you sleep: only be sure of this,
These debts will fall on your own head at last.
(30)   Alas! alas! For ever cursed be that same matchmaker,
Who stirred me up to marry your poor mother.
Mine in the country was the pleasantest life,
Untidy, easy-going, unrestrained,
Brimming with olives, sheepfolds, honey-bees.
(35)   Ah! then I married—I a rustic—her
A fine town-lady, niece of Magacles.
A regular, proud, luxurious, Coesyra.

----

[1]source of irritation
[2]a brownish-gray horse; also a mayfly; also a creditor
[3]two-seated carriage drawn by horses
[4]the twentieth of the month, when bills were due
[5]taxi ride

This wife I married, and we came together,
I rank with the wine-lees, fig boards, greasy woolpacks;
(40) She all with scents, and saffron, and tongue-kissings,
Feasting, expense, and lordly modes of loving.
. . . Well, when at last to me and my good woman
This hopeful son was born, our son and heir,
Why then we took to wrangle on the name.
(45) She was for giving him some knightly name,
"Callippides," "Xanthippus," or "Charippus:"
I wished "Pheidonides," his grandsire's name.
We compromised it in Pheidippides.
This boy she took, and used to spoil him, saying
(50) *Oh! when you are driving to the Acropolis, clad*
Like Magacles, in your purple; whilst I said
Oh! when the goats you are driving from the fells,
Clad like your father, in your sheepskin coat.
Well, he cared nought for my advice, but soon
(55) A galloping consumption caught my fortunes.
Now cogitating all night long, I've found
One way, one marvellous transcendent way,
Which if he'll follow, we may yet be saved.
So,—but, however, I must rouse him first.

(423 B.C.)

26. The phrase "new customs" (line 5) refers to the

    (A) seemingly endless nights
    (B) speaker's insomnia
    (C) crowing of the cock
    (D) servants' snoring
    (E) servants' indifference

27. Strepsiades' distress and discontent come from all of the following
    sources EXCEPT

    (A) an unsuitable marriage
    (B) a worthless son
    (C) declining health
    (D) burdensome debts
    (E) a fretful nature

28. In line 14, "through" is best understood to mean

    (A) via
    (B) throughout
    (C) because of
    (D) by means of
    (E) depending on

29. In line 24, Strepsiades' unfinished thought would most likely pertain to

    (A) his marriage
    (B) Pasias
    (C) the trip to Corinth
    (D) disrespectful servants
    (E) horses

30. From the context, the reader can infer that Strepsiades is a former

    (A) gardener
    (B) woodcutter
    (C) farmer
    (D) ploughman
    (E) goatherd

31. One effect of lines 28–29 is to suggest Strepsiades' feelings of

    (A) hostility
    (B) impatience
    (C) inflexibility
    (D) jealousy
    (E) humility

32. Most of the passage can best be described as a

    (A) villanelle
    (B) soliloquy
    (C) eulogy
    (D) dramatic monologue
    (E) stream of consciousness

33. Humor in the passage is derived mainly from

    (A) Strepsiades' use of puns
    (B) the banality of the subjects discussed
    (C) the speaker's reliance on clichés
    (D) the background of Strepsiades' wife
    (E) Strepsiades' sarcasm

34. Lines 40–41 are used to convey which of the following about Pheidippides mother?

    (A) Her preoccupation with social status
    (B) Her physical charms
    (C) Her reason for marrying Strepsiades
    (D) Her overweening pride
    (E) Her fancy upbringing

35. The content of lines 50–54 does which of the following?

    (A) Explains why Pheidippides is disobedient
    (B) Illustrates a basic difference between husband and wife
    (C) Compares the clothing of the rich and the poor
    (D) Suggests that Strepsiades blames his wife for Pheidippides' faults
    (E) Shows that Pheidippides is closer to his mother than to his father

Questions 36–45. Read the following poem carefully before you decide on your answers to the questions.

Channel Firing

That night your great guns, unawares,
Shook all our coffins as we lay,
And broke the chancel[1] window-squares,
We thought it was the Judgment-day

Line
(5)   And sat upright. While drearisome
Arose the howl of wakened hounds:
The mouse let fall the altar-crumb,
The worms drew back into the mounds,

The glebe cow[2] drooled. Till God called, "No;
(10)   It's gunnery practice out at sea
Just as before you went below;
The world is as it used to be:

"All nations striving strong to make
Red war yet redder. Mad as hatters
(15)   They do no more for Christés sake
Than you who are helpless in such matters.

"That this is not the judgment-hour
For some of them's a blessed thing,
For if it were they'd have to scour
(20)   Hell's floor for so much threatening . . .

---

[1] area in a church holding the altar and the choir
[2] cow put out to pasture on church land

"Ha, ha. It will be warmer when
I blow the trumpet (if indeed
I ever do; for you are men,
And rest eternal sorely need)."

(25)   So down we lay again. "I wonder,
Will the world ever saner be,"
Said one, "than when He sent us under
In our indifferent century!"

And many a skeleton shook his head.
(30)   "Instead of preaching forty year,"
My neighbor Parson Thirdly said,
"I wish I had stuck to pipes and beer."

Again the guns disturbed the hour,
Roaring their readiness to avenge,
(35)   As far inland as the Stourton Tower,[3]
And Camelot[4], and starlit Stonehenge.[5]

—Thomas Hardy (1914)

---

[3]tower built to honor Alfred the Great's victory over the Danes
[4]King Arthur's castle
[5]prehistoric megalithic circle on Salisbury Plain

36. The dramatic situation of the poem can best be described as

(A) ecclesiastical
(B) ethereal
(C) naturalistic
(D) fantastic
(E) suspenseful

37. In line 14, "Red" metaphorically describes the

(A) bloodiness of war
(B) government's political persuasion
(C) passion with which wars are fought
(D) debt incurred by warring nations
(E) dangers inherent in war

38. God's laugh ("Ha, ha") in line 21 is meant to illustrate that

    (A) God has a sense of humor
    (B) God thinks some men are fools
    (C) God is not above poking fun at Himself
    (D) God's words are all-powerful
    (E) God disapproves of wars fought in His name

39. In line 27 "sent us under" is best interpreted as

    (A) gave us coffins
    (B) returned to bed
    (C) put us to sleep
    (D) took our lives
    (E) took care of us

40. In its context, the word "indifferent" (line 28) can best be interpreted as

    (A) absurd
    (B) reckless
    (C) distracted
    (D) oblivious
    (E) bewildered

41. From line 32 to line 33 the tone of the poem shifts from

    (A) whimsical to ominous
    (B) honest to mendacious
    (C) serious to ironic
    (D) facetious to forthright
    (E) detached to compassionate

42. The allusions in lines 35 and 36 serve all of the following purposes EXCEPT

    (A) to provide the poem with a more poignant ending
    (B) to suggest that men of the past are hardly different from men of today
    (C) to propose that readers do all they can to put an end to war
    (D) to convey a sense of fatalism about men's bellicose nature
    (E) to ground a basically whimsical poem in reality

43. The reference to "Christés sake" (line 15) is echoed in

    (A) the broken windows in the chancel (line 3)
    (B) the trumpet blown on Judgment Day (line 22)
    (C) God's comments in lines 21–24
    (D) Parson Thirdly's words (lines 30 and 32)
    (E) allusions to Camelot and Stonehenge (line 36)

44. The poem's main theme might best be described as

    (A) the universality of death
    (B) the inevitability of war
    (C) the influence of the past
    (D) the power of God
    (E) man's inhumanity to man

45. Which of the following literary devices is most prominent in the quoted passages found throughout the poem?

    (A) References to animals
    (B) The use of onomatopeia
    (C) Repetition of key words
    (D) The use of irregular poetic meter
    (E) The use of everyday, colloquial language

Questions 46–55. Carefully read the following passage and answer the accompanying questions.

> People have wondered (there being obviously no question of
> romance involved) how I could ever have allowed myself to be let in
> for the East African adventure of Mrs. Diana in search of her
Line husband. There were several reasons. To begin with; the time and
(5) effort and money weren't mine; they were the property of the wheel
> of which I was but a cog, the Society through which Diana's life had
> been insured, along with the rest of that job lot of missionaries. The
> "letting in" was the firm's. In the second place, the wonderers have
> not counted on Mrs. Diana's capacity for getting things done for her.
> Meek and helpless. Yes, but God was on her side. Too meek, too
(10) helpless to move mountains herself, if those who happened to be
> handy didn't move them for her then her God would know the
> reason why. Having dedicated her all to making straight the Way,
> why should her neighbor cavil at giving a little? The writer for one, a
> colonial governor-general for another, railway magnates, insurance
> managers, *safari* leaders, the ostrich farmer of Ndua, all these and a
(15) dozen others in their turns have felt the hundred-ton weight of her
> thin-lipped meekness—have seen her in metaphor sitting grimly on
> the doorsteps of their souls.

A third reason lay in my own troubled conscience. Though I did it
(20) in innocence, I can never forget that it was I who personally conducted
Diana's party to the Observatory on that fatal night in Boston before it
sailed. Had it not been for that kindly intentioned "hunch" of mine,
the astonished eye of the Reverend Hubert Diana would never have
gazed through the floor of Heaven, and he would never have undertaken to measure the Infinite with the foot rule of his mind.

(25)   It all started so simply. My boss at the shipping-and-insurance
office gave me the word in the morning. "Bunch of missionaries for
the *Platonic* tomorrow. They're on our hands in a way. Show 'em the
town." It wasn't so easy when you think of it: one male and seven
females on their way to the heathen; though it was easier in Boston
(30) than it might have been in some other towns. The evening looked
the simplest. My friend Krum was at the Observatory that semester;
there at least I was sure their sensibilities would come to no harm.

On the way out in the street car, seated opposite to Diana and
having to make conversation, I talked of Krum and of what I knew of
(35) his work with the spiral nebulaé. Having to appear to listen, Diana
did so (as all day long) with a vaguely indulgent smile. He really
hadn't time for me. That night his life was exalted as it had never
been, and would perhaps never be again. Tomorrow's sailing, the
actual fact of leaving all to follow Him, held his imagination in thrall.
(40) Moreover, he was a bridegroom of three days with his bride beside
him, his nerves at once assuaged and thrilled. No, but more. As if a
bride were not enough, arrived in Boston, he had found himself surrounded by a very galaxy of womanhood gathered from the four
corners; already within hours one felt the chaste tentacles of their
(45) feminine dependence curling about the party's unique man; already
their contacts with the world of their new lives began to be made
through him; already they saw in part through his eyes. I wonder
what he would have said if I had told him he was a little drunk.

(1919)

46. The speaker metaphorically compares himself to

(A) a wheel
(B) a hand tool
(C) a hundred-ton weight
(D) a clock
(E) a machine part

47. The phrase "job lot of missionaries" (line 7) conveys which of the following about the speaker?

    (A) His indifference toward the group of missionaries
    (B) His doubts that these missionaries can find Diana
    (C) His regret about agreeing to participate in Mrs. Diana's "East African adventure" (line 3)
    (D) His disapproval of missionary work
    (E) His antireligion bias

48. Which of the following best describes the tone of the phrase "Meek and helpless" in line 9?

    (A) Disdainful
    (B) Impudent
    (C) Extravagant
    (D) Ironic
    (E) Forlorn

49. Which of the following best describes the function of the clause "her God would know the reason why" (lines 11–12)?

    (A) It proves the fervor of Mrs. Diana's religious commitment.
    (B) It adds weight to the description of Mrs. Diana's powers of persuasion.
    (C) It illustrates Mrs. Diana's ability to make others feel guilty.
    (D) It shows that Mrs. Diana depends on logic to get things done.
    (E) It explains why the speaker has been "let in" to the East African adventure mentioned earlier (line 3).

50. What is the antecedent of the pronoun "it" in the phrase "it sailed" (lines 20–21)?

    (A) "conscience" (line 18)
    (B) "party" (line 20)
    (C) "Observatory" (line 20)
    (D) "night" (line 20)
    (E) "*Platonic*" (line 27)

51. From the statement that "the Reverend Hubert Diana would never have gazed through the floor of Heaven" (lines 22–23), the reader may infer that

 (A) mysticism is an essential ingredient in the story
 (B) an account of the Reverend Diana's dramatic moment appears elsewhere in the story
 (C) the reader's view of the speaker will undergo a change as the story progresses
 (D) the speaker is foreshadowing the demise of Reverend Diana
 (E) the speaker believes that Reverend Diana suffers from delusions of grandeur

52. The speaker's claim that "It wasn't so easy" (line 28) can be explained by all of the following EXCEPT:

 (A) the city offered few places appropriate for entertaining missionaries
 (B) the number of men and women in the party was out of balance
 (C) the speaker misunderstood his boss's order to "Show 'em the town" (line 31)
 (D) the speaker didn't have much time to plan a suitable itinerary for the group
 (E) the speaker was unaccustomed to entertaining groups of missionaries

53. Which of the following best describes the speaker's interactions with Reverend Diana?

 (A) The reverend showed little interest in what the speaker had to say.
 (B) The reverend talked enthusiastically about his imminent departure to East Africa.
 (C) The reverend revealed an intolerance for small talk.
 (D) The reverend expressed gratitude for being escorted to the Observatory.
 (E) The reverend told the speaker that the trip to the Observatory changed his life.

54. Which of the following can be inferred from the speaker's diction in lines 41–47?

 (A) The speaker has contempt for the women in the group.
 (B) The speaker respects the women but is reluctant to admit it.
 (C) The speaker is pretending to be antagonistic toward the women.
 (D) The speaker takes pity on the women.
 (E) The speaker thinks the women slightly absurd.

55. In the last sentence of the passage the speaker implies that Reverend Diana

 (A) had been celebrating the impending departure of his group
 (B) was overly impressed by himself
 (C) had been overcome by his good fortune
 (D) had been drinking in secret
 (E) had lost control of his emotions

SECTION II
Essay Questions

TIME—2 HOURS

Suggested time for each essay—40 minutes
Each essay counts as one-third of the total essay section score

Instructions: This section of the exam consists of three questions that require responses in essay form. You may write the essays in any order you wish and return to work on a completed essay if time permits. Although it is suggested that you spend roughly 40 minutes on each essay, you may apportion your time as you see fit.

Each essay will be evaluated according to its clarity, effectiveness in dealing with the topics, and the overall quality of your writing. If you have the time, go over each essay, checking its punctuation, spelling, and diction. Unless plenty of time remains, try to avoid major revisions. In the end, the quality of each essay counts more than its quantity.

For Question 3, please choose a novel or play of at least the same literary merit as the works you have been assigned in your AP English course.

Essays should be written in pen, preferably with black or dark blue ink. Use lined paper and write as legibly as you can. Do not skip lines. Cross out any errors you make. Feel free to make notes and plan your essay on a piece of scrap paper. Please number your essays and begin each one on a new sheet of paper. Good luck.

ESSAY QUESTION 1

(Suggested time—40 minutes. This question counts as one-third of your score for Section II of the exam.)

Read the following sonnet carefully. Then, in a well-organized essay, analyze the techniques the poet uses to develop the dramatic situation in the poem. Comment on the title, tone, figurative language, rhythm, or any other appropriate poetic elements.

Since There's No Help

Since there's no help, come let us kiss and part.
Nay, I have done, you get no more of me;
And I am glad, yea, glad with all my heart,
Line   That thus so cleanly I myself can free.
(5)   Shake hands for ever, cancel all our vows
And when we meet at any time again,
Be it not seen in either of our brows
That we one jot of former love retain.
Now at the last gasp of Love's latest breath,
(10)   When, his pulse failing, Passion speechless lies,
When Faith is kneeling by his bed of death,
And Innocence is closing up his eyes,
        Now, if thou wouldst, when all have given him over,
        From death to life though mightst him yet recover.

—Michael Drayton (1619)

ESSAY QUESTION 2

(Suggested time—40 minutes. This question counts as one-third of your score for Section II of the exam.)

In the following excerpt from Sarah Orne Jewett's story "A White Heron" the narrator describes a little girl's discovery of a heron's nesting place. Read the passage carefully. Then, in a well-organized essay, analyze the techniques the author uses to show the significance of the discovery to the child.

There was a huge tree asleep yet in the paling moonlight, and small and hopeful Sylvia began with utmost bravery to mount to the top of it, with tingling, eager blood coursing the channels of her
Line   whole frame, with her bare feet and fingers, that pinched and held
(5)   like bird's claws to the monstrous ladder reaching up, up almost to the sky itself. First she must mount the white oak tree that grew alongside, where she was almost lost among the dark branches and the green leaves heavy and wet with dew; a bird fluttered off its nest, and a red squirrel ran to and fro and scolded pettishly at the harmless
(10)   housebreaker. Sylvia felt her way easily. She had often climbed there, and knew that higher still one of the oak's upper branches chafed against the pine trunk, just where its lower boughs were set close together. There, when she made the dangerous pass from one tree to the other, the great enterprise would really begin.
(15)   She crept out along the swaying oak limb at last, and took the daring step across into the old pine-tree. The way was harder than she thought; she must reach far and hold fast, the sharp dry twigs caught

and held her and scratched her like angry talons, the pitch[1] made her thin little fingers clumsy and stiff as she went round and round the
(20)   tree's great stem, higher and higher upward. The sparrows and robins in the woods below were beginning to wake and twitter to the dawn, yet she seemed much lighter there aloft in the pine-tree, and the child knew that she must hurry if her project were to be of any use.

The tree seemed to lengthen itself out as she went up, and to
(25)   reach farther and farther upwards. It was like a great main-mast to the voyaging earth; it must truly have been amazed that morning through all its ponderous frame as it felt this determined spark of human spirit creeping and climbing from higher branch to branch. Who knows how steadily the least twigs held themselves to advantage
(30)   in this light, weak creature on her way! The old pine must have loved his new dependent. More than all the hawks, and bats, and moths, and even the sweet-voiced thrushes, was the brave, beating heart of the solitary gray-eyed child. And the tree stood still and held away the winds that June morning while the dawn grew bright in the east.

Sylvia's face was like a pale star, if one had seen it from the
(35)   ground, when the last thorny bough was past, and she stood trembling and tired but wholly triumphant, high in the tree-top. Yes, there was the sea with the dawning sun making a golden dazzle over it, and toward that glorious east flew two hawks with slow-moving pinions.[2] How low they looked in the air from that height when before one had only seen them far up, and dark against the blue sky.
(40)   Their gray feathers were as soft as moths; they seemed only a little way from the tree, and Sylvia felt as if she too could go flying away among the clouds. Westward, the woodlands and farms reached miles and miles into the distance; here and there were church steeples, and white villages; truly it was a vast and awesome world.

The birds sang louder and louder. At last the sun came up bewil-
(45)   deringly bright. Sylvia could see the white sails of ships out at sea, and the clouds that were purple and rose-colored and yellow at first began to fade away. Where was the white heron's nest in the sea of green branches, and was this wonderful sight and pageant of the world the only reward for having climbed to such a giddy height? Now look down again, Sylvia, where the green marsh is set among
(50)   the shining birches and dark hemlocks; there where you saw the white heron once you will see him again; look, look! a white spot of him like a single floating feather comes up from the dead hemlock and grows larger, and rises, and comes close at last, and goes by the landmark pine with steady sweep of wing and outstretched slender neck and crested head. And wait! wait! do not move a foot or a
(55)   finger, little girl, do not send an arrow of light and consciousness

---

[1]pine resin
[2]wings

from your two eager eyes, for the heron has perched on a pine bough not far beyond yours, and cries back to his mate on the nest, and plumes his feathers for the new day!

(60) The child gives a long sigh a minute later when a company of shouting catbirds come also to the tree, and vexed by their fluttering and lawlessness the solemn heron goes away. She knows his secret now, the wild, light, slender bird that floats and wavers, and goes back like an arrow presently to his home in the green world beneath. Then Sylvia, well satisfied, makes her perilous way down again, not (65) daring to look far below the branch she stands on, ready to cry sometimes because her fingers ache and her lamed feet slip. Wondering over and over again what the stranger would say to her, and what he would think when she told him how to find his way straight to the heron's nest.

(1886)

ESSAY QUESTION 3

(Suggested time—40 minutes. This question counts as one-third of your score for Section II of the exam.)

From a novel or play, identify a character (not necessarily the protagonist) who, regardless of the consequences, takes a significant risk of some kind. Then, in a well-organized essay, describe the risk and its motivation. Also explain how the character's action illuminates the meaning of the work as a whole. Choose any of the titles in the following list, or choose one of comparable literary merit. Avoid writing only a plot summary.

Catch-22	*Lord Jim*
The Catcher in the Rye	*Main Street*
Crime and Punishment	*Moby Dick*
Don Quixote	*The Odyssey*
An Enemy of the People	*One Flew Over the Cuckoo's Nest*
Ethan Frome	*The Red Badge of Courage*
For Whom the Bell Tolls	*The Sea Gull*
Going After Cacciato	*A Streetcar Named Desire*
The Great Gatsby	*A Tale of Two Cities*
Hamlet	*Their Eyes Were Watching God*
Henry V	*War and Peace*
Invisible Man	

STOP

END OF PRACTICE TEST 4

Answer Key
PRACTICE TEST 4

Section I

1. E	16. E	31. A	46. E
2. B	17. C	32. B	47. A
3. D	18. E	33. A	48. D
4. A	19. E	34. E	49. B
5. C	20. E	35. B	50. B
6. E	21. A	36. D	51. B
7. D	22. E	37. A	52. C
8. D	23. D	38. A	53. A
9. A	24. A	39. D	54. E
10. B	25. B	40. D	55. C
11. B	26. D	41. A	
12. A	27. C	42. C	
13. A	28. C	43. D	
14. D	29. A	44. B	
15. C	30. C	45. E	

SUMMARY OF ANSWERS IN SECTION I
MULTIPLE-CHOICE

Number of correct answers _____

Use this information when you calculate your score on this examination.
See page 359.

ANSWER EXPLANATIONS

Section I

1. **(E)** In lines 6–7, the narrator says that Skimpole's words are spoken "with such a captivating gaiety, that it was fascinating to hear him talk." Skimpole's youthful appearance (Choice B) also strikes the narrator, but from the outset it's his speaking style that most impresses the narrator.

2. **(B)** In lines 59–60, the narrator shows his naïveté by admitting to confusion about why Skimpole was free of the usual "duties and accountabilities of life." Moreover, he refers to "that early time" (line 57), an allusion to Skimpole's youth and inexperience.

3. **(D)** The speaker's impression is that Skimpole looks like a broken-down young man rather than a well-preserved elderly one (lines 9–10). (A) accurately describes Skimpole's general appearance, but (D) is a more precise answer.

4. **(A)** *Which* refers to the grammatical subject of the sentence's main clause.

5. **(C)** The use of such words as "captivating" (line 6) and "enchanting" (line 57) suggests that the narrator is quite taken with Skimpole. Rather than being put off by Skimpole's arrant past, the narrator is impressed with his individuality, although he can't quite fathom it. In (E) the word "uncertain" applies to the narrator's basic reaction to Skimpole, but the other adjective "envious" doesn't.

6. **(E)** To one degree or another, the passage accomplishes all three purposes. Almost every sentence adds more details to this portrait of Skimpole. In telling about Skimpole, the narrator reveals his feelings toward his subject, particularly in the first and third paragraphs. At the same time the narrator alludes to differences between himself and Skimpole, especially in lines 58–59 where the narrator's hang-up about "the duties and accountabilities of life" contrast starkly with Skimpole's indifference toward them.

7. **(D)** The first paragraph is dominated by words and phrases that portray Skimpole as an unusual and free-spirited figure, among them "little bright creature," "loose and flowing," and "romantic."

8. **(D)** The first paragraph contains the narrator's observations of Skimpole. The second paragraph consists mainly of an account of Skimpole's life and career.

9. **(A)** A synecdoche is a figure of speech in which a part stands for the whole. In this case the phrase "rosy cheeks" could represent a wife, possibly a few children, and perhaps some close friends.

10. **(B)** The phrase implies that some of Skimpole's friends helped him right away, while others, doubtful that their help would make any difference, waited to see what happened to him.

11. **(B)** In this section of the passage the narrator, rather than passing judgment on Skimpole, simply recounts in his own words the story Skimpole has told.

The statement in lines 39–40 summarizes Skimpole's experiences and state of mind and suggests that in spite of his infirmities he suffered no permanent setbacks. It also serves as a break in the narration between an account of Skimpole's weaknesses and a list of his pleasures.

12. **(A)** The sentence is a series of imperatives leading to the climax, "Let Skimpole live!"—a plea to society to get off his back. Its message—"live and let live"—comes straight from Skimpole's guts and vehemently expresses his frustration. (B) and (C) are implied in Skimpole's plea, but the intent of the sentence is to reveal his state of mind.

13. **(A)** In the last paragraph the narrator offers a brief summing up of his introduction to Skimpole. The phrase "at that early time" (line 57) suggests that the story of Skimpole had just begun and that the narrator's confusion alluded to in lines 57–62 will eventually be cleared up.

14. **(D)** The passage emphasizes that Skimpole is an unusual fellow. Among other things, his appearance differs considerably from a man "who had advanced in life, by the usual road of years, cares, and experiences." In other words, Skimpole appears to have taken a less-traveled road through life.

15. **(C)** The passage portrays Skimpole as a nonconformist. The more expected of him, the more he rebelled. A case in point is his stint as a physician in the home of a German prince. Lacking the know-how to cope with two essentials—time and money—Skimpole could not successfully meet the customary demands of life. In consequence, he created a life and a style of his own.

16. **(E)** The speaker is alluding to artists (and others, too) who subscribe to the stereotypical notion that creativity is enhanced by sadness and suffering. Lines 5–10 say that the speaker has cautioned his artist friends against pursuing sadness for its own sake because it will come to them naturally. As he says in line 2, it's "in the air." (A) also relates to seeking sadness, but merely asking for it requires far less effort than embracing it. Likewise, (B) describes a casual action far different from pursuing sadness with the aim of wrapping your arms around it.

17. **(C)** The idea that sadness is pervasive and unavoidable dominates the poem, although the speaker suggests that it need not completely color our lives. He advises friends to fight it (lines 32–33), and he tells us how he tried—unsuccessfully—to overcome it (lines 27–29).

18. **(E)** In lines 32–35, the speaker urges his artist friends to give up voluntary, self-imposed feelings of sadness because the state of their emotion will be reflected naturally in their art—that is, in their strokes of paint.

19. **(E)** Lines 1–10 deal with sadness as it relates to others, particularly to artists. In line 11, the speaker begins to focus on his own encounters with sadness.

20. **(E)** The speaker can't talk about his own sad experiences. As he puts it, his own "sad stories . . . made [him] quiet" (lines 11–12). But others talked about "unspeakable," private matters such as the failures of the speaker's parents (line 13).

21. **(A)** The speaker, commenting on the effects of sadness, is saying that feelings of sadness can almost always be read in the face. That is, it's difficult to hide your emotions.

22. **(E)** In lines 19–25 the speaker describes how, after a sad event, he wore sadness on his face. As a compassionate person he felt sadness, too, for the woes of others, suggesting that sympathy for others begets still more sadness. It also indicates that, whether he wanted it or not, the sadness that he felt for others would be reflected in—or "get in"—his "mouth and eyes" (line 23).

23. **(D)** That sadness is "everywhere," including "the air itself" (lines 1–2), indicates its persvasiveness. Add to that the speaker's assertion (line 3) that sadness "had come from history and we were history," and sadness becomes inescapable. It is a natural part of our lives. This idea is reinforced by the speaker's statements to artists that sadness "would be naturally theirs" (line 9) and that their sadness will be unmistakably apparent in the strokes of paint they apply to canvas (lines 33–35).

24. **(A)** Lines 25–31 recount the speaker's attempt to distract himself from sadness. He failed, however, because it found him, or he found it (line 31).

25. **(B)** The speaker is reiterating the advice he gave to his artist friends earlier in the poem to cease "courting," or pursuing, sadness and "not to fall in love" with it (lines 5–8).

26. **(D)** According to Strepsiades, his servants have recently acquired the habit of snoring, a development that he interprets as their lack of concern for his well-being. (E) is a possible choice because the servants' snores suggest an indifferent attitude toward their master, but in the context, Strepsiades is reporting the snores, not commenting on their significance.

27. **(C)** Strepsiades' monologue illustrates that he is uptight, especially about his wife, his son, and his debts. He has nothing to say about the state of his health.

28. **(C)** Strepsiades blames Pheidippides for his insomnia.

29. **(A)** Pheidippides' utterance briefly distracts Strepsiades from discussing his wife, whom he talks about beginning in line 30. Had he completed his thought, he would probably have said that his eyes should have been hacked out before he saw the woman who eventually bore Pheidippides.

30. **(C)** Lines 32–34 provide evidence that Strepsiades was "a rustic" who once grew olives, raised sheep, and kept bees.

31. **(A)** In effect, Strepsiades is telling his son, "One day, you'll pay for your errant ways," a vindictive but human reaction to a son who has thoroughly grieved his father.

32. **(B)** Unlike a dramatic monologue, in which a speaker engages in a one-sided conversation with a silent listener, this passage finds Strepsiades talking to himself except for a few lines addressed to his sleeping son and a demand

for a lamp made to a servant. Although some of Strepsiades' language is poetic, his words are not presented in the stanzaic structure of a villanelle. A eulogy is a tribute to someone who has died, which this passage is definitely not. Nor is it an example of stream of consciousness writing, for it is far too coherent and structured.

33. **(A)** Among several puns are "bitten" (line 12), which in the context means chomped on by insects and also financially damaged. In line 13, "duns" has a double meaning: a mayfly and a brownish horse. In line 43, "hopeful" refers both to the parents and to the son. In line 55, "galloping" alludes to the swift consumption of Strepsiades' fortune and also to the horses that contributed to the loss of his fortune.

34. **(E)** Strepsiades' description of his wife supports the idea that she was a "fine town-lady" (line 36) accustomed to a life of luxury.

35. **(B)** The quotations reveal each parents' approach to child rearing. Strepsiades favors hard work and discipline; his wife prefers coddling.

36. **(D)** A poem in which skeletons are awakened by the sound of guns and God speaks as though he's just a neighbor is pure fantasy. (A) is a possible answer because the poem's setting is a church. (E) also has some merit because the speaker and his fellow corpses didn't know what the noise was all about. Yet, neither answer describes the poem's overall dramatic situation as scrupulously as (D).

37. **(A)** While "red" has many connotations—from the political left (communism) to love's passion—in this case "red" alludes to blood.

38. **(A)** In lines 17–20, God has humorously explained why some souls will not welcome "the judgment-hour." (Basically, they haven't finished atoning for their sins.) The chuckle He emits in line 21 suggests a slightly sardonic sense of humor.

39. **(D)** The speaker, formerly a person but now a skeleton, is referring to the time when he or she died.

40. **(D)** The adjective *indifferent* modifies the noun *century*, signifying that during the previous century, known as a time of war, people paid no attention to the horrors they perpetrated. To some extent, every choice is correct, but the best one reprimands humans for being blind to the senselessness of killing one another.

41. **(A)** Until the final stanza, the poem, while dealing with a serious subject, namely mankind's inability to live in peace, is pure fantasy. The last four lines, however, focus on the chilling reality of war's destructiveness.

42. **(C)** The place names conjure up poetic or historic associations. Readers are meant to cringe at the prospect of bombing Stonehenge and the other places. (Yet, two of the sites—Stourton Tower and Camelot—stand as memorials to human conflict not much different from that described earlier in the poem.)

Mentioning specific places also turns an abstraction into reality. While the poem may open readers' eyes to the implications of war, it stops short of urging readers to actively oppose war.

43. **(D)** Parson Thirdly picks up God's observation that men pay lip service to Christ but ignore his teachings. He himself regrets having devoted his life to preaching instead of to pipes and beer.

44. **(B)** God's words in lines 11–16 and the reactions of the dead reflect the fatalistic view that war, being an aspect of human nature, is inevitable.

45. **(E)** Both God and the skeletons express themselves in everyday speech, as, for example, "Mad as hatters" (line 14) and "'I wish I had stuck to pipes and beer'" (line 32).

46. **(E)** In lines 5–6, the speaker claims to have been "the property of the wheel of which I was but a cog." In other words, he saw himself not as his own master but as a minor piece of a turning wheel.

47. **(A)** The speaker's use of "job lot" may be slightly derogatory, but it is not insulting enough to conclude that the speaker disapproves of missionary work. At best, it suggests that the speaker views the missionaries impersonally, not as individuals but as an odd collection of do-gooders—a "bunch of missionaries" as his boss says (line 26)—whose lives happen to have been insured by his company. There is no evidence in the passage to support the other choices.

48. **(D)** The speaker uses the phrase to describe Mrs. Diana's affect—that is, the image she projects when she wants something. As the speaker makes clear, Mrs. Diana's meekness and helplessness is but a pose, a pose she uses to manipulate people to do things for her. In short, she is anything but meek and helpless. Thus, the phrase is being used ironically.

49. **(B)** The expression functions like a threat. That is, if the people Mrs. Diana asked "to move mountains" for her failed to do so, they would be subjected to her wrath or possibly worse—the wrath of God. Because she is doing God's work, God is on her side. Notice that the clause refers not to God in general but specifically to "her God"—that is, to her personal and no doubt vengeful version of the Deity.

50. **(B)** The pronoun refers to the noun "party." Diana's party sailed off to East Africa the day after the speaker escorted its members to the Observatory.

51. **(B)** In the context of the second paragraph, the reverend's visit to the Observatory must have been an exciting and eye-opening experience for him. It is unclear precisely what took place that night, but he must have felt that he had "gazed through the floor of Heaven," or at least he claimed as much. As the storyteller, the speaker will provide, or has already provided, details of the incident.

52. **(C)** Because the boss gave him the task of showing the missionaries around that very morning (lines 27–28), the speaker had to devise a suitable plan on

the spur of the moment. His decision to take the group to the Observatory was an inspired choice. By providing a tasteful, uplifting experience acceptable to both men and women, the speaker kept his charges away from everything in the city that might have offended their sensibilities.

53. **(A)** The speaker's interaction with Reverend Diana is described only in lines 33–34, as the two ride the street car en route to the Observatory. Reverend Diana appears to listen to the speaker's account of Krum's work, but his mind is elsewhere, or as the speaker claims: "He really hadn't time for me." The other choices (B–E) may well describe what occurred between the speaker and the reverend, but the passage fails to say so.

54. **(E)** By using the phrase "galaxy of womanhood" (line 43) the speaker conveys an image of women circling around the only man in their midst. Comparing them to creatures with "chaste tentacles" (line 44) demeans the women still further. In effect, the women have given themselves over to the Reverend Diana. The speaker doesn't despise the women for having done so, nor does he take pity on them. Rather, he seems to think their actions are silly and foolish.

55. **(C)** In context, "drunk" does not mean inebriated in the usual sense. Yes, Reverend Diana appears to be intoxicated, but intoxicated by the situation in which he finds himself: He's about to sail off to do God's work with his new bride, and he's surrounded by a "galaxy" of women who adore him. Line 37 captures the essence of his rapture: "That night his life was exalted as it had never been, and would perhaps never be again."

Section II

Although answers to essay questions will vary greatly, the following descriptions suggest an approach to each question and contain ideas that could be used in a response. Perhaps your essay contains many of the same ideas. If not, don't be alarmed. Your ideas may be at least as valid as those presented below.

Note: Don't mistake these descriptions for complete essays; essays written for the exam should be full-length, well organized, and fully developed. For an overview of how essays are graded, turn to "How Essays Are Scored," on page 45.

ESSAY QUESTION 1

Because the poem is a sonnet written during the Elizabethan era, its structure is familiar: fourteen lines, three quatrains, a concluding couplet, and a prescribed rhyme scheme. But unless you can tie the structure to the dramatic situation that the question asks you to write about, try to avoid a stock structural analysis. Instead, you might focus on the speaker's changing attitude. In the first quatrain he (or perhaps, she) firmly asserts the end of the love affair. As the title says, "there's no help"; love has vanished. The second quatrain refers to a future time when the couple may meet again. (Evidently, the breakup was not as hopeless as it seemed at first.) In the next four lines the speaker engages in a flight of poetic fancy, writing what amounts to an allegorical scene in which figures representing Love, Passion, Faith, and Innocence are about to pass on. (Notice that the speaker has wandered from his insistence that he's through with his love.)

In the final couplet the speaker shifts the responsibility to his beloved, telling her, in effect, it's up to you to save our affair. His earlier conviction has dissolved. Not only the sentiment but the diction has changed. At first, short, crisp words convey the speaker's uncertainty. The first four lines consist only of one-syllable words. As the speaker vacillates, the words grow longer, the tempo slows, and speech rolls off his tongue less smoothly, as though he is grasping for a way to postpone the final resolution.

ESSAY QUESTION 2

Climbing a very tall tree in search of a heron's nest in its upper branches is a significant adventure for a small child. The author uses images and figures of speech that emphasize the enormity and the peril of the undertaking. Early in the passage, a simile compares Sylvia's "bare feet and fingers" to "bird's claws." Later Sylvia is characterized as a "light, weak creature" (line 30). Paradoxically, the delicate little girl conquers a tree that the narrator has described metaphorically as a "monstrous ladder" that reaches (hyperbolically) "up, up almost to the sky." Twigs scratch Sylvia with "angry talons" and pitch causes her little fingers to grow "clumsy and stiff" (line 19). To further emphasize the magnitude of Sylvia's quest, the author compares the tree to "a great main-mast to the voyaging earth" (lines 25–26), and as Sylvia ascends heavenward, her face becomes "like a pale star" (line 34). Below her she sees flying hawks. No longer earthbound, she feels the urge to fly "away among the clouds." In effect, she has had a transcendent experience, the drama of which is heightened by a switch in the point of view beginning in line 49. Instead of continuing to tell Sylvia's story, the narrator, like a coach or mentor, addresses her directly: "And wait! wait! do not move a foot or a finger," says the narrator just as Sylvia locates the heron's nest.

ESSAY QUESTION 3

Each of the works discussed below contains material appropriate to answering the question.

McMurphy in Ken Kesey's novel, *One Flew Over the Cuckoo's Nest*, is an inmate in a mental hospital. He embodies the individualist willing to do battle against institutional rigidity and oppression represented by Nurse Ratched and administered by a fear-inducing system that mercilessly controls the destiny of the poorest, sickest, and least resilient members of society. Risking punishment, McMurphy fights for freedom and respect. He brings laughter into the life of his wardmates and incites them to join him in breaking the rules. As a consequence, he is given electroshock therapy and a lobotomy that turns him into a human vegetable. The parallel between McMurphy and Christ is self-evident; both sacrificed themselves for others.

Early in *Lord Jim* by Joseph Conrad, the title character deserts a ship that he believes is about to sink, an act that in retrospect he considers scandalous and cowardly. As one who had long fantasized about being a hero, he cannot escape the aftereffects of his conduct. One could argue that Jim's actions were justified. He hadn't a doubt that the ship was doomed and that his presence on board was superfluous. Besides, his escape was driven not by rationality but by impulse. Yet, Jim can't forgive himself. Disgrace lingers in his memory. By novel's end Jim has demonstrated that he's unafraid of death. He has walked fearlessly into perilous situations and undertaken death-defying risks. To prove his courage once and for all, he confronts an adversary whom he knows will kill him. While Jim's bravado serves no purpose other than to bolster his ego, his story raises issues of morality. Jim himself is difficult to judge. He may have done something inexcusable, but his subsequent behavior mitigates the odiousness of his act. Jim's experience raises such moral questions as whether there are circumstances under which supposedly fixed standards of morality may be violated. And if standards shift, how can they serve as guides for human conduct?

Ibsen's play *An Enemy of the People* focuses on Stockmann, a physician in a small Norwegian town, who discovers that the municipal baths are badly contaminated and insists that the condition be corrected. The burgomaster refuses, citing the high cost of repairs and a loss of revenue stemming from closing the baths for two years. Ignoring the health threat to the town's inhabitants, the burgomaster tries to keep Stockmann from informing the public. In fact, he condemns the doctor, officially declaring him "an enemy of the people." Stockmann fights back, putting his reputation on the line, but the townspeople blindly follow their self-serving leaders. Defeated, Stockmann considers leaving town, but changes his mind and founds a school meant to teach young people to think freely and resist corruption. The play advocates the value of truth. Untruth, hypocrisy, fraud: these are crimes against the public and against society; in the end, they are the real "enemy of the people."

SELF-SCORING GUIDE FOR PRACTICE TEST 4
Scoring Section 2 ESSAYS

After referring to "How Essays Are Scored," on page 45 of this book, use this guide to help you evaluate each essay. Do your best to evaluate your performance in each category by using the criteria spelled out below. Because it is hard to achieve objectivity when assessing your own writing, you may improve the validity of your score by having a trusted and well-informed friend or experienced teacher read and rate your essay.

On the following Rating Chart, enter a number (from 1 to 6) that you think represents your level of performance in each category (A–F).

Category A: OVERALL PURPOSE/MAIN IDEA
6 clearly establishes and cogently defines an insightful purpose
5 clearly establishes and generally defines an appropriate purpose
4 identifies and defines an appropriate purpose
3 identifies and develops a mostly appropriate purpose
2 attempts to identify but falls short of defining a clear purpose
1 fails to identify the purpose of the essay

Category B: HANDLING OF THE PROMPT
6 clearly and completely addresses and directly answers each part of the prompt
5 directly addresses and answers each part of the prompt
4 answers each part of the prompt directly or indirectly
3 answers most parts of the prompt directly or indirectly
2 fails to address important parts of the prompt directly or indirectly
1 does not address the prompt or misinterprets requirements of the prompt

Category C: ORGANIZATION AND DEVELOPMENT
6 insightfully organizes sequence of ideas according to the purpose of the essay; presents a cogent analysis using fully-developed, coherent paragraphs
5 organizes material clearly and develops ideas with generally insightful evidence in unified paragraphs
4 organizes conventional evidence or commentary in appropriate but perfunctorily arranged, formulaic paragraphs
3 organizes material with little relation to the point or purpose of the essay; develops ideas adequately but with occasional irrelevancies
2 organizes weak material in a confusing manner; generally ignores appropriate paragraph development
1 lacks discernible organization; ignores relevant development of ideas

Category D: SENTENCE STRUCTURE
    6 uses clear, precise, and appropriately varied sentences to convey meaning and create effects
    5 uses clear sentences with appropriately varied structures to create interest
    4 consists of mostly clear sentences with some structural variety
    3 contains minor sentence errors and little sentence variety
    2 includes sentence errors that sometimes interfere with meaning
    1 contains serious sentence errors that obscure meaning

Category E: USE OF LANGUAGE
    6 uses precise and effective vocabulary extremely well-suited to the subject and the audience
    5 contains vocabulary that clearly and accurately convey meaning
    4 uses conventional but generally correct and appropriate vocabulary
    3 uses ordinary vocabulary with some errors in diction or idiom
    2 contains awkward word choices and frequent errors in diction or idiom
    1 uses words that often obscure meaning

Category F: GRAMMAR AND USAGE
    6 avoids all or virtually all grammar and usage errors
    5 includes occasional minor errors in standard English grammar and usage
    4 uses standard English grammar and usage but with several minor errors in standard English
    3 contains errors in standard English grammar and usage that occasionally obscure meaning
    2 contains errors in standard English grammar and usage that frequently obscure meaning
    1 contains several major errors in standard English grammar and usage that block meaning

RATING CHART

RATING CHART			
Rate your essay:	Essay 1	Essay 2	Essay 3
Overall Purpose/Main Idea	_____	_____	_____
Handling of the Prompt	_____	_____	_____
Organization and Development	_____	_____	_____
Sentence Structure	_____	_____	_____
Use of Language	_____	_____	_____
Grammar and Usage	_____	_____	_____
Composite Scores (Sum of each column)	_____	_____	_____

By using the following chart, in which composite scores are converted to the 9-point AP rating scale, you may determine the final score for each essay:

Composite Score	AP Essay Score
33–36	9
29–32	8
25–28	7
21–24	6
18–20	5
15–17	4
10–14	3
7–9	2
6 or below	1

AP Essay Scores   Essay 1 _____   Essay 2 _____   Essay 3 _____

TEST SCORE WORKSHEET

Calculating Your AP Score on Practice Test 4

The scores you have earned on the multiple-choice and essay sections of the exam may now be converted to the AP 5-point scale by doing the following calculations:

I. Determine your score for Section I (Multiple-Choice)

    Step A: Number of correct answers _____

    Step B: Multiply the figure in Step A by 1.2272 to find your
               Multiple-Choice Score _____. (Do not round)

II. Determine your score for Section II (Essays)[1]

    Step A: Enter your score for Essay 1 (out of 9) _____

    Step B: Enter your score for Essay 2 (out of 9) _____

    Step C: Enter your score for Essay 3 (out of 9) _____

    Step D: Add the figures in Steps A, B, and C _____

    Step E: Multiply the figure in Step D by 3.0556 _____
               (Do not round). This is your Essay Score.

III. Determine Your Total Score

    Add the scores for I and II to find your composite score _____ .
                          (Round to the nearest whole number)

To convert your composite score to the AP 5-point scale, use the chart below. The range of scores only approximates what you would earn on the actual test because the exact figures may vary from test to test. Be aware, therefore, that your score on this test, as well as on other tests in this book, may differ slightly from your score on an actual AP exam.

Composite Score	AP Grade
114–150	5
98–113	4
81–97	3
53–80	2
0–52	1

---

[1]After the AP exam, essays are judged in relation to other essays written on the same topic at the same time. Therefore, the score you assign yourself for an essay may not be the same as the score you would earn on an actual exam.

Glossary of Literary and Rhetorical Terms

Knowing these terms can help immeasurably when you take the AP exam. Multiple-choice questions often refer to literary devices and techniques defined in these pages. Still more important, essay questions ask you to analyze, among other things, the tone, style, language, and form of prose pieces and poems. As you write your responses, these literary and rhetorical terms are not just handy references but the very tools you need to accurately and cogently express your ideas.

abstract   An abbreviated synopsis of a longer work of scholarship or research.

adage   A saying or proverb containing a truth based on experience and often couched in metaphorical language. See also *aphorism* and *maxim*.

allegory   A story in which the narrative or characters carry an underlying symbolic, metaphorical, or possibly an ethical meaning. In works such as Spenser's *The Faerie Queen* and Bunyon's *Pilgrim's Progress*, the story and characters represent values beyond themselves.

alliteration   The repetition of one or more initial consonants in a group of words or lines of poetry or prose. Writers use alliteration for ornament or for emphasis, as in words such as *flim-flam* and *tittle-tattle*. Also used in epithets (*fickle fortune, sunless sea*), phrases (*bed and board*), and slogans (*Look before you leap*). Alliteration generally enhances the aesthetic quality of a prose passage or poem, as in these lines from Coleridge's "Rime of the Ancient Mariner": *The white foam flew/ The furrow follows free.*

allusion   A reference to a person, place, or event meant to create an effect or enhance the meaning of an idea.

ambiguity   A vagueness of meaning; a conscious lack of clarity meant to evoke multiple meanings and interpretation.

anachronism   A person, scene, event, or other element in literature that fails to correspond with the time or era in which the work is set.

analogy   A comparison that points out similarities between two dissimilar things.

annotation   A brief explanation, summary, or evaluation of a text or work of literature.

antagonist   A character or force in a work of literature that, by opposing the protagonist produces tension or conflict.

antithesis   A rhetorical opposition or contrast of ideas by means of a grammatical arrangement of words, clauses, or sentences, as in the following:

> "They promised freedom but provided slavery."

> "Ask not what your country can do for you, but what you can do for your country."

aphorism   A short, pithy statement of a generally accepted truth or sentiment. See also *adage* and *maxim*.

Apollonian   In contrast to Dionysian, it refers to the most noble, godlike qualities of human nature and behavior.

apostrophe   A rhetorical device in which a speaker addresses a person or personified thing not present. An example: "Oh, you cruel streets of Manhattan, how I detest you!"

archetype   An abstract or ideal conception of a type; a perfectly typical example; an original model or form.

assonance   The repetition of two or more vowel sounds in a group of words or lines in poetry and prose. Note the assonance in "*Meet Pete Green; he's as mad as a hatter.*"

ballad   A simple narrative verse that tells a story that is sung or recited. Popular ballads include Coleridge's "Rime of the Ancient Mariner," Keats's "La Belle Dame sans Merci," and Wilde's "The Ballad of Reading Gaol."

bard   A poet; in olden times, a performer who told heroic stories to musical accompaniment.

bathos   The use of insincere or overdone sentimentality.

bibliography   A list of works cited or otherwise relevant to a subject or other work.

Bildungsroman   A German word referring to a novel structured as a series of events that take place as the hero travels in quest of a goal

blank verse   Poetry written in iambic pentameter, the primary meter used in English poetry and the works of Shakespeare and Milton. It is "blank" because the lines generally do not rhyme. See also *free verse*.

bombast   Inflated, pretentious language used for trivial subjects.

burlesque   A work of literature meant to ridicule a subject; a grotesque imitation.

cacophony   Grating, inharmonious sounds.

caesura   A pause somewhere in the middle of a verse, often (but not always) marked by punctuation.

> Note the caesura (after the word *loosed*) in these lines by William Butler Yeats:
>
> *The blood-dimmed tide is loosed, and everywhere*
> *The ceremony of innocence is drowned.*

See also *enjambment*.

canon   The works considered most important in a national literature or period; works widely read and studied.

caricature   A grotesque likeness of striking qualities in persons and things.

carpe diem   Literally, "seize the day"; enjoy life while you can, a common theme in literature.

catharsis   A cleansing of the spirit brought about by the pity and terror of a dramatic tragedy.

classic   A highly regarded work of literature or other art form that has withstood the test of time.

classical, classicism   Deriving from the orderly qualities of ancient Greek and Roman culture; implies formality, objectivity, simplicity, and restraint.

climax   The high point, or turning point, of a story or play.

coming-of-age-story/novel A tale in which a young protagonist experiences an introduction to adulthood. The character may develop understanding via disillusionment, education, doses of reality, or any other experiences that alter his or her emotional or intellectual maturity. Examples include Harper Lee's *To Kill a Mockingbird*, Thomas Wolfe's *Look Homeward, Angel*, and Cormac McCarthy's *All the Pretty Horses*.

conceit   A witty or ingenious thought; a diverting or highly fanciful idea, often stated in figurative language.

connotation   The suggested or implied meaning of a word or phrase. Contrast with *denotation*.

consonance   The repetition of two or more consonant sounds in a group of words or a line of poetry.

couplet   A pair of rhyming lines in a poem. Two rhyming lines in iambic pentameter is sometimes called a *heroic couplet*.

denotation   The dictionary definition of a word. Contrast with *connotation*.

dénouement   The resolution that occurs at the end of a play or work of fiction.

deus ex machina   In literature, the use of an artificial device or gimmick to solve a problem.

diction   The choice of words in oral and written discourse.

Dionysian   As distinguished from *Apollonian*, the word refers to sensual, pleasure-seeking impulses.

dramatic irony   A circumstance in which the audience or reader knows more about a situation than a character. King Oedipus, for example, unwittingly kills his own father, yet later declares that he shall find and punish his father's killer.

elegy   A poem or prose selection that laments or meditates on the passing or death of something or someone of value.

ellipsis   Three periods (. . .) indicating the omission of words in a thought or quotation.

elliptical construction   A sentence containing a deliberate omission of words. In the sentence "May was hot and June the same," the verb *was* is omitted from the second clause.

empathy   A feeling of association or identification with an object or person.

end-stopped   A term that describes a line of poetry that ends with a natural pause often indicated by a mark of punctuation, as in these lines from "The Waste Land" by T.S. Eliot:

> *In the mountains, there you feel free.*
> *I read, much of the night, and go south in the winter.*

enjambment   In poetry, the use of successive lines with no punctuation or pause between them, as in these lines from Dylan Thomas's "Poem in October":

> *A springful of larks in a rolling*
> *Cloud and the roadside bushes brimming with whistling*
> *Blackbirds and the sun of October.*

See also *caesura*.

epic   An extended narrative poem that tells of the adventures and exploits of a hero that is generally larger than life and is often considered a legendary figure such as Odysseus or Beowulf. Homer's *Iliad* and Vergil's *Aeneid* are examples of epics.

epigram   A concise but ingenious, witty, and thoughtful statement.

euphony   Pleasing, harmonious sounds.

epithet   An adjective or phrase that expresses a striking quality of a person or thing; *sun-bright topaz, sun-lit lake,* and *sun-bright lake* are examples.

eponymous   A term for the title character of a work of literature.

euphemism   A mild or less negative usage for a harsh or blunt term; *pass away* is a euphemism for *die*.

exposé   A piece of writing that reveals weaknesses, faults, frailties, or other shortcomings.

exposition   The background and events that lead to the presentation of the main idea or purpose of a work of literature.

explication   The interpretation or analysis of a text.

extended metaphor   A series of comparisons between two unlike objects.

fable   A short tale often featuring nonhuman characters that act as people whose actions enable the author to make observations or draw useful lessons about human behavior. *Aesop's Fables* are obvious examples. In some respects, Orwell's *Animal Farm* is also a fable.

falling action   The action in a play or story that occurs after the climax and that leads to the conclusion and often to the resolution of the conflict.

fantasy   A story containing unreal, imaginary features.

farce   A comedy that contains an extravagant and nonsensical disregard of seriousness, although it may have a serious, scornful purpose.

figure of speech, figurative language   In contrast to literal language, figurative language implies meanings. Figures of speech include metaphors, similes, and personification, among many others.

first-person narrative   A narrative told by a character involved in the story, using first-person pronouns such as *I* and *we.*

flashback   A return to an earlier time in a story or play in order to clarify present action or circumstances. An author may simply state: "There was a time when Henry loved June with great passion . . . ." A flashback might also be a character's account of the past, a dream, or a sudden association with past events. Willie Loman in *Death of a Salesman,* for example, repeatedly relives events that occurred in the past.

foil   A minor character whose personality or attitude contrasts with that of the main character. Juxtaposing one character against another intensifies the qualities of both, to advantage or sometimes to disadvantage. In *Pride and Prejudice,* for example, Lydia serves as a foil for her sister, Elizabeth Bennet. Lydia is a flighty and immature flirt. In contrast, Elizabeth is sensible and insightful, qualities that she demonstrates again and again in her relationships with Darcy and other characters.

foot   A unit of stressed and unstressed syllables used to determine the meter of a poetic line. While scanning the meter of a poem, mark unstressed syllables with U; mark stressed syllables with /. For example:

> U / U / U / U /
> *She walks in beauty, like the night*

> U / U / U / U /
> *Of cloudless climes and starry skies . . .*

foreshadowing   Providing hints of things to come in a story or play.

frame   A structure that provides premise or setting for a narrative. A group of pilgrims exchanging stories while on the road is the frame for Chaucer's *Canterbury Tales.*

free verse   A kind of poetry without rhymed lines, rhythm, or fixed metrical feet. See also *blank verse.*

genre   A term used to describe literary forms, such as novel, play, and essay.

Gothic novel   A novel in which supernatural horrors and an atmosphere of unknown terrors pervades the action. Mary Shelley's *Frankenstein* is a popular example.

harangue   A forceful sermon, lecture, or tirade.

heroic couplet   Two rhymed lines written in iambic pentameter and used widely in eighteenth-century verse, as in this stanza from "An Essay on Criticism" by the English poet, Alexander Pope:

> *True ease in writing comes from art, not chance,*
> *As those move easiest who have learn'd to dance.*
> *'Tis not enough no harshness gives offence,*
> *The sound must seem an Echo of the sense.*

hubris   The excessive pride that often leads tragic heroes to their death.

humanism   A belief that emphasizes faith and optimism in human potential and creativity.

hyperbole   Overstatement; gross exaggeration for rhetorical effect.

idyll   A lyric poem or passage that describes a kind of ideal life or place.

image   a word or phrase representing that which can be seen, touched, tasted, smelled, or felt.

in medias res   A Latin term for a narrative that starts not at the beginning of events but at some other critical point.

indirect quotation   A rendering of a quotation in which actual words are not stated but only approximated or paraphrased.

irony   A mode of expression in which the intended meaning is the opposite of what is stated, often implying ridicule or light sarcasm; a state of affairs or events that is the reverse of what might have been expected.

kenning   A device employed in Anglo-Saxon poetry in which the name of a thing is replaced by one of its functions or qualities, as in "ring-giver" for king and "whale-road" for ocean.

lampoon   A mocking, satirical assault on a person or situation.

light verse   A variety of poetry meant to entertain or amuse, but sometimes with a satirical thrust.

litotes   A form of understatement in which the negative of the contrary is used to achieve emphasis or intensity. Example: *He is not a bad dancer.*

loose sentence   A sentence that follows the customary word order of English sentences, i.e., subject-verb-object. The main idea of the sentence is presented first and is then followed by one or more subordinate clauses. See also *periodic sentence.*

lyric poetry   Personal, reflective poetry that reveals the speaker's thoughts and feelings about the subject.

maxim   A saying or proverb expressing common wisdom or truth. See also *adage* and *aphorism.*

melodrama   A literary form in which events are exaggerated in order to create an extreme emotional response.

metaphor   A figure of speech that compares unlike objects.

metaphysical poetry   The work of poets, particularly those of the seventeenth century, that uses elaborate conceits, is highly intellectual, and expresses the complexities of love and life.

meter   The pattern of stressed and unstressed syllables found in poetry. See Part 3 for a full discussion of meter.

metonymy   A figure of speech that uses the name of one thing to represent something else with which it is associated. Example: *"The White House says . . ."*

Middle English   The language spoken in England roughly between 1150 and 1500 A.D. Chaucer wrote *The Canterbury Tales* in Middle English.

mock epic   A parody of traditional epic form. It usually treats a frivolous topic with extreme seriousness, using conventions such as invocations to the Muse, action-packed battle scenes, and accounts of heroic exploits. An example is

Alexander Pope's "Rape of the Lock," a poem that portrays a woman applying makeup and fixing her hair.

mode   The general form, pattern, and manner of expression of a work of literature.

montage   A quick succession of images or impressions used to express an idea.

mood   The emotional tone in a work of literature.

moral   A brief and often simplistic lesson that a reader may infer from a work of literature.

motif   A phrase, idea, or event that through repetition serves to unify or convey a theme in a work of literature. Tolstoy, for example, repeatedly uses descriptions of nature to reflect the personality and emotions of his characters. Similarly, Hemingway often uses rain to evoke feelings of death and despair.

muse   One of the ancient Greek goddesses presiding over the arts. The imaginary source of inspiration for an artist or writer.

myth   An imaginary story that has become an accepted part of the cultural or religious tradition of a group or society. Myths are often used to explain natural phenomena. Almost every culture has some sort of myth to account for the creation of the world and its inhabitants.

narrative   A form of verse or prose that tells a story.

naturalism   A term often used as a synonym for realism; also a view of experience that is generally characterized as bleak and pessimistic. Characters in naturalistic works often struggle unsuccessfully to exercise free will. Examples include Henry Fleming in Crane's *The Red Badge of Courage* and the title characters of Norris's *McTeague* and Dreiser's *Sister Carrie*.

non sequitur   A statement or idea that fails to follow logically from the one before.

novella   A work of fiction of roughly 20,000 to 50,000 words—longer than a short story, but shorter than a novel. Popular novellas include *Daisy Miller* by Henry James, *Billy Budd* by Herman Melville, and *Heart of Darkness* by Joseph Conrad.

novel of manners   A novel focusing on and describing the social customs and habits of a particular social group. *Pride and Prejudice* by Jane Austen and *The Age of Innocence* by Edith Wharton are prime examples.

ode   A lyric poem usually marked by serious, respectful, and exalted feelings toward the subject. Keats wrote odes on melancholy, a Grecian urn, and a nightingale, among others. His poem "On First Looking into Chapman's Homer" is an ode honoring the translation of Homer's works by the Elizabethan poet, George Chapman.

Old English   The Anglo-Saxon language spoken in what is now England from approximately 450 to 1150 A.D.

omniscient narrator   A narrator with unlimited awareness, understanding, and insight of characters, setting, background, and all other elements of the story.

onomatopoeia   The use of words whose sounds suggest their meaning. Example: *bubbling, murmuring brooks.*

ottava rima   An eight-line rhyming stanza of a poem.

oxymoron   A term consisting of contradictory elements juxtaposed to create a paradoxical effect. Examples: *loud silence, jumbo shrimp.*

parable   A story consisting of events from which a moral or spiritual truth may be derived.

paradox   A statement that seems self-contradictory but is nevertheless true.

parody   An imitation of a work meant to ridicule its style and subject.

paraphrase   A version of a text put into simpler, everyday, words.

pastoral   A work of literature dealing with rural life.

pathetic fallacy   Faulty reasoning that inappropriately ascribes human feelings to nature or nonhuman objects.

pathos   That element in literature that stimulates pity or sorrow.

pentameter   A verse with five poetic feet per line.

periodic sentence   A sentence that departs from the usual word order of English sentences by expressing its main thought only at the end. In other words, the particulars in the sentence are presented before the idea they support. See also *loose sentence.*

persona   The role or facade that a character assumes or depicts to a reader, a viewer, or the world at large.

personification   A figure of speech in which objects and animals are given human characteristics.

plot   The interrelationship among the events in a story; the *plot line* is the pattern of events, including exposition, rising action, climax, falling action, and resolution.

picaresque novel   An episodic novel about a roguelike wanderer who lives off his wits. Popular picaresques include *Don Quixote* by Cervantes, *Moll Flanders* by Daniel Defoe, and *The Red and the Black* by Stendhal.

point of view   The relation in which a narrator or speaker stands to the story or subject matter of a poem. A story told in the first person has an *internal* point of view; an observer uses an *external* point of view.

protagonist   The main character in a work of literature.

pseudonym   Also called "pen name" or "*nom de plume*," a pseudonym is a false name or alias used by writers, such as Mark Twain (Samuel Clemens), George Eliot (Mary Ann Evans), and George Orwell (Eric Blair).

pulp fiction   Novels written for mass consumption, often emphasizing exciting and titillating plots. Literary scholars regard most novels by such authors as Tom Clancy and Stephen King—as well as the deluge of contemporary romances by Nora Roberts—to be pulp fiction.

pun   A humorous play on words, using similar-sounding or identical words to suggest different meanings.

quatrain   A four-line poem or a four-line unit of a longer poem.

realism   The depiction of people, things, and events as they really are without idealization or exaggeration for effect. See also *naturalism*.

rhetoric   The language of a work and its style; words, often highly emotional, used to convince or sway an audience.

rhetorical stance   Language that conveys a speaker's attitude or opinion with regard to a particular subject.

rhyme   The repetition of similar sounds at regular intervals, used mostly in poetry.

rhyme scheme   The pattern of rhymes within a given poem.

rhythm   The pattern of stressed and unstressed syllables that make up a line of poetry. See also *meter*.

roman à clef   French for a novel in which historical events and actual people appear under the guise of fiction.

romance   An extended narrative about improbable events and extraordinary people in exotic places.

sarcasm   A sharp, caustic expression or remark; a bitter jibe or taunt; different from *irony*, which is more subtle.

satire   A literary style used to poke fun at, attack or ridicule an idea, vice, or foible, often for the purpose of inducing change.

scan   The act of determining the meter of a poetic line. The pattern is called *scansion*. If a verse doesn't "scan," its meter is irregular.

sentiment   A synonym for *view* or *feeling*; also a refined and tender emotion in literature.

sentimental   A term that describes characters' excessive emotional response to experience; also nauseatingly nostalgic and mawkish.

setting   The total environment for the action in a novel or play. It includes time, place, historical milieu, and social, political, and even spiritual circumstances.

simile   A figurative comparison using the words *like* or *as*.

sonnet   A popular form of verse consisting of fourteen lines and a prescribed rhyme scheme. Shakespeare wrote what has become known as the Elizabethan sonnet. Other poets follow a form called the Italian sonnet, attributed to Petrarch. See Part 3 for a discussion of sonnets.

stanza   A group of two or more lines in poetry combined according to subject matter, rhyme, or some other plan.

stream of consciousness   A style of writing in which the author tries to reproduce the random flow of thoughts in the human mind.

style   The manner in which an author uses and arranges words, shapes ideas, forms sentences, and creates a structure to convey ideas. See Part 4 for more on writing styles.

subplot   A subordinate or minor collection of events in a novel or play, usually connected to the main plot.

subtext   The implied meaning that underlies the main meaning of a work of literature.

symbolism   The use of one object to evoke ideas and associations not literally part of the original object. The letter *A* worn by Hester Prynne in Hawthorne's *The Scarlet Letter* is an obvious symbol of Hester's adultery.

synecdoche   A figure of speech in which a part signifies the whole (*fifty masts* for *fifty ships*) or the whole signifies the part (*days* for *life*, as in *"He lived his days under African skies."*) When the name of a material stands for the thing itself, as in *pigskin* for *football*, that, too, is synecdoche.

syntax   The organization of language into meaningful structure; every sentence has a particular syntax, or pattern of words.

theme   The main idea or meaning, often an abstract idea upon which a work of literature is built.

title character   A character whose name appears in the title of the novel or play; also known as the *eponymous* character, such as Hamlet, Oedipus, and Gatsby.

tone   The author's attitude toward the subject being written about. The tone is the characteristic emotion that pervades a work or part of a work—in other words, the spirit or quality that is the work's emotional essence. Turn to Part 4 for a full discussion of tone.

tragedy   A form of literature in which the hero is destroyed by some character flaw and a set of forces that cause the hero considerable anguish. Macbeth, for one, is brought down by his own ambition.

trope   The generic name for a figure of speech such as image, symbol, simile, and metaphor.

verbal irony   A discrepancy between the true meaning of a situation and the literal meaning of the written or spoken words.

verse   A synonym for poetry. Also a group of lines in a song or poem; also a single line of poetry.

verisimilitude   Similar to the truth; the quality of realism in a work that persuades readers that they are getting a vision of life as it is.

versification   The structural form of a line of verse as revealed by the number of feet it contains. For example: *monometer* = 1 foot; *tetrameter* = 4 feet; *pentameter* = 5 feet, and so forth.

villanelle   A French verse form calculated to appear simple and spontaneous but consisting of nineteen lines and a prescribed pattern of rhymes.

voice   The real or assumed personality used by a writer or speaker. In grammar, active voice and passive voice refer to the use of verbs. A verb is in the active voice when it expresses an action performed by its subject. A verb is in the passive voice when it expresses an action performed upon its subject or when the subject is the result of the action.

ACTIVE: The crew raked the leaves.

PASSIVE: The leaves were raked by the crew.

Stylistically, the active voice produces more economical and vigorous writing.

wit   The quickness of intellect and the power and talent for saying brilliant things that surprise and delight by their unexpected cleverness; the power to comment subtly and pointedly on the foibles of the passing scene.

Acknowledgments

The author gratefully acknowledges the following copyright holders for permission to reprint material used.

Diagnostic Test
Excerpt from Alice Adams, *To See You Again*, copyright © 1982 by Alice Adams. Used by permission of Alfred A. Knopf, a division of Random House, Inc.

Poem: Carol Ann Duffy, "In Your Mind," from *The Other Country*, Anvil Press, London, 1990.

Poem: Chris Forhan, "Gouge, Adze, Rasp, Hammer" in *The Actual Moon, The Actual Stars*, pp. 50–51. © 2003 by Chris Forhan. Reprinted by permission of University Press of New England.

Excerpt from William Faulkner, "Dry September," from *Collected Stories of William Faulkner*, copyright 1930, 1958 by William Faulkner. Used by permission of Random House, Inc.

Poem: Hart Crane, "Forgetfulness," from *Complete Poems of Hart Crane*, edited by Marc Simon. Copyright © 1933, 1958, 1966 by Liveright Publishing Corporation. Copyright © 1986 by Marc Simon. Used by permission of Liveright Publishing Corporation.

Poem: Billy Collins, "Forgetfulness," from *Questions About Angels*, Copyright © 1999 by Billy Collins. Reprinted by permission of the University of Pittsburgh Press.

Test 1
Excerpt from Henry Fielding, *Tom Jones*, New American Library, 1963, pp. 489–490.

Excerpt from "The Baker's Bluejay Yarn," from *The Family Mark Twain*, Harper and Bros. New York, 1935, pp. 1139–1140.

Excerpt from Edith Wharton, "New Year's Day," from *Edith Wharton: Novellas and Other Writings*, The Library of America, 1990, pp. 491–492.

Test 2
Excerpt from George Bernard Shaw, *Man and Superman*, in *Major British Writers*, ed. G. B. Harrison, Harcourt Brace, 1959, pp. 717–718.

Test 3
Poem: Irving Layton, "Berry Picking" from *A Wild Peculiar Joy: The Selected Poems* by Irving Layton, © 1982, 2004. Used by permission of the publishers, McClelland & Stewart, Ltd.

Index

Hedda Gabler, 209
Hemingway, Ernest, 185, 190
Henry VI, 154
Heroic couplets, 166, 168
Herrick, Robert, 161
Hesse, Herman, 180
"Hillside Thaw, A," 149
Hippolytus, 189
Homer, 196
Hopkins, Gerard Manley, 119, 140, 141
Housman, A.E., 153
Huckleberry Finn, 182, 188
Hugo, Victor, 190
Hurston, Zora Neale, 206–207
Hyperbole, 156

I
Iamb, 142
Iambic pentameter, 117, 143, 168
Ibsen, Hendrik, 190, 209
Images, 152
Imperative sentences, 43
"In a Station of the Metro," 165
Informer, The, 200
"in just," 119
Internal rhyme, 138
"Intimations of Immortality from Recollections of Early Childhood," 171
Inversions, 43
Invisible Man, 190, 207
Irony, 159
"Is My Team Ploughing," 153
Italian sonnet, 172
"It's No Use Raising a Shout," 137–138

J
"Jabberwocky," 120
Johnny Got His Gun, 192
Joyce, James, 193, 199–200, 206
Julius Caesar, 156
Jungle, The, 190

K
Kafka, Franz, 184, 201

L
"Latest Decalogue, The," 158
Lawrence, D.H., 192

Lee-Hamilton, Eugene, 151
Les Miserables, 190
"Lilacs," 145
Limerick, 171
"Lines Composed a Few Miles Above Tintern Abbey," 164
Literary present, 44
Literature
  antagonist, 189–190
  characters, 186–188
  conflict, 181–183
  description of, 179
  initial responses to, 180
  narration. *See* Narration
  narrator, 44, 187, 189
  plot, 181
  protagonist, 189–190
  real-life connections, 197–198
  setting, 183–185
  structure, 194–195
  themes, 190–192
  unity, 195–196
  writing style, 198–199
Litotes, 156
Lord Jim, 188, 197
"Love Song of J. Alfred Prufrock, The," 148
Lowell, Amy, 145
Lyric poem, 161–162

M
Madame Bovary, 185, 192
Mamet, David, 210
Marlowe, Christopher, 145, 154
Marvell, Andrew, 119
Masefield, John, 152
McCarthy, Cormac, 207–208
Medea, 209
"Meeting at Night," 157
Melville, Herman, 160, 193
Metaphors, 147–150, 200–201
Metaphysical poetry, 163
Meter, 142
Metonymy, 153
Millay, Edna St. Vincent, 120, 172
Milton, John, 145, 173
Miltonian sonnet, 174
Mixed metaphors, 149
Moby Dick, 186, 193, 201

How to Use the CD-ROM

The software is not installed on your computer; it runs directly from the CD-ROM. Barron's CD-ROM includes an "autorun" feature that automatically launches the application when the CD is inserted into the CD-ROM drive. In the unlikely event that the autorun feature is disabled, follow the manual launching instructions below.

Windows®

1. Click on the Start button and choose "My Computer."
2. Double-click on the CD-ROM drive, which is named **AP_English_Literature.exe.**
3. Double-click **AP_English_Literature.exe** to launch the program.

Macintosh®

1. Double-click the CD-ROM icon.
2. Double-click the **AP_English_Literature** icon to start the program.

SYSTEM REQUIREMENTS

(Flash Player 10.2 is recommended)

Microsoft® Windows®	**MAC OS X**	**Linux® and Solaris™**
Processor: Intel Pentium 4 2.33GHz, Athlon 64 2800+ or faster processor (or equivalent).	Processor: Intel Core™ Duo 1.33GHz or faster processor.	Processor: Intel Pentium 4 2.33GHz, AMD Athlon 64 2800+ or faster processor (or equivalent).
Memory: 128MB of RAM.	Memory: 256MB of RAM.	Memory: 512MB of RAM.
Graphics Memory: 128MB.	Graphics Memory: 128MB.	Graphics Memory: 128MB.
Platforms:	Platforms:	Platforms:
Windows 7, Windows Vista®, Windows XP, Windows Server® 2008, Windows Server 2003.	Mac OS X 10.6, Mac OS X 10.5, Mac OS X 10.4 (Intel) and higher.	Red Hat® Enterprise Linux (RHEL) 5 or later, openSUSE® 11 or later, Ubuntu 9.10 or later. Solaris: Solaris™ 10.